RELIGION AND POLITICS
IN
MODERN IRAN

RELIGION AND POLITICS IN MODERN IRAN

A Reader

Edited by Lloyd Ridgeon

I.B. TAURIS
LONDON · NEW YORK

Published in 2005 by I.B.Tauris & Co. Ltd
6 Salem Road, London W2 4BU
175 Fifth Avenue, New York, NY 10010
www.ibtauris.com

International Library of Iranian Studies 3

ISBN: 1 84511 073 0 (Hb)
EAN: 978 1 84511 073 4 (Hb)
ISBN: 1 84511 072 2 (Pb)
EAN: 978 1 84511 072 7 (Pb)

A full CIP record for this book is available from the British Library
A full CIP record for this book is available from the Library of Congress

Library of Congress catalog card: available

Typeset in Garamond Classico by Initial Typesetting Services, Edinburgh
Printed and bound in Great Britain by TJ International Ltd, Padstow, Cornwall

For my beautiful daughter, Hattie

Contents

Acknowledgements

Chapter 1. Jamal al-Din al-Afghani, 'The Reign of Terror in Persia', *Contemporary Review*, LXI (1892), pp. 238–48. Published with permission.

Chapter 2. Mirza Malkam Khan, *Mirza Malkum Khan* (Berkeley, CA: University of California Press, 1973), pp. 278–99. Translated by Hamid Algar. Published with permission.

Chapter 3. Fazl Allah Nuri, 'Shaykh Fazl Allah Nuri's Refutation of the Idea of Constitutionalism', *Middle Eastern Studies*, XXIII.3 (1977), pp. 327–39. Translated by Abdul-Hadi Hairi. Published with permission.

Chapter 4. Ahmad Kasravi, *On Islam and Shi-ism* (Costa Mesa: Mazda Publishers, 1990), pp. 64–77. Translated by M.R. Ghanoonparvar. Published with permission.

Chapter 5. Sediqeh Dowlatabadi, *Zaban-e Zanan* (17/11/1920, 2/12/1920, 2/23/1944, 6/1944, 10/1944, 30/6/1920, 23/6/1920, 25/5/1945, 22/4/1951). Translated by Mansoureh Ettehadieh.

Chapter 6. Mirza Hasan Safi 'Ali Shah, *'Erfan al-haqq* (Tehran: Safi 'Ali Shah, 1999), pp. 62–8, 102–9. Translated by Nile Green.

Chapter 7. Ahmad Kasravi, *Baha'igari, Shi'igari, Sufigari* (Tehran, 1943–44). Translated by Lloyd Ridgeon.

Chapter 8. Sayyid Muhammad Husayn Tabataba'i, *Kernel of the Kernel: Concerning the Wayfaring and Spiritual Journey of the People of Intellect (Risala-yi Lubb al-Lubab dar Sayr wa Suluk-i Ulu'l Albab)* (Albany: SUNY Press, 2003), pp. 119–30. Translated by Mohammad H. Faghfoory. Published with permission.

Chapter 9. 'Abdollah Entezam, 'Nazari tazeh be 'erfan va tasavvof', *Majalleh-ye Vahid* (211/212, 209, 206, 207) (Tehran, 1977). Translated by Matthijs van den Bos.

Chapter 10. Jalal Al-e Ahmad, *Gharbzadegi (Westruckness)* (Costa Mesa: Mazda Publishers, 1997), pp. 11–23. Translated by John Green and Ahmad Alizadeh. Published with permission.

Chapter 11. 'Ali Shari'ati, *Tamaddon va Tajaddod (Civilisation and Modernisation). (Ittihadiyah-i Anjumanha-yi Islami-i Danishjuyan dar Urupa va Anjumanha-yi Islami-i Danishjuyan dar Amrika va Canada)*. Translated by Lloyd Ridgeon.

x · *Religion and Politics in Modern Iran*

Chapter 12. Ayatollah Khomeini, *Islam and Revolution* (London: Kegan Paul International, 1985), pp. 40–54. Translated by Hamid Algar. Published with permission.

Chapter 13. Ziba Mir Hosseini, *Islam and Gender* (London: I.B. Tauris, 2000), pp. 213–46.

Chapter 14. Mehrangiz Kar, *Women's Political Participation: Obstacles and Possibilities* (Tehran: Rawshangaran va Mutala'at-i Zanan, 2001). Translated by Haleh Anvari.

Introduction

This book covers a period of roughly 125 years of modern Iranian history, a period that has witnessed two revolutions, a civil war, *coups d'état*, and the emergence of Iran as the *bête noire* of the superpowers of the age (most recently of the United States whose President George W. Bush felt it necessary to include Iran within the 'axis of evil'). The problems that Iran has had to face in this period are not merely a reflection of its relations with external powers (whose interests in Iran are due to its strategic importance and oil reserves); they are also due to the modernising and centralising tendencies that have been occurring globally. Yet it is virtually impossible to bracket the West out in an attempt to identify how Iranian intellectuals and reformers have responded to the challenges they have faced in these past one hundred years. It might appear that some topics (such as Sufism) have not been directly influenced by the West (typified in Chapter 8 by Tabataba'i), although the indirect pressure for a more ethical and demystified Sufism may have filtered into society during the Pahlavi era and resulted in a new variety of Sufism, or at least Sufism with a new emphasis that has been expressed by 'Abdollah Entezam (Chapter 9). However, there can be little doubt that most Iranian responses to the challenges and difficulties of the modern age reflect the influences that have emanated from the West. It is not without reason that in one of the most useful surveys of modern Iranian thinkers, Mehrzad Boroujerdi called his book *Iranian Intellectuals and the West: The Tormented Triumph of Nativism*. Since the beginning of the Second World War, each generation of Iranians has believed that it has had to grapple with forces beyond its power, commencing with the British and Soviet occupation of Iran in 1941, the *coup d'état* that ousted Mosaddeq (which was supported by the British and the USA), the corrupt regime of Mohammad Reza Pahlavi that was supported by the West, and in the aftermath of the Islamic Revolution of 1978 the 'imposed' war with Iraq, which was being armed by the West. It should be of little surprise that most of the chapters in this book address the problems of Iranian society that are related in some way to the West, as thinkers as diverse as Kasravi and Khomeini have been at pains to indicate. Reform of society and its cherished beliefs and standards (including ossified forms of religion) and the need to adapt to changing circumstances are themes that run throughout most of the chapters presented here.

It is beyond the scope of this introduction to summarise Iran's relations with the West and the main historical events of the past hundred years of Iranian history, for in this short space I wish to focus on the contents of this reader. This work is an attempt to flesh out some of the themes that have been portrayed in the chronological histories that have been published recently, including two excellent books, Ali Ansari's *Modern Iran Since 1921* (Longman, 2003) and Nikki Keddie's *Modern Iran: Roots and Results of Revolution* (Yale University Press, 2003). In addition, this reader provides closer focus on the topics of gender and Sufism, the latter being virtually ignored in the general works on modern Iran.

This reader is pitched at undergraduate and postgraduate students of Iranian studies, Islamic studies, Middle Eastern studies, anthropology, politics and students of other social sciences. This is not to say that it is specific to the university environment, as I am confident that the book will be of interest to a whole range of specialists and non-specialists who find Iran and its modern history and intellectual legacy a challenge or an enigma. However, I confess to structuring this reader to reflect the themes that I address in my course on modern Iran at Glasgow University. The contents of this course change from year to year (although there is a constant core of the 'usual suspects'); however, I have been able to indulge myself in this book by concentrating on my interest in Sufism, and I have also responded to the increasing demand from students for more works by women on women.

The individual authors of the texts in this reader are among the most important religio-political figures in modern Iranian history. A reader on this topic without the inclusion of essays by Jamal al-Din al-Afghani, Jalal Al-e Ahmad, 'Ali Shari'ati and Ayatollah Khomeini would be unforgivable. Some of the texts are well known, such as those by Al-e Ahmad and Khomeini, but given their importance I found that I could not omit them from this work. Other chapters are difficult to locate (al-Afghani) or else are new translations (Shari'ati). I have attempted to provide a balance between those who advocate what I would describe as a more traditional and literal version of Islam (Fazl Allah Nuri) and those whose vision of Islam reflected a form of modern, secular religiosity. I am conscious of the difficulty in using nomenclature to categorise forms of Islam (such as 'Fundamentalist', 'Conservative', 'Liberal', 'Reformist'), and for this reason I have refrained from dividing the chapters into sub-divisions, as many readers do. Instead, I have structured the chapters more or less on a chronological pattern with the exception of the four Sufi chapters in the middle of the book.

I am particularly pleased with the chapters on Sufism because three of the four appear in English for the first time (the chapters by Safi 'Ali Shah, Kasravi and 'Abdollah Entezam). I would like to extend my gratitude to Nile Green and Matthijs van den Bos, who translated two of the chapters and who also contributed short introductions to their translations. Likewise, there are two chapters on women's rights that appear for the first time, and I would like to thank Mansoureh Ettehadieh who not only suggested and translated a chapter on Sediqeh Dawlatabadi, but also introduced me to Haleh Anvari, who translated the final chapter of this reader by Mehrangiz Kar.

My choice of topics and individuals was deliberate, as I wanted to include authors who had a direct religio-political message to convey. It would have been easy to compile a book of studies by academics writing in English, who live in the West and analyse the writings and speeches of people such as al-Afghani, Khomeini and Sorush. However, my aim has been to give readers primary material so that they can draw their own conclusions about the significance of the texts, recurrent themes and possible future trends. (Of course, I am aware that my choice of the contents of this book may lead the reader towards my own understanding of modern Iranian history, but I am often pleasantly surprised by the reactions and conclusions drawn by students who take my course on modern Iran, and who offer different views from those that I expected.) Another of my aims in this book has been that each chapter should be of an adequate length to engage the reader sufficiently. I shall refrain from mentioning the names of certain recent readers on Islam, but I have seen some works that include chapters of between two and three pages. It is hoped that each chapter in this book will stimulate and provoke the reader to contemplate its significance and even to investigate the topic further, which is the reason for the inclusion of the further reading sections at the end of each introduction to each chapter.

As mentioned above, all the chapters have been written by Iranians, although two of these were composed in European languages. The first was by al-Afghani, the second by Ziba Mir-Hosseini. Yet both articles should not be considered as conveying a view of Iran that is removed from the 'reality' of Iran. Al-Afghani's chapter reflects the general message that he espoused to his circle of initiates and resulted in his exile from Iran. Ziba Mir-Hosseini's chapter contains a lengthy conversation with Abdolkarim Sorush, who reiterates his general Islamic hermeneutic which has caused him so much difficulty over the past ten years. This reader does have several non-Iranian voices, however, in some of the introductions that precede each chapter (unless otherwise stated, I have written these introductions).

For the translations that are published here in English for the first time I have adopted a phonetic transliteration system. There are some exceptions, which conform to the general English rendering of terms (such as *ulema*, Isfahan and Mu'awiya).

Lastly I would like to express my gratitude to a number of institutions whose financial assistance has made it possible to actualise this project. Producing a reader is an expensive business, as it is necessary to obtain copyrights for reproducing material, and I have also felt duty-bound to offer small financial encouragement to the translators. I am grateful to the John Robertson Bequest (Glasgow University) and also to the British Institute of Persian Studies. Without their assistance it is unlikely that this reader would be as complete and full as it now is. I make no claims that this book is comprehensive, as there are many other individuals who could have been represented in it. I am aware that it would have been possible to include the works of socialists, such as Taqi Arani, or the writings of the secular-leaning 'Ali Dashti or even the speeches of Mohammad Khatami. However, in a single volume such as this, choices have to be made, and perhaps a second volume might not be such a bad thing.

CHAPTER 1

The Reign of Terror in Persia[1]

Jamal al-Din al-Afghani (1838–98)

The reign of Naser al-Din Shah (reigned 1848–96), the fourth monarch of the Qajar dynasty, coincided with increasing competition between the two superpowers (Britain and Russia) to extend their influence in Iran. While both attempted to gain the upper hand through trade, acquiring economic concessions and granting loans, neither power was prepared to guarantee the defence of Iran, which was perceived as a potentially dangerous over-expansion of military resources. Instead, each power sought to block any advantage that befell the other. This unhealthy competition was one of the factors that perpetuated the stagnation of the Iranian economy, and contributed to the inability of Naser al-Din to finance any reform. Increasing contact with the West through trade, diplomatic missions, missionary activity and the emergence of the printing press resulted in the realisation of how far Iran (and other Middle Eastern regions) lagged behind European countries such as Britain, France and Russia not only in economic, but also in military and educational spheres. Attempts at reform were made in the Ottoman Empire, Egypt and Iran, the most notable attempt in the latter case being the modernising and centralising reforms made by Amir Kabir, one of Naser al-Din's ministers during the early part of his reign. However, opposition to centralising reforms was a great barrier to overcome, as the clergy, the various Iranian tribes, the court and the aristocracy all had vested interests in maintaining a decentralised system of government.

The problems facing Iran during the second half of the nineteenth century cannot therefore be laid squarely upon the shoulders of the Shah, although his three expensive journeys to Europe and his granting of economic concessions to Europeans were misguided policies, and his lack of the ambition and bravery to initiate reform points to a certain weakness of character. It is not surprising that he was subject to much criticism from those native Iranians who were familiar with Western methods and norms, although the differences between these reformers were vast. Some advocated a virtual blind imitation of the West, while others wished to adopt Western sciences to advance Iran while at the same time rejecting the imperialist hegemony enjoyed by Britain in particular. Typifying the latter reformers was Jamal al-Din al-Afghani, a remarkable figure who has become famous as an advocate of Pan-Islam, who at times had the ear of several of the leading rulers of the Middle East, and who engaged the finest European intellectuals of the age in discussion of the merits and otherwise of religion.

Afghani was an Iranian born into a family of seyyeds (*descendants of Mohammad*) *in Asadabad near Hamadan, and it is likely that he also studied Shi'-ism in the holy cities in Iraq. In his late teens, Afghani was in India, where it is possible that his dislike for the English grew, following the events of the Indian 'Mutiny' in 1857. After spending some time in Afghanistan and Mecca, Afghani emerged in Istanbul, where he must have enjoyed something of a reputation as he was invited to give a speech at the opening of the new university in 1870. In praising the Westernising* Tanzimat *reforms of the Ottoman Empire, Afghani made friends among the modern elite, and he was invited onto the Council of Education only to be expelled to Egypt on the grounds of blasphemous remarks he made in a public speech. Afghani settled in Cairo from 1871 to 1879, during which time he established a small circle of reformists, but following anti-British agitation he was expelled, and so he returned to India where he rallied against Sir Sayyid Ahmad Khan, who was advising Indian Muslims to live peacefully within British India. In 1882, he left India for Europe, and by 1884 he was involved in the publication of an Arabic newspaper* (al-'Urwa al-Wuthqa) *in which European imperialism was castigated. In 1886, Afghani was invited to Tehran by the Shah, who developed a negative view of the reformist on their meeting, and so Afghani left for Russia in 1887. Agitating for a Russian–British war, Afghani made no headway, but once again he caught the eye of the Shah of Iran. He joined the royal party on the Shah's trip in Europe in 1889, and he returned to Tehran. However, when he realised that the Shah had little sympathy for his policies, Afghani took sanctuary at a shrine just south of Tehran. Against the prevailing tradition, the Shah had Afghani dragged out of his sanctuary and marched to the border, from where Afghani went to Basra and started to agitate against the Shah among the Shi'-ites.*

It was at this time that the Shah had granted a concession to a British subject that delivered a monopoly for the purchase, sale and export of tobacco, Iran's most lucrative agricultural product. Afghani responded by writing to one of the leading Shi'-ite clerics in Iraq, Mirza Hasan Shirazi, urging him to agitate against the concession. Shirazi did indeed write a letter to the Shah, denouncing the concession, and he went further by issuing a fatwa *in which he instructed his followers to refrain from the use of tobacco. This boycott was observed on a nation-wide scale, including the Shah's own wives, and huge demonstrations erupted in Tehran, which forced the Shah to cancel the concession. The tobacco protest was a watershed in modern Iranian history because it indicated the weakness of the Qajar monarchy and the strength of the opposition, including the clergy, the bazaar and the reformers. It is notable that the complaints in Afghani's letter 'The Reign of Terror in Persia' foreshadowed those that were heard in the movement leading up to the Constitutional Revolution in 1906 when Mozaffer al-Din Shah was forced to grant a constitution. Of particular note is Afghani's demand for the implementation of law and justice (or the deposition of the Shah). The economic ruin of Iran is highlighted, caused in part by corruption (tax farming), and blame is laid at the feet of the Shah and his chief minister. Another point of interest is Afghani's view of the English, and he states that behind Britain's reluctance to chastise the Shah for the reign of terror is the belief that it will have detrimental economic effects in Britain if there is an acknowledgement of a rift between the Shah's ministers and British diplomats. Afghani's distaste for the hypocrisy evident in the British espousal of liberalism and democracy on the one hand and its economic pursuits on the other is not hard to discern, and this identification of double standards and mistrust of Britain is a theme that has regularly appeared in Iranian politics up to the present day.*

Afghani was expelled from Iran and subsequently settled in Istanbul, where he was the 'guest' of the Ottoman Sultan, Abdulhamid (who harboured his own Pan-Islamic dream), and he remained under virtual house arrest until his death from cancer in 1898. Although Afghani suffered the humiliation of exile, he had a revenge of sorts as Naser al-Din Shah was assassinated by Mirza Reza Kermani, who on shooting the Shah is supposed to have exclaimed 'Take this from the hand of Jamal al-Din.'

It was as an advocate of law and justice that Afghani achieved his fame, but if his views on religion were known by Muslims in Iran, Egypt and the Ottoman Empire, it is likely that he would have been regarded as an unbeliever, as his exchange with Ernst Renan reveals Afghani as a severe critic of religion (Islam included). Nevertheless, he played a significant role in highlighting the deficiencies of Middle Eastern rulers, and his bravery in opposing European imperialism has been a source of inspiration for many Muslims in their struggles against colonialism and neo-colonialism.

Note

1. 'The Reign of Terror in Persia' first appeared in *The Contemporary Review*, LXI (1892), pp. 238–48.

Further Reading

Albert Hourani, *Arabic Thought in the Liberal Age, 1798–1939* (Cambridge: Cambridge University Press, 1962), Chapter 5, 'Jamal al-Din al-Afghani', pp. 103–29.

Nikki Keddie, *Religion and Rebellion: The Tobacco Protest of 1891–2* (London: Frank Cass, 1966).

——*Sayyid Jamal ad-Din "al-Afghani": A Political Biography* (Berkeley and Los Angeles: University of California Press, 1972).

——*An Islamic Response to Imperialism: Political and Religious Writings of Sayyid Jamal ad-Din "al-Afghani"* (London: University of California Press, 1983).

Elie Kedourie, *Afghani and 'Abduh: An Essay on Religious Unbelief and Political Activism in Modern Iran* (London: Frank Cass, 1966).

THE eminent Oriental statesman, scholar, orator, and reformer who contributes this article, the substance of which was lately delivered in French, at Queen's House, by the request of the Rev. H. R. Haweis, belongs to one of the Afghanistan tribes. He has travelled all over the world, and from the time when he took an active part in the wars between the father of Abdul Rahman Khan and Sheer Ali, he has devoted himself zealously to reform both at Teheran and Constantinople, travelling incessantly throughout Europe in order to acquire the elements of our civilisation, and leaving no stone unturned to adapt the modern idea to the needs of Asiatics. He is a man of cosmopolitan sympathies and encyclopaedic learning, with a special gift for languages, which enables him to preach his doctrines in many tongues; and above all he is a man of action. For some time he was a member of the Council of Public Instruction at Constantinople, where his ardent spirit, his hatred of corruption, and his large philanthropy at last got him into trouble with the authorities. He then visited Persia, where he holds high rank as Ulema and 'Son of the Prophet', by virtue of which dignity he has the privilege of remaining seated in the presence of the Shah. For some time he was treated by his Majesty with high distinction; but again his enthusiasm for reform, coupled with his vast authority with the people, got him into difficulties with the Shah's Ministers; and, after a most brutal arrest, banishment, and imprisonment – from which he has but recently escaped – the adventurous Moolah finds himself for a season the honoured guest of Prince Malcom Khan, the late Persian Minister at the Court of St James. His paper speaks for itself: he is here to push the claims of an oppressed and outraged people, with whom we have increasingly important political and commercial relations – upon the diplomatic consideration of those European statesmen who have the intelligence and penetration to see that England's Imperial interests in the East are closely connected with the safety and independence of Persia. The Sheikh is fifty years of age, in prime vigour, and in the full flush of his first important victory over cruelty and corruption in Persia, as evidenced in the abolition of the iniquitous and unpopular Tobacco Régie or concession to Europeans, an abolition which has been extorted from the Shah entirely by the brave and concerted action of the Moolahs, who have encouraged the people to stand together in resisting this latest form of Imperial robbery, until the Shah perceived that further resistance on his part was not only impolitic but impossible. – H. R. H.]

THE Reign of Terror? – Yes, it has come. My country is laid waste. Persia is decimated. Her irrigation works are ruined. Her soil unplanted. Her industries undeveloped. Her people scattered. Her noblest sons in prison, tortured, bastinadoed, robbed without pity, murdered without trial, by the Shah and his Vizier. This man, lately the son of his cook, is now the absolute disposer of the life and property of those who remain alive and have anything left. The England which received the Shah with all honour, supposing him to be bent on progress and civilisation, must at last be undeceived, and the sooner the better. Truth is stranger than fiction. No accounts of the horrors now going on in Persia can be overstated: not a tenth part will ever leak out – underground dungeons, torture-rooms, devils in human shape, greed, avarice, unbridled lust, unscrupulous violence, and the Shah himself the careless spectator or interested perpetrator of the worst crimes that sully human nature, and defile the page of Eastern history. I come from Persia; my friends lie there in dungeons. I speak that I know; I am not an obscure individual. My title, 'Son of the Prophet', may serve to signify to all Europeans that I am known and well accredited throughout the dominions of the Shah, recognised in my high religious dignity by the Shah himself and all his Ministers and ambassadors and upholders of our holy religion, and accepted as one of the chief teachers of the people. I have come over here to tell all Europeans who are interested in Persia – I will not say in humanity – that the grievances of my countrymen can no longer be hid; that they concern Russia and England, for to Russia and England the Persian turns, knowing well that both these great nations have interests in Persia, and that it can be for the interest of neither to see Persia depopulated and ruined; for, whilst neither Russia nor England will be permitted to conquer Persia, both for their own sakes should aid her to development. Let it be known that under the present Shah we have no law, and of late, I may add, no government. In former times the Grand Vizier used to stand between the Shah and his people; he represented, and to some extent respected, the interests of both; he was a high noble, and sometimes a great Minister and a great man; he mixed on equal terms with the high Persian aristocracy, who exercised a kind of feudal authority, and lived in a sort of patriarchal state on their well-cultivated lands. Now all that is changed; the Shah has ruined the nobles, seized their wealth, crushed their authority, scattered their people. The Vizier is a man none of them care to sit at table with, he is of the dregs of the people; he respects no one, and is respected by none; he robs openly for the Shah and himself. Another Minister is so illiterate that he cannot sign his name. Such is the 'Court'; the old strain of Persian aristocracy is almost extinct, a few hide away, some are banished, some are in prison, some are dead – all are degraded, crushed, lost to Persia.

Then I say there is no law. A patriarchal government without a written code is tolerable; but neither law nor government, only cruel, rapacious, unscrupulous and sleepless tyranny, that is not tolerable; yet that is our lot. The Persians have borne much; they are, like most Eastern nations, accustomed to high-handed rule of thumb and rough dealing, and some spoliation; but the over-bent bow has snapped at last. They cry out for redress. The insurrections *The Times* makes so light of are evidences of a fire that smoulders, and is ready to burst out all over Persia. The attitude of the people at this moment means European protection or Persian revolution. One stifled cry is ready to burst from the heart of every Persian: it is 'Justice! May we not live, untortured, unrobbed? If not, it is better to die.' The other day a Persian gentleman, overcome, driven mad with the misery of the times, forced himself before the Shah and committed suicide in his presence. If complaints are not universal it is due to the fact that over-caution, bred of past experience, has become a characteristic of the Persian people, and of late another cause has operated. The Shah's Government, especially since his Majesty's reception in Europe, has industriously circulated the report that the present unfair system and the Shah's personal power are guaranteed and fully approved of by Russia and England. 'What use,' say the Persians, 'if those all-powerful nations help the Shah to rob and murder, and doubtless get a share of the spoil in the way of concession to banks and tobacco dealers – of what use for us to rebel? We are murdered, lost, if England is for the bastinado, slavery, torture, assassination without trial, and robbery without redress. The great countries, the Queen, the Emperor of Russia, are after all not the friends of progress, justice, liberty. They look as if they too were great banditti, like our Shah.'

This is what the Persians say, hoodwinked by the Shah's Ministers. They are also whispering – and that opinion too, is gaining ground, as it is the only one which explains the facts – 'The Shah is no longer responsible for his actions.' By a strange fatality, he has chosen a Vizier who is also not responsible. Brandy, hashish, and the lowest women and men have done their work. The Shah is ruined in mind and body. The Shah must be deposed. That is what, for the first time in the Shah's reign, the people of Persia are now saying. Why has it come to this? Why has it *not* come to this before? I will tell you. For years the people have been hoping that the Shah will fulfil some of his many promises, and give them some law and the elements of justice. These were years ago formulated in many admirable State papers addressed by Prince Malcom Khan to the Shah, and the Shah seemed to approve and fully countenance all the ideas of his eminent Minister, who has occupied the most exalted diplomatic positions, in almost all the Courts of Europe, for thirty years.

I, Sheikh Djemal ed Din, on my return from Europe, also endeavoured to formulate the modest and reasonable aspirations of the people exactly in the sense suggested by Malcom and approved by the Shah. The people gathered around me as about their deliverer. 'A code of law! a code of law!' was all their cry; 'no matter what, only some law; we have no law, no courts of justice, no security of life and property; let us be taxed, squeezed, and oppressed in moderation; but let us have some law and we will submit!' The Shah still smiled; Ministers, mudjtahids, officers, merchants, every one began to scent the sweet odour of coming liberty. The dream was short-lived. The Shah suddenly drew in. The stormy tide must be stemmed – and stemmed at once. He saw his absolute tyranny would be checked. A dark frown succeeded the transitory smile. The frown was permanent. Soon came words, soon came actions. *The Times* calls this the '*Shah standing firm*'. The Shah tottering to his fall would be a truer description of his attitude. I, Sheikh Djemal ed Din, and Son of the Prophet, was suddenly arrested, simply because I had formulated propositions approved by the Shah himself – most moderate, most possible – the minimum of concession, most wise, and in full accord with all that was respectable and intelligent in Persia – a description which unhappily excluded the Shah and his present Ministers.

Now you must remember that until lately we not only enjoyed a patriarchal aristocracy, interested in the cultivation of their lands and the welfare of the people, and a noble body of teachers and preachers, intent on learning and education; but also *sanctuaries*, or places to which those persecuted or out of favour at Court might flee; and these sanctuaries have always been respected by our rulers. Well, the Shah has destroyed and desecrated this ancient and pious institution. There was one sanctuary especially sacred, not far from Teheran. To that, on hearing of his Majesty's displeasure, I had retreated; but to such a despot nothing is sacred. Three hundred of my devoted disciples were with me; we lived there, studying, praying, working, believing, watching. In the middle of the night the sanctuary was violated by the emissaries of the Shah. I was seized, well-nigh stripped in mid-winter, and hurried away over the frontier. All Persia seethed with indignation and fury. It meant a blow to reform, to justice, to the national hopes and aspirations. The Shah was afraid. His Vizier diligently published that I had been escorted with all honour by my own wish to the frontier; that special supplies of money and stores had been despatched after me that I might lack no comfort. Lies! – I was half naked, half starved, in chains till I escaped to Bagdad; I came to England; I resolved to tell the shameful story, not for myself, but for my people. Allah! let the light shine in on the dark places of the earth. I do not know your language, but in broken French I have spoken to some of your people. I now write, and friends help me to produce my cause in your generous and liberal *Review*.

I continue. My companions, some of the best, most learned, and honoured in Persia, were now thrown into prison. They had done nothing, made no revolution, only reminded the Shah of his formal promises, which were daily most grossly violated by the Vizier and his governors and soldiers. Three hundred of my companions now languish in dungeons, from which they are pulled at intervals to be bastinadoed – their feet beaten into a jelly (these are refined students, men of brain and heart, and some are nobles and ex-Ministers, and the best blood of Persia) – others have their ears cut off, their eyes taken out, their noses slit, their joints wrenched, and so they linger and so they die. As I write news comes to me: my dearest and oldest friend has had his head cut off without accusation, without trial, or defence of any kind. So I am entitled to speak of all this at first hand. The African slave trade, the worst atrocities of the past, pale before what is at this moment going on in Persia under the very shadow of the English and Russian legations. But facts, dry facts, are needed.

Remember, then, you law-abiding English, that up to the present time there has never been a single line of written law for the guidance of such departments as the criminal, civil, municipal, or in any of the revenue branches – never been any equitable government at all: everything centres in the Shah. And suppose he is mad, or generally drunk, or both – what then? I tell you nothing rules him but the passing whim of the moment. That is what it has come to at last, and his example is faithfully copied by his Government and Ministers, koyemakams, sub-mudirs, etc. etc. Justice is therefore non-existent. The Minister who is in power today may be called upon to undergo the bastinado, the burning by red-hot iron, or other torture tomorrow. Punishment for supposed misdeeds and mutilation of the various members of the body is the order of the day; so no one is ever sure of his ears, nose, hands, feet, or head, not to mention his property or liberty.

This is the present reign of terror; do you think this a misnomer of the situation I am describing? Under such a system it would require demigods to steer clear of the grossest abuses; but when creatures below humanity – drunkards, maniacs, dullards, and debauchees – are entrusted with it, a reign of terror is the only possible result.

We suffer in Persia bodily from the abuse of power, but that abuse is the direct consequence of the constitution of power in Persia. Behold what takes place: a man is desirous of obtaining the governorship of a certain province, say Khorasan or Aidarbjau. His first step is to lay at the feet of the Shah his *pishkash* (offering), the amount of which varies, according to the post sought for, from thirty to one hundred thousand tomans – a toman equals, roughly speaking, seven shillings. He then has to guarantee the raising of a sum representing the annual revenue of the particular province exceeding that of the previous year – i.e., the amount for which the late governor was responsible; at this stage, and if he is not outbidden, or the Shah does not demand more, the applicant for power succeeds in obtaining the curt consent of the Shah expressed in the word 'Bali' – all right! Armed with this powerful disyllable from the lips of the shadow of Allah, the aspirant to office has next to conciliate the Ministers, whose approval can only be bought by more sums of ready cash, or *pishkash*. Having at last succeeded in receiving his appointment, he becomes suddenly transformed into an irresponsible tyrant and oppressor. It is his turn now to receive *pishkash* from the underlings who seek places in his train, and in the case of a governor of a province his retinue generally amounts to three hundred. He has his chamberlains, his secretaries, his pipe-bearers, his body-servants, his ferrashes (military servants), his executioners, his master of the horse, grooms, cooks, and the rest. From the chamberlain down to the stable-boy each in turn has to make his offering to the newly appointed governor, who of course appoints the highest bidder. Everything being thus pleasantly settled, they proceed to their destination, and the province then becomes a scene of sub-robbery and spoliation, the heavy hand being lifted only when nothing more can be discovered to steal.

How is it likely to be otherwise? No wise Vizier, to ensure tenure of office, to support the nobles in their beneficent influence; no nobles to support; no check upon the rapacity of the governors, or the cupidity of the Shah – how can it be otherwise? Remember, no governor, nor any single person in his employ, ever receives a farthing in salary or wages. That is, and has been from time immemorial, the method of the East. Up to a point the people are content and take it as a matter of course, but the system is only tolerable when tolerably worked. The people expect to be ground down – granted, but within limits; and in the old days there were popular governors who remained long in power, and bad governors who were complained about and dismissed, and a Vizier who listened to reason. But now all this temporising has given way to unbridled extortion. The governor aims, of course, not only at getting enough to cover the *pishkash* he has had to give for his appointment, but enough to live on sumptuously whilst in office, and a round lump on departure to enable him to pay upon some future occasion.

Now these officials, from the governor downwards, are quite uncertain as to the length of time they may be permitted to retain their posts, for, in the case of a higher bidder presenting himself, they at once receive their dismissal: no consideration of fitness being entertained nor the good of the people in the least consulted. In order to prolong their term of office they are constrained to send periodically additional sums of *pishkash* to the Shah and his Viziers.

In the absence of any rule for the imposition of taxes or tithes, or for the payment of penalties, the Governor and his subordinates naturally extract and squeeze as much as they possibly can out of the people.

Now, what has been stated regarding the case of a governor equally applies to minor governors and sub-governors, lieutenants, mudirs, and others. The amount of *pishkash* to the Shah, Viziers, and principal governors varies according to the extent and capacity of the province, division, or town. It is, in fact, systematic extortion all round. Promotion amongst officers in the army is on the same plan. They have to outbid one another, and their pay is spasmodic and uncertain. Private soldiers would consider themselves lucky if they got one or two months' pay in the year. The only way they can live is by robbing the people and shifting for themselves. These burdens, with their attendant horror of false imprisonment and torture, fall heavily upon the shoulders of the Persians when they submit, but worse is their fate now if they venture to remonstrate. There is no friendly Vizier, no wise Shah, no interceding nobles, no just and long-established governors. It is not to be wondered at, therefore, if the oppressed Persian nation, once amongst the proudest and most enterprising in the world, should for the time be such an apparently abject race. Descendants of warriors and conquerors are now only fit to be tillers of the earth, hewers of wood and drawers of water, and right glad of the opportunity of being allowed to do even that unmolested. The sons of our nobles, I say, are ready to be employed in any of the meaner capacities in their own country, about what was once their own lands, in order to obtain their daily bread. This boon, however, they are often unable to secure. Many are driven out by hunger, whilst the few who still possess any property live in hourly dread of being deprived of it; but they are few and far between. As to the majority, they live continually insecure, not only in the possession of the good things of this life, but of life itself.

Our wives and daughters are at the mercy of the Shah and his minions; our girls are violated by the police without redress; our treasure extorted under torture by the soldiers. Fathers are afraid to tell their sons where lie the buried jewels, and the hoard of gold coins bricked or tiled up. In a moment our shops are broken up and the merchandise scattered; our wives and children wander like beggars along the highways, and drop and die in the caves, or swell the pauper crowds in Constantinople or Baghdad. Poor and mean, squalid, timid, secret, and panic-stricken is the small remnant of Persians who remain. Is it the fault of Persia, land of the sun; land of the date, the pomegranate, the barley, and the wheat; Persia, with her coal-mines, and none to work them; her wealth of iron, and none to smelt it; of copper, of turquoise; her wells of virgin petroleum; her arable land, so fertile that one has but to scratch the soil and harvest after harvest springs as fast as one can reap; and her so-called deserts which need but the restoration of her irrigation works? But all is undone, ruined, blackened, curst. I wander through a land of sparse and rapidly decreasing population; deserted villages, now silent, untenanted, lonely, wrecked hamlets; bones whitening by the wayside, bones of emigrants who have never emigrated. Thousands of us during these last years of the Shah have been compelled to take refuge in the Caucasus and the Transcaspian countries, while thousands more are to be found in the streets of various towns in Turkish Arabia, Anatolia, and as far as Turkey in Europe. At Constantinople I met Persians with delicate hands employed in the meanest capacity, such as water-carriers, street-sweepers, drovers, etc. It will be found, on examination, that the number of emigrants out of Persia exceeds one-fifth of the total population!

I have now to make a terrible and incredible admission: the moral of which should strike home to those thousands of English men and women who received the Shah with such acclamations. However *bizarre* it may seem, it is nevertheless a fact, that after each visit of the Shah to Europe he increased in tyranny over his people. Probably this may be more or less due to his arrogant estimation of his individual power and importance, based upon the flattering receptions which he received in Europe. The result is that the masses of Persia, observing that after each European tour the Shah became more intolerant and despotic, naturally but ignorantly attributed their increased sufferings to European influences, and hence their dislike of Europeans became yet more intense, at the very moment when a *rapprochement* might easily have been effected, and when, more than at any previous time, Persia stood in need of the kindling and liberalising influences of wisely directed British statesmanship.

England does not know what a blow is being dealt to her prestige in the East. She has at present done nothing to disabuse the minds of Persians of those erroneous notions which at this moment distort their judgement.

The real or affected ignorance of your English press on the true condition of Persia is another source of confusion and annoyance to those who desire her welfare. You depend, for instance, on certain wires from Teheran. Nothing could be more misleading at the present moment. Those wires are filtered through the Imperial Bank. The bank means the interest of the shareholders. The legation and the bank echo the views of the Ministers for the time being about the Shah. For them Persia is well governed – the masses are content, the Shah is the father of his people, the concessions to Europeans, especially the Tobacco Régie, merely graceful attempts to fall in with European ways and foment the *entente cordiale* between distant peoples or friendly allies. Here and there may be a few malcontents; no doubt these must be put down with 'a firm hand'. The Shah, patient and kind as he might be, would not be trifled with. A deep-seated revolt, ready to break out, and which has already broken out, north, south, east and west, is described as 'a local difficulty with the police'. Look at the way in which quite lately your newspapers have treated the furious indignation with which the tobacco concession has been received in Persia. You simply don't grasp the situation. Your journalists, for instance, make uncommonly light of the extraordinary action of the 'chief priest at Kerbala', who has forbidden the faithful to smoke in order to show the contempt and hatred with which the Persians view the detested monopoly in tobacco granted to English speculators by the Shah, and sold by the Shah for a larger sum. One would think the English press really did not know what the monopoly meant, or who the 'chief priest at Kerbala and the chief merchant at Teheran' really were. And as to the Shah's 'great firmness' in exiling one and defying the other, one would really suppose that 'folly' and 'firmness' were, in the journalist's estimation, convertible terms.

Well, then, first as to the tobacco monopoly. The prescriptive and inalienable right of the Persian to sell his tobacco or other wares to whom he will, was grossly violated by the Shah when he sold, or allowed his venal Ministers to sell, the tobacco monopoly to a foreigner. The Shah soon saw his mistake, but having pledged his word he dared not offend the European speculators, who hide under the aegis of your legation at Teheran. Nevertheless, as I write news reaches me from Teheran that arrangements have been made – the Shah, 'who stood so firm', getting alarmed at the action of the 'chief priest at Kerbala', and the Tobacco Régie has been cancelled. As to the 'chief priest of Kerbala', he is practically a Persian Pope, the presiding power at Kerbala. His Anathema means far more than the excommunication of the King of Italy by Pius IX or Leo XIII. In short, it is the undisguised opinion of all who know Persia, and are not taken in by the telegrams, that the Shah is hurrying blindly to his fall, which will be hastened by one mad act after another, unless he gets frightened and yields inch by inch.

I come now to this last point, What made the Persians believe that England meant to help them? I pray you, did not your Ministers a year or two ago urge upon the Shah a firman granting security of life and property to his subjects? Did not the Shah issue such a firman, and, after considerable pressure and long debate and hesitation, frankly communicate it to the Powers? Did not her Majesty upon hearing this express to Malcom Khan her profound satisfaction, and was not your Minister at Teheran regarded as a party to the transaction? All Persians believed that a firman thus issued and *communicated* to the European Powers gave the Powers, England first and foremost, the diplomatic right to insist upon its due observance, or at least to demand the explanation for any gross violation of it. Well, what followed? I, Sheikh Djemal ed Din, soon after became the natural and respectful mouthpiece of the people's joyful aspirations. I am received with favour by his Majesty, my words are approved, the regeneration of Persia is at hand; law is to be given, life and property are to be safe, our wives and daughters protected from outrage, our bread-winners from cruel and ruinous exactions – all is going well. Suddenly I am seized, banished, imprisoned; my friends are imprisoned and tortured, without explanation, without trial. After this, the people's eyes were opened; they felt they could place no reliance on the Shah and his promises. But their eyes were then turned to the Powers, to England first and foremost. Now would the British Minister, at least, certainly speak one little word at Teheran, if only to ask for some explanation of so gross a violation of the blessed firman. But no, not a word! Persia still waits for a message at this crisis. But you are afraid of your pockets. The bank interest might go down if any rumour of disagreement between the Shah's Ministers and your diplomatists at Teheran got wind. Therefore you are all as mum as mice, as the saying is, at Teheran; and as for your Parliament, it cares for none of these things – who knows or cares about Persia? You gaped at the Shah, he was amusing and a novelty. But the Persian people you exploit. Still it is not believable to them that England intends to do nothing, not so much as lift her voice – England, so ready to help Garibaldi – so willing to sacrifice untold wealth in order to put down the slave trade. Yet England refuses a word of remonstrance or advice when the firman to which she has been made a party through communication is torn to pieces before her eyes.

I come here to ask your people at this crisis to get questions asked in Parliament about the 'alleged' atrocities – that is the word, I believe – now going on in defiance of the Shah's own firman in Persia. Your Minister would then be instructed to approach the Shah's Ministers, and ask for an explanation on behalf of Her Majesty's Government. The moral effect of such an action would be immense, so great is still the prestige of England. But the Shah thinks you don't care how he acts, and if you will not or dare not help us anyhow, Russia is on the alert. If, at the present moment, she does not want to get direct to India, she is at least obliged to get first to the Persian sea-board, and for the furthering of this project she will certainly not hesitate to avail herself of the present disposition of the Persian people. You stand by helping yourself to odds and ends – here to tobacco, there to bank shares; you prove neither the open friend nor the open foe, and Persia, who cannot believe you foe, but almost doubts you friend, waits and waits for a word from you, which would cost no ships, no money, and would not really endanger your banking or your trade; a word from a free, powerful people on behalf of a beleaguered and enslaved, but noble, active-minded, and capable people. This is all we want at present; but that word must come soon, ere more victims are immolated in prison, more hearts broken, more resources squandered, more thousands banished; change, change, any change would be for the better. That is what Persia demands. The word will out which has been smouldering in a million ruined homes, but now rolls like the roaring of the sea full of ominous thunder and of irresistible rush; its echo has at last reached England: 'Change the Government, or dethrone the Shah!'

CHAPTER 2

A Traveller's Narrative[1]

Mirza Malkam Khan

The exact date of composition of Malkam Khan's 'A Traveller's Narrative' is unknown, although it must have been written in the second half of the nineteenth century. As a critique of certain sections of society, namely the clerics and the literati (including court intellectuals, scribes and poets), this work provides an alternative view of the backward state of Iran to that offered by Afghani, who focused on the Shah and his chief minister. Aside from these criticisms of certain societal groups, Malkam composed several treatises in which he championed both political reform along Western, liberal lines, and European civilisation. He also believed that illiteracy in Iran could be reduced by reform of the Persian alphabet, and he devised his own alphabet, which failed to attract much attention.

   Malkam Khan's life was as colourful and eventful as Afghani's, with whom he collaborated for a period. Born into an Armenian Christian family in Isfahan in 1833, Malkam was sent to an Armenian school at the tender age of ten in Paris, and on his return to Tehran he was initially employed as a translator at the newly established college, the Dar al-Fonun (House of Arts), and was soon a teacher there in his own right. Malkam was able to establish himself further as a translator at the Paris peace treaty between Britain and Iran following the conflict between the two over Herat. On his return to Tehran he impressed Naser al-Din Shah and was made special translator to the monarch. From this point on, Malkam assumed a more politically active stance, and he presented the Shah with a proposal for governmental reform as well as establishing an institution based on European freemasonry (although there were no official connections with European lodges). The aims of this institution, the Faramush-khaneh (House of Oblivion) included the search for truth, promotion of human rights and the establishment of lawful government. The secrecy of the organisation aroused the suspicion of the clerics and the Shah, and eventually Naser al-Din prohibited the Faramush-khaneh. Malkam was exiled to Ottoman territories, but was appointed the adviser to the reformist Iranian ambassador in Istanbul, Mirza Husayn Khan, where he remained for ten years until 1871. Although the Faramush-khaneh was dissolved, its lasting influence may have been influential in the succeeding generation of reformists, including clerics (ulema). Indeed, Malkam Khan had been able to attract influential clerics to the institution, including the Imam

Jom'eh (Friday prayer leader) of Tehran, and also Seyyed Sadeq Tabataba'i, who was the father of Seyyed Mohammad Tabataba'i, one of the leading clerics supporting the Constitutional Movement in the first decade of the twentieth century.

Mirza Husayn Khan became Naser al-Din's chief minister in 1871, and Malkam once more enjoyed royal patronage, as he became a councillor and was awarded the title Nazem al-Molk (Regulator of the Kingdom). Sent to London with the title 'Minister Plenipotentiary in London' to organise the Shah's trip to Europe in 1873, Malkam subsequently attained the post of ambassador in London, and was given the title 'prince'. After sixteen years in London, Malkam's fortunes began to wane with the controversy over the lottery concession in 1888–89. The Shah granted Malkam the monopoly for a state lottery in return for £1,000, and Malkam then sold this lottery to a British syndicate for £40,000. By this time, the protection and influence of Mirza Husayn Khan had long vanished, and the Shah's chief minister of the time was unsympathetic to Malkam and was able to acquire a fatwa *from the clerics that denounced the lottery as un-Islamic, and so the lottery was rescinded and Malkam was dismissed from his ambassadorial rank.*

Malkam then devoted his energies to criticising the Iranian state through his newspaper Qanun *(law) (the first issue of which appeared in 1890) and to promoting the idea of lawful, constitutional government. The guiding principles of Malkam Khan's views were expressed in* Qanun's *slogan of 'Unity, Justice and Progress'. The theme of unity is of interest because it was the major element in the world view of Ahmad Kasravi some half-century later; he, like Malkam, desired to see the end of sectarian conflicts in Iran.* Qanun *was banned in Iran, but its discussion of politics and the contemporary situation in Iran attracted like-minded reformists. One of these reformers was Afghani, and these exiles shared a distaste for the corruption of the Shah's ministers, and both were impressed by the advances and progress of the West and desired a reform of Islam. After the assassination of Naser al-Din Shah, Malkam was once again called upon to serve Iran, and he was appointed ambassador to Italy. He passed away in Switzerland in 1908.*

There is little doubt that Malkam Khan was a major influence on the intellectuals and reformists in the period leading up to the Constitutional Revolution, mainly because of the ideas expressed in Qanun. *These ideas included a bicameral Parliament, the lower house being elected by the people with an upper chamber being composed of the notables. However, some scholars have criticised Malkam for his greed, insincerity and trickery, which are typified in his conversion to Islam, his involvement in the lottery scandal, and his seeking for high office which when successful in 1898 was followed by his closure of* Qanun. *Even if it is accepted that Malkam was a self-promoting charlatan, his impact on and contribution to the discussion for reform should not be underestimated, as copies of* Qanun *were reprinted by constitutionalists, and his articles were also reprinted in the leading newspapers of the day.*

Note

[1.] 'A Traveller's Narrative' was translated into English by Hamid Algar, and appeared in his *Mirza Malkum Khan* (London: University of California Press, 1973), pp. 278–99.

Further Reading

Hamid Algar, *Mirza Malkum Khan* (London: University of California Press, 1973).

Malkum Khan, 'Persian Civilisation', *Contemporary Review*, LIX (1891), pp. 238–44.

Iraj Parsinejad, *A History of Literary Criticism in Iran (1866–1951)* (Bethesda, MD: Ibex Publishers, 2003), pp. 95–118.

—⁕—

[THE following translation is offered as a specimen of Malkum's style as essayist. The translation is based on the text entitled 'Sayyāḥī Gūyad', in *Kullīyāt-i Malkum*, pp. 187–212. It cannot be regarded as strictly representative of his work, for unlike most of his treatises and essays, it has little to say on political and economic matters. 'A Traveller's Narrative' is, by contrast, a lively treatment of the subjects it sets out to discuss, despite obvious literary short-comings, and is inspired throughout by an acute sense of satire.

The piece constitutes a sustained attack on two classes of men: poets and men of letters and religious scholars. Government officials, physicians, and astrologers all receive passing blows, but are not on this occasion the chief objects of satire. It is regrettable that the exact date of composition of the essay is unknown, for the views on traditional poetry and eloquence expressed in it form one of the earliest protests against that subordination of content to form which characterized much of Persian letters in the Qajar period. The establishment of the Qajar dynasty had followed by a few decades the formation of the Isfahan school of poetry, which aspired to imitation of the classical masters, particularly the panegyrists of the Seljuq period.[1] When the Qajar court was established in Tehran and came to function as a new centre of patronage, the school of Isfahan transferred to the capital, and the imprint of its ideals can be seen on most Persian poetry until late in the nineteenth century. The poetry in imitation of classical masters produced by men such as Saḥāb (d. 1808), Ṣabā (d. 1822), and even the greatest of the school, Qā'ānī (d. 1854), was for the most part forced and unconvincing; the search for rhetorical ingenuity became frantic and sometimes took the poet beyond the bounds of comprehensibility. It is verse such as this that Malkum ridicules by means of the rhymed absurdities the poets in his piece recite. Later in the nineteenth century, the transformation of Persian poetry began with the introduction of political and social concerns into the corpus of accepted poetic themes and the subordination of form to content, of word to meaning. Although Malkum never tried his hand at verse, in this essay he foreshadows some of these developments which were to revivify Persian poetry.

The view of the ulama expounded at length in this piece is of great interest for revealing Malkum's sincere opinion of that class. He ridicules even their title of 'learned men' (*'ulamā*), preferring instead to coin the word *jahlmandān* (ignoramuses) as a more appropriate designation. Their concern with points of ritual and branches of the law (*furū'āt*) is depicted as inherently absurd, and they are accused of having divided the community into warring sects merely for the sake of selfish interest. They do the bidding of kings by proclaiming their self-seeking wars to have religious sanction and, while turning a blind eye on the failings of the powerful, visit all their harshness on the weak. All objections to their misdeeds they silence by denouncing the protester as an infidel, and their minds are closed to all new knowledge, particularly that emanating from non-Muslim sources.

Although the justice of many of Malkum's accusations, once shorn of polemical exaggeration, may be accepted, it is none the less clear from the piece that he was impatient with the whole apparatus of traditional culture and religious learning. With his background of European education and his concern for a radical westernisation of Iranian life, he could have had little sympathy for a class which, in the nature of things, was bound to absorb and elaborate a transmitted body of learning (*naql*) and to cultivate a knowledge of Arabic.

The class none the less has its uses, even for a reformer such as Malkum, for he suggests that they form the best support for the honour of the nation and are capable of rendering 'unlimited services to people and to state'. They need, however, one to guide them (*murabbī nadārand*), 'to reduce their affairs to order, and regulate and determine the tasks they are to fulfil'. It is clear from other evidence that Malkum himself aspired to the position of 'guide' of the ulama and hoped to direct their attention away from *furū'āt* to matters he considered more pressing. It is by no means certain that this would have resulted in truer service by the ulama to the cause of religion: Malkum's profession of belief that 'the perspicuous faith of Islam is perfect and the best of all paths for men to follow' rings as hollow as all his other utterances on the matter.

Malkum's view of the ulama has anticipated certain more recent attitudes towards them. His mocking of their heavily Arabicised speech bears comparison with Jamālzāda's depiction of a shaykh in his celebrated story 'Fārsī Shikar Ast' (Persian is sugar-sweet).[2] The shaykh expresses himself with greater grammatical accuracy than the figures in Malkum's piece, a fact which doubtless reflects Jamālzāda's superior command of Arabic. It is also of interest to note that the complaint that the ulama devote excessive attention to minor matters of ritual and the details of ablution still is heard frequently in Iran.

Despite the interest of its contents and the satirical verve apparent in its wording, the essay is weak and unconvincing in its structure. It lacks the masterly coherence and control that alone would qualify it to rank with masterpieces of Persian satire such as the work of 'Ubayd Zākānī (d. 1371). There is no real transition from one episode to the next, and the ending is abrupt and unexpected. Too many characters make their brief appearances, and not all have a clearly defined function. Thus, the narrator, his friend, and the 'ill-mannered youth' are all positive figures, observing and criticising the lunacy around them, with no apparent difference of outlook or belief. This structural weakness is less apparent in Malkum's shorter dialogues, 'Rafīq va Vazīr' and 'Shaykh va Vazīr', where a clearly circumscribed topic is discussed by only two persons.

The translation is inevitably free at those points where it was necessary to construct whole sentences of nonsense approximately corresponding to those in the original. Those sentences which in the text are written in a barbarous pseudo-Arabic are marked with an asterisk in the translation. – H. A.]

I once had occasion to witness a sublime and wondrous gathering in one of the cities of Iran, which I attended in the company of a friend. Not long had passed after my arrival before a certain dignified *ākhūnd*[3] joined our gathering and settled himself down in the place of honour. An hour later, a person adorned in costly garments with embroidered hems entered the room and took his place beside the *ākhūnd*. With an earnest frown on his face, he exchanged the customary greetings and compliments with all present and then, to all appearances, subsided in an ocean of thought.

I asked my friend: 'Who is this lofty personage?'

He replied: 'Our host, one of the gentry of this city.'

Soon after arrived another person, who was wearing a white robe decorated with silver thread, over his robe, a cloak, and on top of the cloak, a coat of squirrel fur. Instead of trousers, he had chosen to clothe his legs in a nondescript, dark blue undergarment. He sat down directly facing our host. Then came another guest, a man of impudent bearing, with a fur hat set at a jaunty angle on his head, clad in military attire and a green cloak with golden epaulettes. He went and stationed himself next to the *ākhūnd*.

It was at this point that I saw our host suddenly emit a roar of such dimensions that I feared for myself and turning to my friend requested an explanation.

He replied: 'Our respected host was simply calling for his water pipe.'

Soon I saw a host of servants rush in and jostle each other with such abandon that the guests were almost trampled underfoot. I was waiting for the imminent collision when I observed the *ākhūnd* angrily preparing to quit the gathering. He had arisen and was beginning to deliver a furious oration.

Our host, slightly unknitting his brow, addressed him in conciliatory tone and finally succeeded in seating him anew. The *ākhūnd* replied with a strange mixture of ceremonially polite and intentionally offensive phrases. The gentleman in the white robe took the side of our host, but the guest who was clad in a green cloak took up the cudgels for the *ākhūnd*, and an hour passed in pleasant conversation between them.

I was not well acquainted with their manner of expression and therefore asked my friend to explain the substance of the dispute. His reply was as follows: 'The reason for the *ākhūnd*'s attempted departure was the laxity of his host's servants in bringing him his accustomed water pipe. This aroused his anger and caused him to arise and prepare to leave. And his parting words were: "May God have mercy on past generations! I spit on times such as these!"'

'Then our host responded: "Patiently to forbear is a duty for you. Exert yourself in patience, I beg of you! Do you not constantly recommend this lofty quality to us? How can it befit your spiritual dignity to be filled with such pride that you find delay in the simple matter of a water pipe to be quite intolerable? You consider yourself an exemplary model for all men and invite us to learn pleasing morals and conduct from your person, but is obedience truly incumbent on us? In what chapter of the law is it stipulated that you should always receive your water pipe before all others, never once having to wait?"'

'The *ākhūnd* replied: "If you imagine yourself to have acquired some dignity from service to the state, I too have earned much honour from service to the Sacred Law.[4] Disrespect shown to me is tantamount to disrespect of God's Law, let none gainsay it! And if this matter is not spelled out in the lawbooks, it is none the less present in the Glorious Qur'ān. To honour the believer is to revere the values of religion. Did not the Prophet say: 'The learned among my people are as the Prophets of the Children of Israel'? You have not, like me, expended toil and trouble and the light of your eyes in the dark corner of a madrasa! Come now, tell us, what worthy service have you performed for government and people to deserve all this pomp and grandeur? What have you done but cause your depredations to descend throughout the land and usurp the people's hard-earned wealth? All you have to show for your efforts is a manner of speech befitting your station and the joy and glee of foreigners that the affairs of our land go according to their desires!"'

The gentleman in the white robe, who was evidently an accountant in government service, turned to the *ākhūnd* and said: 'Respected sir! You have let your anger pass beyond all reasonable bounds. Now you saw fit to mention madrasas; tell us, pray, who builds madrasas for you and your like? Who pays the cost of your dignity and rank? You who claim to be a servant of the effulgent Law of God, tell us honestly, what service have you performed? What flawless, well-argued book have you composed to remain as a monument in time to come? How many thousand traditions of the Prophet do you know by heart? With how many Arab masters have you studied the Glorious Qur'ān, its recitation and interpretation? How many thousands of the straying and lost have you led to the haven of true guidance? What service, indeed, have you performed other than this, that you have divided our Twelver Shi'i community, which once was one, into two parties, and called them Shaykhī and Uṣūlī?[5] You have forced these wretches to contend with and condemn each other; you have severed the ties of love and fraternity between them. And this, so that "guides" and "elders" might constantly be in demand and all kinds of hostility continuously erupt.

'Tell me, what mosque have you built, what madrasa established? And what unknown *imāmzāda*[6] have you discovered and honoured with a worthy tomb?

'Now you say that disrespect shown to you is tantamount to dishonouring the Sacred Law, but this you have yet to prove. You are not yourself the law; you claim only to be a *mujtahid*,[7] so tell us clearly what you mean. As for what God has ordained, His commands are general in scope; specific provisions may freely be discussed. Why should you alone qualify for the rank of "believer" and of "scholar"; cannot we also aspire thereto? Or are you of those believers and learned men whom God has mentioned in His Book?[8] And as for the saying of the Prophet – may the peace and blessings of God be upon him – that "the learned among my people are as the Prophets of the Children of Israel", we will know that it refers to you when you transform your walking stick into a snake and when you restore the dead to life! Only then will you qualify as one of the learned intended by the Seal of Prophets!'

On hearing this, the military man laughed and said: 'Glorious and Exalted is God Almighty! See what a pass we have reached! His excellency the clerk, who always spells Āshtīān[9] with an *'ayn* and *ṭā*, has taken it on himself to explain a Qur'ānic verse, and started to mumble about "general" and "specifc". My dear sir, it is quite enough that you should scrawl out your illegible *siyāq*,[10] be innocent of all the principles of accountancy, unable to perform the simplest arithmetic, and yet hold the position of chief accountant in the land! To manage the accounts while quite incapable of accountancy is indeed a staggering feat. "Deduct therefrom" is the extent of your learning; "the lofty ministry", your only adornment. Come now, leave aside "general" and "specific"!

'Besides, the meaning of the *ḥadith* is not what you imagine. Comparison does not imply complete identity between objects or persons compared. If the ulama are the best of men in their seeking of proximity to God, in learning and in wisdom, it is enough to justify the comparison. Then, too, consider this: the Prophets of the Children of Israel were issuing a challenge, were laying claim to prophecy. They performed miraculous deeds only to bear witness to their claim. If you should imitate Pharaoh and deny the word of God, then will it be a duty for the ulama to bring forth miracles and to turn a stick into a snake!'

All this brought his excellency the accountant to a pitch of fury, and he replied: 'Your true calling is that of a poet! Now nonchalance and carelessness may be part of the poet's profession, but they should not always be on display. It is no cause for surprise that when they wish to enumerate the true servants of the state, they write: Mīrzā the mouthful, Mīrzā the fragment, Mīrzā the particle, Mīrzā the drop and Mīrzā the invisible.[11] In youth such persons are sensualists and libertines, but in old age they set themselves up as sages and preceptors. Their talents lie in patching words together, and when they come to compose history, it becomes all too clear that the sum of their knowledge is the four dynasties of ancient Iran. Were you to ask them what celebrated persons were alive in the first year of the reign of Parvīz, and what great events befell at that time, they would be unable to give you satisfaction. Out of all the occurrences in the history of the world, they are content to be familiar with the tale of Rustam and Isfandiyār[12] and what passed between Khusrau and Shīrīn.[13] Of prosody, rhyme, and rhetoric, they know nothing, and of the poetry and literature of foreign peoples they are entirely unaware. Whenever they cannot fit a verse to its proper metre, they pass it off as a "pleasing pause".[14] Any weird fancy that is contrary to the rules of both Persian and Arabic they regard as proof of the utmost eloquence. Despite all this, they are not content with a stipend of 300 *tomans* and a hundred *kharvārs* in kind!'[15]

When the *ākhūnd* saw the turn that affairs had taken, he said: 'Gentlemen! I have abandoned all my complaints, and so now leave each other in peace.' The guests asked and granted each other forgiveness, and the gathering dispersed.

Leaving that seat of argument and dissension, I emerged into the street and fell into the clutches of sundry classes of madmen, each one separately of perverse disposition and each afflicted with a different species of lunacy. Some hoped to cure the sicknesses of the body by the use of magic formulas. Others wished to deduce the fate of men from the conjunction and disposition of the planets. Still another group was of the belief that language was invented not for the purpose of conveying ideas, but for the construction of rhyming phrases and other devices for squandering men's time.

This latter species of lunatic was celebrated among the commonalty for its wordy blabbering. In strict adherence to their beliefs, the members of this group paid no attention to meaning, whether in speech or in writing. They considered obscurity of speech the highest degree of accomplishment and spent most of their life in the study of rare and uncommon words. When they listened to someone speaking, it was not in order to grasp the purport of his speech; rather they were on the lookout for some new and unfamiliar word that he might utter.

Because of their innate stupidity, whenever one of them knew twenty different words for one meaning, instead of using only one, he would employ all twenty in succession, considering eloquence to repose in peculiarity of expression. All their energy and attention were devoted to striving after the utmost degree of obscure complexity.

The more incomprehensible a statement was, the more lustre it gained in their eyes, and if they wished to praise the accomplishments of some writer, they would say: 'That rascal is so eloquent that none can understand his writings.'

Because they reckoned rhymed prose to be the finest of all literary artifices and had no purpose in their writings other than the production of rhymes, they would frequently string together whole lines of nonsense, just for the sake of rhyme.

Whenever the word *vāṣil* (arrived) occurs in their compositions, after it you will find *ḥāṣil* (obtaining); all beings (*vujūd*) are generous (*dhī-jūd*); dispositions (*mizāj*) are invariably effulgent (*vahhāj*). A word in isolation they clearly thought as tasteless as dough; it had to be rhymed with another in order to ferment. Every wretch who was qualified by some adjective had another affixed to him for all eternity. Any falsity or lie (*durūgh*) had to be like the darkened sky (*bi-furūgh*); to serve and to bear (*khidmat*) without trouble and care (*ẓahmat*) was quite out of the question, and whosoever's rank was lofty and high ('*ālī*), his rank was sublime as the sky (*muta'ālī*).

They had certain inherited words which all the idle blabbers recorded and unvaryingly used in their correspondence. Thus even when cholera was raging, they would write: 'Your noble missive arrived at the best and fairest of times'; and none thought of asking them: 'You unjust blabberer! If cholera is the fairest of times, then what is the worst?'

According to the custom prevalent in correspondence up to this day, in all their communications they wrote as follows: 'We submit that our real concern is your effulgent disposition. Should you intend to inquire after our condition, we enjoy the blessing of health and are busied with praying for your well-being. We suffer from no manner of misfortune, except separation from the pleasures of conversation. We entertain great hope that such may soon be allotted us and come within our grasp.'

They had written books which even after a second earnest attempt at understanding left the reader confused and uncertain as to their meaning. I have myself read a hundred of their books and not found a single new idea in any of them. When your glance fell on the page, you would encounter a Joseph lost in the well of the dimple on the chin; the moth of the heart was melting on the fire of love; and a snake-like tress was twisting round the cheeks of the beloved. In every line a goblet was being drained; the arrows of the eyelashes were being fitted into the bow of the eyebrows; and with the polo stick of the tresses the hearts of the lovelorn were being snatched up.[16]

I saw ten thousand panegyric odes which all in one manner and style began with the spring. Then, racing back and forth between mountain and plain, sea and river, after a thousand adventures, the poets arrived in the patron's presence. Then, from his eyelashes to his horse's tail, all would be praised in a flurry of rhyme. After limitless and unbounded extravagances, they would finally petition the cerulean vault to halt the course of time that the life of their patron might be eternal.

Whatever tyrant they praised, inevitably the wolf and the sheep would practise fraternal love from the auspicious effects of his justice, and in awe of his anger, amber would no longer stretch out the hand of aggression against straw.

They told lies in praise of every scoundrel, spinning together extravagances a lunatic would not dare repeat. But when these blabberers recited them, none thought of objecting, rather everyone said together: 'How true!' All this, I failed to understand. Was it that they had contrived some meaning for the poet's words that had never occurred even to him?

Once I chanced on the most celebrated of this species in a garden where they had convened a gathering. They were busy praising each other with the most elevated flattery and making a show of their art and talent with the most awesome extravagance. One of them was particularly celebrated among his fellows for his facility in coining rhymes and in conceiving unlikely turns of phrase. As his eye fell on me, he said:

> Truly the world is now my darling, for now from the fourfold clime,
> The caravan has arrived before visage of imperious speech!

He had hardly delivered himself of the second hemistich when the blabberers began to exclaim: 'Well done! A masterpiece! What a mind! Truly you are the mother and father of all eloquence! Mercury, the celestial scribe, in hopeless envy of your turn of speech, casts away his meteorite quill! Venus dances enraptured on the throne your pen has furnished! The world is reborn from the life-giving drops shed by the bounteous raincloud of your fancy!'

Upon hearing the lavishing of so much praise, another of the blabberers thought good to make his contribution. He said: 'Indeed your excellency has spoken well. Your humble servant, too, has an offering to make which he trusts will be worth the hearing:

> Be swift as the soul, but not swift-footed;
> swallow a hundred morsels, yet never chew.
> Thou art not that body, thou art a seeing eye;
> be free of the body, thou hast beheld the soul,
> The animal spirit knows naught but sleep;
> men's bodies are but shade and shadow.
> My mother of invention grieves at her own decease;
> she suffers the pangs of labour, as the lamb is
> born of the ewe.'

The participants in the gathering came close to fainting, such was their joy and so intense their pleasure. From every side arose murmurs of approval, and all were astonished at the profound wisdom of the blabberer's utterances. Someone swore by the heads of all those present that never had any diver thus penetrated the ocean-depths of meaning.

Meanwhile, another of the poets had firmly secured his hat, and adopting a heroic stance he began to intone:

Lofty tree of Kayanid stock! Spread copiously
    your seed; no harm can result.
Triumphant shall I be in every warlike clash;
    in sleep and in waking, like heroic Rustam
    and swift-paced Bīzhan.[17]
The champion turns black to white and white to
    black; puts up a shield to all your arrows.
He makes captive the emperor of the world;
    enslaves unto himself the tongue of praise.

Not pausing to let the gathering express its appreciation of this piece, yet another rhymester sprang up and with a wealth of exaggerated gesture began to wail:

O blood of my liver, trickling forth from the phoenix!
    Who in this earthly abode is beyond thy gaze?
When the steed of thought enters the land of heat,
    the swift-turning heavens begin to melt.
The firmament revolves, unceasingly alert; the light of
    guidance is concealed within the serpent's skin.
Life he has gained from that pre-eternal spread; but
    the friend averts his gaze, and passes on.
The dust of the world settles on the mouth of heaven;
    the rich banquet is gathered up.
Every jewel that the stone's jaws emit, is like a
    tooth from the mouth extracted.

At this point, one of the blabberers who had particularly high standards and had not yet seen fit to praise any of the works recited, drew a scroll of paper out of his belt and, with much pride and complacency, began to read the following:

'The lofty-soaring falcon of talent and learning adorned thus its tongue, that perpetual diminishment of fine and noble speech was contrary to the pearl-like drops of the fresh and verdant quill of growth, and the resourceful scribe, throughout the revolution of days and nights, brought forth gems of bright and glowing truth.

'The finely prancing meteors of fate stood unjustly accused in that feast of fine speech and eloquence. Truth, forsooth, shone like a gleaming tooth; nor could the eye perceive aught uncouth. The virgin bride of speech, groomed by the comb of thought, emerged from the veil of men's imagining into the broad hall of eloquence, and there, with all manner of sweet scent, and still sweeter sentiment, the cheek of that cherished idol was made pure and free of sorrow and gloom, of smoke and fume. With the auspicious blessings of noble quality, all hewn from the mine of honour, she snatched the desire of her heart from the jaws of the dragon of time. There, in the springtime of her youth, in the fourth clime of the terrestrial globe, she gave utterance to her fivefold eloquence, arising from the six directions of thought and mounting to the seventh heaven of fame and fair renown.'[18]

The complacent blabberer was preparing further to slacken the reins on the steed of eloquence, so that it might gallop beside the swift-flying bird of subtle and diaphanous thought, when some ill-mannered youth of distraught aspect leaped up from his corner and tore aside the curtain of modesty and shame.

'O blabbering idiots!

'What mean you by so much absurdity? Why this earnest intent to squander your time and cause your fellows pain and discomfort? Is time your deadly enemy? Shall men's thoughts always turn on empty words? Why torment our wretched people who would gladly know what it is you have to say? Where is the lofty-soaring falcon? And who is the virgin bride of speech? Why not express matters in such a way that your words are clear to yourselves and instructive to others?

'Obscure verbiage and rhyming phrases have no charm: your effort is wasted and your pride misplaced. Anyone who commands a wide vocabulary can render his speech so complex and obscure that no intellect may comprehend him. Yet true eloquence does not reside in obscurity. A good style of composition derives from clarity of thought and results in ease of comprehension; it does not come from the studied obscurity of those absurd writings you take as model and authority.

'Have you never sifted the fair from the ugly in their works, never asked the ancient versifiers and chroniclers: "O shameless scribe! O honourless poetaster! O fraudulent fool! Why squander your time on these absurdities and afflict mankind with worthless, empty words? What sense is there in this, that you waste twenty years of precious life in learning endless words and then ponder three days over a line of rhyming nonsense?"

'Now you claim to worship the ancients in all regards; why not observe, then, their rules in what you write? In all matters you refer to their pronouncements as final proof and evidence; yet in the art of composition – the true area of their excellence over later generations – you flout their basic rules! They insisted on clarity of expression and ease of understanding; you strive for obscurity and extravagance. In all tongues, expression is subordinate to meaning; but you defy the principles of composition approved by all mankind and make meaning dependent on expression.

'All too often you go beyond what needs to be said simply for the sake of having a rhyme. Do you not see how blind it is to regard obscurity as the highest feat of the written word? Every lunatic knows that the real task of a writer is not to hinder comprehension. His words should be as clear, concise, relevant, and coherent as possible. His meaning should be expressed in such a manner that it is capable of retaining stylistic excellence in any language into which it is rendered.

'From childhood on you have been accustomed to mere blabbering and are unaware of the ugliness of all you write. But were you to read your writings translated into other tongues and beheld the mere ideas, stripped of the adornment of rhyme, then truly would you understand what nonsense it is you write! When foreigners read your writings, they wonder how it is that you pass as sane.[19]

'As for the viceregents of good fortune,[20] no class of men ever benefited from the common people as they have done, nor has any people suffered on account of its great and noble ones as ours has done. Yet, instead of being thankful for the toil others endure that they may enjoy their ease, they strive only to multiply their pain and care. For the sake of no conceivable advantage they bring down every day a new disaster on the people. They send abroad the goods we need ourselves and purchase in exchange luxuries for their narrow, selfish pleasure. They trade our rice for paper flowers and to obtain a cubit of four-eyed[21] granite part with a hundredweight of silk. They buy dog skins from the West for their weight in silver and sell our whole cotton crop for a fistful of earth!

'As for our religious scholars, instead of studying the souls of men, they investigate the methods of cooking *kūkū*[22] and halva. Were you to ask them concerning the immortality of the soul, they would respond with an exposition of the finer points of ritual ablution. And should some unbeliever request from them a proof of prophecy, they would offer him the principles of ethical behaviour. Though the perspicuous faith of Islam is perfect and the best of all paths for men to follow, the ignorance and stupidity of this herd has hidden the principles of God's law beneath a mass of petty rules and secondary concerns, such that the truths of this noblest of faiths remain unknown to most nations of mankind. They have imposed on men all kinds of minor duty that are of no use in spreading the faith or securing the public good, and in elaborating them they have spent years in argument and dissension.

'If someone were to say that four thousand years ago, in a certain village, a certain shaykh's donkey spoke so many words to his master, these respected ignoramuses[23] would immediately gather their books together and dispute interminably whether the ass in question, at the time of speaking, was facing west or east.

'I have seen as many as three hundred different books, all contradicting one another, on the approved manner of washing one's hands and performing ablution after an act of nature. One said that the right hand has to be washed first of all, and another claimed that if you started with your left foot, you went beyond the pale of the faith. Another of these idiot scholars maintained that whosoever offers a greeting in squint-eyed style[24] is an apostate and deserving of death. Yet another had succeeded in establishing that whoever fails to remove his stockings at a certain hour of the day, will burn in hellfire for all eternity.[25]

'For two thousand years these learned men have spent night and day discussing the attributes of a certain king of the West. One advanced the theory that the monarch in question sprouted horns from his forehead. Another pointed out that his parentage was unknown. Some said that he was an exceedingly ascetic man and an ineffably just ruler, while others attempted to prove by sheer weight of verbiage that he was the most cruel and vicious of warriors. All parties wrote books in defence of their assertions.[26]

'Another task of the learned ignoramuses was from time to time to please their compassionate overlords by drowning the nations of the world in blood and making them fodder for the sword. This they saw fit to call jihad.

'They did not examine the affairs and objects of this world in accordance with their true and obvious nature; rather, the basis of their investigations was what had been said concerning them. Realities men had observed with their own eyes, they deemed unworthy of credence, but any absurdity they read in some rotting book they would immediately believe. If, for example, some idiot read in a book that another idiot had forty years before proclaimed the sun to be triangular in shape, it would be impossible to persuade him of its circularity. Anyone who expressed doubt concerning the truth of the written word was, without delay, stamped an unbeliever.

'Merely on account of some virtue allegedly possessed by an ancient writer – one quite irrelevant to the point at issue – they would deny the plainest facts. Any wisdom they claimed to reside in some unintelligible phrase they would explain by repeating: "Truly God is omnipotent!"

'Such people it is who still regard themselves as the legitimate heirs of all worldly wealth and the apportioners of eternal felicity.'[27]

One day I was sitting in a room with a group of these ignoramuses when that same ill-mannered youth whose acquaintance I had made at the previous congress of lunatics and who clearly never lost an opportunity to be impolite, interrupted the learned discourse, saying: 'The four-eyed nation has made more progress in all manner of wondrous art and industry than the squint-eyed people.'

He had hardly completed his utterance when one of the ignoramuses leaped two feet in the air and said:

'Refinement of the form imprinted on man's character depends on the permanence of the souls of the community. Innovation and deficiency are suspended for it has been said "asceticism and self-denial in things small yet great shall cause you loss of selfhood". By virtue of this irrefutable proof, he is accursed and an infidel!'

The youth replied: 'No, you are the infidel!'

Here I interjected: 'He is right. He understands and expresses matters better than you are able. You imagine learning and scholarship to consist in complexity of expression and try to reduce all factual knowledge to a play of words.'

The ignoramus began to scream: 'The degree of conduct and behaviour, the excellence of formality and favour, result in the succession of man's allotted fate. For as Platakunos, who hailed from the most luminous of cities and was one of the most accomplished pupils of Buqmatinos, once had occasion to remark: "each scent is affected by a body and each body affected by a scent." Therefore, because of the descent of intelligences, which necessitates composition of the body and the merging of all souls, the simple body cannot receive subtle, immaterial result. I thus conclude that the soul is immortal and you are an infidel!'

The youth replied: 'It may well be that the soul is immortal and that I am an infidel. But this you should know for certain, that the use of obscure and unfamiliar words and the mention of a few Greek philosophers are no proof of real knowledge. Appeal to every Platakunos and Buqmatinos in the world; still your words will be meaningless and absurd! Your God-given natural tongue is capable of expressing any thought or idea, and if you were truly learned you would exercise your talent in that tongue. But your true aim is not to acquire and transmit learning. Rather, with a show of knowledge, you try to adorn or conceal your one true accomplishment – the science of deception. It is for this that your speech is deliberately obscure!'

The eloquent ignoramus exclaimed in fury: 'We have made a promise to those who disbelieve! The corporeal treachery of innate disposition and the guile of nature have proven the qualities of the carnal self. For the greatest of all bounties is the tongue of our ancestors, and likewise the supreme exemplar of rhetoric manifest to all men is traced out in the bonds of the generous one of eternal essence. Hence it is clear that the peoples of the occident have borrowed their sciences from our ocean of learning.[28] Aeons and eras will pass before they ascend from the lowest depths of ignorance to the lofty degree of intelligence!'

The youth retorted: 'It is precisely because of claims such as these that you remain devoid of all true learning. Your pride and complacency cause you to stay ignorant of the state of other peoples and the progress they achieve. You have restricted the learning of mankind to a few books of the ancients which you imagine can never be surpassed. The falsity of this belief is apparent to all possessed of true insight. The wisdom of the Creator and Sustainer has disposed our powers of intellect in such manner that progress is continuous and perpetual. It is the most signal instance of His creative power that He has inclined the intellect of man to unceasing progress, and this inclination alone secures our superiority over the animal realm. You wish none the less to make of the slight and insubstantial knowledge of the ancients, together with the whole mass of their absurdities, the ultimate limit of human progress! The worst of it is that you know nothing even of what they knew!

'Once you have committed to memory some obscure name or unknown word, you imagine yourselves to be a compendium of all learning and accomplishment. But this you should know: that if you and all your kind should join forces and come together, a mere schoolboy of four-eyed race could worst you all in argument.

'For a thousand years you have been pretending to the possession of intelligence, yet never have you uttered a word to justify your pretension. The most learned among you, exerting their minds to the utmost, are capable only of repeating what has been said ten thousand times before.

'The truth of the matter is that you excel only in consuming the people's wealth.'

The accomplished ignoramus, beside himself with rage, glared threateningly at the youth and shouted incoherently: 'May the curses of God be upon infidels and His wrath upon these cursed wretches! Infidels, unbelievers! Denunciation of abomination! Paper blackened with the deeds of the heretics! The evil and vicious encompassed by damnation! By the Omnipotent One, you have surpassed all unbelievers in unbelief and become an unbeliever even in their eyes, unbeliever!'

The youth said: 'This manner of speech neither lessens my unbelief, nor adds to your degree of learning. If what you say is true, express yourself in such a way that even if we cannot understand you, at least you should be able to understand yourself, instead of thus wasting a lifetime on empty words. If you had ever engaged in serious study, you would not have become the laughing-stock of the people, nor would our nation have been thus humiliated at the hands of foreigners. You who claim to be the educators of the people and their guides upon the path – your duty is not done merely by mounting the pulpit to make a show of piety and asceticism! In every respect you must aid and protect the people. Lay the foundations for prosperity; shorten the hand of the tyrant and oppressor; deliver the people of the Prophet from the grasp of the infidel. To show people how to wash and ostentatiously to tell one's beads are not fit occupations for the exponents of the Law of God!'

When the ignoramus heard these words, he bade farewell to all restraint and patience, the flame of his anger leaped ever higher and, loudly intoning the *takbīr*,[29] he lifted his stick to bring it down on the head of that shameless, cursed wretch and give him his just reward.

But the eloquent youth saved his skin by nimbly quitting the gathering, and the champion of the faith was left victorious and unchallenged on the field of battle.

I too left the assembly, and outside I encountered another pack of ignoramuses who were dragging some wretch along in the most ignominious fashion. I asked one of them who the man was and what offence he had committed.

He replied: 'The vile, accursed wretch was so full of vice and so forgetful of the rites of religion that not only did he associate with the unbelievers, but even learned their language. Today he was reading a book in the four-eyed tongue, and so we are preparing to chastise him that none other may commit the same abomination.'

I proceeded on my way and beheld another man groaning helplessly as his feet were bastinadoed, invoking God, the Prophet, and the Imams as he pleaded for mercy. In amazement and full concern for the wretch's fate I went forward and asked the ignoramuses who were standing there loudly condemning him: 'Who is he, and what is his offence?'

They answered: 'We found the mother of corruption[30] in his pocket; now we are inflicting the penalty prescribed by law.'

I had still not recovered from my astonishment at their reply when I saw another youth being dragged along in fetters. I inquired the nature of his crime from one of the ignoramuses. After repeated and emphatic denunciation of him as an unbeliever, he answered: 'This accursed fellow is a Sufi[31] and an unbeliever. He does not believe all that he reads and is convinced that most of the ancient historians were liars. In addition, he has been heard on several occasions to say that the sun never rises in the west.'

I said to my friend, in whose company I still was: 'Glorious and Exalted is God Almighty! What kind of creatures are they that they have no fear of God? They commit all the proscribed and forbidden acts, in public and in private, but they torture and torment these powerless wretches on account of some minor slip, some simple human weakness! They pass over altogether the sins and errors of the great and deem the lowly and defenceless deserving of every kind of harshness. Thus they become partners of the viceregents of good fortune inflicting on others the punishment they themselves deserve. Truly I am astounded! How is it that God, the Lord of the Worlds, permits such people to exist and thrive?'

My guide and friend warned me against my audacious thoughts and said in awesome tones: 'Seek not the secrets of the unseen world beyond, and question not the wisdom of God's decree! Put not such trust in your own mind and reason! Some benefit follows on every harm, and every error contains the seeds of its own correction. If a thing appears ugly to you, then hasten to give your fellows fair advice, that it may be remedied. Yet what do men truly know of ugly and of fair? The wisdom of the Peerless Creator is not of such low degree that one ignorant like you should be able to examine the destinies of the world.

'The existence of these ignoramuses, which you deem void of use and profit, is productive of numerous beneficial effects, one hundredth part of which the human mind cannot grasp. Without this class, how could the nation survive and prosper? Even if they have deviated completely from their true and original path of conduct and fallen from that high position of respect they ought duly to command, it remains a fact that their very turbans are a better protection for the realm than all the "victorious brigades"[32] put together.

'If the oppressors have still not stretched out their hands in every direction, the only reason is their fear of the fanatic rage of the ignoramuses. Or else by now the squint-eyed would have done their worst.

'For the honour and respect of our nation, no better support and prop than these ignoramuses can be imagined. Alas, there is none to guide them, none to reduce their affairs to order, to regulate and determine the tasks they are to fulfil. There is no doubt that they could render unlimited services to people and to state. Worldly concerns and care for livelihood keep them constantly distracted; yet even now they are the source of much benefit to the nation. It is only the unseemly actions of a few that have brought the whole class into disrepute, for among the ignoramuses are to be found persons who, by their high moral qualities, more than compensate for the failings of their fellows. These reputable ignoramuses, even though few in number, are a source of pride for all humanity: pious, learned, godfearing, protectors of the oppressed, upholders of the faith, deadly enemies of wrong belief, truthful in speech, free of all human failings, and adorned with every virtue.'

I said: 'Up to now I have encountered no one endowed with qualities such as those you mention.'

My friend replied: 'The good and noble in every class are always absent from public view. They shun the crowd whenever possible and have no desire to put themselves on display. If these truly learned men whose sole aim is the truth and who are worthy of implicit faith and trust were to put their wares up for public sale, what would be left to distinguish them from the ignoramus mass?'

As we were speaking thus, my eye fell on an ignoramus who was seated with his devotees and engaged in expounding the principles of justice and the requirements of the law. A merchant on whose face piety and honesty were clearly written entered the assembly and began talking to the ignoramus in a humble, pleading fashion.

Their conversation became protracted, and, advancing stealthily in such manner as to remain unnoticed, I gave ear to their words and recorded them in my notebook.

The merchant was saying: 'By your blessed head, if I did not need it, I would never mention the matter. True, at the time when I entrusted the five hundred tumans to your excellency, I had no need of them, but recently I have come into straitened circumstances. If you do not now kindly return the money, I will stand disgraced!'

The ignoramus replied: 'The acquisition of property once obtained is quite impossible, for partnership is dependent on the severance of rational objections and secondary ideas. The proof of this is that possession needs manifest support, just as vision requires effulgent light and brilliance.'

The merchant said: 'All that your excellency says is true and to the point, but your servant is in urgent need. Please give instructions that my deposit be returned.'

The ignoramus responded: 'Our guides in matters of the faith have always considered disaster as a form of recurrent blessing, and, having regard for the axiom that "the deprived are secure against being led astray", they conclude that denial of witness devolves upon cloistered learning. Were it not so, why should our souls, which may be likened to lightning flashes, be restricted, stable, and composite all at once?'

To which the merchant answered: 'Sir, the truth of the matter is, I cannot understand your idiom. I have several creditors awaiting me; my mind is distraught; I must go. So permit me to receive my money and take my leave.'

The ignoramus replied: '"Words are more precious than glittering treasure." It is therefore incumbent on you to subject the accursedness of stupidity to the star of good fortune.'

The merchant exclaimed: 'My lord and master, I beg of you! A thousand tasks await me!'

The ignoramus resumed: '"He who confines your property is the best of righteous men." It is as if you wished to thin the martyrs' ranks!'

The merchant protested: 'My dear sir, what do you mean to say? To what end have you delayed me here from morning until now? Is it so lengthy and difficult an affair to restore to people the money they entrusted to you? Tell them to bring my money, and I'll be gone about my business.'

The ignoramus responded: '"Deceit with facility, the reward for ignorance." Hearken to this fragrant counsel, for the wise have said . . .'

The merchant exploded: 'I spit on the tombs of all the wise and all their cursed sires! What game is this you wish to play? I did not come that you might rejoice at my wretched plight.'

The ignoramus gravely said: '"Anger, anger upon anger, ruins man's affair." The advice of scholarly investigators has been in all cases, and on all bases, "whatever you take from God's servants, a small share for yourself".'

The merchant cried out: 'You idiot! What are all these words? You hope by this idiotic drivel to cheat me of my money? By God Almighty, until I have every last *dīnār*,[33] I'll leave you not in peace!'

The ignoramus replied: 'Refutation of accusation! Denial of attribution! "We shall beat you in fury!" Legal penalty, plentifully applied!'

The merchant shouted in despair: 'Truly you are mad! Your brain has suffered damage! What is it you have to say? Why will you not return my money?'

The ignoramus then declaimed: 'O cursed dog! O filthy wretch, impure, unclean, through and through! You dishonour the treasurer of the Sacred Law, impute evil to ignorance-dispelling light! Thrash the abominable infidel! Torment and chastise the hell-bound apostate!'

The master's obedient disciples, in a fine fit of anger, set on the merchant from every side and expelled the guiltless wretch, bleeding and half-dead, from their lofty midst. The unfortunate merchant staked all that he had upon his claim, but wherever he turned, he was thrust away, with nought to show for his troubles but fresh beatings and chastisement.

Notes

1. See Malik ush-Shuʿarā Bahār, 'Bāzgasht-i Adabī', *Armaghān*, XIII (1311 solar/ 1932), pp. 441–8; XIV (1312 solar/1933), pp. 57–69.

2. *Yakī būd, yakī nabūd*, 5th edn (Tehran, 1339 solar/1960), pp. 22–37.

3. *Ākhūnd*: one distinguished by dress and possession of religious learning, or pretension thereto, as a member of the religious classes.

4. Compare with this fictitious statement the words of Mullā Muḥammad Ṣāliḥ Burghānī (d. c. 1850), addressed to the governor of Qazvin: 'Rule and rank last as long as your appointment by the king; after your dismissal, the pleasures you enjoyed are exposed to loss. But the ulama are constantly in the presence of the Creator. As soon as you and your like see us, you act with humility and submission to us, treating us with respect . . . This, then, is a divine power, and superior to all other pleasures' (Muḥammad b. Sulaymān Tunukābunī, *Qiṣaṣ ul-ʿUlamā* [Tehran, 1304 lunar/1885], p. 64).

5. The Shaykhīs, a sect established by Shaykh Aḥmad Aḥsāʾī (1154/1741–1241/ 1826). The most distinctive feature of his teaching was the doctrine of a 'fourth pillar' (*rukn-i rābiʿ*) of the faith, that is, an intermediary between the community and the Hidden Imam, whose existence tends to lessen the absoluteness of the Occultation. Shaykh Aḥmad was denounced as an infidel by a number of the ulama of Qazvin (see Tunukābunī, op. cit., pp. 31–32). On his life, see the work of his son, ʿAbdullāh b. Aḥmad Aḥsāʾī, *Sharḥ-i Ḥālāt-i Shaykh Aḥmad ul-Aḥsāʾī* (Bombay, 1310 lunar/1893). A concise description of his teachings is given by Henri Corbin in 'L'Ecole Shaykhie en Théologie Shiʿite', *Annuaire de l'Ecole des Hautes-Etudes (Section des Sciences Réligieuses), année 1960–1961*, pp. 1–60.

The Uṣūlīs: the mass of the Twelver Shiʿi community, those who held to the principles (*uṣūl*) of jurisprudence authoritatively expounded for the Qajar period by Āqā Muḥammad Bāqir Bihbihānī (1117/1705–1208/1803). Clashes between the Uṣūlīs and Shaykhīs repeatedly occurred in a number of Iranian cities, especially Tabriz and Kirman, down through the early years of the twentieth century. See Aḥmad Kasravī, *Zindagānī-yi Man* (Tehran, 1340 solar/1961), p. 22; and Gianroberto Scarcia, 'Kerman 1905: la "guerra" tra Šeihī e Bālāsarī', *Annali del Istituto Universitario Orientale di Napoli*, XIII (1963), pp. 186–203.

6. *Imāmzāda*: a relative or descendant of one of the Twelve Imams, as well as the tomb enshrining his remains.

7. *Mujtahid*: Shiʿi jurisprudence provides for the guidance of the believer in matters of practice by a *mujtahid*, a scholar competent to deliver judgment on the legality of a course of action, in accordance with the Qurʾan, the Traditions of the Prophet, and those of the Twelve Imams of the Shiʿa.

8. Malkum is presumably alluding here to the verse 'truly among His bondsmen the wise [or learned, *'ulamā'*] fear God' (Qur'ān, 35:28).

9. Āshtīān, a village near Arāk in north-west Iran, properly spelled with *alifmadda* and *tā*, not *'ayn* and *ṭā*.

10. *Siyāq*: a system of notation traditionally used in accountancy, based upon abbreviated forms of the Arabic words denoting numerals.

11. The meaning of this statement is obscure. It may be that here the accountant wishes to belittle his adversary's profession: the ranks of the military, as entered on the payroll, range from 'mouthful' to 'invisible', and thus all represent insubstantial quantities.

12. Two heroes of the Iranian epic tradition.

13. The hero and heroine of a romantic episode frequently celebrated in Persian verse.

14. 'Pleasing pause' (*sakta-yi malīḥ*): a poetic licence consisting in a pause in the metre of a verse, corresponding to the rest in music.

15. *Kharvār*: a unit of measure equivalent to 300 kilograms.

16. All stock images in the vocabulary of Persian lyrical poetry.

17. Two more heroes from the epic tradition.

18. To mention the numerals four, five, six, and seven in successive lines of verse was a much practised artifice in classical Persian poetry. So stylised did the practice become that mere mention of the numeral served to indicate associated objects: thus 'four' alluded to the four elements, or the four humours of the body; 'five', to the five senses; 'six', to the six directions; and 'seven', to the seven heavens of the traditional cosmology.

19. This station of Malkum's piece invites comparison with an episode occurring on pp. 51–64 of a novel by the contemporary Iranian writer, Fereidoun Esfandiary, entitled *The Identity Card* (New York, 1966). A quintessentially Iranian gathering of complacent poets and their uncritical admirers is portrayed with convincing and economic skill. The poets recite verse of lofty and elevated tone but banal and outworn content, which all lavishly applaud. The tranquil atmosphere of the flawlessly formal ceremony is shattered by the hero of the novel, like Malkum's 'ill-mannered youth', who when invited to appreciate the works recited abruptly declares that poetry is dead and embarks on a eulogy of modern science.

The nonsense verse Malkum has his poetasters recite is also reminiscent of some of the pieces in *Vaghvagh Sāhāb* by Ṣādiq Hidāyat and Mas'ūd Farzād (Tehran, numerous editions).

20. 'The viceregents of good fortune (*khulafā-yi iqbāl*): a sarcastic term by which Malkum evidently intends to denote the government of Iran, or the ruling class as a whole.

21. 'Four-eyed' (*chahār-chashmī*): by the use of this term, here and at other points in the piece, Malkum appears to mean 'European'. Because the designation 'squint-eyed' is used in a contextually similar sense, it may be that the two terms are intended to refer to two European nations. We may conjecture that the English are the 'four-eyed', and the Russians the 'squint-eyed', for later in the piece Malkum implies that

but for the 'fanatic rage of the ignoramuses', the 'squint-eyed' would have entirely absorbed Iran.

22. *Kūkū*: a kind of omelette, usually filled with spinach or other vegetables.

23. 'Ignoramuses': thus I render Malkum's coinage *jahlmandān* (sing., *jahlmand*), composed of *jahl* (ignorance) plus suffix -*mand*, and intended as the counterpart of *dānishmand* (learned: *dānish* [learning, knowledge] plus suffix -*mand*).

24. See n. 21 above.

25. Malkum is here alluding to a conflict of views on a certain detail of the ritual ablution: whether it is necessary to wash the bare feet or simply pass moistened hands over one's stockinged feet (the practice known as *mash* from Qur'ān, 5:6).

26. The 'king of the west' to whom reference is made is Alexander the Great, sometimes identified with the figure of Dhūl Qarnayn, 'the Possessor of Two Horns' (Qur'ān, 18:33 ff.). In traditional Persian literature Alexander is depicted not so much as a warrior and conqueror as a seeker after ultimate truths, who finally discovers the 'water of life' in the mountains of Qāf, on the farthermost edge of the world. See art., 'İskender Nâme', *Islâm Ansiklopedisi*, fasc. 52 (Istanbul, 1951).

27. 'Heirs of all worldly wealth': presumably in the sense that the ulama would take charge of the estates of those who died intestate, and possibly too in the sense that sums of money contributed for religious or charitable purposes (*zakāt, ṣadaqa, khums*, etc.) would be entrusted to them. 'Apportioners of eternal felicity': in the sense that they arrogated to themselves the judgment of the blessed and the damned.

28. Malkum's insertion of the claim that 'the peoples of the occident have borrowed their sciences from our ocean of learning' in a passage of nonsense, uttered by a figure of absurd and unlimited ignorance, is an interesting indication of his own attitude to the claim. If he himself seriously asserted the sciences and institutions of modern Europe to be the long-forgotten achievement of the Muslims themselves, it was for tactical purposes that he explicitly confessed.

29. *Takbīr*: pronunciation of the words *Allāhu Akbar*. Their use here by the 'ignoramus' as he raises his stick signifies his belief that the youth is an enemy of the faith and that chastisement of him will constitute jihad.

30. 'The mother of corruption' (*mādar-i fasād*, cf. Arabic *umm al-khabā'ith*): an epithet commonly applied to wine.

31. Sufis were frequently thought in Qajar times to be unbelievers because of the antinomian tendencies some of them displayed. Clerical hostility to them was particularly marked early in the period. Sayyid Muḥammad Bāqir Bihbihānī prided himself on the title *ṣūfīkush*, 'Sufi killer' (see Tunukābunī, op. cit. [n. 4, above], p. 148); and his eldest son, Āqā Muḥammad ʿAlī Bihbihānī, encompassed the death of two prominent members of the Niʿmatullāhī order, Nūr ʿAlī Shāh and Maʿṣūm ʿAlī Shāh (see Muḥammad ʿAlī Tabrīzī Khiyābānī, *Rayḥānat ul-Adab* [Tehran, 1326 solar/1947], II; pp. 245–7).

Partial justification for the view of Sufis held by the ulama is supplied by the testimony of a number of European observers, who compared the state of belief of Sufis they encountered to that of European freethinkers (J. B. Fraser, *Narrative of the Residence of the Persian Princes in London in 1835 and 1836* [London, 1838], I: 231; Arthur de Gobineau, *Les Religions et Les Philosophies dans l'Asie Centrale* [Paris, 1865], ch. v; A. Sepsis, "Quelques Mots sur l'Etat Religieux Actuel de la Perse," *Revue de l'Orient*, III [1844]: 107–109).

[32.] 'Victorious brigades' (*afvāj-i qāhira*): the term by which the Iranian army was conventionally designated in Qajar chronicles, irrespective of the fortunes of battle.

[33.] *Dīnār*: a monetary unit equivalent, in the Qajar period, to one thousandth of a *qirān*, and in present-day Iran to one hundredth of a rial.

CHAPTER 3

Shaykh Fazl Allah Nuri's Refutation of the Idea of Constitutionalism[1]

Shaykh Fazl Allah Nuri

[1.] Introduced and translated by Abdul-Hadi Hairi, first appeared in *Middle Eastern Studies*, XXIII.3 (1977), pp. 327–39.

DISCONTENT with the tyrannical regime in Iran was overwhelmingly expressed by all groups of people, the most influential of whom was the clergy. However, after the declaration of the constitution on 5 August 1906, opposition gradually appeared on the part of the new Shāh, Maḥammad ʿAlī, and amongst a number of the respected *ʿulamā*. Opposition was initiated mainly by Shaykh Faẓl Allāh Nūrī (1842–1909) as soon as he came to understand that a constitutional regime was not necessarily in accordance with Islam.

Shaykh Faẓl Allāh was an established *mujtahid* of Tehran. He had migrated to Najaf in his youth and studied there for several years. In 1875 he went to Sāmarrā, studied under the great *mujtahid*, Ḥājī Mīrzā Ḥasan Shīrāzī, who is famous for his *fatwā* issued against the 1890 Tobacco Concession. In 1882 the Shaykh moved to Tehran where, as a *mujtahid*, he enjoyed a great measure of influence and respect among the people. During the constitutional movement, Shaykh Faẓl Allah allied himself with the other two Tehran *mujtahids*, Sayyid Muḥammad Ṭabāṭabāʾī and Sayyid ʿAbd Allāh Bihbahānī, and supported the establishment of a constitutional form of government. However, when the supplementary fundamental law (made in 1907) was tabled in the first parliament Shaykh Faẓl Allāh turned against the constitutionalists.

The Shaykh declared that the Islamicised constitution (*mashrūṭah-i mashrūʿah*) for which he had been fighting was different from that which came out of the constitutional revolution. Shaykh Nūrī's opposition caused a number of the *ʿulamā* in Iran and Najaf, the most influential amongst them Ḥājī Sayyid

Muḥammad Kāẓim Ṭabāṭabā'ī Yazdī, to give him support.[1] This conflict which led to a split amongst the leading *'ulamā* and strengthened the tyrannical tendencies of the existing royal circle, can be rated as the first effective drawback the young Persian constitutional regime suffered.

Writers on modern Iran present various reasons for the division among the *'ulamā*; interested students of the subject can find authors' viewpoints in their works. It seems, however, that a most important reason for the conflict was ideological. It is generally held, and rightly so, that the most influential factor which led to the declaration of a parliamentary regime was the *'ulamā*'s support of the constitutional revolution. Despite this fact, however, not much attention has been devoted to the ideological and theoretical foundation of the *'ulamā*'s participation in the Revolution. It seems that it has not been considered important to see what were the *'ulamā*'s reasons for supporting or opposing constitutionalism, or what was the *'ulamā*'s own interpretation of the principles of a modern constitution.

The constitutionalist *'ulamā* thought that democratic constitutionalism could be in agreement with Islam by designating at least five *mujtahids* in Parliament to . . . reject and repudiate, wholly or in part, any such proposal which is at variance with the Sacred Law of Islam.[2] Whereas the *'ulamā* opposed to the constitution considered constitutionalism to be against Islam.[3]

This ideological conflict gave rise, among other things, to a considerable volume of political literature, both for and against constitutionalism. This literature appeared mainly within the first decade after the declaration of the constitution in Iran. Among the various books, papers, and leaflets, with titles such as *'Ibrat-nāmah* (The Book of Warning), *Ghayrat-nāmah* (The Book of Zeal), *Shab-nāmah* (Night Paper), *Ṣubḥ-nāmah* (Morning Paper), *Rūz-nāmah* (Newspaper) and so on, which were being published during that period by the Persian Secret Societies, there appeared a number of publications written by the *'ulamā* and the Persian religious students of Iran and Iraq.

It is difficult to determine how many works were written on this subject by the clergy because many of them are hardly known. The works of the *'ulamā* in favour of constitutionalism are of considerable volume and will engage us in another study. In this article, an attempt will be made to give a brief introduction to some of the works written in condemnation of constitutionalism and the Persian Constitutional Revolution. Then, an English rendering of the most coherent and systematic treatise of this kind will be presented. Literature of this sort was also of considerable quantity but because of the victory of the constitutionalists, though it was mainly a victory in theory only, fewer numbers of the anti-constitutional works have been known to observers. The following are representative examples:

1. A handsomely printed little book entitled *Tadhkirah al-ghāfil wa irshād al-jāhil* (A Reminder for the Negligent and a Guide for the Ignorant) was written

some time after the bombardment of parliament by Muḥammad ʿAlī Shāh in 1908. The author praises the shāh because he demolished the *majlis* which the author called 'the house of infidelity' (*khānah-yi kufr*).[4] The book does not bear any author's name, but we accept the words of Sayyid Shahāb al-Dīn Najafi Marʿashī who believes that its author was Shaykh ʿAbd al-Nabī Nūrī (d. 1925).[5] The book itself indicates that it was written by one of the *'ulamā*, because at its opening the following *ḥadīth* is mentioned as a motive for writing the book: 'When innovations appear in the world, it is the duty of the *'alim* to manifest his knowledge; otherwise, the curse of God will be upon him.' It is interesting to note that two opposing parties based their argumentations on the same *ḥadīth*. The absolutists called the constitutional regime an innovation and fought against it; but the constitutionalists, Mīrzā Muḥammad Ḥusayn Nāʾīnī for instance, saw an innovation and betrayal of Islam in the position that the absolutists upheld in favour of tyrannical governments.[6] In his discussion, this supporter of the old regime took liberty, equality, and representative government as heresies, and accused the advocates of a constitutional regime of having been led astray.

2. Another clerical writer who condemned constitutionalism was Shaykh Abū al-Ḥasan al-Najafi al-Marandī whose treatise is called *Barahīn al-furqān fi buṭlān qawanīn nawasikh muḥkamāt al-Qurʾān* (The Theorems of the Qurʾān on the Falsity of the Laws which Abrogate the Well-Established [Verses] of the Qurʾān). On the title page the author also made reference to the above-quoted *ḥadīth* as his motive for undertaking his work. Basing his argument on certain other *ḥadiths*, he described *shūrā*, *majlis*, and *mashrūṭah* as detrimental to Islam. This book was written *circa* 1921.

3. There are recorded a considerable number of *istiftāʾs* (requests for a formal legal opinion), which had been sent to several different *'ulamā* during the period when the Persian Constitution was abrogated by the Shāh (1908–09), requesting an opinion on the lawfulness of a constitutional regime. In reply, the *'ulamā* had declared *fatwās* against constitutionalism. There are also many supporting telegrams which the *'ulamā* sent to the Shāh and other authorities during the same period, expressing their opposition to constitutionalism.[7]

4. The writings of Shaykh Faẓl Allāh Nūrī and his assistants in the form of leaflets, treatises, and manifestos, are good sources in which the position of the supporters of the old regime is very well expressed.

A few of the declarations (*lāʾiḥahs*) are recorded by Kasravī.[8] Nūrī's views are stated in a number of publications issued during Nūrī's stay in Shāh ʿAbd al-Aẓīm. The followers of Nūrī published a newspaper called *Al-Daʿwah al-islamīyyah* (The Islamic Call), and another one entitled *Tanbīh va īqāẓ* (Admonition and Awakening).[9] Apart from these papers which appeared on a regular basis, a declaration was also issued on 28 July 1907.[10]

The most important and coherent treatise which Shaykh Faẓl Allāh wrote in condemnation of constitutionalism is that which is reproduced in Malik-Zādah's book.[11] It appears to be an eloquent expression of the clerical ideological position *vis-à-vis* the idea of constitutionalism. In this treatise, Shaykh Faẓl Allāh takes issue with the constitutionalists very systematically and refutes them on the ground that a constitutional form of government violates the *Shī'ah*. Nā'īnī, who wrote the best book in favour of constitutionalism, addressed himself to the contents of this treatise without mentioning the name of the treatise or its author.[12]

In his treatise, Shaykh Faẓl Allāh ridicules the idea that Jews, Muslims, Zoroastrians, etc. may be equal before the law. He is forthright in denying the validity of any legislation passed by a body of ordinary people such as 'drapers and grocers'. He thanks God for helping Muḥammad 'Alī Shāh to bombard the parliament in 1908. The Shaykh holds that freedom of the press is detrimental to Islam because it does not allow any punishment for malicious accusation (*iftirā'*), backbiting (*ghaybat*), slander, obsession, abusive language, insult, and the like.

The treatise includes some Arabic passages and Qur'ānic verses. One full paragraph is composed in Arabic, and the rest of the work is written in a relatively unfamiliar Persian. It is preceded by a question directed to Shaykh Faẓl Allāh. He is asked to declare his opinion of constitutionalism, the extent of its applicability to Islam, and the reasons behind the shaykh's withdrawal from constitutionalist activities.[13] – [A. – H. H.]

The [following] question will be directed to the sacred presence of highness, the proof of Islam and Muslims, reviver of 'nation', truth, and religion, the reformer of the path of the chief of the prophets and messengers, the striver in the path of the Tradition (*al-sunnah*) and the indisputable Book (*al-Kitāb al-mubīn*) [i.e. the Qur'ān] with his heartblood and wealth; the one whose lifetime is limited to the Time of God (*ayyām Allāh*): [the man who is] the remnant of the worthy predecessors, the expert in Islamic jurisprudence, the divine learned man, the second *Vaḥīd*,[14] the greatest chief, that is to say, al-Ḥājj Shaykh Faẓl Allāh al-Nūrī al-Ṭabarī al-Māzandarānī, may God prolong his protection and make him reach his aims by giving currency to the truth.

In our days the subject of 'constitution' [with a French pronunciation], which is an innovation of foreign nations, has come into view through the efforts of a number of people who consider themselves politicians and 'civilisé'. [This phenomenon] divided the inhabitants of Iran into three groups: one group was fascinated by the speeches of the orators and the founders of this principle welcomed [their call] and received [it]. Another group denied [it] outright; they argued that this situation is one of the innovations of the countries which do not have a compiled divine law and do not truly believe in the laws of the prophets and messengers, though outwardly they belong to [certain] creeds. The third group, having heard the contradictory talk of the [above] mentioned two groups, have become hesitant and have stayed still and [uncertain].

At the beginning of the diffusion of this subject [i.e. the idea of constitutionalism], your highness, the proof of Islam, assisted them seriously, but suddenly, in the middle of [your] activity, you disassociated [yourself from them], withdrew and refused to make an appearance in the consultative assembly. Not much time was passed when, because of the opposite party's attempt on [your] life, you, together with a group of *mujtahids*, prayer leaders, pious people and the like, took refuge in the sacred shrine of Ḥazrat-i ʿAbd al-ʿAẓīm. The fame of this migration [to the shrine] reached all over the guarded country. Most of the supporters [of constitutionalism] fell into a state of uncertainty, and some [of them] were vanquished, so that the serious pressures of the constitutionalists and the evil consequences of the aforesaid assembly did what they did, and [then] happened what happened.

Of the subject matter presented [here], the point in question is why that serious support was replaced by disagreement and migration. Did [your change] have any religious reason or was it only expediency? Did you oppose [them] because you found constitutionalism in opposition to Qurʾānic laws and the rules of the Divine *Sharī ʿat*, or did your withdrawal and opposition have ordinary reasons and accidental purposes? If you enlighten [us] you will be rewarded.

The Answer
In the Name of God, the Beneficent,
the Merciful

Praise be upon His friend [ʿAlī Ibn Abī Ṭālib], and blessing be upon His Prophet and the Prophet's virtuous family, and may God's curse be upon all their enemies, until the Day of Judgment.

This is to bring to the notice of my religious brothers and fellow-believers, may God strengthen their faith and [increase their] success, that first of all I thank the Master of the universe, may His greatness be exalted. Who in this great calamity [which is like that] of the end of the world, and in this gigantic test [which is given to] the Muslim people and to the believers – a calamity which ages the minors and makes the old decrepit – granted this feeble and helpless [writer] such a great grace, and honoured [him] with such a lofty honour, despite the volume of the enemies, to announce the truth of Islam to the people of all cities with a sufficiently loud voice in the meetings, from the pulpits, and by [writing] communiqués. [This duty was done despite the fact that] the corrupt people were in a thoroughly victorious position, and the commotion [which resulted from] this fiery world calamity was stirred by pig-headed people. [This task was performed] by way of obedience to the command of the master [ʿAlī Ibn Abī Ṭālib] and by refraining from [personal] interests and desires. When these 'great' men, whose foundations are shaky, [in the words of the Qurʾān, had their] 'hearts reach to the throats' [33:10], I did not fear, and performed my necessary duty; thanks to God, first and last, outwardly and inwardly.

Secondly, the corrupt aspects of this affair are not so limited that they can be treated within these [few] pages. Rather, [many] comprehensive treatises should be written on this problem, as at the request of this prayer [i.e. the writer], a number of learned men are [presently] occupied [compiling such comprehensive works]. God willing, they will finish and publish their works.

However, to answer the question within the scope of this paper, considering the appropriateness of the time, and in order to increase the knowledge of all Muslims and their insights into the proper *ḥukm* and *fatwā* concerning this accidental problem (*qaẕiyyah-yi ḥadīthah*), I shall briefly declare [the following]: The sources of this calamity [the Persian constitutional revolution] were the new sects and the naturalists who received the idea of constitutionalism from [our] neighbours [i.e. Russia and Ottoman Turkey], and presented it in a very appealing manner. Obviously, anyone who was fascinated by this [pleasant] presentation, and was a lover of [justice, and saw a number of people] seeking justice, automatically made an effort to earn it [as soon as] he heard this agreeable word; he did not refrain from giving his life and wealth as much as he could. This writer, for example, took part in this affair and experienced a lot of trouble while travelling or at home. [There were] also [some] means which were agreeable. When we began to put the matter into effect, I noticed that a group of people who had always been accused of deviations [from the right path], involved themselves in the affairs. Little by little I heard some equivocal words from them, but I interpreted them as [sound] ideas. Then they unveiled the matter to an extent and established the [fact] that the representatives [of parliament] should be elected and the majority of the votes relied upon. Again I ignored [these things], interpreting that these [measures might have been taken] to establish order and to promote justice.

Gradually it was decided to make a constitution and to write a [fundamental] law. At times the [matters] were being discussed with some [of the people involved and the question would arise]: 'What is the meaning of this system?' [I would tell them]: 'It seems that [the constitutionalists want to forge an innovation and to lead [people] astray. 'Otherwise, what is the meaning of a representative system (*vikālat*)? Who is the elector and for what is the representative elected (*muvakkalun fīh chīst*)? If the problems concern secular affairs, there is no need for these religious arrangements.[15] If general religious matters are to be treated, then these matters are related to *vilāyat* [i.e. the rulership which is authorised by God through His Prophet and the *Imāms*, that is to say, the *'ulamā*] not *vikālat*. During the [Greater] Occultation of the [Twelfth] *Imām*, may God hasten his happy ending, [i.e. his return], *vilāyat* is within the capacity [only] of the specialists in *fiqh* and of the *mujtahids*, not of a certain grocer or draper. [Also], relying on the opinions of the majority is wrong according to the Twelver

Shī' ī religion. What does it mean to 'write a law'? The law for us Muslims is only Islam which, thanks to God, the exalted, traditionists and the *mujtahids*, generation after generation, have taken pains to protect and keep in order. Thanks to God, the exalted, there are also many protectors of Islamic law at the present time.

[The constitutionalists] used to answer these questions with seductions and procrastinations until that anathematised constitution, named fundamental law (*qānūn-i asāsī*), was written and I was asked to make it conform to Islamic principles. In defiance of my disappointment about the salvation of these arrangements, I condescended and, together with a group *of 'ulamā*, spent some time on this matter until we made [that law] conform [to Islam] as far as possible. The printed [draft], which included expressions and corrections, remained with this writer. However, the groups of people who were exercising a controlling power over all the affairs were not co-operative. Rather, they clearly and openly said that it would not be possible to make constitutionalism (*mashrūṭah*) conform with Islamic divine principles. [They added that] these corrections and applications [of the constitution to Islam] would cause foreign states not to recognise our country as a constitutional state.

Since I thus saw the situation, I, with the assistance of a group, presented the second article of the supplementary fundamental law which authorises the supervision of the *mujtahids* over the decisions of the assembly in all epochs. They accepted that article because they could not have rejected it. Then, enjoying the agreement of everyone, I painstakingly wrote, printed, and distributed in all the cities a separate chapter in order to confirm the fact and prevent any [later] revisions [of the article].

When they saw [the chapter] and understood that [if the article] remained without any change, they would be completely prevented from reaching their corrupt aims, they did what they did and I faced what I faced and suffered what I suffered. [These developments] resulted in the incident [of our refuge in the] sacred shrine of ['Abd al-'Aẓīm].

During the entire ninety days of our stay in the shrine, I, together with a large number of *mujtahids*, high-ranking people, and the *faqīhs,* said and wrote what had to be said and written; [everything, from beginning] to end, was communicated to all. Afterwards, they gave [us] a [written] paper in which a commitment had been made not to deviate from Islamic provisions. Then, I and [other] distinguished *'ulamā* returned [to Tehran].

After [our] withdrawal [from the constitutionalists' camp] and the cooling of the fierce hostilities, [the constitutionalists] found the atmosphere ready to distort that anathematised law which was corrected [by us]. Being led astray by a group of people, who were like the *Khawārij* of *Nahravān,* they tampered with the letters of the article regarding [the *'ulama*'s after supervision], to the extent that they benefited from it as they had wanted, but [its] outward [composition appeared] agreeable to credulous people. What an excellent poem this is [for this occasion]:

> The thief who steals the breath of air is [a real] thief.
> [And also the one who] steals the carpet from the *Ka'bah* is [a real] thief.

After they finished the [business of] establishing the innovation and compiling the misleading [constitution], they began to take actions. They performed what they performed in the way of obscenities, reprehensible actions, insulting Islam, distorting [its] provisions, degrading the divine *'ulamā,* violating the *sharī'ah* and religion, enjoining indecency and forbidding right conduct (*al-amr bi al-munkar wa al-nahy 'anal-ma'rūf*), consolidating the false and making propaganda for every erroneous and ignorant man. [They also] denied respect for the Book of God, [created satanic] temptations in the minds of the common people about the elevation of cultic practices [ordered by] God (*sha'ā'ir Allāh*), they shed blood, and put [their innovative] ideas into operation. All these actions [were performed] before the Eye of God and His friends (*bi 'ayn Allāh wa naẓar awlīyā-'ih*). So God let them grow their sinfulness and [publish] blasphemous writings. They did not limit themselves to these [things]; rather, they attacked the king of Islam (Muḥammad 'Ali Shāh] and surrounded him from all sides and insulted him with certain [words] which do not merit mentioning. But the king was patient and considerate in all the occasion. The wise men of the state and the majority of the people were astonished by his patience and tolerance. This crisis [finally] reached its extreme point, and [the people] openly turned away from the path of guidance. At this point the command of God, the exalted, was issued for their extinction: 'He brought their stratagem to naught' (105:2) and the just king treated them as the owners of the Elephant were treated.[16]

In brief, this great sedition, from its beginning to the day of its extinction, passed through three stages: the first stage was that of discourse and presentation (*taqrīr va 'unvān*). The second stage was that of writing and declaration (*taḥrīr va i'lān*); the third stage was that of practice and test ('*amal va imtiḥān*).

In the first stage, people followed the evil-decorating satans [i.e. the constitutionalists]. Their presentation was so pleasant that it fascinated every learned and illiterate man. To obtain [such a pleasantly presented theory of government, many people] became ready to sacrifice their lives, let alone their wealth. In the second stage, i.e. that of writing and declaration, they first limited themselves to summaries and ambiguities. But, after deeper consideration, [we saw] the secret disclosed either directly by the malicious board [the *majlis*] itself through law making and doing other things, or, under the indirect influence of the board, through lifting the chain of the *Sharī'ah* from the fearless dirty people. So that, they may say, write, and publish in their manifestos and newspapers whatever they can against any respected thing, i.e. religion, religious leaders, the '*ulamā* of [good] conduct, and religious people.

They were occupied with these obscene actions. However much this writer and other '*ulamā* and Muslims supplicated (*istighāsah kardīm*) it did not have any effect. If one wants to collect the nonsense [that was published] in the newspapers during this period [he would have to compile volumes of] books.

As for the third stage, which was the stage of actions; on this [problem], it would be sufficient [to refer to] the injustice which emanated from them and is called 'administration of justice' ('*adlīyyah*). Thank God that the very passage [of the law], which deals with a punishment for [shedding] the blood of a Zoroastrian, caused the wrath of God and destroyed their malicious works.

It may not be hidden that there are many reasons for the unlawfulness of constitutionalism and for its repugnance to Islamic provisions and to the Prophetic path, peace may be upon their executors, in [all] the aforementioned stages. First of all, [both the writing of] a constitutional law and the following of the opinion of the majority [are against Islam. The idea of depending on the majority] even though it is originally allowed in permissible affairs (*umūr-i mubāḥ*), is an unlawful legislation; it is an innovation in religion because it is made as a law to be obeyed. [And of course] every innovation is a straying from the right path. Also, it is unlawful to make a permissible action as a person's duty to be obligatorily performed and to punish the person for his refusal of performing that duty. 'Say: Hath Allāh permitted you, or do ye invent a lie concerning Allāh?' [10:60]

Governmental matters and orders have always existed, but it has been obvious that those were irreligious principles. But [in our age] everyone witnessed that adherence to the 'lawful' nonsense and absurd opinions of the [national] assembly was considered by all Muslims as one of the most obligatory duties, and opposition to the assembly was seen as worse than apostasy. What innovation can be more serious than this?

It is not possible to deal [fully] with what [the constitutionalists said and did]. In this paper, however, a short allusion will be made only to the [relevant] *fatwā* and *ḥukm* in opposition to the corrupt aspects of the second stage, that is to say, the writings and declarations. [In our discussion] we will not touch upon the matters which are beyond the scope of the Assembly. We shall [deal only with] what came out of the Assembly, to be more specific, those malicious fabrications which were called the 'fundamental law', and only a few articles of it will be treated here. The rest [of the problems] should be found in the works which are being compiled by the distinguished '*ulamā*. We [only] say them, and seek God's help.

One of the articles [No. 8] of that 'book of errors' (*zalālatnāmah*) [i.e. the constitution] rules that all the individuals in this country have equal rights. In its latest edition this phrase is given as: 'The inhabitants of the country of Iran will have equal rights before the state law.' The word 'equality' spread and was circulated until it perforated [all] ears. Equality is one of the pillars of constitutionalism; [the latter] would vanish without equality. I remember, when this article was being under discussion, one of the few distinguished members of the assembly said to me that this article was extremely important. [He added]: 'If this article is included in the constitution, foreign states will recognise it even if we change all other articles. If this article disappears [from the constitution] but the rest remain, our constitutional system will not be recognised.' I answered immediately: 'then it is all over with Islam' and stood up and said: 'Oh! People who are sitting, you should know that the Islamic country [of Iran] will not accept a constitutional government because it is impossible to have equality in Islam.'

Oh! [My] religious brothers, now think attentively over the Islamic provisions [and see] how many differences they established among the subjects concerning the persons obligated to observe the precepts of Islam (*mukallafin*). [In Islam there are differences among the *mukallafin*] in religious observances (*'ibādāt*), *mu'āmalāt*,[17] trades, and policies. [There are differences between] minors and those who are mature, the rational and the irrational, the sane and the insane, the healthy and the ill, the one who has free will and he who is compelled, the satisfied and the dissatisfied, the authentic [client] and the lawyer [or representative] and the guardian, the slave and the free, the father and the son, the wife and the husband, the rich and the poor, the learned and the ignorant, the doubting person and the convinced, the imitator [of a *mujtahid*] and the *mujtahid*, the descendant of the Prophet (*sayyid*) and the *non-sayyid*, the distressed and those at ease, the Muslim and the infidel, the infidel under [Muslim] protection (*zimmīs*) and the infidel who is at war [with the Muslims], the originally non-Muslim person and the apostate, the national [*sic*] apostate and the apostate by nature, and so on, none of which is hidden to the expert *faqīh*.

For instance, the *zimmī* infidels are subject to special provisions in their marital relations with Muslims. It is not allowed for a Muslim to marry an infidel, but Muslim men can have non-Muslim women as concubines and on a temporary basis. Also, apostasy of either partner of the married couple entails the cancellation of the marriage.

Conversion of either partner of a [non-Muslim] couple to Islam also has special different provisions. With regard to the problem of inheritance, unbelief (*kufr*) denies a person inheritance. An infidel may not inherit from a Muslim, but the reverse is permissible. Also, an apostate has special definite provisions; his property will be transferred to his heirs, his wife [automatically] is divorced, his body becomes unclean, and it is obligatory to punish him with death. Also, there are different provisions concerning usurious transactions. The *zimmī*'s transactions in lands require the payment of the *khums* [one fifth of the net income] if the *zimmī* buys the land from a Muslim. About crimes, punishments, and blood money, various provisions have been made.

Oh! [my] religious brother! How can Islam, which thus distinguishes among provisions of different matters, tolerate [the idea of] equality? [One only has to admit that] it is intended to open a business over against the founder of the *Sharī'ah,* and to establish new rules; may God, the exalted, protect us from it.

The principal part of this game – constitutionalism – was played by the erroneous group [i.e. the non-Muslim citizens and most probably the *Bābīs*] in order to escape from the four definite provisions which are made for those who renounce Islam. What a wrong idea! What a [set of] vain thoughts! The house [i.e. the territory of Islam] has a lord and the religion has [its] master. Strangely [enough], they ascribe their misrepresentation and their own casting of doubt on the people to the state law [because, having in mind the proverb] 'the liar has a poor memory', [they want to be safe from any objections regarding their possible contradictory remarks – *sic*].

Oh, heretics! If this state law is in conformity with Islam, it is not possible to include equality in it, and if it is at variance with Islam, it would be against what is written in the previous part [of the constitution], that is: 'whatever is against Islam cannot be lawful.'

Oh, knavish and [individuals] devoid of zeal! See how the master of the *Sharī'ah* has granted you honours because you have been embellished with Islam. He has granted you privileges, but you deny them by saying that you must be equal brothers with Zoroastrians, Armenians and Jews; God's curse may be upon those who approve this [equality]!

Strangest of all is that they say that the articles of the law can be changed. Is this change from Islam to infidelity, or from infidelity to Islam? Both alternatives are obviously wrong.[18] One may argue that this change [only] consists of a change from Islam to Islam, that is to say, from a permissible [action] to another permissible [action]. Although this [kind of] change can be conceived, it is wrong to make and put into effect a law which regulates a permissible action, the performance and non-performance of which is all the same to the founder of the *Sharī'ah*. [It is wrong especially if] a punishment may be given to those who do not obey such laws. The secondary meanings (*'anāvīn-i Sānavīyyah*), which are considered in order to explain the basis of the differences among the provisions, such as the obedience [of a child to his] father, or vows, oaths, and the like, are limited in *fiqh*, and are beyond [the authority of] the votes of grocers and drapers.[19]

Oh, irreligious [individual]! You want to establish a new innovation in religion and change [it] by these guiles and impostures. God forbid! [Your idea would never] enjoy any success, because false [ideas] have a limited period; [as the Qur'ān says:] 'Those who do wrong will come to know by what a [great] reverse they will be overturned!' [26:227] Within two astronomical hours (*du sā'at-i nujūmī*)[20] all the erroneous devices they had made for a long time were ruined. I praise God with all His commendable [attributes], and [thank Him] for all His graces.

Another erroneous article of the constitution concerns freedom of the press. After a series of changes and alterations, the text [of the article finally] went as follows: 'All publications, except erroneous books and matters harmful to the perspicuous religion [of Islam], are free and censorship of them is forbidden.[21] According to this article, many of the unlawful things which should be forbidden have been made lawful because only two matters are excepted, whereas [in fact] one of the imperatively unlawful things is malicious accusation (*iftirā*'). Another indisputable unlawful matter is backbiting of a Muslim (*ghaybat*). Also, slander against a Muslim, harm, abusive language, insult, intimidation, threatening, and the like, are forbidden by the *Sharī'ah* and are considered unlawful by God. Is freedom in these things not solely declaring lawful what God has made unlawful? And [of course] the status of one who declares lawful what God has made unlawful is obvious, and the provision concerning him is clear.

It is strange that in cases other than those which have been excepted, censorship has been forbidden [in the law], whereas forbidding indecency (*nahy-i az munkar*) is one of the basic principles and the writer or opinion-giver [who supports the idea of censorship over evil publications may want] to carry out the Islamic duty of *nahy-i az munkar*. More strange than this is that at the bottom of this article [no. 20] a punishment has been laid down for one who may disobey [the law], and [in this case] reference is made to the press law. This is also wrong and is an innovation because in matters related to the *Sharī'at* we do not have [any provision for] a cash penalty for committing unlawful things; whereas there [in the article] cash penalty has been laid down.

Oh, Muslim brothers! It is an annoying situation (*zāqa al-ṣadr*); all these non-sensical and extravagant statements are given in order to destroy the foundation of religion and to cause the disappearance of the *Sharī'at* of the master of the messengers. I swear to the One [i.e. God] Who split the seed and exhausted the breath that religious thieves have entered [the scene] and their only concern is to take [our] religion and to destroy its adherents. Otherwise, giving currency to justice does not need these arrangements.

In order to remove any obscurity related to [the idea of] justice, a term which has been the most important means of attracting most of the people to this incident [i.e. the constitutional revolution], here we give some explanation:

Know that heaven and earth depend on justice, the necessity of which is obvious according to both reason and the *Sharī'ah*. The question, however, is to find out its applicability. This famous phrase [which says]: 'equal oppression is justice' seems to be incorrect. Oh, Muslims! Islam which is our religion and the religion of [all] adherents of the Prophet is more complete than all other religions. It is based on perfect justice, as God, the exalted, says:

'Lo! Allāh enjoineth justice and kindness. '[16:90] Thanks to God, the exalted, that in Islam, there is but justice. Prophecy and kingship among preceding prophets were different; sometimes the [two authorities] were centred [in one person] or were divided. [The two authorities were centred] in the blessed person of the most honourable Prophet, the last of the prophets. [God's] blessing may be upon him and his family as long as the universe lasts. Such was [also] the case with the caliphs of that magnanimous [personality, i.e. Muḥammad], either lawfully or unlawfully. But several months after the occurrence of accidents, these two affairs, namely the assumption of religious affairs and the using of power and glory, and alertness over the security [of the state], centred in two [separate] authorities.

In fact, these two authorities are complementary and supplementary to each other, that is to say, the foundation of Islam is laid upon these two [sets] of affairs: deputyship in the affairs of prophecy and kingship. Without these two, Islamic provisions would be inactive. As a matter of fact, kingship is the executive power of Islamic provisions, and doing justice depends on executing them. In Islam warnings, promises, and threats, and carrying out punishments are all used as executive procedures. Even warning is more important [because] it consists of fear of God and believing in the origin and return [of creation] (*mabda' va-maʿād*), from which will result the [state of having] fear and hope. These two things which have to do with heart, soul, and conscience, are more influential in taking good actions and in avoiding indecency, [both of which] form the truth of justice. The stronger [one's] certainty may be about the origin and return [of creation], and the more fear of God, and hope [one may have of God's mercy], the more widespread justice will become. [By the same token], the more [the state of fear and hope] diminishes, the more injustice will be increased.

In early Islam, due to the closeness of the time of the Prophet and manifestations of God's Agents (*awlīyā-ʾi-ḥaqq*) [i.e. the *Imāms*], justice was more widespread. However, after the Occulation of the *Imām* of the universe, peace may be upon him, when his Specified and General Agents were entrusted with the affairs, a gradual weakness appeared in the [people's] beliefs because of certain accidents. Therefore, injustice increased [in various ways] depending on the different circumstances and the existence and non-existence of the endeavour [both] of the *ʿulamā* and the kings.

According to these preliminary remarks, it has become evident that, if justice is to spread, it is necessary to strengthen these two groups. That is to say, those who know [Islamic] provisions and those who possess power among Muslims. This is the way for earning the correct and useful justice.

Yes, in our epoch, currency has been given to a subject which [falsely] sounds like justice. Thus, a number of naturalists who deny the origin and return [of creation] and consider [our] life limited only to this world, saw that with anarchy and without setting up a 'law' they would not be able to achieve their benefits of life. Therefore, they made [a mixture of] sacred heavenly laws, as well as [the devices created by their own] defective minds, and called it 'law'. They accepted this law in order to satisfy their desires. With this arrangement they established order, [but] the commander and prohibitor in this order are the same law, plus the punishment which has been considered in the law. It does not create any commander and prohibitor inside one's heart. It is for this reason that shameful actions are current in keeping with the [established] system, and equal oppression given to all has been increased. As soon as they find themselves in security of the law they commit treason and injustice.

Now, Oh Muslims and children of the Muslims who do not appreciate the divine grace, what a firmly [founded] religion we have; what benefits one can enjoy from it: and what reforms can be made [through it] on [the affairs related to] this world and to the world to come! Is it proper to recant this straight path and to follow these defective-minded people whose deficiency is, if you pay attention, testified by the assembly (*hay'at*) itself? [Should] we bear this great oppression that, simply because of its omnipresence, has been called 'justice'? [Are we to] become preoccupied with worldly [affairs], to turn away from the origin and return [of creation], and to seek only worldly improvements and wealth?

So many prophets were appointed by God to persuade the children of Adam to [be concerned with] the world to come and [induce them] to abstain from this ephemeral world (*dunyā-yi fānī*). On the contrary, whatever our [constitutionalist] orators have said to the people during the past two years [consists only of the suggestion that] one should go after these worldly [affairs], and earn wealth and have pleasure. At one time one of these devils, out of 'sympathy', said in private to [some] of our countrymen that the removal of poverty in this country depends on two things: firstly, the decreasing of expenses, and secondly, the increasing of incomes. The most important thing which limits expenses is the lifting of veil from women, [because] the home dress would be sufficient for outside and inside. [They also argued that] one set of servants is enough; needs would be met with one carriage;[22] one party with both women and men would be enough, and other things of this sort. Oh, zealous [people]! [Do] deliberate [and see] what [evil] thoughts they had about you. Many examples of these evil thoughts were found [in the writings of] newspaper editors and [the speeches of] orators. Thank God that they did not reach their aim, and [let us] hope that by divine favour, they [also] will not reach [their aim] in the future. 'So, of the people who did wrong, the last remnant was cut off. Praise be to Allāh, Lord of the Worlds!' [6:45]

The reason for extending this discussion was that the religious and believing brothers, may God increase their success and protect them from the evils of the devils of the human and the spirit world, may know and understand some of the corrupt thoughts, evil intentions, words and deeds of these human satans. [I pronounced the foregoing statement] in order that [people] may not listen to those words, [which sound] charming but are nonsensical and destructive to religion, [and may not] hold to the overworn string of this group who are suffering a loss in this world and the world to come.

Oh, brothers! [Do] deliberate! If the subject [which the constitutionalists presented] was of [any] virtue, why were its supporters the people who had corrupt opinions and [performed] corrupt actions? Yes, some of them looked virtuous, but, out of credulity, they were deceived or they were of the type of the *Khawārij* of *Nahravān*.

In fact, it was a great test given by God. Those devils were acting so skilfully that [their actions] disguised their real nature. The strangest of all was that they considered that malicious incident [the revolution] as a victory of the *Imām* the Epoch, peace be upon him. They addressed dissolute and even disbelieving people with attributes and respects which [only] suited the friends of God (*awliyā' Allāh*), martyrs, and virtuous people. Indeed it was one of the great calamities destined for the time when the end of the world is to be expected (*ākhir al-zamān*).

If one refers to the books which deal with [the Twelfth *Imam*'s Occultation, the history of bloody fights, and the signs of the advent of the *Imām* of the Epoch, may God, the Exalted, hasten and facilitate his return, one would see several traditions which are applicable to the situation which existed during the [past] two years. One can consider [the recent events] as some of the excellent signs [of the coming of the *Imām*]. If I gain an opportunity by the will of God, I will collect those traditions from the books of the *ḥadīths* and the commentaries [of the Qur'an] and will publish them in an annotated form. [I shall take this step] in order that the knowledge of [my] religious brothers may increase and their beliefs may be firmly established. Oh, God! Grant me success with Your graces; put me into operation in the way which may please you; keep me away from whatever displeases You. [I hope these wishes may be fulfilled] through the dignity of Muḥammad and his pure family, may God's peace be upon them all until the Day of Judgment.

Another article included in that erroneous book [i.e. the constitution] says that no punishment will be ordered and executed except according to the law. This provision is in contrast with the sect of *Ja'far*, peace may be upon him, because during the [Greater] Occultation of the *Imām*, peace may be upon him, [only] the *Shī'ī fuqahā* are authorised to handle new problems (*ḥavādis*) and to control [all] the affairs. They would find the truth and execute [necessary] punishments after ascertaining the principles; [this procedure] does not at all depend on the approval of anyone.

Another article [of the constitution] divides the powers of the state into three, the first of which is the legislative power; this is also an innovation and a downright aberration, because in Islam, no one is allowed to legislate or to establish a provision. Islam does not have any shortcomings that require completion. Concerning new incidents [i.e., problems: *vaqā'i'*] which may emerge, it would be necessary to refer to the gate of the provisions, that is the [General] Agents of the *Imām*, peace may be upon him. The Agents, [then] would deduce [the relevant provision] from the Qur'ān and the *Sunnah* [of the Prophet], but they cannot make law. Many articles of this type can be found in this erroneous book.

In defiance of the fact that the constitutionalists made efforts to mislead people by their abstract writings and by referring everything to the law, there are about twenty points [in the constitution] which stand in contrast to the explicit rules of Islam, and which cannot ever be interpreted as favourable [to Islam].

This was the nature of the ambiguously written [constitution]; the state of the detailed law would obviously be [worse]. The constitutionalists wrote a law for judicial affairs, but hid it for several months without having the courage to sign and publish it. This was a summary of the details concerning this great calamity and innovation. [I am] presenting [this communication] to [my] believing brothers in order to increase their insights and to make them understand the [correct] *fatwās* and provisions [relating to the problems of constitutionalism].

In sum, my aim [in dealing with the above discussion] is that there may remain no uncertainty or doubt that constitutionalism is against the religion of Islam [which was given to us by] the best of mankind, upon him may be peace and thousands of salutations. It is not possible to bring this Islamic country under a constitutional regime except by abolishing Islam. Therefore, if any Muslim attempts to impose constitutionalism upon us Muslims, his attempts will be taken as destructive to the religion. Such a person is an apostate, to whom the four provisions regarding the apostate may be applicable, regardless of his being knowledgeable or illiterate, strong or weak.

This is the *fatwā* and the opinion to which I do not think anyone would be opposed: I [hereby] command and enjoin them [on the people]. May God have mercy upon those who assist Islam and its adherents.

Oh, God! [Do] corroborate our king and his army; eternalise his life; immortalise his kingship and rule: and establish him on the straight path. May God's curse be upon those who disdain Islam or are willing to disdain or change it.

Notes

[1.] To the best of our knowledge no critical study has yet appeared on Shaykh Faḍl Allāh Nūrī's life and political activities. The literature of the constitutional period is biased about him. He has been strongly attacked and praised by the constitutionalists and absolutists respectively. The British official reports are not sympathetic about him (see F.O. 416, the volumes related to the years 1905–09). Some biographies exist which include Sayyid Muḥammad Mahdī al-Mūsawī al-Iṣfahānī, *Aḥsan al-wadī 'ah fi tarājim mashāhīr mujtahidī al-Shī'ah* (Najaf: Al-Ḥaydariyyah, 1968), and Ḥāj Mullā 'Alī Vā'iẓ Khīyābānī 'al-Tabrīzī, *Kitāb-i 'ulamā'-i mu'āṣirīn* (Tabrīz, 1946) pp. 94–95, and which have no critical value. For details concerning Nūrī's opposition and Sayyid Kāzim's involvement in the opposition, read Ahmad Kasravī Tabrīzī, *Tārīkh-i mashrūṭah-yi Iran* (Tehran: Amīr Kabīr, 1951), pp. 294. 381–5, 496–8.

2. E. G. Browne, *The Persian Revolution of 1905–1909* (London: Cambridge University Press, 1910), p. 373, quoted from Article 2 of the Persian Supplementary Fundamental Law written in 1907.

3. The motives of the various groups who supported the two opposing parties, the constitutionalists and the absolutists (*mustabiddīn*), are discussed in Ervand Abrahamian. 'The Crowd in the Persian Revolution', *Iranian Studies: Journal of the Society for Iranian Studies,* II (1969), 128–50. For a detailed study of the constitutionalist '*ulamā*'s view of modern political institution, consult Abdul-Hadi Hairi. *Shī'ism and Constitutionalism in Iran,* (Leiden, 1977).

4. See pages 33–4 of the above book.

5. The suggestion which was made to this writer is worth considering, because Najafi not only is a well-read religious leader (in Qum, Iran), he is also a distinguished genealogist and bibliographer. Besides, there is an indication that attests to the correctness of Najafi's suggestion because Shaykh 'Abd al-Nabī Nūrī was one of the supporters of Shaykh Fazl Allāh in his campaign against the constitutionalists; of Mahdī Malik-Zādah, *Tārīkh-i inqilāb-i mashrūṭiyyat-i Iran* (Tehran: Suqrāṭ, 1949). Vol. III. p. 30.

6. See his book which he wrote in defence of constitutionalism entitled *Tanbīh al-ummah wa tanzīh al-millah* (Tehran: Firdawsī, 1955), pp. 4–5. Nā'īnī was the most systematic author among the '*ulamā* on the subject of constitutionalism. On his life and political thought consult the present writer's book described in no. 3.

7. Malik-Zādah, *Inqilāb*, Vol. IV, pp. 222–78.

8. Kasravī, *Mashrūṭah,* pp. 409–38.

9. A sample of *Al-Da'wah al-islamīyyah* can be found in Muḥammad Ismā'īl Rizvānī, 'Bīst-o-Du Risālah-yi Tablīghātī az Dawrah-yi Inqilāb-i Mashrūṭīyyat', *Rāhnamā-yi Kitāb,* XII (1969), 234–5; photographed copies of a few issues of *Iqaz va Tanbīh* were consulted by the present writer in Tehran, in the summer of 1970.

10. Kasravī, *Mashrūṭah,* pp. 415–23.

11. Malik-Zādah, *Inqilāb,* Vol. IV, pp. 209–20.

12. Nā'īnī. *Tanbīh, passim.*

13. For the text both of the question and the Shaykh's treatise, see no. 11 above.

14. Reference is being made here to Aqā Muḥammad Bāqir Bihbahānī who is noted for his long effective campaign against the *Akhbārīs*. On this man and the *Akhbārī-Uṣūlī* controversy, cf. Gianroberto Scarcia, 'Introno alle Controvarsi tra Ahbārī e Uṣūlī Presso Gli Imāmiti di Persia', *Rivisia degli Studi Orientali,* XXXIII (1959), 211–50, and 'Alī Davvānī, *Ustād-i kull Aqa Muḥammad Bāqir lbn Muḥammad Akmal Ma'ruf bi Vaḥīd-i Bihbahānī* (Qum, Iran: Dār al-'llm, 1958).

15. Here, Shaykh Fazl Allāh is referring to the constitution, which the constitutionalists were making an effort to Islamicise by including some special articles in it.

16. This is a reference to the Qur'ān and the story of *aṣḥāb al-fīl* (105: 1–5).

17. On the definition of this term, the Shahīd al-Awwal has this to say: 'Every religious precept, [*ḥukm shar'ī*], which principally aims at worldly affairs, whether it involves attraction of benefits or avoidance of loss, is called *mu'āmalāt*. Cf. Muḥammad Ibn Makkī al-'Amilī, al-Shahīd al-Awwal, *Kitāb al-qawā'id* (n.p., 1890), p. 5.

18. Since Islam meant the absolute truth to Shaykh Faẓl Allāh he, as a *mujtahid*, was fully right to consider false any deviation from Islam. Deviation from infidelity to Islam was also called false by the Shaykh, perhaps because he was assuming that Iran was already a Muslim country. Therefore, to him, it was absurd to think that the change of law involved a deviation from infidelity to Islam.

19. The expression '*anāvīn-i sānaviyyah* applied in *fiqh* to the actions which are originally obligatory or forbidden, but which under certain circumstances will change. For example, if a man forbids his son to ride a bicycle it will become obligatory for the son not to ride a bicycle despite the fact that riding a bicycle was not originally forbidden by God.

20. This means only two hours; here the Shaykh is referring to the bombardment of the first *Majlis* which he considers as a religious victory.

21. Article 20 of the supplementary fundamental law.

22. I.e., there would be no need to appoint female servants for women and to allot separate carriages for them.

CHAPTER 4

The Detrimental Consequences of Islam[1]

Ahmad Kasravi

Ahmad Kasravi was born in 1890 in the Azeri-speaking city of Tabriz in north-east Iran. He received a traditional, religious education, and at the age of twenty he graduated as a preacher in Tabriz. In 1911 the Russians occupied Tabriz, and the anti-constitutionalist former monarch Mohammad 'Ali Shah attempted to reinstate himself on the throne. Kasravi gave sermons in Tabriz in which he encouraged people to take up arms against the Russians, and supported the aims of the Constitutionalists, while other clerics in Tabriz were suspicious of constitutionalism because of its supposed connection with secularism. Some clerics collaborated with the Russian forces in order to take revenge on their religious opponents, and Kasravi described how he forced himself to watch the executions of these supporters of constitutionalism so that he would never forget the savagery of the bigoted clerics.

In additional to his religious learning Kasravi was attracted to modern sciences and knowledge which emanated from the West, and he realised that it was necessary to learn European languages to further his knowledge of the modern world. To this end he began to learn English from the teachers of the American Memorial School in Tabriz where he was employed as a teacher of Arabic. However, he resigned from this school because of the sectarianism between Muslim and Christian students.

The Russian Revolution in 1917 inspired many movements in Iran with socialist leanings, and one of these was the Azarbayjan Democrat Party, and Kasravi was involved in mediating between the various factions within this party, indicating his standing within the region. He also organised the Democrat Party's local food relief committee during the severe famine of 1918. However, Kasravi distanced himself from the Democrat Party when it adopted a more separatist position and declared the independence of the Republic of Azadestan. Kasravi felt that his life was threatened because of his political and religious views, and since most of those who sympathised with his opinions were in prison, he decided to flee to Tehran.

Once in the capital in 1919 he was offered a job as an Arabic teacher in a high school, but he returned to Tabriz and in 1921 he entered the Ministry of Justice, where he worked for the next ten years in various locations within Iran. This gave him the opportunity to become acquainted with the languages and histories of these regions, providing him with the background for his academic works. Kasravi was uncompromising in establishing justice and rooting out corruption in his work within the Ministry of Justice, and unsurprisingly he made some powerful enemies which resulted in his recall from several locations and his relocation in remote areas. His commitment to pursuing justice resulted in his judgment against Reza Shah (the first Pahlavi monarch who reigned between 1925 and 1941), in which he defended the farmers of land in Mazandaran against the claims of the Shah. However, as a result of the pressure against him, Kasravi resigned from the Ministry, and he decided to pursue the career of a lawyer, while at the same time teaching Iranian history. As a lawyer he was involved in a number of high-profile cases, including his defence in 1938 of the so-called 53, a group of Marxists led by Taqi Arani.

During the 1930s Kasravi's activities in the fields of journalism and academia intensified. He set out his world view in 1932–33 in a work called A'in (Creed) which also served as a refutation of left-wing ideas that were becoming increasingly popular in Iran. In 1933–34 he published 'The Five-Hundred Year History of Khuzestan' and between 1934 and 1941 he published the 'The Eighteen Year History of Azarbayjan', the aim of both works being to denigrate separatism within Iran. Moreover he launched a monthly journal in December 1933 entitled Payman, *of which he was editor and almost sole writer. Recognised as one of Iran's leading academic figures, Kasravi was a target for the Ministry of Education, who were seeking to staff the newly established University of Tehran. However, Kasravi's views on the detrimental effects of classical Persian poetry (including Hafez, Khayyam and Sa'di) on Iranian society, which he made public in his writings and speeches, resulted in the Minister of Education denying Kasravi a lectureship. Kasravi was not prepared to compromise and he remained an iconoclastic figure among literary circles, breaking with many of the most respected figures of the era.*

In 1941 Reza Shah was forced to abdicate as Britain and the Soviet Union desired an Iran secure from the threat of the influence of Nazi Germany. Reza Shah's young son Mohammad Reza became the new Shah, and after the stifling period of his father's reign there ensued a period of relative political freedom which permitted greater public expression through books, periodicals and newspapers. From 1941 until his death in 1946 Kasravi published a remarkable number of pamphlets and articles. Many of these were composed of articles that had already been published in Payman, *and this accounts for much of the repetition that one finds in Kasravi's writings. The political freedom permitted Kasravi to establish an organisation called the* Azadegan *(the Free) that served to promote his ideology throughout the country, with branches in all major cities. Kasravi believed that reform of Iran could be achieved only through educating the masses, and the main elements of reform were contained within sixteen points that he outlined in a speech in 1941, the main essence of which was the promotion of democracy, economic welfare, education and social and personal life. These points were further disseminated within the official newspaper of the*

Azadegan, Parcham, *edited by Kasravi, and variations of* Parcham *were printed between 1942 and 1945. The perceived radicalism of the ideas espoused by the Azadegan, and their ritualistic book burning resulted in members being beaten up, imprisonment, dismissal from governmental jobs and denial of promotion. The strength of the Azadegan was limited and at its height the party could attract no more than a few thousand supporters.*

By 1945, Kasravi believed that having awakened Iranians to the problems facing the country, the Azadegan were ready to take control of Iran, however, a month later an attempt was made on Kasravi's life. The individuals responsible for the assassination attempt were members of a group called the Feda'iyan-e Islam *(Devotees of Islam), a radical group of Shi'-ites outraged by Kasravi's 1944 critique of traditional Shi'-ism. Yet the public disquiet caused by the Azadegan resulted in greater opposition from the clerics, who forged an alliance with elements within the government, including the speaker of the Parliament who publicly accused Kasravi of advocating anti-Islamic views, while Premier Sadr brought charges of propagating 'heretical ideas' against him. On 11 March 1946 Kasravi was shot dead by members of the Feda'iyan during the last session of the preliminary hearings of the heresy charges brought against him.*

The text provided here is the first chapter from Kasravi's short book entitled On Islam *which was first published in 1943–44. Kasravi's own belief in Islam was far removed from what he perceived to be the traditional interpretation that was accepted by Muslims of his own age. His own understanding of God resembled that of the Deists, who envisaged God as a remote creator who did not intervene in the matters of the world, which was governed according to laws. Kasravi also accepted the prophethood of Mohammad, and seemed to have a genuine respect for the 'noble Arab', which suggests that he was not influenced by the anti-Arab racist ideas found in Iran at this time. On Islam elaborates on the kind of criticisms levelled against the clerics (which we have witneseed in Malkam Khan's writings), such as superstitious beliefs, too much concern with jurisprudence, and a tendency to glorify the past at the expense of adapting to existing realities. Kasravi's ideal Islam comes near to the Wahhabi form that rejects Sufism and Shi'-ism, although even the Wahhabis were criticised by Kasravi for not being forward thinking. The governments of the Middle East are also criticised for promoting the traditional forms of Islam, for this not only serves their limited and selfish interests, but also enables Europeans to expand their influence in the region. His critique of the Islamic tradition, the Iranian government and Western influence, although polemical and theologically unsound, was influential upon subsequent generations of lay intellectuals such as Jalal Al-e Ahmad and 'Ali Shari'ati.*

Note

1. 'The Detrimental Consequences of Islam' was translated into English by M. R. Ghanoonparvar in *On Islam and Shi-ism* (Costa Mesa: Mazda Publishers, 1990), pp. 64–77.

Further Reading

Ervand Abrahmian, "Kasravi: The Integrative Nationalist of Iran", *Middle Eastern Studies*, 9 (1973), pp. 271–95.
Ahamd Kasravi, *On Islam and Shi-ism*, translated by M. R. Ghanoonparvar (Costa Mesa: Mazda, 1990).

———•———

[We are speaking of the Islam of today. Not only does this so-called Islam – an establishment run by the clerics – not do any good, it does a great deal of harm and is a source of misery. If we consider the Easterners' problems and their sense of helplessness to have three causes, one is this very establishment. Because of the constraints of time and space, I will confine myself to discussing a few major detrimental consequences of Islam.

This Islam is the Source of Misguided Ways and Ignorance

Moslems everywhere and of every sect have sunk into a state of misguided ignorance. If I were to enumerate their ignorant beliefs and practices, I would need to write a large book. Here, I will only briefly list some of them.

A. The first source of their devious ways is their lack of understanding of the true meaning of religion. Despite the interest they exhibit in religion, they are ignorant of its true meaning. Religion consists of 'understanding the meaning of the world and life and living in accordance with the dictates of *kherad* [rational faculties]'. They have not understood this. They consider religion as comprised of a series of baseless superstitions and harmful practices. To them, religion is something marginal to life.

For instance, as mentioned above, Moslems today divide themselves on the basis of ethnic group in most places and live according to European laws and customs. They study European sciences, which are not compatible with religious beliefs. They hang on to their religions and are still bound by them, because they think of religion as something separate from life, the result of which is happiness and salvation in the next world.

Even more interesting is the fact that there are still clerics in Najaf, Karbala, al-Azhar University, and in other places, who study *feqh* and write books on the subject without offering any reason whatsoever for doing so. Is this not a sign of their misguided ways and ignorance?

B. Understanding the Creator is basic to religion, but these people do not know Him. They have fabricated a god out of their own imagination, who sits up in Seventh Heaven, running the world through the angels, a god who, like a selfish, autocratic king, goes into a rage at the slightest disobedience on the part of the people, sending sickness, famine and earthquakes, but later, when the people turn to him and begin to plead and wail, his wrath subsides and he ends his punishment.

Such is the god that they imagine, a god who has created the world for the sake of a few, a god who bestows favours, accepts mediators, and speaks to the people through prayer beads and verses of the Koran (*estekhareh*).

C. *Kherad* [rational faculties] is the most valuable gift of God, and everyone must recognise and follow it. The truth is that the purpose of religion is to strengthen the rational faculties. Moslems neither recognise nor value them. Indeed, because their beliefs and practices are irrational, they are hostile towards rational faculties and minimise their value. They have frequently come and argued with us as to why we place so much importance on rational faculties. We have heard them say: 'The rational faculties [*aql*] of different people differ.'[1]

D. Prophethood is one of the bases of religion and is, indeed, one of the secrets of the universe. They do not know its correct meaning and maintain a number of groundless beliefs about it. In their opinion, when God chooses a person, Gabriel appears to that person and speaks to him. The barriers between him and God disappear and angels continually visit him. The prophet then announces his claim to the people and the people demand 'miracles' from him in order to test him. If he is capable of performing them, they will accept him, and henceforth accept whatever he says. This is what they understand of prophethood – which is, it must be said, totally nonsensical.

The books of Moslems are full of stories of miracles attributed to the noble founder of Islam: He splits the moon in two; he ascends to Heaven to see God; he brings the sun up again after it has set; he makes a spring flow from his fingers; and he speaks to a lizard.

If you ask a Moslem the reason for believing Mohammad to be a true prophet, he will immediately respond: 'He performed miracles; he split the moon; he had knowledge of the invisible.' We respond, 'We read in the Koran that whenever the Prophet was asked to perform miracles, he clearly stated his inability to do so, so how can you say that he performed miracles, and on what basis do you write all those stories in the books?' Here they are at a loss and have no answers.

E. As for the next world, they have filled their minds with nonsensical delusions about it: when a person dies, he comes to life again in the grave; two angels – one called Nakir and the other Monkar – fiery clubs in hand, come to him and ask him certain questions in Arabic, such as, 'Who is your God? Who is your prophet?' He must answer each question properly, otherwise the fiery clubs will descend upon his head. If he is a sinner, the grave will close in on him very tightly. On Resurrection Day, everyone will rise out of his grave and all will gather in a desert. God will sit on a throne, with prophets lined up on both sides. Sins and acts worthy of reward will be balanced on a scale. Each prophet will mediate for his 'people'. Then, people will have to cross the very thin, sharp 'Bridge of *Serat* '. One group will go to Paradise, and the other will fall to Hell.

F. In religion, if people understand God, they must also understand His laws (about how the world operates). Understanding God without understanding His laws is useless. However, Moslems are ignorant of God's laws. Here are some examples:

(1) This world operates systematically and everything is the result of something else; nothing can occur without a cause. But Moslems are forever seeking acts without causes, those which are contrary to the laws.

For instance, they treat illnesses with prayers; they consider their leaders to be capable of 'miracles' or 'wondrous acts'; they believe in the second coming of Christ, the reappearance of the Imam in Occultation, and the immortality of Elias, all of which are contrary to the laws of the universe. And if you object, they respond: 'It is not outside the realm of God's power.' These ignorant people do not know that God has established boundaries for His ability and laws for all His work, which do not allow everything which could be to be.

(2) This world is constantly progressing. Progress is a significant part of the laws of the universe, so that at any given time, other improvements occur. But, Moslems understand the reverse to be true. To them, the past is better than the present or the future. It is in the light of this misconception that they fail to value their own time, always thinking about the past. This is one of the causes of their backwardness.

(3) It is the will of God that every once in a while a godly movement occurs, a righteous path is opened to the people of the world, and misguided beliefs and practices are eliminated. But Moslems consider this process to have ended with Islam. In their ignorance, they perceive that the hands of God are tied, believing that even if millions of years go by, God will no longer concern Himself with the world.

(4) While they hold such beliefs about time and think as they do concerning religious movements, they expect that at the end of time, Jesus will descend from Heaven or Mahdi will appear and change the world. They do not understand the laws of nature and have fabricated such ignorant beliefs.

These were six areas in which Moslems are misguided. Each one of these is a separate, rooted, misguided belief, which is worse and more harmful than worshipping the idols of Lat and Hobal.[2]

These are the ignorant practices that can destroy the world and make the nations inferior. The purpose of religion, which human beings need, is to prevent such beliefs and practices.

These are the misguided beliefs in which most Moslems are entangled, and which comprise the ignorance of the sheikhs of al-Azhar University and the religious scholars of Najaf, in addition to the many other misguided beliefs in which the common people are entangled, or other false teachings and misguided beliefs, including Shi'ism, Batenism, Sufism, Kharabatism, Greek philosophy, Aliollahism, and Baha'ism, which are common in most Moslem countries, and each group claims one of these as its sect. In addition, in recent years, materialism has also come from Europe to the East and has become very common among

Moslems. Today, most of the educated (clerics among them) are irreligious and materialistic. The only thing is that some of them openly display their irreligiosity; but many, despite their irreligiosity, will not let go of religion, living with weak beliefs in doubt and helplessness.

Moslems Submit to Subjugation

Worst of all is the degrading and abject state in which Moslems live. Today, Moslems everywhere, with the exception of Turkey, are under the control of Europeans and have submitted to this degradation, none of them even thinking about freedom. To put it more clearly, today, Moslems have given up the idea of having a country in the name of Islam and do not even hold such a hope in their hearts. Indeed, today, there is a contradiction between being a Moslem and loving freedom. Moslems, in every country, are divided into two groups. One group is made up of those who desire freedom for their country and the honour and dignity of their nation, and who strive towards this end. This group has turned away from religion. The other group consists of those who are devoted to religion (or pretend to be), but whose hearts are devoid of the desire for freedom, honour and dignity, and who are hostile to those who seek freedom.

Why is this so? Allow me to briefly retrace the history of this phenomenon. Fifty or sixty years ago, when European sciences and the new ideas of the Europeans spread among the Moslems, and in every country there appeared movements in the name of patriotism or representative government and the like, clerics or leaders of Islam everywhere found such ideas and movements incompatible with their establishment and everywhere expressed their hostility towards them. Consequently, a gulf was created between religiosity, on the one hand, and the desire for freedom and patriotism, on the other. In order to preserve their establishment, the clerics tried everywhere to make their followers (who are the religious people) abandon love of such things as country and nation, even to make them become hostile to such ideas. This is the history of that separation.

The truth is that in the world as it is, Islam is not suitable for a large free country called the Islamic world. Nor is it suitable for people in the countries which are populated by Moslems to retain that religion, operating their countries in accordance with its laws, and at the same time to be free. The political institutions of Islam were not meant for today's world. It is not possible to run a country with them. Those who understand and value the meaning of the freedom and independence of a country and whose sense of honour and dignity prevent them from submitting to the control of foreigners will inevitably turn away from religion. On the other hand, clerics and others who cannot or do not want to turn away from religion will have no choice but to give up such notions as freedom, independence, and patriotism. In order to be able to retain their religion, they happily accept subservience to foreigners.

If you examine the situation carefully, you will see that the ideals of Moslems (the practising ones), wherever they are and no matter to what ethnic group they belong, consist of having their mosques respected, not having their way to Mecca blocked, having their domes (or, as they call them, their holy sites) remain intact, having respect shown to their Friday and Islamic holidays, having the Koran recited on the radio in the evening or morning, and occasionally having some European write in praise of Islam and its founder. It is just these few things that comprise the ideals of the religious Moslems. Under these few conditions, they are all willing to be subservient to any government, European or Asian. This is so obvious that it requires no further elaboration.

Moslems Boast of Their Ignorant Beliefs and Practices

As we said, the beliefs held by Moslems today, which they consider religion (whether about God and the prophets or about life and the hereafter), are all false and all founded in ignorance. It is precisely these ignorant beliefs which keep them from progressing and which have caused them to become so wretched and degraded. On the other hand, as we shall see, the progress of time has left Islam and other religions behind. But Moslems themselves do not know this. Indeed, they are so ignorant that they boast of their ignorance, thinking of themselves as possessing salvation and hoping that Europeans will convert to Islam. They have heard that when Islam appeared, people converted to it in droves, and they assume that the same thing should happen now. They do not realise that neither Islam nor the times have remained the same. We have often seen that over-zealous novice clerics entertain the futile wish of going to Europe to engage in the propagation of Islam. Some have often been heard to say in despair, 'Why on earth do these Europeans not become Moslems?'

Many of them hope that sooner or later some powerful European leader will convert to Islam and will spread it far and wide. During the last World War, when the German Kaiser – purely in order to deceive the Moslems – pretended to support Islam, Moslems, smiling with delight, congratulated each other and everywhere displayed their support for Germany. Later, when Mussolini and Hitler appeared, they focused their hopes on them. In the beginning of the present war, when the Germans were advancing rapidly, most Moslems everywhere engaged in 'Hitler praising'. Some were saying: 'God has chosen him, and you will see that he will even become a Moslem.'

One day, a merchant who had travelled to India and Russia came to me, and among other things, began to praise Hitler. He then added: 'There is only one thing left, that is, for him to become a Moslem and bring Islam to the height of its glory.' This was not something that deserved an answer from me. It deserved nothing but silence. However, he would not stop, continuing with even more nonsense. In an effort to stop him, I said: 'How could Hitler bring Islam to the height of its glory?' He answered: 'He has power. He is able to do anything.' I saw that it was getting worse, so I just said: 'Let us not continue this conversation.'

If the readers will consider this response carefully, they will have an example of the extent of the ignorance of Moslems. Note how many erroneous beliefs are mixed together in this argument.

(1) Because he has heard of Hitler's gains in the war, he is attracted to him from this distance, placing irrational hopes on him, supposing him to be a man of God.

(2) He thinks that religion cannot spread except through force, and that is why he expects Hitler to help spread Islam.

(3) He finds no shortcomings in his own religion, which is full of misguided beliefs and practices, and hopes it will spread in Europe.

(4) He is totally ignorant of the problems which the sciences have created for Islam and other religions. When Moslem youths are educated and become acquainted with European sciences, they become irreligious. Yet, this person expects European scientists to convert to Islam.

(5) There have been movements in all Islamic countries where Islamic laws have been abandoned and, through revolution and bloodshed, European laws and ways of life have been introduced. Yet, this person wishes the Europeans to accept Islam and its laws and to use them among themselves.

On another occasion, a cleric said the same thing about Hitler, expressing the same hope for the spread of Islam through Hitler. I asked him: 'Is the number of Moslems larger today, or was it larger at the dawn of Islam?' He answered: 'It is a hundred times larger today than at that time.' I said: 'If this is true, why is it that they were able to make such conquests then, while today they are wretched and subservient to others?' He said: 'Well, today, Islam is weak.' I asked: 'Why is it weak? Why were they strong at that time, with their small numbers, while today, despite their large numbers, they are weak? What is the secret?' He could not answer. I continued: 'If you do not know the answers to these questions, you should remain silent rather than insisting on debating in ignorance.' Then I said: 'You may not know the secret of the Moslems' weakness despite their larger number, but we do. At that time, the source of Islam was clear. Moslems knew nothing but Islamic beliefs, were steadfast in them, made sacrifices, and, despite their small numbers, made many great conquests. But, today, the source of Islam is vague and obscure. Islamic beliefs have been polluted with hundreds of ignorant and misguided beliefs and practices, and Moslems are disunited and in disarray, not to mention the fact that their beliefs are weak. That is why, despite their numbers, they are incapable of doing anything and live under the control of others.

'Hence, the problem is with Islam itself, with the beliefs and the teachings themselves. Could Hitler solve this problem? Is this the kind of task he can accomplish?'

When I made these observations, he hung his head, rose to his feet and left. This was another example of the ignorance of the Moslems and the boasting of their misguided beliefs. Not only is this kind of boasting a sign of ignorance, but it has the harmful consequence of Moslems not realising their problems and not searching for salvation. In their boastfulness, they forget their wretchedness and degradation.

Moslems Resist Any Good Ideas and Any Salvation

Because of their certainty of the truth of their misguided beliefs and their reliance on the strength of those beliefs, Moslems resist any good ideas and any salvation, show hostility, and create obstacles.

In the past forty or fifty years, we have witnessed the Constitutional movement, or the government of the people, which is itself the result of world progress and the advancement of ideas. Moslems have opposed such movements in Iran, in the Ottoman Empire, and in other places to the point of bloodshed. They engaged in disruptive and deplorable actions when schools and colleges were established. They have opposed the establishment of offices for records and documents. They have refused to accept the use of the solar calendar. There have been countless actions such as these.

Worst of all is their reaction to the Pakdini movement.[3] Today, the world suffers from materialism, which destroys the roots of religion, belief in God, good deeds, uprightness, tranquillity of life, and everything else. Materialistic philosophy, which has deep roots, considers the world nothing more than this tangible material system and does not believe in God, the soul, and the afterlife, or *kherad*, which are the bases of religion. It lowers human beings to the status of animals, considering them incapable of good deeds. It considers life a battle and the world a battlefield. It teaches everyone to think of nothing but his own pleasure. We have raised the banner to fight this philosophy – the most powerful and frightening of all misguided philosophies the world has ever seen, one which is in every way incompatible with religion and its objectives – and we respond to it from every angle. However, we see that Moslems, instead of being pleased and supporting us, react with hostility and create all sorts of obstacles. Why? Because we do not say these things in the name of 'Islam'; because these things are different from their irrational beliefs.

See what this religion has come to, whose followers fight the efforts made to eliminate irreligiosity, but allow themselves to be hostile and to create obstacles in their way.

Many readers may not be aware of the meaning of these observations and of our purpose in making them. I will state them more clearly.

Since the scientific movement began in Europe two or three hundred years ago, it has resulted in the failure of religions, for several reasons.

(1) The contradictions between the sciences and what is contained in religious books concerning the earth, the sky, the stars, and so on.

(2) The philosophy of materialism appeared because of the advancement in sciences and became widespread along with the sciences. Materialism is the enemy of religion; it is contrary to religion in every respect. This philosophy considers the world nothing more than a superficial, material system, placing human beings in the same category as animals, without the potential for improvement, and regards life as nothing more than a fight for survival among the living.

(3) As a result of the spread of sciences, ideas have progressed and human life has changed with the new inventions. That is why religions have become obsolete and the laws that they offer for life have become inferior.

The result of all this has been that religions have been defeated and devalued. The masses of the people have turned away from religion and those who did not (some ignorant old men and women) have become weak in their beliefs and have begun to doubt. The religious leaders realised that they were impotent and did not try to prevent the situation. Rather, they allowed this situation to happen and withdrew from it. It must be said, frankly, that religion became like 'contraband'. The religious people have not merely gone into a kind of hiding here and there, they actually pretend not to hear the hundreds of criticisms lodged against religious books and even the foundations of religion and do not respond to them. They do not pay attention to the contradictions that exist between religion and science.

Since a hundred years ago, this has been the situation with regard to Judaism, Christianity, Islam, and other religions. Their leaders are content that some organisation – even one of wretchedness and degradation – has been established, one which is supported by old women and simpletons or tricksters and evil persons who profit from religion.

An examination of the issue reveals that most priests in Europe and many clerics in Asia are irreligious or weak in their beliefs, because they have read the books of the materialists or have listened to their statements. Since they are like impotent smugglers, despite their awareness that modern sciences are incompatible with their religious beliefs, and that the young people who study will become weak in their beliefs and even irreligious, priests, mollas, rabbis, and others, nevertheless, send their sons and daughters to schools and colleges to study those sciences.

In Europe, Nietzsche, Bakhner, and other standard-bearers have risen and written so many books on materialism and irreligion. Thus far, no response has been made by priests – a response, that is, which is of acceptable scientific value. In Asia, in Egypt, Shebli Shamil and Salameh Musa and others have published books which have shaken the foundations of theism and religion. The scholars of al-Azhar University and the clerics of Najaf have only pretended not to hear and have merely tried to preserve their own organisation.

If a high-school student goes to al-Azhar University or Najaf or Karbala, which are considered religious centres, to engage in debates with religious scholars and clerics, he will receive no response to any criticism or question he may set forth. That is why I say that these religions have all become like contraband.

The wretchedness and worthlessness of religions reached a point that some reformists, like Marx, regarded them as harmful to the world and considered it an obligation to fight them. In the opinion of such reformists, religions are remnants of the human Age of Ignorance and a continuation of idol worshipping and superstition. They think that prophets were charlatans who took advantage of the people's ignorance and taught them a series of superstitious beliefs. As proof, these reformists state that in the present time, the age of sciences, no one can claim any longer to be a prophet, and no one mentions God and His having a hand in the affairs of the world.

Much has been said and written on the issue of religion and science having been at odds since ancient times, until, finally, science has triumphed and totally destroyed its rival.

In Iran, much has been written on the issue of Europe being a place for science and learning, while Asia always gives rise to 'religion, superstition, and delusions'. Religion has become so debased that some people, in order to avoid being considered ignorant, openly proclaim to be irreligious. Separation and incompatibility between religion and science have reached the extent that no one would even suppose that 'religion and science could coexist, both pursuing the same ends'.

In short, at such a time when religion has been so debased, by the will of God, we raised the standards, stood up against materialism, and responded strongly to each one of its false teachings. We clarified a series of very important truths and showed that religion itself is a system superior to science. Thus, we honoured the pure name of the Creator and silenced the unenlightened. For more than ten years, we have been working in this vein and, with the help of God, we have overcome all the misguided beliefs and practices. But what can be said when we see that Moslems – those helpless and ignorant people – instead of being pleased with our efforts and victories, are displeased, and the clerics engage in all sorts of hostility. What we have done is in accordance with the will of God, and what they do is motivated by their ignorance and misguided beliefs.

As we said, they do not understand religion in the sense that we are saying and do not seek the same end as we do. In their opinion, religion is a system by which to show the glory and place of the Prophet of Islam and his family.

They recite such quotes as, 'Had it not been for you, We would not have created the heavens and the earth,' and the Shi'ites add that 'Had it not been for Ali, We would not have created you.' In their opinion, God created the world for the sake of the Prophet of Islam, Imam Ali ebn Abi Taleb, and their family.

And religion functions merely for the purpose of making them and their status known, as well as for mourning them and visiting their shrines, the reward for which will be nothing more than their mediation on the Day of Resurrection and going to Paradise.

That is why in their minds, no matter what happens to Islam, it will remain eternal, it will not be harmed by the ignorant and misguided beliefs and practices which have found their way into religion, and they have no fear of the wretchedness and degradation of the Moslems.

The question is whether religion is for the sake of the people or the people are for the sake of religion. We say that religion is for the sake of the people. But they do not accept this and consider the people to be for the sake of religion. We say that religion should show the highway of life to the people, make them aware of the useful truths of the world and prevent them from being misguided and disunited. That is why we say that religion, which has lost its essence and has been mingled with misguided beliefs and ignorance, can be considered as having been destroyed. But they say that religion is for the purpose of acquainting the people with those 'revered' by God – that is, the Prophet of Islam and his family – and their status, to have the people accept them, always repeat their names, demonstrate love and fondness for them, keep their stories alive without allowing them to get old, and make their domes places of worship to which they will make pilgrimages from far and near. For them, this and only this is religion and its end.

But I have been digressing. The hostility of the Moslems towards the correct path to salvation is itself one of the great detriments of this establishment they call Islam. Furthermore, the behaviour of the Moslems is the result of their religious beliefs, not merely a passing whim: let the world be as it may, they should not allow this tainted establishment to be eliminated and the myth of God's love for those He reveres be disrupted.

Politicians Have Made a Tool for Themselves of This Establishment

Another detriment of this establishment they call Islam is that powerful governments who wish to conquer the world and have set their eyes on the impotent and helpless Islamic masses have made of this establishment a tool for the advancement of their objectives.

It is imperative to speak at length on this subject (in fact, to say everything there is to say on the subject would require a separate book); however, since time does not permit me, I will try to be brief.

These governments, which do not stop at using cannons, guns and tanks for the advancement of their policies, but follow every path and employ every means to do so, are well aware that various sects that exist under the name of Islam create great problems for Moslems and on the whole afford these governments several distinct advantages:

(1) They create disunity rather than unity and alliances and instigate conflicts and hostility among the people.

(2) They degrade ideas, greatly hindering Moslems from living in full equality with Europeans.

(3) European sciences and certain beneficial movements which have appeared among the Europeans (such as constitutionalism and patriotism), and which have also reached the East, became ineffectual as a result of coming in contact and being incompatible with these sects.

Because these governments are well aware of this, they support many of these sects, and in doing so, they reap much benefit; which is to say that since the followers of these sects and their leaders find such governments supportive of their sects, they are inclined to rally behind them and willingly submit to being subservient. (We have frequently witnessed in Iran that whenever foreigners have set foot in this country, the clerics and their followers engage in joyful celebrations.)

It is with this idea in mind that Europeans give a free rein to these sects wherever they are, value their leaders, and support them both openly and secretly. In addition, Orientalists, a group of political government employees, continually write and publish books about these sects. In the guise of non-partisan research and historical assessment, they strive to stabilise the foundations of each sect, as we have seen them do in regard to other misguided beliefs, including Sufism and Kharabatism, writing books in support of these ideas.

For instance, in regards to Sufis, they try to show that Sufis have been profound thinkers pursuing certain truths; whereas, we know for a fact that the substance of Sufi ideology has consisted mostly of fabrications. Hence, their teachings are like deadly poison for the people at a time such as ours. More surprisingly, Europeans have based their lives on hard work and self-sacrifice, and we witness how they struggle, how they fight their wars against each other, and in order to gain superiority over others, how they have thousands even hundreds of thousands of their young people killed without remorse. But, in regards to the Easterners, they praise Sufism or Kharabatism, which are based on the degradation of the world, carelessness about life, idleness and laziness, or they show their support for sects the consequences of which are nothing but backwardness in life. From this point, you can deduce their hidden motives.

The same is also true of Islam. In truth, this establishment called Islam serves the interests of greedy expansionist governments at every turn. Besides, as we said, religious Moslems are prepared to live subservient to any government, and only wish to be free in their religion (or better said, their own sects). That is why when Mussolini rose to power in Italy and wished to take over some Islamic countries, we saw that he pretended to be a supporter of Islam. One could say that he was practising to be a shepherd of these scattered flocks. Also, the

Japanese government, which for many years desired to take over Burma, Java, Indochina, and India, displayed its support for Islam, practising to be a shepherd.

Although there were many Moslems in Japan, the motives of the Japanese government were purely political. It would be impossible for Japan to have an Islamic government one day.

This Islam Degrades the Name of God

The greatest detriment of this establishment called Islam (and also other religions and sects) is that it degrades the pure name of God. Such religions and sects offer a series of unfounded ideas and useless instructions – which neither conform to science nor benefit life – in the name of 'religion' or the 'path of God', providing the irreligious and unenlightened an opportunity for criticism.

Today, the important question is whether or not God truly concerns Himself with this world and shows a path to the people. Obviously, since science is founded on materialism, they have not accepted such questions and scientists have dismissed them as irrelevant.

As we said, today, the masses of the people are irreligious and do not submit to the belief in the existence of God, let alone accept His guidance. But we have spoken much in this regard and have provided solid responses to these materialist scientists. We have shown that every so often a divine movement must appear and a new highway open to life.[4] But this highway must not only conform to the rational faculties and science, it must also be above science and act as a teacher to the rational faculties. It must teach the people the laws of life and be a source of comfort to the people and the prosperity of the world. Such a valuable system can be called 'the path of God' or 'religion'. If religion comes from God, it must be comprised of ideas higher than those of the people.

How can the teachings of sects – most of which oppose the sciences and the rational faculties, are incompatible with life and, on the whole, consist of empty and pedestrian ideas and futile and irrational instructions – be called religion? How could this wretched contraband establishment deserve to carry the name of God?

Will calling such teachings religion not turn the people away from religion? Could ascribing such ideas to God result in anything but the destruction of His pure name?

These are the great detriments of this establishment, known as Islam in name only, which we have briefly enumerated. These are the detriments which emanate from each sect and are common to all of them. However, some sects have other exclusive detriments. For instance, the Shi'ite sect, which is the Islam of the Iranians, has particularly detrimental attributes, the enumeration of which would be lengthy in itself.[5] In this sect, ignorance has reached such a level that the sect considers government, as it exists and should be, as 'illegitimate' and prohibits the payment of taxes and service in the military without realising the ultimate consequences. On the other hand, they give money in the name of religious taxes [*zakat* and *mal-e emam*] to the clerics, who have absolutely no responsibility in this world. According to the beliefs of this sect, anyone who makes a pilgrimage to Karbala, Najaf or Mashhad or sheds tears in religious mourning ceremonies will be absolved of all sins, which is why most of the religious people commit price-hiking, hoarding and violations of the law, and have no regard for their country. In fact, some of them are thieves, tyrants, and swindlers, who, relying on making a pilgrimage to Karbala or holding religious mourning ceremonies, live unabashedly and with peace of mind. Of this kind of detriment, much can be found in this sect.

Notes

[1.] *Kherad*, as Kasravi's text shows, is the power to distinguish between good and evil, right and wrong, and so on. *Aql* is quoted by Kasravi here as a synonym for *kherad* [tr.].

[2.] The idols of Lat and Hobal were worshipped in pre-Islamic Arabia [tr.].

[3.] The Pakdini movement: *Pak*, literally 'pure' or 'total' (according to Kasravi's lexical explanations provided in 'Vazhehnameh-ye Zaban-e Pak') and *din*, meaning 'religion'; hence, Pakdini may be translated as 'pure religion'. 'Pakdini' refers to a system of beliefs advocated by Kasravi in his writings, and which found some followers in Iran [tr.].

[4.] On this matter, see *Varjavand Bonyad* (Kasravi). *Varjavand Bonyad* (Sacred Foundation) is a book which Kasravi, in an advertisement at the end of *Bekhanand va Davari Konand*, calls 'the most valuable of our books' and urges readers to read [tr.].

[5.] See *Davari* on this point (Kasravi). *Davari* is the shortened title of *Bekhanand va Davari Konand* (Let Them Read and Judge), which has also appeared under the title *Shi'igari* (Shi'-ism) [tr.].

CHAPTER 5

Sediqeh Dowlatabadi: An Iranian Feminist (1882–1961)

Introduced and Translated by Mansoureh Ettehadieh[1]

The position of women was always demeaning and insecure. They were considered as weaklings and were the ward of the father, brother or husband. They were married off young and were generally illiterate or half educated, being able to read but not write. The oppression of women was worst in the lower echelons of society. They had no security and no freedom. They could be easily divorced and their fate depended on the kindness or humanity of their husband or family. In the upper classes women could enjoy the protection of their family, but they were just as insecure.[2] Things began to change with the Constitutional Revolution at the beginning of the twentieth century, and Sediqeh Dowlatabadi played an important role in the developments which gradually changed the conditions of women.[3]

Sediqeh Dowlatabadi stands out among other Iranian proto-feminists of her generation such as Mohtaram-e Eskandari,[4] Agha Baygom,[5] the daughter of Shaykh Hadi[6] or Maryam Mozayan al-Soltaneh.[7] She is the most significant personality among them because of her clearcut ideas on the position of women, her uncompromising attitude, her courage, steadfastness and perseverance. In contrast to Mohtaram-e Eskandari, who died young, or Mrs Kahalzadeh,[8] who in fact worked with her husband, or Shams Kasma'i or the daughters of Imam al-Hokama or Shams al-Mu'ali[9] who seem to disappear from view, Sediqeh lived a long life, continued her fight and was involved with the developments which changed the position of women in Iran.[10]

Sediqeh was born in Isfahan when Naser al-Din Shah the fourth Qajar monarch had been on the throne for thirty-six years. He was assassinated in 1896 and was succeeded by his son Muzaffar al-Din Shah. During the last decades of Naser al-Din's reign, government tyranny, despotism and foreign political and economic dominance alienated large groups of people. Criticism by liberal Western-oriented thinkers and reformers presented the alternative of a better government, which contrasted with the current mismanagement of affairs. Led by the ulema, *the religious body, who had their own reasons for dissatisfaction, there were strikes in Tehran and some other provincial towns until the Shah was obliged to accept the establishment of a Majles or parliament. The electoral laws were enacted immediately, elections were held and the Majles was opened on 6 October 1906. The deputies then proceeded to enact the Constitutional Laws and a year later the Supplementary Fundamental Laws, which were modelled on Western laws.*[11]

The Constitutional Revolution not only triggered an awakening among men in Iran; it also affected women. Although women were not given the right to vote, and were classed with madmen and children in this regard, the Fundamental Laws granted the right to education, free speech, free press and the right to organise without discriminating against women, and this gave them the opportunity to become active.[12] *Imbued with great enthusiasm, women claimed they were awakened too. They founded schools, published journals and newspapers and organised societies where they made patriotic speeches in support of the Revolution, or discussed their conditions, demanding that the government pay attention to their needs, a plea which fell on deaf ears. They were not discouraged, however, and continued their activities, arguing that not until women were educated could they nurture useful patriotic citizens. By thus expressing their common problems and working together, women came to discover their affinity as a social class.*[13]

These activities were not popular among men, except in some liberal circles. At best women were limited to educational and other feminine pursuits. Political activity was out of the question and they were either discouraged or prohibited from interfering in what was considered a masculine domain. This fact was generally accepted by women, who declared that they had no interest in politics. Sediqeh Dowlatabadi was an exception in this regard and she kept a lifelong interest in political affairs of the country although she was prohibited from active participation.

Sediqeh Dowlatabadi's life and work can be divided into three periods. The first period is from her birth in 1882 to the Constitutional Revolution of 1906. The second period is from the Revolution to the fall of the Qajar dynasty in 1925, and the third period covers the reign of Reza Shah Pahlavi and his son Mohammad Reza, till her death in 1961.

Sediqeh came from a highly educated religious family. One of her brothers, Yahya, was a prominent educationalist and together with another brother, 'Ali Mohammad, they were active political figures in the Constitutional Revolution. Sediqeh was educated at home but was encouraged by her father and took her studies seriously. She was married at twenty and went to live in Tehran, where she witnessed the tempestuous course of the Revolution, which also generated a lot of activity among a number of women. No doubt her dislike and distrust of politicians and her deep conviction that education was the only road for women's advancement were acquired at this time.

The marriage did not last, and Sediqeh returned to Isfahan, where she opened a school for girls in 1915. But Isfahan was a very conservative city and she was obliged to close it, soon afterwards. She also organised the Patriotic Women's Society, which was dedicated to the promotion of home-manufactured cloth, and she campaigned against early marriage for girls.[14]

In 1917 Sediqeh began to publish a journal, Zaban-e Zanan *(women's tongue). Afsaneh Najmabadi, who has co-edited her work, points out that although this was not the first women's journal, it was the most daring, for not only did it mention women in the title, but Sediqeh called it 'women's tongue', which by tradition was to be discreet and not heard.*[15]

Sediqeh's ambition as a journalist went beyond women's questions. She began to discuss political issues and claimed she had taken up the pen in order to defend Iran's independence, a claim made by male journalists, too. According to her, writers and journalists fought with their pens and she declared she did not fear death for this cause.[16]

What Sediqeh wrote denigrated politicians, but was tolerated for a time, due no doubt to her brothers' influence. As a consequence of her attack on the government's agreement with the British in 1919[17] *and her vehement criticism of the Ministry of Education over its disregard for girls' education, especially in Isfahan, her journal was confiscated and she was obliged to leave for Tehran, where she published* Zaban-e Zanan *for a short period. In 1923 she went to Europe for medical treatment and to study education in France. She was over forty at the time.*[18]

Sediqeh studied with enthusiasm and enjoyed her new-found freedom, although she was unwell for most of the time, and was short of money and homesick. Apart from studying, she was a keen observer of life around her, curious in particular about women's lives, and she wrote long, eloquent letters to the two young sisters she had adopted.[19] *She returned to Iran in 1927, and found employment as an inspector of girls' schools, in the Ministry of Education. By this time Reza Pahlavi had ousted the Qajars and been crowned Shah, and a new dawn was breaking for women.*

Reza Shah had long-term plans for the modernisation of Iran, which included women, particularly in the field of education, which could not but meet with Sediqeh's approval. Primary and secondary schools for girls were opened in the main cities of Iran and in 1936 women were admitted to the newly founded University of Tehran. The marriage age was increased to fifteen and the sensitive question of the unveiling of women was broached in January 1936.[20] *Sediqeh was very much in favour of the unveiling of women, or as she put it the freedom of women, and since her return to Iran she had not worn the veil. In 1935 Sediqeh was made the director of the* Kanun-e Banuvan, Ladies Society, *a post she retained until her death twenty-six years later.*

The Kanun *was an educational and vocational school for girls and young women. But Sediqeh did much more than run a school. There were literary classes for adults and she organised conferences and invited prominent people to talk and discuss current issues. One interesting course of study she initiated was the education of the wife and mother. The girls were to study, for instance, good manners, economy, health, decoration, sewing, cooking, the relationship of wife and husband, the psychology of men, the relationship of the individual with society, the mother's role in the upbringing of children and youths etc.*[21] *According to Sediqeh, a woman's ultimate duty was to be a good housewife and mother, but when she came to discuss the question of work for women she had a dilemma. She considered work gave women dignity and independence; however, this ran counter to her ideals of the good wife and mother, a question which still perplexes Iranian women to this day.*

Once Reza Shah abdicated in 1941, Sediqeh began to publish Zaban-e Zanan *once again. The first issue came out in December 1942. It soon became the organ of the Kanun, and the exponent of her ideas and where she tried to come to terms with the many contradictions in the status of the modern Iranian woman. As a journalist she was fearless, but having experienced male animosity, she was cautious and generally spoke as a moralist and not as a critic and claimed* Kanun-e Banuvan *and* Zaban-e Zanan *worked for a peaceful transition. She particularly claimed that* Zaban-e Zanan *had become active once again as the position of women was endangered and she felt it her duty to take up the challenge. However, she also delved in political and social matters and ran into difficulty with the authorities, which once again banned the paper for eighteen months when she criticised the government because of shortage of bread.*[22]

Sediqeh Dowlatabadi *was above all an educationalist and consistently believed in the importance of education as the key to women's independence and advancement. In fact education was the core of her ideas, and all her other views about the position of women in society or the politics of the country emanated from this basic assumption that education was at the centre of all development. As a feminist she was critical of the low marriage age, polygamy and the male right to divorce, and campaigned assiduously to have the stigma attached to women in the Electoral Laws – which classed them with madmen and children – removed. She was particularly opposed to the* hejab, *or the veil, as demeaning to the dignity of women.*

Sediqeh's political ideology was that of the reformers of the Constitutional periods: she believed in Western liberalism, she was a passionate nationalist and an idealist with socialist leanings. She was, however, realistic enough to realise that the dictatorship of Reza Shah had its advantages for the cause of women, and while it lasted she co-operated fully with the government.

She knew French and had studied in Europe, a rare privilege for Iranian women at the time. She attended two international conferences, in 1924 and in 1947, in Paris. She met and was admired by a number of European and American feminists.[23] *In 1932 she chaired the Conference of the Women of the East in Tehran.*[24] *These advantages gave her confidence and strength and perhaps explain the superior stance she took in the articles she wrote and the talks she gave, which today might appear somewhat moralistic and domineering.*

Sediqeh was born when women's position was one of subservience and powerlessness. She died two years before women were granted the right to vote in 1963. All her active life she was closely tied to the cause of women and was responsible to a great extent for its development from isolated timid beginnings involving a few women to an effective government-sponsored national policy. But when she came to review her life's work she greatly deplored the way the movement had taken shape and was disappointed by and critical of the image of modern Iranian women. Nevertheless, the next generation of

Iranian feminists, taking their cue from her, were better educated, clearer about their goals and the methods to employ. Chief among these women one could cite Dr Mehrangiz Manuchehriyan, who was a diehard feminist, a lawyer, a senator and the first woman to receive the Human Rights Peace Prize of the United Nations in 1968 and the Peace Prize of the Centre of World Peace Through Law in 1971.[25]

In order to understand Sediqeh's ideas and her goals, with all their weaknesses or strengths, it is fitting to dwell on some of her work as expressed in letters, speeches and articles. The pieces introduced here are chosen to give the core of her ideas on three topics: women's education, the question of the hejab (the veil), and her political ideas.

━━•━━

Education

('We are Writing Again', *Zaban-e Zanan*, 52, 17 November 1920)

Education was the core of Sediqeh's ideas as the only means by which women – and indeed all society – would advance. The following articles in Zaban-e Zanan, *and letters exchanged with the Director of the Ministry of Education in Isfahan in November 1920, led to the banning of the journal on January 1921. Sediqeh objected vehemently and the order was rescinded in June on condition that she should keep to her lawful duties and publish only on literary moralistic matters, and to change the name of the journal from plain* Zaban-e Zanan *to the* Journal of Zaban-e Zanan. *However, Sediqeh probably found the atmosphere in Isfahan too restrictive, and moved to the relatively more liberal Tehran.*

Perhaps we have not written of the need for founding more free government schools for girls (especially in Isfahan, which is totally deprived in this regard) in every issue of *Zaban-e Zanan*, but we have at least shouted and screamed about this need during the first and second year this journal was published. During the first years we wrote publicly to the previous Minister of Education, Mr Asadallah Mosafa, and we printed his reply in the thirteenth issue of *Zaban-e Zanan*, but we have seen no results until now. It is possible that some of our readers have grown tired from the repetition of this problem. Perhaps some people are opposed to women out of spite, but we say that we shall never desist from repeating and writing that this is the only remedy and sole treatment for achieving the happiness of our nation and our country.

Even if you do not listen to us and do not react as you should, and even if you stop the education and nurturing of girls, out of spite or enmity, or even if you obstruct the obvious duty you have towards the nation and its happiness, we shall persevere and fight you.

It is obvious to all educated and liberal persons that the advancement of the nation and country depends on the education and the nurture of girls. Today's girls are tomorrow's mothers and children grow up and are educated and are nurtured in the bosom of the mother. They learn the characteristics of humanity from her and God willing they will climb the ladder of knowledge with love and purity.

This is the future, which confronts us. If our forebears had begun this charitable work, no doubt our fathers would have reached this goal by now and we would have been among the happiest people on earth and our country would have been considered one of the luckiest in the world. However, they did not do so. But the idea took shape in the minds of a few of our fathers and resulted in a movement which threw Iran into educational conflict and turmoil, a conflict between a lofty and a lowly contradiction. We have to try to escape the lowly state and to take permanent steps with regard to the whole country, and with a single mind and purpose endeavour to move towards this holy principle, so that we shall safeguard our future and the future of this country and the future of Iran's children. You should know that we have no other remedy but this. What is the excuse of the mighty Ministry of Education? And what is the reply of the Department of Education of Isfahan? We are addressing the Director of the Department of Education of Isfahan who has attended school himself, has taught as a teacher and is well known as an educator. What is his reply to our request?

To the Director of the Department of Education: Sir, do you really pity the unfortunate girls of this land and country? Will you do what your duty and your conscience and your love of your country bids you to do?

We suggest that a number of free government-sponsored schools for girls should be founded, which would follow the programme of the Ministry of Education and the tenets of Islam. Their budgets should be provided by taxation and, according, to Islam, the share of boys' schools should be twice that of the girls' schools. Although today the needs of the girls are more than those of the boys, still we do not suggest that you should open as many schools for girls as you do for boys. What we say is that if you open six schools for boys, open three for the unfortunate girls.

Taxes are paid by the peasants and the peasants are your pride. Peasant women work harder than peasant men; don't these mothers deserve half of their heritage for their girls? How long will injustice and tyranny be perpetrated?

How long should this city, this ancient capital of Iran, the geographic centre of the land of Iran, remain in darkness and complain and not be heard by Tehran. O you learned *ulema* and you patriots, O you Iranian liberals, O you governor, O you educators, O you learned women, O you sisters who hold education dearly, O you modern people, hear the cry of Isfahan and take pity on the mothers of tomorrow and the children of this land.

Although informed people know that the only remedy for this nation and the best medicine for its prevalent sickness and the best means of strengthening the independence of the country and the greatest happiness for all of us is to have schools and to educate the boys and girls, still the authorities procrastinate. Still the budget assigned to the police force is higher than the budget of our Ministry of Education, and we still do not have sufficient government-sponsored schools for girls and boys in all the cities of Iran to meet our needs, and to this day our political parties have not established even one nightly literacy class for adult education.

By now, fifteen years after the achievement of our freedom, there should have been a university in each province and different types of schools as needed in each city and town for boys and girls, and there should have been agricultural schools in each village and adult literacy classes (two hours nightly) to educate all men and women.[26]

Alas for this weakness, alas for this negligence, alas for this animosity.

It is surprising we have taken no heed of all the trials and pains of the past. But despite the screams and shouts and the time wasted, despite all that may happen, we are still optimistic and we say and repeat again and again, schools, schools, schools.

The Director of the Department of Education of Isfahan replied to Zaban-e Zanan, *which published the letter in* Zaban-e Zanan, *54, 2 December 1920.*

To the Honourable Editor of the journal *Zaban-e Zanan*, may your journal flourish!

An article was published in the fifty-second issue of your journal about the need for girls' schools. It is necessary to assure you that the view of the mighty Ministry of Education is to increase and develop schools and to advance the centres of learning in this country. However, it depends on present-day conditions; it is necessary first to organise and plan this undertaking in order to bring about its achievement. You should know that this is why, for the last three years, the government endeavoured to increase the number of centres of learning. With regard to the education of boys and girls, important and remarkable steps were taken, though they were far from sufficient and did not meet the needs of the country. Therefore if public schools for girls have not been founded in Isfahan, it is not because of a lack of attention. Perhaps you will agree that the reason for this delay is the lack of means.

As for myself, responsible for this department and according to my conscience, I assure you that, as far as my duties are concerned, I shall not desist from serving with sincerity the cause of education within the limits of lawful regulations. As for the education of girls, it is obvious that when the preliminary and necessary means are ready and religious conditions are completely satisfactory, I shall not hesitate to make useful suggestions to the authorities, with the hope of achieving this goal in the near future.

Lastly, I offer my thanks to the righteous pen of the journal whose main concern is the advancement of education. I take the opportunity to point out that the best thing that should adorn the pages of all our journals is to pay attention to education which, according to the views of the honourable author of the article, is the only remedy for all the ills of our country.

The Director of the Department of Education of Isfahan

Sadeq Ansari

Sediqeh was not to be intimidated and answered back. Her tone is combative and challenging (Zaban-e Zanan, *27 November 1920).*

Our Reply to the letter of the Department of Education

The honourable Director of Education, your honourable letter number 25 in reply to the article entitled 'We are Writing Once Again' in issue number 52 of the journal *Zaban-e Zanan*, with which you adorned our office, carried three points, which are as follows:

1. It reiterates that 'the view of the mighty Ministry of Education is to increase and develop schools and advance the centres of learning in this country', although it is conditional on the possibilities of the times.
2. It assures us that if no girls' schools have been established in Isfahan, it is not because of a lack of attention to this end, the reason for its delay being the lack of means.
3. The honourable Director of the Department of Education assures us that according to his responsibilities as governor and his conscience, when the preliminary means are ready he will not hesitate to recommend to the Ministry the necessity of taking action with regard to schools for girls.

Now we shall give our reply with due respect.

First, the fact that at the end of the letter, the pen of *Zaban-e Zanan* has been called righteous and has been praised is no doubt greatly encouraging and gives hope to the employees of our journal, so please accept our gratitude.

As to the reply to the first part of your letter, where 'present-day conditions' are mentioned, we do not understand what the intentions of the authorities are. Does it mean that after fifteen years conditions do not allow that a tenth of the country's income be spent for the advancement of our children, the boys and girls of Iran, which is the only means to strengthen the independence of our country and achieve progress, freedom and lasting happiness? Does 'present-day conditions' mean that the police force of Tehran should have a larger share of income than the province of Tehran, and that the important suggestions of the Ministry of Education for safeguarding and defending the rights of all the children of this country should go unheeded? No doubt the budget assigned to this Ministry with all its branches is not as large as that of the jails of Tehran.

The fundamental rights of the children of this country have been put in the care of the Ministry of Education. Is this how it should perform its duties? Are these 'the conditions of the times' as seen by the authorities of that Ministry?

As to the second point, mentioning 'lack of means': according to you, what are lack of means? Are numerous illiterate girls walking the streets, orphans poor and in rags, who run after fancy carriages, not sufficient? Could you not provide them with teachers and books from Tehran? Our eyes behold so much misery and poverty among the children of our country that we have grown used to it and we make no haste to overcome it.

It is winter now; perhaps more than 3,000 poor but intelligent boys and girls are homeless, bare, hungry, shivering by the side of the street or on the doorsteps of shops, or sleeping with the dogs and cats and taking refuge in some rubbish pile or hole. They have always been there, they have died there and probably been replaced by others. Were there no means?

Come now, gentlemen, let me explain. These are excuses and subterfuges and rhetoric of the pen. You all know well that in Europe there are homes for homeless dogs, food, education and a bed. But millions of the children of our land are like fodder in this unfortunate land of Iran, and still the time has not come and the means are not available to take serious steps.

As to the third point you write, promising to open free government schools for girls in Isfahan in the near future, although it includes a condition, that is 'useful suggestions should be made', we shall wait and see whether happiness shall be brought to the unfortunate girls of Isfahan, in order to express our gratitude to the authorities of the Department of Education of Isfahan and its honourable Director, for the fulfilment of his governmental and conscientious responsibilities. We shall then express our congratulations in the pages of *Zaban-e Zanan*, in the name of the unfortunate girls of Isfahan. (vol. 1, pp. 225–30).

Hejab

The question of the hejab, *(veiling of women) was always a political and a controversial question. In 1936 Reza Shah unveiled women arbitrarily and all opposition, especially from the* ulema *and the conservative section of society, was put down forcefully. When he abdicated in 1941, many women took up the veil again. Sediqeh Dowlatabadi, who had been a vocal opponent of the veiling of women, did not keep quiet and, as a proponent of morality and decent public behaviour, she argued that in fact the* hejab *gave women a better opportunity to commit all kinds of vices. Naturally she was well aware of the religious overtones of the question, therefore she trod carefully. In June 1944 she wrote an article in* Zaban-e Zanan *on the return of the veil.*

'The Social Position of Women' (*Zaban-e Zanan*, 2, 23 May 1944)

The position of women in the world has generally been uncertain. Ever since men organised themselves in tribes, women were positioned behind men. If we study ancient history, we notice that women's position did improve and once they achieved an honourable position they never regressed to the previous barbaric conditions.

Since the creation of the world, women have traversed three stages.

The first stage was that of savages. At this stage women were given no rights. They were slaves and beasts of burden in the household of the men. Just as a guilty slave was tied to a tree and beaten, women too were punished harshly for the smallest trespass. The father or husband was the owner of the girl or woman – in fact the weaker sex was crushed under the foot of the stronger one.

The second stage was when the inhabitants of the East began to believe in a single God. Iran, too, was among these religious nations. At this stage no worthwhile share was assigned to women, but in the monotheistic religions, women were considered the partner in life, which was an improvement for women.

The third stage began with Islam. The true religion of Islam gave a legal status to women, but unfortunately to this day women have not reached their legitimate and permanent status and have not been able to gain a legal and social personality. It could be questioned, how is it that women still have no legal and social status, when for nine years they have enjoyed the benefits of freedom and legal status? This is the answer: yes, it is nine years since women won freedom, but this is meaningless, because now that the power which bestowed that freedom by force on the women of Iran is shaken, their opponents (selfish men) targeted their first arrow at the heart of women's freedom. The unfortunate thing is that the first article against the freedom of women was written in the name of women. In this way they want to put the banner of opposition in the hands of those women who have the least knowledge of the rights of humanity, or to mislead them so they cause harm to others. They ignore the fact that by this act they not only target the personality and position of women, but also harm the personality of great men, for it is impossible that great and famous men can emerge without great and knowledgeable mothers. The influence of the character and mentality of the mother on the child is an accepted fact. It is impossible to deny the importance of the milk and nurturing of the mother and it is obvious that if a woman is deprived of all human rights she will not be a worthy mother. Then why do men wish to curtail their own progress? Why do they oppose the freedom of women and their participation in social matters?

I do not deny that since women obtained their freedom no extraordinary improvement has occurred and nothing unexpected has happened. But as I know that in every revolution there are disturbances, one should fight against these disturbances, not undo the causes of progress. I also believe time is needed to remove defects. Despite this fact, I have often paid attention to the principles of good behaviour in conferences and articles and I have criticised the behaviour of young women. Unfortunately I see that, contrary to the past, they encourage women to regress to barbaric times. Despite the fact that we live in dangerous and sensitive times, the question of the *hejab* has kindled a fire among progressive and benighted women. Fathers and daughters, wives and husbands quarrel. The road to immodesty is being cleared for capricious women who, clad in their *hejab*, incur a thousand other wrongdoings, and pay not the slightest attention to the opinion of the foreigners.[27]

Many things need reform, such as stopping prostitution, which would be a great and useful step to benefit public health, enforcing social virtues, caring for orphans, ceasing unnecessary spending, stopping the stealing and stabbing of vagrants and villains, forbidding the use of opium in all coffee shops and public drinking, forbidding bribery and the taking of bribes and public and private thefts, which is so prevalent that it can be said to have become second nature to Iranians. All these things are against the religion of Islam, but the ignorant and pessimists allow all these things to happen and only discuss the veil, although according to Islam the face and hands are allowed to be free and women are ordered to be virtuous and modest. It is obvious that anyone who respects the lofty position of women is not satisfied with the immodest behaviour of some shameless and dishonest women. Furthermore, civilisation and religion do not allow women to appear with dishevelled hair and half clad in public; rather, they must appear clean and orderly and wear respectable clothes worthy of the honourable position of women. As mentioned at the beginning of this article, imperfections must be removed gradually and will be so. In order to further these goals we need other things, such as good teachers and worthy mothers and we must draw the attention of the Ministry of Education to this particular point and urge the enforcement of the law of compulsory education, because it will produce important reforms (vol. 2, pp. 336–8).

'The Return of the Veil' (*Zaban-e Zanan*, 3, Tir 1323 S/June 1944)

'*A God believing man who seeks righteousness may wear black or white clothes.*' The above poem means that righteousness and morality do not depend on clothing. Those who make faith and religiosity dependent on clothes use the women of Iran each day and each moment according to the needs of the times and for their own personal aims, but they are mistaken and have taken the wrong way. I believe a strong and righteous society must have a true faith. Black or white clothes are not signs of faith or corruption. Did wearing felt hats or fur hats make a society more virtuous? Did the change from fur hats to the Pahlavi hats[28] reform our shortcomings? Did the change from the Pahlavi hats to European *chapeaux* change our public character? I declare bravely that the answer is no.

First we must diagnose the disease and then seek a remedy for it. I remember very well that at the beginning of the Constitutional period, a number of people cried that the Constitution was based on religious laws and that the laws of true religion were equivalent to the Fundamental Laws. However the despots argued that the Constitution was opposed to Islam and believed that the despotic monarchy was according to the tenets of Islam. The Constitution triumphed, but was it able to change the public character or the ways of selfish godless people? No.

The holy religion of Islam, which is pure philosophy, contains comprehensive decrees on how to remedy all the ills of humanity, it decrees that praying is a duty and that each person who performs his duty five times daily and heeds such conditions as regards food, clothes, place – even the water he makes his ablutions with – and is absolutely clean, that person will be redeemed and his family too will benefit. But it does not decree that that person, be it a man or woman, should wear black or white. Unfortunately Islam has been interpreted for us in such a way and certain points have been added to it so that the actual decrees have practically disappeared. For instance, previously it was said that if a virtuous woman was obliged to talk to a man, she should curl her tongue like a nut so her voice would not sound alluring or attractive and be the cause of corruption. This is foolish. A righteous person who does not change her voice can meet a thousand corrupt and evil people but her strong belief will not waver.

Sakineh, the daughter of Imam Hosayn the son of Imam 'Ali,[29] was prominent among the learned, and most Arab poets took their poems to her for correction in public gatherings. She never changed her voice and did not use her tongue in an unnatural way. The speeches Zaynab, the daughter of Amir al-Mu'menin,[30] gave in the audience of Yazid[31] were nothing less than miraculous. They were so poised, strong and logical that even her enemies said it was the voice of 'Ali which was being heard from heaven. No doubt, had it been unnatural or faked, it would never have impressed the audience and they would not have thought it to be heavenly.

If we should wish to eradicate the corrupt characteristics of society, we should first eradicate greed and cupidity and stop unnecessary and unlawful rapacity. Clothing has not the slightest importance; on the contrary, the veil gives a better opportunity to commit corrupt acts.

When the women's movement began, people were of two minds. A number said unveiling would increase dishonesty, but a group believed that the co-operation of women in social life and their unveiling would teach them manners and improve both men and women. But as this act was done by decree, the result was unsuccessful. However, if we judge its advantages and disadvantages we shall realise that its advantages are greater. A certain veiled but corrupt woman could pass unnoticed in front of her husband or father and go to a meeting place, whereas if unveiled she would be unable to go. The veiled woman who, under her face mask, could eat a cucumber or munch seeds, must now behave properly and not eat while walking in the street. The one who could steal something from a haberdashery shop must now discontinue her evil acts.

Even liberal ladies are more mindful of their behaviour in public, and do not desist from giving advice and morally helping more ignorant women. Therefore one can hope that in the light of our freedom gradually the lives of women of whatever background will come to be based on stronger foundations. But the change of clothes and veil, after ten years of being unveiled, will no doubt kindle the fire of corruption and will have disadvantageous results. *Kanun-e Banuvan* and *Zaban-e Zanan* will spare no efforts in order to stop the resumption of this overt corrupting act. (vol. 2, pp. 348–51).

Speech on Public Morality and the Question of the Veil, published in *Zaban-e Zanan*, 6, Mehr 1323 S/October 1944.

Sediqeh took the opportunity during a speech she gave at the Kanun-e Banuvan *to make a plea for public morality, which was a recurring theme of her ideas, once again equating immorality with the return of the veil, which she said gave women the possibility of cheating and misbehaving. She also insinuates that some people wanted to imperil the independence of Iran by putting women back under the veil. In fact what she was saying was that the independence of the country depended on the independence of women. The speech is a passionate argument against the veil, with strong political and nationalistic undertones, a reminder that she was always politically oriented.*

History teaches us that need and necessity are the essence of progress. It was necessity that turned the savage nomad into the inhabitant of palaces. Need often creates other needs. When we build a house we realise that we need rooms and rooms need cupboards and furniture. At times this need is so sensitive that it equals the life and death of a nation. If such needs are not met, the life of the nation might be imperilled.

If we take into account the deeds of leading reformers in the world at any time or place, we notice that when any of them acted it was because necessity brought to their attention the fact that it was a question either of death or independence. We had such leaders in Iran too. For instance we can mention Kaveh[32] the ironmonger, who rebelled when the situation became precarious. Of course the idea of self-sacrifice was his, but it was the help and the assistance of the people that made it possible to reach their goal.

Now let us think a little. Do we have needs or not? No doubt everyone will say we have many urgent needs. It is obvious that these needs are of different degrees. Our most urgent public need is our poor public morality, which stems from lack of knowledge and easy credulity. When I read the most sensational articles in the newspapers, about the worst, selfish acts of some people, I am not surprised. Why? Because I know very well that the person who acts in this way has no feelings other than his selfishness. This is what he was taught at whichever school he went to, or whichever family he came from. Therefore what else can we expect from him but what he does?

Don't think the needs I mention today are material needs. I refer to moral needs. During the past three years that we have enjoyed freedom of the pen[33] you have all read what our writers have written and pointed out the short-comings of Iran and the Iranians. Indeed our chests and cupboards are filled with the historical documents about the worthlessness of Iranians. Our ears are deafened and our eyes blinded by hearing and reading all this. I am an Iranian woman who has no other political motive but the independence of Iran. I read carefully all the articles I can obtain. I feel regretful and saddened by the descriptions of selfishness. Listen carefully and correct me if I am wrong. Experienced ladies and gentlemen know that the conferences at the *Kanun-e Banuvan* are the occasion for discussion and I am proud to say that anyone can freely express his ideas about the topic being debated.

Ever since I remember and have observed the conditions of the times, I have come to believe that public morality has greatly deteriorated. The morality and mental needs of Iranians has changed during the last thirty or forty years. The origin and cause of this deterioration is not relevant. What is relevant is that, unfortunately, few people remain today who retain the best characteristics of Iranians: bravery, decisiveness and truthfulness. What is needed is that those few who still possess these attributes should at least unite.

For 2000 years our motto has been good deeds, good thoughts and good speech. Truth and decisiveness give rise to bravery. Individual needs are not so complex, although it is individual needs that create public needs. Public needs must be met by the support of the people. Do you think this support means intrigue? No. Chaos and disorder? No. Do you think political parties and factions are the answer? No. What is it then? The answer is bravery, truthfulness and decisiveness. Not until these attributes are widely disseminated will our poor public morality disappear. Unless we develop strong morality we shall remain in the clutches of this or that.

[*Sediqeh went on to talk at length about Joan of Arc and her fearlessness in the defence of France. She concluded thus:*]

Was it anything else other than the feeling of need that prompted this girl to bravery and self-sacrifice? No. Therefore, we must conclude that need gives rise to sacrifice especially if that need is safeguarding the independence of the country and the prestige of the nation.

Today the greatest need is the safeguarding of women's liberty. Therefore it is my duty to remind you ladies that we face a great danger. That danger is imminent and frightening. What danger? The danger of the demise of the liberty and independence of women. If we do not prevent this danger, we shall face a worse danger tomorrow: the demise of the independence of Iran. Why? Because the safety and independence of the country are linked to the safeguarding of the character and prestige of the people of this country. If the inhabitants of a country have no will, if they are indecisive and timorous, if they lack prestige which is a necessary human quality, if they lack character, the independence of that country will not last; others will allow themselves to take it under their tutelage. Today intrigue for the return of the veil is increasing daily and the despots are reaching their evil goals, but they do not know where they are heading.

Unfortunately, ignorant women are blindly stepping in their footsteps. I assure you that in various places people are getting ready to strangle women, that is half of the body of the Iranian people. They are preparing to strangle you and me, and after they have killed our right to independence and have proved that half of the Iranian body is paralysed, they will sit at the table of official peace-making and sign away Iran's right to independence and they will be vindicated. If a nation in which half of the people fight the other half with their pens and that other half is lifeless like this table, upon which I do as I like – one day I cover it with a tablecloth and the next day I take it off – that nation is unworthy to stand alongside the men of this world who are alive. Just because our country has been the corridor for war, does it mean we have no right to independence? No. Anyone can pass through the desert created by God, but they don't have a right to it. If we are ignorant of our rights, and if the charter which proves our sickness and worthlessness is registered, will we not be condemned before the society of world peace?

Dear and honourable ladies, will you now not agree that we have a dire need and a heavy duty and that in order to meet our needs we must really unite and perform our duties so that we shall not be introduced to the world as wooden doors or tables? However, we still have another need: to unite with our liberal-minded men. One hand makes no sound, therefore it is necessary that we should act in unison and step on the battleground together and fight the frightful shape-shrouded men. What kind of a fight? A fight fought with intelligence, not with scandal. Today, our numbers are too few and the numbers of old-fashioned women larger. Are you ready to be trampled by stupidity?

It is said that those who love flattery, who wish to fill their pockets, who are demagogues, are waiting to be sure that when they begin to act, the authorities will stay silent. It is then that unveiled honourable ladies will be attacked in the street.

Now I wish to conclude my speech. First of all, be assured that my discourse and my information are not baseless and unfounded. Secondly I cannot assign the duties of you ladies. My only duty is to review the personality of women and to warn you if your social rights are attacked. This small house called the *Kanun-e Banuvan*, to which all Iranian ladies have a right, has never deviated until now from the straight path and its policy has never been its polemics. But if it keeps quiet in times of darkness and trouble, it will recede to the days of Shah Soltan Hosayn,[34] who announced that the city of Isfahan was sufficient for him. In that case it had better close its doors and not remain standing. I repeat: I do not wish to point out your duty to you, but I know my own duty is. If a day comes and those evildoers who sit in darkness try to undo ten years of freedom and stain women's prestige, believe me, without hesitation and without looking back, I shall go with a white banner among the men who do not understand that to blind and deafen their own mothers, sisters and wives and daughters is a great crime. These men do not want to understand that if their mothers are not educated and wise the virtue of Islam will not be maintained and the veil of immorality they wish to put back on women is the veil of dishonesty which prostitutes put on. It is not what religion is made of. Yes, I shall go among these men, and even if I am killed I shall proclaim in a loud voice to the world that Iran does not lack women. I shall carry the honour for ever and I shall have proven my ideas. After the unveiling of women and the events of Khorasan,[35] when I stood in the cemetery in front of the holy shrine of Hazrat-e Ma'sumeh, in Qom, and pronounced women's duty from the podium, a large number of akhunds gathered and listened to me. God is my witness, I didn't think I would come down from the podium alive, but I did not fear death. Even the authorities thought my action was dangerous, that I should be careful. Now also you can be sure that I prefer a violent death to a slow death caused by Iranian women's indifference and worthlessness.'

[*Sediqeh ended her speech by citing a few verses of poem by her late brother Yahya.*] (vol. 2, pp. 373–7).

Politics

Article on the Resignation of the Prime Minister Vosuq al-Dawleh (*Zaban-e Zanan*, 32, 30 June 1920)

As mentioned, in the summer of 1919, the government headed by Vosuq al-Dawleh negotiated an agreement with the British government, which was very unpopular.[36] Liberal politicians and newspaper editors were critical of this agreement and Sediqeh was no exception. In fact, her criticisms of the government occasioned several attacks on her office in Isfahan. The government eventually resigned in June 1920. This is when Sediqeh wrote this article.

It is a few days since the resignation of Mr Vosuq al-Dawleh was accepted and until now a number of people have put up their candidature for the post of Prime Minister. But as we take up the pen and write, none has been accepted. It is heard, however, that our fate and the distraught conditions of Iran will eventually be entrusted to Mr Moshir al-Dawleh.

The news worth hearing about is that in the north of the country banners of independence and freedom are being flown especially in disapproval of Tehran.[37] Patience is running out. For instance in one of the headlines of the newspaper *Hallaj*,[38] dated 3 July 1920, it is written: 'Yes, for a long time, Azarbayjan or

Azadistan have been disappointed with Tehran, and wish to take their fate into their own hands.'[39] Gilan has risen in a bloody rebellion[40] and is angrily threatening Tehran. Mazandaran is falling quickly into chaos. Khorasan is beleaguered by Bolshevik forces and is preparing its own defence.[41] News from Zanjan and Kurdestan is not good. This is the present-day condition.

Yes, in the words of our brother Hallaj, we say this is the present-day condition. If our readers remember, we have always said directly or indirectly that lies are bad, that we should support liberty, that despotism is evil, that common people should not be misled, that education should improve etc., and practically from the first issue of *Zaban-e Zanan* until now we have shouted and repeated what should be done.

The amazing thing is that there are people who still believe that the world will allow them to do what they want as they did before the World War, and in their unfortunate way oppress the poor, exploit the dispossessed, take the clothes off the backs of workers and labourers and rule over them. Despite all the cries which arise from everywhere, it can still be observed or read that people of such and such a place complain of such a department or of the director or his titled assistant, but no one hears that anything substantial has been done, or perhaps there are no such things to hear about.

Of course sensitive people will grow tired of all this indifference, oppression, pressure and deceit, and their patience will run out and one day they will act and find a solution for themselves and those who will come after them. If Tehran wishes to retain its distinction it has to promote freedom; instead of spending extra sums on the police, who arrest someone or banish another every day, it should spend more on education, increase the number of schools, help the children of the labourers, expand knowledge and stop nepotism and treason and truly start to promote the cause of humanity. Perhaps then the government can retain its hold; otherwise it is possible that Tehran will be condemned before the free national tribunal of Iran.

The seventh article of the Fundamental Laws reiterates that neither the whole nor any part of the principle of the Constitution can be altered. We see no reason to write about this because it is obvious to all what the principles of our country are, how it has been governed and in particular how our country and its children, all our products, wealth and our being have been at the mercy of this or that, and however much people from the various corners of the country spoke or cried or wrote about it, they were either not heard or were silenced directly or indirectly. Is this not sufficient? We cannot explain the deceit more openly. It is not right to forbid writing or explaining what is just and to find excuses to put a stop to it. Many people are aware of all these problems, even we women, who are far from public affairs, know and understand.

If a number of people are silent it does not mean they are ignorant or satisfied with these matters; rather it is because they have chosen to remain silent. Even if some people say yes, it is not evident that they do not understand or are resigned. No, this is not so. Iranians are patriots and nationalists; only a few influential people wish to keep their power and accept this situation. They are despots who are well known to all those who seek freedom. In order to maintain their power, these people will seek the destruction of their country and the disappearance of order and the weakness of the Constitution. They wish to keep their position and the wealth of their relatives, which they well know their family or ancestors took from the people by force. They rely on other influential men in order to undermine freedom and strengthen despotism. Yes, but free Iran will allow them no time to overthrow liberty. No! They should know that the shackles of despotism are broken everywhere.

And once again I repeat the words of Hallaj: these are present-day conditions (vol. 1, pp. 204–6).

'Our Mother Iran' (*Zaban-e Zanan*, 31, 23 June 1920)

Sediqeh Dowlatabadi remained deeply influenced by the Constitutional Revolution she had experienced in her youth and she retained a lifelong interest in politics, which had undertones of socialism.[42] *But she never lost sight of women's interests and the role education should have in their lives. According to her, motherhood was the ultimate goal of womanhood and in an article entitled 'Our Mother Iran', she equated mother country Iran with a man's natural mother, who should be defended and loved.*

The name of Iran is dear to the ear of anyone who loves her. Those of us who understand how worthy our mothers are and know that it is due to their nurturing and care that we enjoy peace, understand the lofty position of the mother country and do not refrain from being happy when she is happy and cry when this great mother is old and miserable.

Each person or group of persons, even birds and other creatures love their mother and as a child knows his mother among a crowd of women and runs to her from afar, so the children of a nation run to embrace their mother country. All the wars and battles have been fought to defend and keep the honour of the mother country. Even the principle of social democracy, which wants everyone to have an equal share in the world and invites the children of the world to unite socially in the bosom of the mother earth, considers that each parcel of land belongs to the children of that beloved land.

Yes, but how long are the children of Iran going to put up with despair and bear the injustices and misery inflicted on their mother? Till what year, month, hour, minute or second are we to mourn and bemoan the loneliness and desperation of our old mother?

The poet Sa'di says when one member of the body hurts, the whole body aches.

From a socialist point of view, Iran is a member of the great world community, the world mother. How will the other members progress if she remains injured and sick for centuries? If we leave this point of view aside, we still should not ignore our responsibility and look at it from a selfish point of view: we cannot shun our responsibility and remain indifferent about saving the virtue of our mother.

For several years now we hear or read an often repeated word: betrayal. Does our country not have enough servants to stop the hands of traitors? God forbid that there should be more traitors than servants. In that case what should we do? Which is the way of redemption? What is the remedy for our sick mother?

O honourable sisters! Do you know how many centuries our brothers never called on us to serve our mother, rather they barred the way to us and we committed the sin of remaining silent while they did nothing but add to this misery.

Thank God we now have many educated and progressive sisters. Don't you think the time has come to lift yourselves up and try to serve the mother country? To gather around her to nurse and remedy her illness?

You all know the best remedy is schools. We must open small and large schools in villages and cities. They should be mostly free government schools. Compulsory education is one of the articles of our Fundamental Laws and we should demand that the government implement it. Our educated sisters from Tehran and other cities should travel to the villages and towns where girls and women are uneducated and try to find easy ways to bring education and knowledge to these unfortunate people.

Societies should be organised to see that these matters are put into action. Cultural societies should be organised to achieve these goals in a hurry. However much we distrust the social and public attitude of our brothers, we still know and believe that some are liberal-minded and nationalists, and we expect them to hear our call and to come to the aid of the mother country and to ignite the light of optimism so that with God's help we shall be able to push modernism in Iran through the road of knowledge and reach the plain of affection, happiness and freedom. (vol. 1, pp. 199–201)

'The Weakness of Our Constitution' (*Zaban-e Zanan*, 3, 25 May 1945)

The life of the Majles was two years, and according to the electoral laws the orders for the renewal of the next elections were to be announced before the current session of the Majles ended, but often this was delayed and the period between two sessions was several months or even years.

The present conditions of the Majles has excited the writers and nationalists, and they all express their regrets in various ways. They fear the closure of the Majles and fear more the beginning of the elections for the fifteenth Majles while Iran is under foreign occupation, and yet they do not think that the continuation of the fourteenth Majles is advisable. Each of these ideas is honourable and acceptable. Then what is to be done?[43]

If we pay attention to the first, second and third Constitutional periods, we shall notice that there was one particular reason why nothing was ever done in the interests of Iran; rather, everything worked to her disadvantage. That reason is so shameful that we tremble to mention it, and we fear and believe that this is the reason of the blight of our Constitution. It is evident that if the architect lays the first stone crookedly the wall will rise crookedly.

What do you read in the first article of the Fundamental Laws? We read that women, madmen and children have no right to vote.[44]

In the name of justice, the same justice which decrees that it is compulsory for a Muslim man or woman to seek education and knowledge, the lawmakers did a great and shameful injustice to the women of Iran. The first article of the Fundamental Laws, the first stone, was laid crookedly, and thus weakened the basis of our Constitution. Why?

What did women want thirty or forty years ago? Why did the lawmakers class their mothers with mad people? Why did they not heed God who created man and woman together to continue the human race? Isn't it true that if you do not heed God, you will suffer his anger and wrath?

How do you want to enjoy freedom when you consider half of humanity mad? The proof of women's incompetence was registered and signed in the first article of the Fundamental Laws, and it is now thirty years that you have acted according to this same law.

No, no, sirs, we are not surprised that you have not benefited from the fruit of the Constitution and that your freedom does not go beyond the braziers of opium. Forgive me, dear brothers, look around you and forsake your selfishness. The Iranian woman is your mother and the mother of your children. If she is mad, how could a madwoman raise a wise child? Therefore you should begin the remedy from the top.

To fly from one branch to another, and to suppose the way is barred, will eventually lead us to a quagmire in which we shall sink. Therefore the preamble of the Fundamental Laws should be cleansed of the ignominious and dirty phrase, and leave women alone. Be assured that we have no wish to elect or be elected; what we want is that women should not be mentioned at all, rather we want to have the glory of not being a party to your malicious and traitorous policies which weaken the independence of Iran and our good name.

We assure you that if you remove this curse you will reap the fruit from the tree of freedom, on condition that our wise men do not sell or buy the ballots as in the past. (vol. 2, pp. 439–40)

A letter addressed to the Prime Minister Dr Mohammad Mossadeq (22 April 1951)

This letter was written to Dr Mossadeq in 1951. Once again Sediqeh argues about the right of women to vote[45] which was still denied and illustrates the combative mood of her younger days.

I beg permission to ask you confidentially about the electoral laws and the question of women's disenfranchisement. Your Excellency, do you personally believe that today Iranian women should be considered lower and more limited in the views of foreigners, than during the first Constitutional period? If you reply yes, and that you consider this in the interest of the country, I shall obey and keep the 2,000 women entrusted to my care silent for the sake of the interests of the times. However I beg you to consider the rights bestowed on women in three stages during the past half-century.

1. The laws of the first period of the Constitution classed women with madmen and children.
2. The amendment of the Fundamental Laws of 1328 S/1949 by the Constituent Majles, (which also created the Senate),[46] exempted women from being classified with madmen and children and was an improvement, at least in appearance. At the time I questioned His Majesty about this question and what was to be done, through Mr Jam the Minister of Court. The answer was that the Senate would solve this question and women would achieve their lawful rights.
3. The present law, which is enacted in the interest of the public, not only exempts women from the right to vote without reason, but once again classes women with those who have no right to vote, such as murderers, or those condemned as criminals, or those who have corrupt ideas or are bankrupt etc. Despite the fact that the government attaches great importance to the progress and maturity of the Iranian nation, it is limited to men only and no share is given to women.

Dear Prime Minister, I do not want to take up your time, but I wish to understand the situation in order to be able to reply to the women in my care; if maturity and progress is limited to men and if women do not matter, the law being enacted (and God knows for how long women will still be deprived of their rights) then women should not be mentioned and the law should remain silent where it concerns them. If women are a part of the Iranian nation and have a share in the national progress, should they be classed with the lowest of men who have no identity, in the laws being signed by Your Excellency? It would have been better if Your Excellency ordered that certain rights be granted to women. If the questions I ask were asked of you by the United Nations, what would your answer be? If I were to know your reply I would be better able to explain it to the learned ladies.

Finally, I wish to defend my personal right according to my conscience. I am classed with the women named in the law, though I have served the cause of education for the last forty years. For eighteen years I directed the *Kanun-e Banuvan* with a limited budget, and I strove for the progress and education of women. My only lofty goal has been to educate the mothers of future generations and, with the help of God, I directed a difficult institution and served the public and people each year more assiduously than the year before.

I beg you to compare this with the work of any other righteous and eminent director of this country. Who performed his duties and served the cause of humanity better and more? I leave this comparison to Your Excellency's judgement and if I remain silent today due to the requirements of the times and the order of our beloved Prime Minister, and have kept others silent, this is also another which the future will judge too.

I have no other request and I ask your forgiveness for my presumption and await your reply impatiently. On Sunday a number of ladies not only blamed me but have threatened me, and the control of *Kanun* might be problematic in future. I need to give them a convincing reply. (vol. 1, pp. 166–7)

A Speech on the Question of Buying National Bonds

This speech was written to be broadcast on the radio programme of the Kanun-e Banuvan *and probably dates from the end of Dey 1330 S/December 1951. The Iranian government with Mohammad Mossadeq as Prime Minister nationalised the oil industry in May 1951. This embroiled the government in a long controversy with the Anglo Iranian Oil Company and the British government. In September 1951, the British consulates were closed all over Iran, the British workers left Abadan and an embargo was placed by the British government on Iranian oil. The government, in dire need of money, issued national bonds in December.*[47]

In the following speech at the Kanun-e Banuvan, *in support of Mossadeq, Sediqeh proves once again that she had not only retained her verve and combative nationalist spirit, but she had not lost sight of the cause of women. She also manifests her negative attitude to the British government and its influence on Iranian politics, a belief she had always held.*

Honourable listeners,

It is a while since I have closed my lips and in accordance with the saying that '200 words are not equal to half an act' I have concerned myself with the cause of culture and education. I now wish the honourable audience to know the reason why I am taking their time to listen to my talk.

Perhaps it has been proven that I am a servant and a fighter and my endeavours have always been to combat ignorance. I remain an outsider, however. Why? I leave those of you who are astute to find out the reason.

During these recent events I have reached the conclusion that the time has come for all Iranians, high and low, to fight, and if people wish to obtain their lawful rights this is the time they can achieve their patriotic wishes. As I am a reasoning person I must explain my reasons. Previously, whatever was attempted ended in failure and the reason given was that 'they don't want it and will not let us.' Perhaps this answer was justifiable to a certain extent. But now with these irreversible events there is no reason to give such an answer. 'They don't want it and will not let us' is no longer an acceptable answer. It is necessary to try very hard for things to progress and it is up to us to decide to implement our wishes.

Why do I say that recent events are irreversible? Some people will perhaps say that when the government changes these developments will change also. This is possible in ordinary cases, but in the case of Abadan and the hands-off policy which ensued, it is irreversible and will never change back unless God forbid …

The second question concerns the closure of the British Consulate, which is also irreversible. Even if Iran in a friendly gesture should accept that a limited number of consulates should be opened again in certain places, it is inconceivable that they should act as before and have the same meaning as in the past.

In order to relieve the boredom of our listeners I shall delve a little into history. In 1920, when *Zaban-e Zanan* had been published for two years in Isfahan, the question of the agreement of Vosuq al-Dawleh emerged. Though the policy of *Zaban-e Zanan* was educational and tuitional and advocated the achievement of equal cultural rights for women and men, when the agreement became known *Zaban-e Zanan* felt it to be its duty to publish it and to point out the danger to the independence of the country inherent in each article. *Zaban-e Zanan* was a weekly journal and was popular with the young merchants of Isfahan. At that time, with the indirect interference of the Consulate of Isfahan headed by Mr Hague, the Consul, these same young merchants were persuaded to gather in the telegraph office[48] and to ask the late Ahmad Shah to sign the agreement. They pitched their tents in the telegraph grounds, pots of soup and rice[49] were set up and the adulators gathered round blustering. At that time – it was near noon – one of the merchants took up a copy of *Zaban-e Zanan* and cried, 'Listen and look what this paper is writing and be assured that what it writes is the truth because its author neither wants to be a minister nor a deputy, she has no other worry than her love for her country and education.' When the paper was read and people understood that the agreement of Vosuq al-Dawleh was contrary to the independence of the country and that it was the propaganda of the Consulate of Isfahan, which had misled simple people, the tents disappeared and no traces of the soup and rice pots or the ashes from the fire were to be found. By the next day *Zaban-e Zanan* was robbed.

On the following day – it was Saturday 30 Mehr 1299 – *Zaban-e Zanan* published an article entitled 'Enemies Fire Their Guns'.[50] The leading article began thus: three groups – the despots, thieves and the enemies of Iran – have the same policy. Of course despots attack the liberals, the thieves attack the innocent and our enemies attack the patriots and so on. On Thursday 5 Aban, at eight o'clock at night, there was an armed attack by a number of people on the office of *Zaban-e Zanan* while the police put up a defence. All through the night until morning seventy-two rounds of fire were exchanged. At daybreak three people escaped from their hiding place. The following night the same thing was repeated. But with the perseverance of the police the three men were arrested. One of them was the personal servant of the Consul. After several hours the Consulate of Isfahan demanded their release and the police released them on condition they should leave the Consulate. These events are recorded in detail in the book about *Zaban-e Zanan*.

My aim by mentioning this history is to draw attention to these facts as I remember them, this is how the Consulate acted and interfered in the affairs of patriotic Iranians during the last thirty-two years. Therefore the time has come that *Kanun-e Banuvan* should join the campaign, which has God's approval, and help the government by buying national bonds.

[*Sediqeh ended her speech by detailing her own contribution and that of the other teachers of the* Kanun, *and invited other ladies in Tehran and in the provinces to do the same.*] (vol. 2, pp. 306–9)

Notes

[1.] In this chapter, the translator has included an introduction and has made comments on sections on the text in various locations. These sections are all discernible by use of italics, while the texts of Dawlatabadi are not italicised (ed.).

[2.] M. Ettehadieh, 'Zan dar Jame'eh-ye Qajar, Moqe'yat-e Ejtema'i-ye Zanan dar Aghaz-e Qarn-e 14 H.', *Inja Tehran Ast, Majmu'eh-ye Maqalat dar bareh-ye Tehran* (Tehran, 1269–1344 HQ/1998), pp. 251–85.

[3.] The information on Sediqeh Dawlatabadi used here is based on the three volumes entitled: Sediqeh Dowlatabadi, *Nameh-ha, Neveshteh-ha, va Yad-ha* (Sediqeh Dawlatabadi, Letters, Writings, and Remembrances), ed. Mahdokht San'ati and Afsaneh Najmabadi (Chicago: Midland Press, 1998).

[4.] Mohtaram-e Eskandari was a Qajar princess who set up the Patriotic Women's League (*Anjoman Nesvan Vatankhah*) in 1922, which had an Islamic flavour and promoted female education, assistance for orphans and hospitals for women. Sediqeh Dowlatabadi was to join the executive committee of this association. Mohtaram-e Eskandari died in 1925 (ed.).

[5.] Agha Baygom was one of the organisers of the Women's Society (*Anjoman-e Nesvan*), which developed into the National Ladies Society in 1910. She advocated women's education, prevention of foreign interference and the promotion of nationalist issues (ed.).

[6.] Shaykh Hadi Najmabadi was a pro-constitutionalist cleric (ed.).

[7.] Maryam Mozayan al-Soltaneh was the editor of a woman's newspaper called *Shokufeh*. It contained articles on literature, education, child-marriage, house-keeping and also on nationalist issues and the struggle against foreign influence. Maryam Mozayan died in 1919 (ed.).

[8.] Mrs Kahal was the editor of the first woman's newspaper, called *Danesh*, which commenced publication in 1910 (ed.).

9. Mrs Dorrat al-Mu'ali opened *Omm al-madares* (Mother of Schools), a female educational institute in Tehran, in the first decade of the twentieth century (ed.).

10. For more information on the women's movement see: 'Bidari-ye Zanan, Fa'aleyat-e Zanan dar Enqelab-e Mashrutiyat', ibid., pp. 289–308. Also, E. Sanasarian, *Women's Rights Movement in Iran, Mutiny, Appeasement and Repression 1900 to Khomeini* (New York: Praeger, 1982).

11. The Constitutional Laws were passed on 30 December 1906 but as they soon proved inadequate, the Supplementary Fundamental Laws were enacted on 7 October 1907.

12. The disenfranchisement of women was actually mentioned in the fifth article of the Electoral Laws passed in September 1906. Those excluded from the right to vote included criminals, bankrupt people, thieves, those who had to be under someone's tutelage, and those accused of corrupt opinions.

13. Ettehadieh, 'Bidari-ye Zanan'.

14. *Sediqeh Dowlatabadi*, vol. 1, p. 12.

15. Ibid., vol. 3, p. 669.

16. Ibid., vol. 1, p. 220.

17. At the end of the First World War, the British and Iranian governments made an agreement whereby the British government was to supply Iran with experts for the reform of the army and its finances, and also pay it a loan. This agreement, which came to be known as the 1919 Agreement, was very unpopular and was not ratified. The government of Vosuq al-Dawleh, which had negotiated the agreement, fell on 20 June 1920. For more information see: W. J. Olson, *Anglo-Iranian Relations During World War One* (London: Frank Cass, 1984).

18. Sediqeh was to have been accompanied by one of her brothers on this journey, but neither could go, and she undertook the trip accompanied by a French doctor who was also on his way to Europe. At the frontier, she was arrested by the local governor, on the ground that a woman could not travel outside Iran unaccompanied by a man of her family. She wrote a very angry letter to the authorities objecting strongly to the ill treatment she had met with and the personal insult to her good name and dignity, and the expenses she had incurred. *Sediqeh Dawlatabadi*, vol. 1, pp. 28–34.

19. After her father's death, Sediqeh adopted her two younger sisters, whose mother was an illiterate woman who remarried. She kept a close control over the girls, supervising their education and subsequent marriage. She wrote to them frequently while she was in Europe, directing them in their emotional, social and everyday life. These letters are a good example of her perception of the ideal of woman. (Ibid., vol. 1, pp. 43–122)

20. The policy of unveiling women was undertaken by the government on 8 January 1936. It was not passed as law, rather by decree. There was much resistance in certain quarters, but the government was adamant and unveiling was pushed through by force in many cases. But as soon as Reza Shah abdicated on 17 September 1941 in favour of his son Mohammad Reza, many women took up

the veil again. This time the government had too much on its hands and overlooked it. As a result, the female population was divided between those who aspired to the modern image of womanhood, and those who retained their religious and traditional attire.

21. *Sediqeh Dowlatabadi*, vol. 2, p. 437.

22. The shortage of bread was due mainly to war conditions, the occupation of Iran by allied forces and particularly because wheat was sent to the Soviet Union.

23. *Sediqeh Dowlatabadi*, vol. 1, pp. 13, 111.

24. This conference was attended by a number of women from Arab countries, also Japan and Australia. It was presided over by one of the Shah's daughters, Princess Shams.

25. For more information see: *Senator, Fa'aleyat-ha-ye Mehrangiz-e Manuchehriyan*, by N. Ahmadi and P. Ardalan (Tehran 1382 S/ 2002).

26. Article 19 of the Supplementary Fundamental Laws decreed education to be compulsory; however modern schooling was opposed by conservative elements and the government, with a lot of trouble on its hands, took no initiative for a long time. At last in 1911 a number of schools were founded for boys in Tehran and in 1918 for girls, but these were timid steps. The real breakthrough came during the reign of Reza Shah, when serious steps were taken to open schools in the major cities of Iran.

27. This refers to the allied occupation of Iran during the Second World War.

28. Men were obliged to change their traditional clothes and headgear in the winter of 1928; they were made to wear a hat with a brim in front. This was called the Pahlavi hat. In June 1935 orders changed and men were obliged to wear the European chapeau.

29. Imam 'Ali, the cousin and son-in-law of the prophet Mohammad, became the fourth caliph to rule over Muslims, but Shi'-ites consider him to be the lawful successor of the prophet, who should have succeeded him.

30. Amir al Mu'menin (Commander of the Faithful) is another of the titles of Imam 'Ali.

31. Yazid was the son of Mu'awiya, the second Umayyad caliph. He was designated by his father to succeed him, but upon the death of Mu'awiya, Hosayn the grandson of the prophet did not accept his succession and was slain in battle by Yazid in 63 HQ/ 820. He has always been considered by Shi'-ites as the worst villain of all time.

32. Kaveh is a legendary hero in the *Shahnameh*, or 'Book of Kings', composed by Ferdawsi in the eleventh century. Kaveh, who was a modest ironmonger, rebels against the tyrant Zuhak, who was ruling over Iran, and slays him. He is the epitome of those who resist tyranny and despotism.

33. Article 20 of the Supplementary Fundamental Laws granted the freedom of the press and the pen. However, while Reza Shah's dictatorship lasted, this freedom of the press was non-existent. When he abdicated, the newspapers once again began to be active. This was the time when Sediqeh too began to publish *Zaban-e Zanan* once again.

[34.] Shah Soltan Hosayn was the last Safavid king, defeated by the Afghans. His capital, Isfahan, was sacked in 1722. He has become the epitome of cowardice and indecisiveness.

[35.] There were some protests over the unveiling of women, which was enforced by the police, but when European hats were imposed in the summer of 1935, there was an uprising in Khorasan which was put down violently.

[36.] See n. 11 for the agreement, 1919.

[37.] The 1919 agreement being unpopular, there were protests in Tehran and other cities. In general the Prime Minister Vosuq al-Dawleh acted forcefully, exiling the leaders who were fomenting discord.

[38.] The newspaper *Hallaj* was published by Hasan Hallaj in 1919.

[39.] At the end of the war, Azarbayjan fell under the sway of Shaykh Mohammad Khiyabani, a Democrat politician who went so far as to declare the government in Tehran illegal. There was an uprising in Tabriz, and danger of cessation.

[40.] The uprising in Gilan had a long history, but it had been dormant until the 1919 agreement when, with Bolshevik influence, it flared up once again.

[41.] As a protest over the agreement, there was a Communist-inspired uprising in Khorasan. The example was followed in a number of other cities.

[42.] The spread of socialist ideology made its debut during the Constitutional Revolution. It took its inspiration from Baku, and was limited to a small political party in the Majles. It also found some adherents among intellectuals and political activists, but it never developed into a popular movement.

[43.] The fourteenth Majles, which was elected while Iran was under occupation, ended in February 1944. According to the electoral laws, elections should have been called while the Majles was still sitting. However, due to the occupation of Iran and inherent difficulties it was delayed. It had been agreed that the allied forces would evacuate Iran at the end of the war, but when it ended in May 1945, the British and American occupying forces left, but the Soviet troops remained until May 1946. It was after the evacuation that elections began in October and the fifteenth Majles met in July 1947.

[44.] Sediqeh here mistakenly mentions the Fundamental Laws, whereas the electoral laws dealt with the question of the right to vote.

[45.] Mohammad Mossadeq, who became Prime Minister in April 1951, presented a bill to the Majles to reform the electoral laws, which is in question here.

[46.] Mohammad Reza Shah was shot at by a member of the Tudeh or Communist party of Iran on 6th July 1948. Immediately a Constituent Assembly was elected on 21 April 1949 to alter the Constitution and give the Shah more powers. A Senate or Majles-e Sena, had been foreseen in the Constitutional Laws but had never been constituted because it bestowed too much power to the monarch, was now set up.

[47.] At the end of the war, when at last foreign troops left Iran, and the Soviet-backed Communist government of Azarbayjan fell to the Shah's troops, the main concern of the Iranian government was the question of its relationship with the

Anglo Iranian Oil Company, which was under growing attack by the nationalists. In April 1951, Mohammad Mossadeq became Prime Minister, and proceeded to nationalise the oil industry. This involved the government of Iran in a long battle not only with the oil company, but with the British government.

48. Taking sanctuary or *bast* was always a way of resisting the government authorities. The places chosen were often holy places such as a mosque or shrine, but it could be the telegraph office, the Shah's stable, or a foreign legation or embassy. Prior to the Constitutional Revolution, the merchants of Tehran took *bast* in the British Legation, which was an effective move that persuaded the Shah to grant a Constitution.

49. While the merchants and shopkeepers (about 12,000) were in the British Legation, they were provided with food, some said by the British. The rice and meat etc. was cooked on the premises. Here allusion is made to this fact and the rumour about the supposed British role.

50. *Sediqeh Dowlatabadi*, vol. 2, pp. 218–20.

CHAPTER 6

A Persian Sufi in the Age of Printing: Mirza Hasan Safi 'Ali Shah (1835–99)

Introduced and Translated by Nile Green

The nineteenth century saw an important revival in the fortunes of Sufism in Iran after a long period of state-sponsored suppression of Sufi masters and their followers during the Safavid era. But while influential Sufi masters were able to find powerful patrons and followers, their doctrines as well as their own persons as sources of religious authority in competition with the religious scholars (ulema) remained controversial throughout the century. Upon the reintroduction of the Ne'matollahi order to Iran in the last years of the eighteenth century after a two-hundred-year 'exile' in India, the Sufi missionaries attached to this order found a hostile reception among the religious authorities in Iran. Nevertheless, a considerable following was built up across the great trading cities of central Iran such that by the middle of the nineteenth century the Ne'matollahi order had managed to entrench itself firmly within Qajar society. Although at face value propagating a mystical or esoteric interpretation of Islam, the leaders of the order also became associated with a number of powerful political and religious figures, including Aqa Khan Mahallati, the leader of the Isma'ili branch of Islam and erstwhile governor of Kerman. Partly as a consequence of these associations (themselves in part born from the need for protection from certain branches of the ulema*) and partly as a result of the swirling debates in nineteenth century Iran over the nature of religious knowledge and authority that also witnessed the emergence of the Baha'i faith, the leadership of the Ne'matollahi order itself became subject to the same rivalries. Political affiliation was therefore in some senses implicit in Sufi doctrines that ultimately tied adherents to the authority of living masters.*

All of these social, religious and political currents were manifested in the career of arguably the major Sufi of the last quarter of the nineteenth century in Iran, Mirza Hasan Isfahani, better known by his Sufi sobriquet of Safi 'Ali Shah. Safi 'Ali Shah was born into a family of merchants in Isfahan in 1835 and as a young man became a disciple of the head of the Ne'matollahi order, Rahmat 'Ali Shah (d. 1861). During the mid-1860s he travelled to India, where he resided for some time before continuing his travels to make the pilgrimage to Mecca and the Shi'a holy cities of Iraq. While in India he kept the company of the Aqa Khan Mahallati and his son the future Aqa Khan II. It was also in India that Safi completed his first major work, Zubdat al-asrar, *a lengthy mystical poem showing the influence of the great masnavi of Jalal al-din Rumi (d. 1273). This work was first published in Bombay in 1872, taking part in a considerable expansion of Persian lithographic printing in Bombay controlled in part by expatriate Iranians such as Safi himself. Other editions followed, allowing Safi 'Ali Shah to make a name for himself by means of the technology of the printing press. After a further visit to India, when he seems unsuccessfully to have sought the patronage of the Nizam of Hyderabad or his courtiers, Safi 'Ali Shah settled in Tehran, where he was able to gather around him a body of disciples that included influential figures at court. Here in the Qajar capital he devoted his time to writing and publishing a number of other long mystical poems, including a monumental mystical commentary on the Qur'an in poetic form. Written in Persian for the benefit of Iranians unable to comprehend the subtleties of the Qur'an in Arabic, this text confirms Safi 'Ali Shah's association with the major intellectual trends of his day. As in much of his work, however, traces of Islamic modernism are engulfed within a mystical reading of Islam. As a self-conscious attempt to transmit an earlier spiritual legacy through time, Safi's mystical writings reveal the complexities involved in the reinterpretation of Muslim tradition in the late nineteenth century.*

Much of what we know of the life of Safi 'Ali Shah is based on a short biography that appeared towards the end of Safi's life in the early Iranian magazine Sharaf *in 1890–91. Given the fact that his literary career had so fruitfully coincided with the growth of printing in Iran, it seems appropriate that an at times picaresque account of the life of this Qajar public intellectual should appear in the pages of a magazine devoted largely to the lives of major figures of the royal family and court. Sufi gatherings during the Qajar period have been compared to the secret societies which flourished in pre-revolutionary Europe, while by the turn of the twentieth century Freemason lodges were also a significant part of Iran's socio-political landscape. It is against this background that we should see the decision by Safi 'Ali Shah's successor, the prominent courtier Zaher al-Dawleh (d. 1924), to transform Safi 'Ali Shah's order into a new kind of modern association known as the* Anjoman-e okhuvvat *(Society of Brotherhood) shortly after the death of Safi 'Ali Shah in 1899.*

The two extracts which are translated below are drawn from Safi 'Ali Shah's major prose work, 'Erfan al-haqq *(The Gnosis of Reality), which was first published in Tehran in 1880. In* 'Erfan al-haqq, *Safi 'Ali Shah discusses a number of important aspects of the Sufi life, which range from such classic themes as the unity of being (*vahdat-e vojud*) and self knowledge (*ma'refat-e nafs*) to questions with a more clear bearing on socio-political life, such as the qualities that define the possessor of religious knowledge and authority. Safi shows himself to be a conscious heir to the earlier Sufi tradition of Ebn 'Arabi (d. 1240) and Jalal al-din Rumi, while also emphasising the consistency between Sufism and Shi'ism in line with Iranian Sufi writers of only a generation before him. At the same time, his arguments in* 'Erfan al-haqq *reflect some of the major intellectual* *debates concomitant with the onset of modernity in Qajar Iran, along with the rivalries and controversies between different religious groups.*

In the first section, Safi discusses the theme of divinely ordained authority, as possessed by the Prophet Muhammad and the twelve Shi'-ite imams. This notion of authority (velayat) as bestowed through a special relationship with God and the Prophet/Imams had a long ancestry in Sufi and Shi'-ite thought and would later be reflected in Ayatollah Khomeini's theory of the unity of political and religious leadership (velayat-e faqih). In the guise of an instructive and at times admonishing presentation of the true meaning of Islam, Safi actually presents what is in some senses a polemic against other versions of Shi'-ite Islam during his lifetime. In classic modernist form, he plays down the importance of miracles and presents Muhammad's mission as one aimed at the advancement or progress of mankind. Like other influential Iranian thinkers a century later, drawing on the Prophet Muhammad and Imam 'Ali, his notion of the religious leader is as someone standing up against the customs of the age and so transforming them. At the same time, his vision of Islam remains a highly esoteric one in which the principles of Shi-ism and Sufism must overlap. Islam means not only accepting the twelve imams but also accepting the saints (awliya) and gnostics ('orafa). Given that the subject of the book is the question of mystical knowledge or gnosis ('erfan), he argues in effect that not only must the true gnostic be a Shi'-ite Muslim but the true Shi'-ite Muslim must also be a gnostic. While drawing on many of the classic themes and terminology of Sufi doctrine to present an esoteric reading of Islam, Safi focuses on the theme of religious authority and the means by which it is achieved. His implicit argument is that it lies in the hand of the perfected gnostic. But a warning is issued to those who would claim religious authority but lack the mystical connection to the first imam and patron of the Sufis 'Ali ibn Abi Taleb, for 'the gnostic who speaks without the assistance (vala) of 'Ali is a heretic (zendeq), just as anyone who ventures onto the sea without a boat is drowned.'

In the second piece, Safi partakes in the long Sufi tradition of composing rules for novices (adab al-muridin). Here is a Sufi moral charter that places a public and private code of behaviour within a wider ontological and epistemological framework that is aimed at unveiling man's true being to himself and delivering higher knowledge in the process. But in an echo of Safi's earlier description of the virtues of the Prophet Muhammad, this set of rules also by extension prescribes the qualities and virtues required of the true religious leader. At the same time, his metaphorical frame of reference offers a template for leadership more generally, suggesting links between his book and aspects of the old Persian genre of the mirror for princes (nasihat nameh). It seems possible that his discussion of the proper virtues of the rampant lion contain, inter alia, a reference to the Qajar dynastic symbol of a warlike lion. While these are in one sense a set of rules for Sufi novices, therefore, the combination of their capacity for broader application and the fact of their publication as a lithograph book also portrays Safi assuming the role of a public moralist. For in a reflection of the moral interface between the Sufi adept and the Persian 'gentleman' more generally, much of this behavioural code echoes normative Iranian rules of social etiquette, as also exhibited in the gallantry of the wrestling club (zurkhaneh).

The place of this moral charter within an emergent public sphere is further suggested by its polemical undertones, by its veiled references to and attacks upon false Sufis, godless ulema and superficial 'masters of ceremony' more generally. Placed within the set of rules, therefore, is a spirited defence of Sufism and the science of gnosis as the truest version of Islam and perhaps also a defence of Shi'-ism itself against the rise of other mystical movements in Iran. A real Muslim would not reject the Sufis any more than a true Sufi would reject the religious law. As the rules reach their conclusion, Safi continues with a series of examples of the nature of esoteric knowledge and the power of the unseen world. Concerned to uphold the esoteric principles of Sufism as a valid epistemological path, like the great Islamic modernists a few decades later he upholds the importance of individual verification of religious knowledge in the face of the weight of tradition. 'He who says there is no higher verification (tahqiq) or investigation (ta'miq) either prefers the dead or his imagination is closed by his own designs.'

Further Reading

Hajj Mirza Hasan Safi 'Ali Shah – *'Erfan al-haqq hamrah ba rasa'el-e asrar al-ma'aref va mizan al-ma'refeh*, with notes by 'Abdollah Entezam and Ehsanollah Estakhri (Tehran: Safi 'Ali Shah, 1378/1999). Section 1 is translated from pp. 62–8 and section 2 from pp. 102–9.

M. Bayat, *Mysticism and Dissent: Socioreligious Thought in Qajar Iran* (Syracuse: Syracuse University Press, 1982).

M. van den Bos, *Mystic Regimes: Sufism and the State in Iran, from the Late Qajar Era to the Islamic Republic* (Leiden: Brill, 2002).

N.S. Green, 'A Persian Sufi in British India: The Travels of Mirza Hasan Safi 'Ali Shah,' *Iran*, 42(2004).

L. Lewisohn, 'An Introduction to the History of Modern Persian Sufism, Part I: The Ni'matullahi Order: Persecution, Revival and Schism', *Bulletin of the School of Oriental and African Studies*, 61 (1998).

Sayyid Muhammad Rizvi, *Shi'ism: Imamate and Wilayat* (Richmond Hill, ON: Al-Ma'arif Books, 1999).

On the Rule of Reason (*'aql*)

[A person once rose up from among the Arabs who in all of his beliefs, actions and mentality was the opposite of his people and so all of the Arab tribes then rose up against him. He gave a command that was the opposite of the tribe's predilections, so no one accepted his commands, not even his family and relatives who offered him only advice and discouragement. Finally the opposition and rebellion reached its extremes and ended in slaughter. He took hold of the bravest ones among the Arabs and overcame and conquered the others and declared his own prophethood (*nubuvvat*) to the sultans of this world.

All those who were conciliatory towards him and accepted the poll tax (*jezya*) were safe from his might, but the stubborn ones were either brought to their knees by the arrow of his prayers or killed by his sword. Yet he conquered most of the land and his command became established. And this was one of the wonders of the world, for such a thing does not happen that a man without any outward possessions stands up against the whole world and wins.

Now, if you say that this was through divine assistance then the argument is already proven anyway; but if you say that it was through the prudence of reason (*'aql*) then you have grasped the intention of the story. If you say it was one of those things that happened by chance, only if such a thing had happened again would you have the right (*haqq*) to say such a thing. But if it was unique, then you do not have the right to think of such a great and wondrous event as being by chance. If you bring as examples the evidence of certain sultans who were like that, such as Nader Shah [1688–1747] who rose from the lowest to the highest position, they were not of this kind. First of all, they were not up against the whole of creation in the path of religion and custom. His intention was the progress (*pish raft*) of mankind and people needed someone like him to become their leader so that their lives, possessions and honour would be kept safe. And secondly when he left he didn't leave behind his own law and whoever became leader after him established a law (*qanun*) according to his own predilections. He was like [the famously just pre-Islamic ruler] Anushirvan in his own time. But what has remained today of all that justice (*'adl*) and fairness (*ensaf*)? So one should not make comparisons. If you say such and such a learned man was accomplished in this or that craft or science and that this was due to his reason and that to follow that person is our duty, I would say in reply that you are right only if there is only one of his kind and if you absolutely need his craft and science. But you are not right if there are many of his kind and you do not need him, that is, if it is not necessary for you to learn his science or craft.

In this I am referring to the people of religion and not those who have gone astray from the path of reason. I have not said words that need careful consideration and I have not spoken of prophetic miracles or wonders, because reason and self-perfection (*kamal-e nafs*) direct everything. Think carefully about what I am saying. At some place on the earth a man without any possessions or a fixed home, who has not studied any science or art and to all appearances does not have any particular strengths or courage, declares all of the religions of the people of the world corrupt and nullified. He says to the people that to follow him is their duty and that whosoever doesn't follow him is an infidel (*kafer*) who will not be given God's mercy. He says that he is the owner of the possessions, lives and honour of the people in this world and the hereafter, has power over kings and their kingdoms and is better than the first and last people. And he says that God has chosen him and that his assistant is a book called the Qur'an and that in half a moment he can travel across all of the skies and that his body is made of subtle spirits (*arvah-e latifeh*). And he makes other claims of this kind, no matter whether anyone had seen a sign or a trace of his claims. But this person single-handedly put forward his claims and when people rose up against him they were defeated and after his death his religion (*din*) became stronger and his command didn't disappear and his work didn't stop. If you think about it, this in itself is a sufficient miracle and there is no need for other miracles.

I do not have anything to do with those prophetic miracles that have been mentioned and talked about in books, which are dubious and arouse doubts and cannot be supported with evidence to the deniers nor be argued for with the antagonists. But whether the reporters have mentioned them or not, I myself believe in all those miracles, not based on the complete laws of the reason but because of my own mystical experiences (*shohud*). And if you ask how reason guides us with regard to prophetic miracles, then I would say 'since there are a hundred there must also be ninety'. But even with self-perfection, good intentions and the strength of reason, prophetic miracles are not habits that can be passed on.

Why did they say about the prophets that they were honest and sincere? Know that in this matter our greatest guidance is the principle of attraction between those of the same kind.

> *The shards within this earth and sky*
> *Are but the same as straw and hay.*

If you are of the same stuff as the prophets, what need is there for miracles? And if you are not, then what do you gain from them? The special prophethood of Muhammad and his being the Seal of the Messengers is proven and today obeying his commands and his book is our duty on the earth. And from that messenger two signs have been left that will remain until the end of the world: the Book of God and the Family. As Muhammad himself has said, 'I am leaving with you the Book of God and my Family,' that is, the Twelve Imams, the first of whom was 'Ali ibn Abi Taleb and the last of whom is the Hidden Mahdi. And that Book and Family are united and manifest and witness one another. They have given guidance and deliverance to mankind and have not alienated mankind so that the surface of the pool that is the totality of authority (*velyat*) can join with its source.

Fact (*tahqiq*): the secrets of the world and of man are contained in the Book [i.e. the Qur'an]. The Book is the repository of divine secrets and accounts for all the souls and horizons of the world. *Nor is there a grain in the darkness of the earth nor anything green or dry but is under His effective protection.*[1] The desire is to analyse the greenery of the world, which are the outward horizons, and the dryness of the world of the most beautiful, which is the soul (*nafs*). The divisions of the world are contained entirely within the human soul (*nafs*) and that is why we interpret their collective unity as 'dryness' and why one human being can explain the entire world. That is why the great division is interpreted as greenery and for that reason we call the Book the Great Discriminator (*furqan-e a'zim*). And in terms of the beauty of the word which is the World of the Beautiful Science (*'alam-e 'elm-e ajmali*), the Book has taken the appearance of words and forms and has analysed the world and been accepted. That is why we call it the Glorious Quran (*qur'an-e majid*), which is a summary of the horizons and the souls and contains the greater worlds and the lesser worlds. It guides souls to understand their state of existence, from the state of dispersion (*farq*) to the state of gathering together (*jam'*). It guides the horizons in their confinement and guides the great ones to freedom. As the King of the Saints ['Ali] has said, the entire Qur'an is contained in praise and the sum of this praise is in the words 'In the name of God (*besmillah*)' and whatever is in the *besmillah* is in the dot of the letter *b*. 'And I am the dot beneath the letter *b*.' That is, when the letters and the lines of discrimination gather together in the Qur'an, and the dust of impotence is lifted from the words, the line reaches the dot and their union becomes complete. And in the Book the world of the heavens and the world of human reality become one.

Explanation (*tawzih*): The World of Interpretation (*'alam-e 'ebarat*) is in itself complete with the overflowing of being (*tajalli-ye vojud*). In the robe of the fixed station of an existent – essentially and physically, invisibly and visibly, omnipotently, angelically and royally – the human being points towards the complete overflowing of being. In the robe of the fixed station of divinity – namely and attributively, secretly and really – the Book is a metaphor for the complete overflowing of being. In the robe of the words – esoterically and exoterically, in meaning and in language – the human being is like a book expressing divine knowledge. And the Book that teaches humankind is great and divine.

A man of truth who has the attributes of God the Great stepped up from the Place of Collective Unity to the World of Becoming (*'alam-e kasrat*) and took upon himself the protection of the Degrees of Possibility. Under the verifier of 'I am the slave of the slaves, Muhammad', he put on the clothes of human appearance and became like other people. *I am about to place a vice-regent in the earth.*[2] So it was settled. The Eternal Book that is the esoteric Word of God and is the Tablet that protects knowledge came down from the World of Divinity (*lahut*) to the World of Humanity (*nasut*) and was accepted. It took the appearance of the lines and words of a book, since a book's truth is entered into through its words and from putting together the letters one returns to the surface of its meanings. In this way mankind comes first, because mankind is the body of divine unity (*tawhid*) and God's vice-regent (*khalifeh*) and leaves the Earth of Vice-Regency to the Heaven of Unity in order to return to its origin, just like the Mother of Books. That is why the Messenger left behind the Words of God and his Family.

Yet things that are on high take on the appearance of being from below. That is to say, do not be satisfied with the words alone. Don't go down the path where the Words of God are not with you. Don't say 'The Word of God is enough guidance for me.' Don't put your claws into those who are the firmest in faith (*'urvat al-vathqa*) in the land, because the vice-regency of the Messenger Muhammad was not only about the everyday commands and policies of Madina. There are thousands of issues here that are finer than a strand of hair. Unless someone becomes aware of the realities (*haqa'eq*) of the affairs of the Gnostic and is presented with the robe of honour of Friendship and Vice-Regency (*vali va khalifati*), he is not worthy of the vice-regency.

According to this introduction and what we have explained so far, after the Messenger Muhammad vice-regency is the right of 'Ali. And from the first people to the last people, and from those who populate the earth and the sky, no one else was more worthy of this than him nor has been so worthy since him. (Otherwise, preferring what is superior over what is preferable becomes necessary and in the religion of God and the heavenly workshop there would be a great deal of excess and carelessness and the descendants of the shaykhs would not have their place and would not be aware of all the commands.) But one cannot behave against proper conventions (*adab*), nor can one at any time reproach those who follow only the externalised forms (*zaher*) of the religious law (*shari'a*).

But let us go to the main topic and speak of the mantle (*kherqeh*). Know that Islam means testifying to the truth of the prophets and the Messenger, and especially to Muhammad being the Seal of the Prophets. And the essence of faith (*iman*) is accepting the Twelve Imams. This means regarding them as the most excellent of all humanity after the Messenger, knowing the necessity of loving each one of them and counting the Twelfth Imam Mahdi as the one with whom the Vice-Regency finishes. Islam also means admitting to the existence of the rightly guided saints (*awliya-ye rashedin*) and perfected gnostics (*'orafa-ye kamel*) and at all times having complete belief in gnosis (*'erfan*). *Allah loves those who perform their duty to the uttermost.*[3] This beneficence is called gnosis and, after studying the true beliefs of Islam, gnosis causes the accomplishment of faith. As a result mankind is introduced to God the Merciful. And the content of this becoming acquainted with God is the acceptance of the Divine Will (*iradat*). Whoever turns away from the Will shall not be acquainted with God. A sign of love (*mohabbat*) and friendship (*velayat*) with the Greatest Friend of God is resoluteness and service to God's Friends, who are guides to mankind and on the road to becoming acquainted with Him and are illuminated with His Light. In Ghadir Khumm, Mohammad the Sultan of Bearers of Good News received the oath of Authority (*velayat*) and Allegiance (*bay'at*) and Love (*mohabbat*) from all creation and so gave the establishment of his religion to the Vice-Regency of 'Ali. In this way he founded the edifice of gnosis so that the gates of mercy would be open to all and the hand of each and any exalted and knowledgeable being would at any time be stretched out to ask for his kindness.

In every age there is a hidden Friend, and the test goes on till Doomsday.

When the seeker (*murid*) with a steady walk imitates his spiritual master and achieves the stage of self-annihilation (*fana*) and his manners become as those of his master and his courage becomes solidified in will and obedience, then no trace will be left of his own existence. Then the signs of God's love will appear on his body and the lights of the appearance of Muhammad will fill his heart (*qalb*). These are the blessings (*barakat*) of purity, the signs of God's kindness. In this way, the seeker's sins turn into endless beauties and he finds entry into the enclosure of God's protection, as it is said in the hadith, 'The Friendship of 'Ali is a fortress and whosoever enters it is protected from punishment.' But do not think that if that is the meaning of the Friendship of 'Ali then others cannot reach out to him or else you will be disappointed. There are stages (*marateb*) to Friendship. The first stage is amity (*dusti*) and the final stage is annihilation in God (*fana fi'l allah*). The lengthened shade of His kindness has spread everywhere and has reached every being, so that everybody's hands can reach out to Him and nobody would be excluded.

God is a creator without any needs and not only would He not deny His slaves despite all of their disobedience but the sinners are even closer to being pardoned. Think of this hadith: 'The love of 'Ali is so beautiful that even sin leaves no mark upon it.' Therefore expect 'Ali to reward any of the sins of the ill-wishers, doubters, deniers and hypocrites with a thousand kindnesses from the merciful Maker and Protector of Slaves (*bandeh navaz*), who will be more kind than you believe. *Convey to them: O my servants who have committed excesses against your own selves, despair not of the mercy of Allah, surely Allah forgives all sins; He is Most Forgiving.*[4] Nevertheless, in my opinion, despite 'Ali's love, there is no sin that would be harmless. But loving 'Ali is to perform a good deed and hating him is a sin. Every good thing (*khayri*) comes from the path through the mountains that is his love and every bad thing (*shari*) comes from the fissures of his enmity (*'adavat*). For all of the potentialities became existent in the authority (*velayat*) of 'Ali and the Prophet made the existence of his authority necessary for the people and made his authority the source of his worship (*'ebadat*). Yet his authority was that of a tender man and was worshipped (*masjud*) by both the Kingdoms of angels and men. Whichever Messenger followed his authority became perfected and was sent forth. And so the gnostic who speaks without the assistance (*vala*) of 'Ali is a heretic (*zendeq*), just as anyone who ventures onto the sea without a boat is drowned.

> *Whoever lacks the friendship* (dusti) *of 'Ali is an infidel* (kafer)
> *Even an eremite of the age or master of the way.*

On the Rejection of the Sufis

A group rose up against the community of Muslims (*umma*) and decorated itself with the clothes of the people of Sufism and yet they were not Sufis. Outwardly they were dervishes, but inside they were wolves dressed as sheep. They sit in the shops, wear wool (*suf*) and connect their initiation (*kherqeh*) back to Abu Bakr and some of them to 'Ali. They talk about miracles (*karamat*) and since there are plenty more nullified seekers than those who possess the truth, many have gathered around them and for this reason discord (*fetneh*) has made its appearance. Truth (*haqq*) and irrelevance (*batel*) became mixed together and when the imprudent ones passed the limits, it became necessary for the followers of truth to refute the people of darkness. This had nothing uniquely to do with Sufism, for among the *ulema* and the superficial people (*ahl-e zaher*) there are also many of that kind. And so contempt for them has entered through the people of the Prophet and among all the reports of transgressions among the godless *ulema*, not even a hundredth part of all these reproaches are towards the blue-clad Sufis.

Know that in reality between the People of the Law (*shari'a*) and the People of the Path (*tariqeh*) – that is, between the exoteric religious scholar (*'alem-e zaheri*) and the true gnostic (*'aref-e haqiqi*) – there is no contradiction. If the scholar of the religious law has no worldly intentions and the Sufi gnostic has purified his heart and soul, they mean the same thing and have no dispute with one another. This is because the essential meaning of Sufism (*tasavvuf*) and what is on the lips of the people of gnosis is that after studying the jewellery box of belief that is Twelver Shi'i Islam one has to take only what is necessary from the world. One should be satisfied with little, train the unruly lower self (*nafs*) to accept the divine injunctions and always remember God with one's heart until God becomes one's master and all that is not God is forgotten. What I am saying in this book is all about this and if a scholar of *shari'a* does not deny this in terms of his own beliefs then he too is a Sufi but simply shuns the language of the Sufis. Even if he denies it, what else can he say but that? Are they rejecting only letters like *sad*, *za* and *fa* or are they rejecting a morality that they see as neither worthy nor laudable?

A Subtlety

Claiming to be accomplished and to have reached a certain station (*maqam*) is the result of ignorance. For the one who has this degree does not claim to have it. A shell that has been thrown to the side of the ocean and is showing off has no pearl within it. So the person who has the elixir of life hides himself from the people and does not sell the jewel for a loaf of bread. Such claimants are ignorant in seeking it. So the undisputed spiritual master (*murshed*) must have the divine power and the life of the heart and not merely a certificate that is in truth only a worldly irrelevance. Even if such worldly irrelevances are compatible with the sum of meaning, they are only a petty thing and do not lead to anything useful or healthy. The verses of the Qur'an are all about describing the perfected self and reproaching the worldly ones who are ignorant of God. If you are perfected, God's expression should be enough. But if you are not perfected, then what is the point of all these things?

O dervish, if you are seeking to become a Sufi, act according to these instructions and that will be enough for you.

The first rule is to meditate on this reality: you are a human being (*adam*) and are superior to all other creatures. Dive into yourself to discover what is the difference between human beings and animals. The first stage of seeking is shunning animal behaviour, for each animal has one bad attribute and many specialities. How terrible is the man who has none of the specialities of any of the animals but has all of the bad attributes of being an animal! The seeker needs to follow the path of humanity (*adamiyyat*) and must shun animal ways.

The second rule is that with all of his powers the seeker should seek a lawful living and should work hard to achieve this, for it is an essential issue. A heart that is not bound by the licit (*halal*) and the illicit (*haram*) becomes hard and the light of divine unity (*tawhid*) does not shine on it. Such a heart will fall into doubting and suspicion and the person will cause trouble to others. Most forms of corruption and evil-doing are due to this. I am trying to be brief and you should be able to understand these things with a little direction. But don't become obsessed with this matter, because all of your time will be busy with it. Earning your living without thieving, cheating, lying or acting tyrannically is enough. In order to keep you away from your work, Satan will make you obsessed with things like not being cautious, needing to be tested again or worrying that you might have been cheated. While you are doing your ablutions before prayers Satan will tell you that you are not really clean and that your impurities have not been removed and that you should do the ablutions one more time. Or when you recite your prayers, Satan will make you doubt that your pronunciation was correct and make you say them again.

The third rule is not to transgress the laws of the king and the laws of the country and other such matters. This too causes conflict and is the opposite of justice. It will molest your soul (*nafs*), your people and your family.

The fourth rule is to be good-mannered with all people out of kindness and compassion and not because you are paying attention to your own designs. The latter is the way of the people of hypocrisy (*nafq*) and means being false to people and to their creator.

The fifth rule is to know that God is present (*hazer*) and to seek refuge in Him at all times from the evils of the lower self.

The sixth rule is to leave behind your envy and desires and to be content with what you are given. Always meditate on death and the unreliability of the world and do not spread the seeds of desire upon the soil of envy. Expansive desires are the opposite of the Sufi way and in the end are the cause of regret.

The seventh rule is not to seek for too much in words (*kalam*) and to speak only as much as is necessary, because talking less is a comfort to the world. This is good in terms of healthy thoughts and good intentions. Speak with wisdom and then be silent as an example to others.

The eighth rule is to eat little and be hungry most of the time. The divine gnostics shun eating in the following way: eat twice and leave out the third time. If you cannot eat only enough food to make you work or be satisfied, then leave this matter. For a dervish is recommended to eat, because being hungry is food for the concupiscent soul (*nafs-e ammareh*).

The ninth rule is to stay awake, for being sleepy is not a part of the craft of spiritual poverty (*faqr*). Too much sleep makes the seeker ignorant and sets him away from his aims. The one who has pain does not sleep and the one who knows the way before him is long exerts himself even harder during the night than the day.

> *Sleep is only for the birds and fish,*
> *But the lovers are drowned by sorrow.*

Rise at the dawn for inward prayers (*munajat*). Your first task is to cry for your lower soul, for the damage you have done to yourself and for your wasted life. Then regret your past ignorance and meditate upon your misery and the imminent arrival of the messenger of death and the loneliness of the grave. Read anything that makes you submissive (*khozu*) and brings you into the divine presence (*hozur*), for according to the thinking of the Sufi this is better than the Qur'an. But read the Qur'an a great deal none the less and dive into it. The eyes of the seeker of truth (*haqq-talab*) should never be dry of tears.

The tenth rule is not to exclude anyone from goodness. One must reward any bad thing with goodness, for God likes this attribute very much and in turn rewards such slaves with goodness. When you are doing a good deed, consider it as a favour but do not make people feel obliged in return. Remember your own badness and the goodness that God has conferred on you and do not stop wanting good things for others. If you have fallen and you see someone who is trapped, whether you can hold his hand or not at least feel sympathy and pray for him, because that is also helping. So help him as much as you can and do not be selfish or self-consumed. Share your earnings with the poor as much as you can and be obliged to God for the fact that you are not mean and do not save your money away. But beware of becoming proud of yourself and admiring yourself after doing a good deed. Only true wayfarers deserve to be admired. Take great care that your behaviour and speech are not based on lies or desire, because to do this is contrary to spiritual poverty (*faqr*). Do not show off because the Angel of Death is always right behind you and looks with mockery at the people of the world. Such is the unreliability of the world that you cannot possibly be proud of anything. Therefore concentrate your attention on divine remembrance (*zekr*) and keep your heart busy with recollection (*fekr*). Soon when your soul appears before the dais of Divine Greatness, the Real One (*haqq*) will ask you what you have done with the resources of existence and how you have spent its endless wealth. Yet our Creator is kind and the Kind One does not ask the empty-handed one what he has brought with him or what he has done with His belongings. You will be embarrassed and ashamed: how could you see the spirit (*ruh*) that was so dear to you in the world become so wretched? And what would you do with your possessions?

Let me give you an example. If you see a rose garden or a green plain or flowing water or something else that raises your spirit, its enjoyment would be a hundred times greater if you saw it in a state of wakefulness rather than through the dreams of your lower soul (*nafs*). Equally, when you dream of the howling and fighting of terrified animals or something that makes your lower soul become worried and hateful, you feel such fear that you wake with a start with your body trembling afterwards, even though in the state of wakefulness you have seen much worse things and never been so terrified. This shows how much more convincing are the fraudulent perceptions made by the naked self (*nafs-e mujarrad*). These are signs (*'alamat*) that truly affect those who have been affected by them, for the hidden world (*'alam-e ghayb*) has equally entered the hearts of those who accept and those who deny, so that there is no being excused from it. If your belief in the traditions (*akhbar*) of the prophets is not complete, then travel within your own being because every part of it is a sign (*'alamat*). If your attention (*havas*) is mostly busy with the fortunes of the self and the issues of the world and you do not pay attention to things of meaning, then you will become suspicious and your fancies will lead you astray. As long as these are your only inclinations, you will remain the way you are. But if you unite yourself with the existence of the hidden world and the perfections of meaning, then you will become like them yourself.

Imagine that when an unappealing thought comes to you or when you are told unacceptable things, it is as though your mind becomes anxious about snakes and scorpions or about a dark and frightening place or a terrifying cemetery. Your memory becomes cloudy, and you say 'enough' and refrain from thinking about it again. In the same way, when by contrast good faces appear in your mind or when you are told about a great master, your attention is turned in that direction so much that if your attention is continuous the good and beautiful angel will enter your lower self and your attention will not be given over to anything else. When this matter becomes true and obvious to you, then unifying yourself with the reality (*haqiqat*) of your naked self is a noble thing. If keeping away from the filth of the world and from perverse and inadmissible thoughts and talk of such matters appears remote and strange to you, it is because your thinking has been irrational (*na-ma'qul*) your whole life. You have devoted your attention to the opposite of your proper purpose. Behaving against what you are used to is quite unpleasant. But if you understand this matter then you have understood the truth about paradise and hell, which is to say that paradise and hell are nothing but the angels acquired within your self (*nafs*) and the usefulness of good or bad morals. So how long do you want to postpone this and on what basis are you rebelling?

O dervish, the one who is a man of battle has to appear on the field of gnosis and the one who is like a woman and only a hero of the tongue had better not show his face. In this affair the lion would leap into action, while the spinner of gnosis (*'erfanbaf*) has nothing but an exaggerating tongue (*zaban-e laf*) and spends too much time just repeating verses.

The brave lion is the one that is the craftsman (*honarpisheh*), not a recitor who recites too much. His thought (*hemmat*) is sublime and his perspective is broad. When a lion gets hungry it goes out to hunt and stops when it is sated and does not keep what is left from other animals. The cow is the opposite of the lion. It eats as long as there is something to eat, grazes without knowledge of what it is doing and when it no longer finds anything goes to sleep in a corner. It has neither honour nor thought, neither leaves anything behind nor gains anything. Its magnanimity is in eating and it is content with just moving about. And so a man who has neither skill nor generosity is lower than a cow and lesser than a donkey. But a brave man becomes known in the battle and not by his buttered tongue. He is both fearless and captivating. He does not show off and is genial to his friends. He would come forward as the first among his followers and would not make a shield of them. He would not be worried or lose heart by the great number of his enemies. He would appear as god-fearing and not as proud of his power, for pride comes from miserliness and has deprivation as its outcome. He would be tactful and not superficial and malicious. He would abhor pettiness and would not forget prayer and dedication. And if his followers showed a certain skill he would not make it his own and deprive them of their rights.

O dervish, the nobility of any action is contained in its content and its purpose. Think about the content of the science of Sufism. What is it and who is the master of this science? Regard my words as invaluable and precious, because in this brief book all the secrets and the proper conventions (*adab*) are contained and not a single point has been left out. He who says there is no higher verification (*tahqiq*) or investigation (*ta'miq*) either prefers the dead or his imagination is closed by his own designs. My words are for the people of Sufism (*tasavvuf*) and not for the masters of ceremony (*takalluf*) who believe like blind men and refrain from things with lightning flashes (*'arz*) and dread. Such a person has no wisdom in friendship and no generosity (*futuvvat*) in enmity.

Notes

[1.] Qur'an 6:60. All translations are from *The Quran*, Arabic text with translation by Muhammad Zafrulla Khan (Richmond: Curzon Press, 1971).

[2.] Qur'an 2:31.

[3.] Qur'an 5:94.

[4.] Qur'an 39:54.

CHAPTER 7

The Detrimental Consequences of Sufism: Extracts from Sufism[1]

Ahmad Kasravi

The introduction to Chapter 4 outlined the main contours of Kasravi's life, so in this introduction more space can be devoted to his views on Sufism. Between 1925 when Reza Khan was crowned Shah of Iran and 1946 when Kasravi was shot dead, Iranians were engaged in a struggle to establish their self-identity. The Shah and many intellectuals believed that it was necessary to drive Iran towards the West and modernise, which involved far greater centralisation and the adoption of Western sciences and civilisation. Included in this was the subordination of religion to the state, and the diminution of religion from a way of life in the public sphere to a private, personal realm. Moreover, just as religion in the West was becoming demystified, so, too, many Iranians believed that religion in Iran should follow the same pattern. This was a challenge to Sufism, which seemed to some to be something of an anachronistic vestige from the Middle Ages, with its uncontrolled emotional ritual practices, such as the mystical dancing (sama'), and its belief in the miraculous powers of Sufi masters.

The ideologies that challenged Sufism included not only that of a nationalistic state but also the left-wing 'materialist' views of young intellectuals such as Taqi Arani, and the existentialist-inspired world views of writers epitomised by Sadeq Hedayat. In its defence, the Sufi tradition was supported by many who believed that Iran could utilise Persian mystical literature in its quest to strengthen its position in the world of nation states. This, according to Kasravi, was the opinion of Mohammad 'Ali Forughi, who was one of Reza Shah's prime ministers. Kasravi believed that such a policy only served the interests of the foreign powers whose objective was to maintain a weak Iran, and thus preserve their political and economic hegemony in the area. It was partly because of the promotion of Persian literature that endorses fatalism, passivity and immorality that Iranians had not been able to compete with Western powers in terms of education, science and many other elements that comprise modern life.

Kasravi's criticisms of Sufism were presented in his Sufigari *(Sufism), a booklet of some eighty pages in Persian which was published in 1943–44. The text includes eight sections which are entitled: how Sufism appeared; the evils attributable to Sufism; Sufism's evil conduct with Islam; Sufism has been nothing but a source of the spirits' weakness; the Sufis have not had the least fear in lying; how the Iranians were vanquished by the Mongols; the benefits gained by the Sufis from Mongol rule; the truths that can be found in Plotinus's discourses. Later editions of* Sufigari *included an introduction which appears here.* Sufigari *is not a sound piece of academic writing, rather it is very selective in its selection of examples of Sufi ritual and belief, and anyone with the slightest knowledge of Sufism can see beyond the generalisations made by Kasravi. Nevertheless, the text is an important example of the type of criticism that Sufism has had to face in the modern age. Much of this criticisms is of course not new, for opponents of the Islamic mystical tradition, including Ebn Taymiyya and Ebn Jawzi, attacked Sufism in the medieval period. Yet the distinguishing feature of Kasravi's world view is his rejection of tribal, ethnic, linguistic and religious differences and his promotion of nationalism in Iran. Although* Sufigari *may be read as a defence of Islam, Kasravi's prime concern in his writings was Iran and Iranian society, and Islam was a secondary consideration.*

As Kasravi admits in his text, the Iran in which he lived did not suffer the same Sufi problems as in previous ages when Sufis wandered the length and breadth of the Islamic world, begging and sponging. However, he maintained that the evil teachings of Sufism caused untold damage to Iranian society and that the Sufis were no more than charlatans who were self-seeking opportunists who changed their opinions in order to curry favour with the rulers or with society. In the early twentieth century and with the centralising reforms of Reza Shah Sufism had indeed undergone profound changes. There are fewer references in travel writing and in Persian literature to the wandering dervishes, and many modern leaders of the main Sufi order in Iran, the Ne'matollahis, exhorted their followers to seek employment. Although there existed several branches of Ne'matollahi Sufis, they demonstrated that rather than stagnate and remain isolated from modernity and its challenges, they fully embraced the opportunity for change. Perhaps this is best illustrated with reference to the spiritual successor of Safi 'Ali Shah, namely Zahir al-Dawleh (1864–1924), who established the Society of Brotherhood, which preserved the Sufi traditions of zekr *rituals, belief in the traditional Sufi doctines such as* fana *(annihilation) and* baqa' *(subsistence in God) but which at the same time supported the Constitutional Movement, provided charity for the needy who had been caught up in the ensuing civil war, promoted a social conduct based on brotherhood and equality, and – perhaps most telling of all – adopted the trappings of a modern organisation with registers and financial accountability. Under Zahir al-Dawleh's successor, Binesh 'Ali Shah, the Society of Brotherhood even rejected the traditional form of single spiritual leadership of the Sufi master and adopted a consultative council to decide on significant issues. The Society of Brotherhood was not the only branch of Ne'matollahi Sufism to display modernising tendencies, for another major group, the Gonabadis, revealed similar responses to the new era.[2]*

The validity of Kasravi's attacks against Sufism, whether from a theological, political or sociological perspective, is difficult to substantiate. Nevertheless, one wonders if his biting criticisms, which commenced in the mid-1930s, contributed to the acceleration in reform within organised Sufism. The continued existence, support and sympathy for Sufism and the Persian mystical tradition testify to Kasravi's failure in persuading Iranians to turn aside from Sufism. Indeed, his world view in general was sterile, emotionless and he wished to impose a single, austere vision upon Iranians, a vision which was the antithesis of the Persian Sufi tradition. However, it would be unjust to conclude this brief introduction by castigating Kasravi, for he should be applauded for critiquing the Sufi tradition and calling into question the motives of those who supported it. Even if the answers that he reached seem pre-meditated, surely he should be applauded for desiring a truly free Iran, independent from both the shackles of European hegemony and uncritical acceptance of the traditional mind-sets.

One final point about the text below (from Sufigari *– or "Sufism", which was published in Iran in 1943–4) is that Kasravi does not help his reader by inserting explanatory footnotes. He assumes that his reader will have a reasonable degree of knowledge of Sufism. Most of the footnotes that appear in the text, therefore, are my additions unless stated otherwise.*

Notes

1. The original text is from *Sufigari* (Tehran: 1943–44).
2. See Matthijs van den Bos's *Mystic Regimes*.

Further Reading

Matthijs van den Bos, *Mystic Regimes: Sufism and the State in Iran, from the Late Qajar Era to the Islamic Republic* (Leiden: Brill, 2002).

Mohammed Ali Jazayery, 'Ahmad Kasravi and the Controversy over Persian Poetry. 1. Kasravi's Analysis of Persian Poetry', *International Journal of Middle Eastern Studies*, 4 (1973), pp. 190–203.

——'Ahmad Kasravi and the Controversy over Persian Poetry. 2. The Debate on Persian Poetry Between Kasravi and His Opponents', *International Journal of Middle East Studies*, 13 (1981), pp. 311–27.

Leonard Lewisohn, 'An Introduction to the History of Modern Persian Sufism, Part I: The Ni'matullāhī Order: Persecution, Revival and Schism', *Bulletin of the School for Oriental and African Studies*, 61 (3), pp. 437–64.

——'An Introduction to the History of Modern Persian Sufism, Part II: A Sociological Profile of Sufism, from the Dhahabi revival to the Present Day', *Bulletin of the School for Oriental and African Studies*, 62 (1), pp. 36–59.

—•—

[Kasravi's] Introduction

[Many readers know that we have taken a stand and made efforts over the past eleven years, fighting against all the erroneous paths and ignorance that exist in Iran and other places. Sufism is among the worst of these erroneous paths. It spread a thousand years ago, sinking roots with which we have also engaged in battle. At first we occasionally wrote about Sufism in the discussions in *Payman*[1] and *Parcham*.[2] Then last year we published a booklet of all my speeches, printed under the title 'Sufism'. Because the copies of this were few in number, we are printing it again with additions and other changes.

Sufism has been interpreted in the book [mentioned above], and whatever was worthy of discussion concerning its lack of foundation and its harmfulness has already been outlined. But there are several things that must be presented in this introduction.

(1). People say, 'The Sufis are a small group and they are scattered here and there, and it is not worthwhile for anyone to bother with them.'

But this is a crude opinion because the Sufis are not few in number. Rather there are many. They have organisations now in several Iranian cities including Tehran, Maragheh, Gonabad, Mashhad and Shiraz. Sufis are not merely those dervishes with felt hats and hair-plaits, nor are they merely those dirty, polluted masters and those beggars who carried an axe or a begging bowl. There are thousands of others without hats and hair-plaits, and there are dervishes without axes and begging bowls whose minds are blemished with Sufi evil teachings.

Among the state employees and bureaucrats you can find many people who are dervishes, and each one considers himself a follower of this 'Mast 'Ali-shah' and that 'Bahman 'Asheq-shah'. Behind office desks are those in charge of people, and these are the kinds of thoughts that have settled in their minds: 'O this world lasts only a few days. Good and bad will pass. The eminent ones have not lifted their heads to bother with the world. (This too will pass, O God).'

In addition, Sufi evil teachings have existed not merely among the Sufis, that is to say, their harm is not only to Sufis. Just as we have described in the book [mentioned above], this erroneous path has sunk roots in all directions, and most people are not Sufis yet they are contaminated by its evil teachings even though they do not realise it.

From this perspective there are many books contaminated by these evil teachings. Moreover, the Sufis have passed on thousands of books, in poetry and prose, as a keepsake which are now in the hands of the people, in their homes. Our poets and advisers have all benefited from Sufism. The poets who have followed the 'content' regarded the evil teachings of the Sufis as a treasure. They had the same attachment to Sufism as those advisers and leaders. Books on the subject of 'morals' in Arabic and Persian have been written, all of them have their basis in Sufism. I'll say just one thing: This old erroneous path has wound its way in all directions, spreading its poison in the body of the people.

Aside from this Sufism is a tool in the political world. For years European Orientalists and the Ministry of Culture of Iran have joined hands in its circulation. *Memoirs of the Saints*[3] of Shaykh 'Attar has been printed in Europe and sent to Iran. The *Masnavi* of Mawlana,[4] his *ghazals* and other poems have been printed and widely circulated. The Iranian Ministry of Culture holds classes on Sufism in places of learning, and money is poured out annually in printing Sufi books.

These are the things that must not go unseen, and one should not consider that the damage and harm of Sufism is slight.

(2). People also have offered a criticism, arguing along the lines that 'the knowledge that develops today will make all of these erroneous paths disappear'.

This is another crude opinion. What is knowledge? According to you knowledge includes those fields of science, physics, natural history, astrronomy, medicine, mathematics, and others like these. Which one of these is it that will make Sufism disappear? Which one of these is it that will stand up in battle with Sufism or other erroneous paths?

We see that in these past forty years, knowledge has increased and advanced in Iran, and despite this, neither Sufism, nor Shi'-ism or any other of the erroneous paths have vanished. They have only weakened. Knowledge has weakened all of these erroneous paths, and they in turn have weakened knowledge. There is a universal rule that when two contrary things oppose each other, they are both weakened.

Now, in the name of dervish-hood and Sufism the humblest among the educated renounced his home and his life, and went to the *khanaqah*. The humblest person sat for the *chelleh*[5] and gave himself hardships, or took up the horn, walking stick, begging bowl and axe, and became [known as] a 'wanderer of the world'. Sufism no longer has that power. But when those educated people became aware of the Sufi teachings, they adopted them and absorbed those evil teachings in their minds. They have learned in lessons that the thing that caused those unfounded and evil teachings has not existed. So it is inevitable that their inner feelings will be contaminated, and their will becomes weak. This is the same state of affairs that pertains to the other erroneous paths, and is something that we witness now in Iran. It is a state we had to explain in discourses elsewhere.[6]

If knowledge could destroy the root of the erroneous paths it would have been done in Europe. But you see that it has not done this, indeed it could not do this. Knowledge has been current in Europe for more than two hundred years, and it has reached into all corners. In addition, the movements for democracy, socialism, communism, and others like this appeared, and each one in its turn has caused some change. In these circumstances they were not able to destroy Christianity, which in its present state is a great erroneous path and mistake. They were able only to weaken it.

Most worthy of our attention is the experience of Russia and communism. The movement appeared with such great depth, and turned the whole country upside down. The communists revealed their enmity to the priests and their establishment, and rose up in great effort and opposition. Yet after all this, it is now clear that Christianity and other faiths have not vanished from that country, and once again, the state has given ground to the priests and *mollas*.

This in itself is worthy of discussion because it is necessary to combat these erroneous paths and cut down the inroads they make, and replace them in those areas with truths. The secret of the task is this: truths should replace errors. If not the errors will never vanish. On this topic too we have presented our opinions elsewhere.[7]

Let us put this to one side. Knowledge itself is twinned with another great erroneous path. Knowledge, wherever it is found, exists along with materialism. We held that knowledge can eliminate Sufism. What benefit would there be in a place where materialism replaces [Sufism]? Materialism is not weaker than Sufism, indeed, it is worse in today's world.

Sufism has made people weak, lazy and cowardly, and arrests the development of the world. Materialism makes people greedy, and cruel, indeed it turns them into thieves and tricksters and ruins the welfare of life. Moreover, successive wars have erupted in the world's present condition, and cities have been destroyed (as we witness today).

There is an incredible story told by one group that the solution to [the problem] of Sufism will be knowledge (or it is better if we say materialism, which is concomitant with knowledge). Another group showing support for the Sufis says, 'The only thing that can save the world from materialism is Sufism.'

If we want the truth, neither knowledge (or materialism) can be the solution to [the problem] of Sufism, and Sufism too will not be able to obstruct materialism. These are two erroneous paths, and both of them can exist together. Each one can take root in a new space in people's minds. A person can be both materialist and Sufi. It is possible that someone may consider life as nothing, and have no care for anyone or anything, and have no concern except for his own enjoyment. And at the same time, the same person may consider the world worthless and ephemeral, and not yearn for its pleasures, and he may withdraw himself, Sufi-like, from any task that requires some effort. This is the condition that we see today in many people.

It is this difficult battle which we have commenced that can destroy both Sufism and materialism, and relieve the world from their harmful effects. It is religion that can soothe the people from these erroneous paths. We can say this in a better way: we have opened a highway of life to the world.

I am so surprised that people have not been satisfied with this deep-rooted and effective struggle, and they have found faults and given advice [to the effect] that knowledge will be the cure. I myself don't know what name to give this.

(3). For many years Sufism has been praised from Europe. I say 'from' Europe and not 'in' Europe because they praise it for us. Whatever Europeans say and write, whether in Farsi or in European languages, is for our benefit. They are traps that are set beneath our feet. It is like something bitter that they want a child to eat. A grown up comes and says something like, 'Give it to me, I'll eat it. O how sweet it is!'

This is a great crime committed by the Europeans who in their political manoeuvrings have joined hands with the Eastern peoples in these matters. In itself, this is a disgraceful blemish that will remain on the skirt of European history. That very Europe which showed the world all that knowledge, and caused all those movements in life. This too is an example of its evil, for it tries to plunge the people of the East further into ignorance. In the history of Europe, in contrast to those bright moments, there will also be these dark ones.

Three years ago, in a European journal that was written in Persian we see opinions printed in praise of the Sufis. For example, one of the articles discusses Fakhr al-Din 'Eraqi and tells the story of how he lost his heart to a child dervish, and his journey to India (which we too have presented in the text of the book). It describes this ugly and irrational story and begins with praise, saying:

> So, these lazy dervishes, dressed in tatters (whose ignominy is derived from their reputation, and their reputation comes from their ignominy),[8] were busy in singing and dancing, and they obtained their daily bread in the dervish path. Today we live in different times. In this rational and mechanical world we are fascinated with other idols. We have another way of life, and we have lost ourselves in this new world to such an extent that it appears that we have totally forgotten the spiritual strength of the old world. Therefore when we hear the story of the *Qalandar*,[9] perhaps immediately we call them mistaken or mad. But what madness is it that (like these vagrant, lazy, dervishes) discovers spiritual beauty with such clarity and goodness, [and] leaves God's deep imprint in the heart?

All of these are sentences that we read in a European journal. European scholars send these to us as presents. They sing these treacherous children's songs for us. I don't see the need to engage in a discussion about them all. I hope the readers have a look at the story of 'Eraqi in the book (on page 26),[10] and then read all of this twice and think well what this European writer is praising, what things he calls 'spiritual meaning' or 'imprint of God'.

It is necessary to reply to this writer, 'If you speak the truth, why don't you tell the same things to Europeans? Why don't you write these things in European languages and spread them among Europeans? Iranians have taken the required share, and more, of Sufism. They have discovered much of that 'spiritual beauty' of which you speak, and there no longer remains any unexplored point. If these things are good, wish them for your own people.'

One must not be deceived by their lies. If the Eastern people are deceived by their lies, in addition to the damage that they want to inflict, those who are deceived will become even more abject in European eyes. They will come together and say to each other, 'You see how we deceived them!'

If one day those Europeans happen to portray Sufism, dervish-hood and the like to us, they will say, 'You still have been unable to stop the begging *Qalandars*. You have been unable to cut the root of Sufism. You are half a desert, you are not worthy of freedom.'

In any case, this kind of clamour from Europe does not arise from well-wishers or the pure in heart. The people in Iran who make the same clamour with them, in writing and publishing books in an attempt to spread Sufism, are those who wish evil on this country. One must not pay them any respect. It is necessary to join hands and with haste and vigour, and dig up the root of this pollution and error.

Sufism has been mistaken in its very root, and during a thousand years and more it has caused damage and harm to Eastern people. Now it is the time to pull up this root once and for all.

It is necessary to destroy these Sufi institutions in Iran and India. And those parasitic *pirs*[11] and those around them must go in search of work and a profession.

Section One: How Sufism Appeared

Sufism, like many other things, arose from the philosophy of the Greeks. The founder, it is said, was Plotinus, who was one of the philosophers of Greece or Rome.

Plotinus wrote many works in a philosophical tongue. A summary of them in a simplified way is that whatever exists in the world is just one thing; God exists and other things have become separate from him; the human spirit has come to this world and has been trapped in matter; it must continually flee from this world and its pleasures, and hope for connection with its source or home.

He said that in this world too, if someone leaves himself in ecstasy, he can connect to that source of existence (or it is better if we say 'God'). 'It is necessary to close the eyes of the head and open the eye of the heart. Then we will see what we find within ourselves, indeed, [that] which is in us.'[12]

These following sentences are the words of Plotinus:

> All of us are of God (*az khoda*), but we have become separated from Him, and we will return to Him. The human spirit descended from a world, free and pure. In this world it became trapped in matter and became impure. Therefore any person who does not pander to the desires of the body but takes care of the spirit will be less impure. And the person who wants to escape from this trap must turn aside from the pleasures of this world and engage in abstinence.

These foundational sentences of Sufism, as we will see, are illusory and there is no proof that they are correct. They are things that Plotinus imagined and said, without producing any proof.

The sentences where he says, 'The human spirit descended from a world, free and pure. In this world it became trapped in matter . . .' is not that far wide of the mark. We can say his meaning is the separation of the spirit from the soul (we also say that too, and several times we have spoken about it). But the first sentences where he says, 'All of us are of God, but we have become separated from Him, and we will return to Him,' is very wide of the mark. One must ask, 'How can you say this? What proof do you have of this?' Likewise, there are other sentences of his without proof.

He says, '[Each person] must turn aside from the pleasures of this world.' One must ask, 'So for whose sake are these pleasures?'

[Plotinus] says, 'If someone leaves himself in ecstasy, he can connect to God.' One must ask, 'How can one leave oneself in ecstasy?' Such a thing, except as an illusion is impossible. In addition, if someone is of God, then he is of God. So what need is there for leaving oneself in ecstasy?

[Plotinus] says, 'Then we will see what we find within ourselves, indeed, that which is in us.' If we analyse this sentence, its meaning is that there is no God, and we ourselves are God. This is something that many Sufis have said:

> *You are those who seek God. You are God.*
> *He is you, not external to you. He is you.*
> *Why do you seek something not lost?*
> *Why are you searching for something you haven't lost?*

But this idea is also nonsense for it ignores the reality of God.

Where is the path that we have taken to God? When have we accepted God's existence? When we ponder and think about this world, we see it cannot exist by itself, and this order and adornment that is apparent is not derived from this world in itself. We see that we are humans and are greater than all existents of this world, each one of us came unwillingly into this world and we will leave unwillingly. Because of this we know that there is something else behind this world. We know there is a hand outside this world. It made it appear and also makes it move. 'We don't know what God is or how He is. This we know, that He exists and He is outside this world.'

In any case, when we have seen that this world and these human beings cannot exist by themselves, we remain helpless. We have said that God exists outside this world, so now how can we say, 'That God is those very human beings.'

This resembles the trees we see in a desert, standing in a line next to each other, and a water channel has been dug beneath their roots. When we realise that the existence [of the trees] cannot be due to the trees themselves, we assume that a gardener has planted them and dug the water channel for them, and so we search for the gardener and his dwelling. Then someone among us who has been shown the trees says, 'That gardener is this very thing.' Wouldn't we laugh at his words? Wouldn't we say that if these trees could exist by themselves what need would we have to believe in the existence of a gardener and go searching for him?

We repeat, Plotinus's words, like the discourses of other Greek philosophers, have been a source of nothing but fancy. Anyway, just as we have said, from the start Plotinus had a number of followers in Greece.

During the first centuries of Islam, when Greek knowledge and philosophy reached the Muslims, this view of Plotinus too reached the East. Here its circulation among Muslims was greater, and it caused a great shock throughout the Islamic lands. When in time reason became weak, many people accepted the discourses of the Greek philosophers and followed them. [They considered that] it was fortunate that they had heard that man was one with God! It was fortunate that they recognised themselves as God, and they boasted, 'I am God.' This was a cry that was heard among the weak-minded.

In time small groups appeared and *khanaqahs* were established. Plotinus, as is clear from his works, used to discourse only about humans, and said that only the human spirit had been separated from God. But it was here that the larger field for 'the unity of existence' opened up. They made its skirt encompass beasts and wild animals, indeed everything. 'There is nothing in existence except existence.'

So, the purity or turning away from the pleasures of the world (about which Plotinus spoke) caused people to exchange these pleasures of the world for a life without work, and remaining unmarried, they crept away to a corner and did not bother with the world, or else, they wandered from city to city, in a nonchalant state, which was another cause for the rapid advancement of Sufism.

Also at this point, the tradition of the master and disciple took hold, for in each group there existed a master, and others were in his hands, or those of his deputies. Each master would have received the *kherqeh*[13] from another master. In this manner, there were groups of men, and many *selselehs*[14] appeared, with various names. Wearing clothes of dark blue wool because they had turned away from the world, they also shaved their heads.[15]

In addition, the Sufi masters claimed that they had reached God. They made extravagant claims, and pretended that the chain of events in the world was in their hands. They could improve a person's fate if they wished, even making him king, and they could do the reverse, turning him into nothing. They claimed to know the hidden, the apparent, and each person's secrets, and they claimed to be able to speak to the animals, in addition to flying in the air. They called themselves 'the friends', raising themselves to an equal footing with the prophets. Many of them considered themselves superior to the prophets.

In their opinion, religion or the ordinances that the learned establish are for the common people, and the pious are nothing but worshippers of the husk. But Sufism is for the elite who worship the kernel, and they regard others beneath their rank.

They named the state of being without work and women (which are among bad practices) 'blindness to the world and to its pleasures', and they lived happily in that state, although it was inevitable (due to their idleness) that they resorted to begging and requesting bread and money from people. They did not consider this a disgrace, rather, they called the people 'people of the world' and they were not slow to describe them with reproach and censure:

May God curse the People of the World, the young and old, all of them.

They called the market in which they begged every day 'Satan's den', and they reproached merchants. A Sufi should not work, and should refrain from activity in the house and everyday life. He should be with others in the *khanaqah*. If someone was inclined to Sufis he had to give up his own wealth and possessions to the dervishes and become penniless like them.

It is worth reading what they wrote in their books about these kinds of people: 'He renounced worldly attachments'; 'he washed the filth of worldly possessions from his hands', 'don't prostrate to worldly goods'.

In the beginning when Sufism appeared among the Muslims, the people were terrified, especially of the foolish sayings they heard from some of the Sufis. One such beggar of the Baghdad market said, 'there is nothing in my cloak except God,'[16] to that very ruffian of the *khanaqah* who said, 'Glory be to me how great is my majesty.'[17] These foolish sayings were very troublesome to the Muslims, and they did not hinder any opposition to the Sufis. Thus, Hosayn son of Mansur[18] was crucified in Baghdad for sayings of this ilk. One of the Turkish kings, Baqra Khan, killed Sufis there.

On the one hand Sufism advocated easiness in life and it accorded with laziness and satisfying one's bodily demands, yet on the other hand many people liked to withdraw from the masses and form a separate group. So Sufism proliferated daily, and gradually the people (with their ears full of the foolish Sufi sayings) lost their fear, and no longer tried to molest them. Indeed many people among the wealthy ranks supported them and built *khanaqahs*, and established bestowments (*vaqf*) of towns and houses. They donated much money. The Sufis also attempted to Islamicise their origins. Thus some of them traced their *selseleh* to Imam 'Ali Ibn Abi Taleb, and others to the Caliph Abu Bakr.

Until the beginning of seventh/thirteenth century, which is the period of the Mongol triumph, Sufism had advanced and built *khanaqahs* in all places, in Iran, India, Khwarazm, Bukhara, Turkestan, Asia Minor, Iraq, Syria, Egypt and others. As we will see, this was one of the reasons for this Mongol victory.

Subsequently, it became even more widespread during the Mongol era. As a result of the stories that the Mongols had killed millions of people, carried off millions of women and girls, plundered and ruined the whole country, Iranians had a choice. They could pluck up courage and devote themselves to protection and unity with one another, and rise up in a great historical movement, emerging victorious over the enemies and taking revenge on them. Alternatively they could close their eyes from everything, entrust their country to the enemies, surrender their lives to merely eating, sleeping and passing time, and they could attach themselves to Sufism or going to the *kharabat*[19] for their peace of mind. There were only these two options. Since the Iranians didn't have skilful and zealous leaders they chose the Sufi option (and so too going to the *kharabat* and other practices like this), and it was this that made Sufism grow.

Indeed, the Mongols wished for that, for it was in their interest that Iranians suddenly closed their eyes to the country and its sovereignty, and engrossed themselves in Sufism and other such activities. The Mongol period was the spring of these mistaken paths and evil teachings.

It was during and after this Mongol era that many large groups appeared in Iran and other places. Some of them performed amazing things such as walking in fire and playing with vipers. One group called the Qalandar shaved all the hairs from their heads (including their beards and eyebrows) and they performed other astonishing acts.

In addition, some of the masters (having their eyes on crowns and thrones), with the assistance of the dervishes prepared the ground of kingship for themselves. In Iran one of them was Mir Qavam al-Din Mar'ashi (or Mir Bozorg)[20] who in Mazandaran founded the Mar'ashi dynasty. Another was Shaykh Jonayd Safavi[21] who rose in the hope [of establishing a dynasty] but he himself and his son Shaykh Haydar[22] were killed in their efforts, and in the end the task of founding a dynasty was left for Shah Esma'il,[23] the son of Haydar.

The Safavid dynasty emerged from a Sufi movement. Despite this, during the Safavid era Sufism did not thrive very much; indeed, it was towards the end of that dynasty that Sufism, whether in Iran or in other places, began to decay. Day by day its glory and beauty diminished, and until the present day it has declined.

Despite this, in our age there are many Sufis, whether in Iran or in other places, and they have put their own institutions in order. Now in Iran, in Tehran, Shiraz, Maragheh and Gonabad there are masters from India, and we hear the names of Mehrbaba, Shah Khamish and others.

This was a short history of Sufism. One can say that in these one thousand and three hundred years that have passed since the beginning of Islam there have been several things that have been very influential in Iranian life and that of neighbouring peoples, and which have been the source of their misfortune. One of the most influential of them is Sufism.

The point here is that Sufism has intertwined with every aspect of daily life, and its poison has polluted everything. It has polluted all aspects of life: in the recognition of the world, daily life and God, nurturing the spirit, wisdom and its pursuit, reading and research, nature and habit, work and business, cultivation of cities and the countryside, householding and wedlock.

There is one thing worse than this. The Sufis have made poetry, which has had much currency in Iran, the tool of their task. They have engaged in weaving long verses, and they have poured out their harmful illusions in the form of poetry. In this way they have occupied people's minds.

During these one thousand years great poetry weavers have appeared in Iran among the Sufis. From Sana'i,[24] Abu Sa'id,[25] 'Attar,[26] Mawlavi,[27] Owhadi,[28] Jami,[29] Shabestari[30] and others – each one composed much poetry, from masnavi, lyric and couplets (to say nothing of the many books that they wrote in prose).

Worse than this is that other poets who have followed the content [of Sufi poetry] in order to compose a poem have taken and used the evil teachings of Sufism as their source. They have told the stories of Sufi masters (from Shebli,[31] Bayazid,[32] Sa'ri,[33] Ebrahim Adham[34] and others), and have written elaborately in poetry.

The result is that the baseless illusions and poisonous evil teachings of the Sufis were united together so that not only the Sufis and their followers, but others too, became polluted by them. Today in Iran there are many people that have these evil teachings in their minds even without their understanding or wanting [them], and they are trapped in its persistent poison.

This is what we say. Sufism has been and is one of the causes of the Iranian people's misfortunes. You see Orientalists who wish evil upon the East, and they make great efforts not to allow this institution fall apart, writing books and making speeches on Sufism. You see that the Iranian Ministry of Culture, which has brought this institution into view, wishes evil upon the Iranian people, and regards Sufism as its cultural source, and therefore has engaged in printing books and propagating Sufi words.

Section Two: The Evils Attributable to Sufism

As we said previously, in addition to being nothing more than baseless illusions, much harm appeared from Sufism when it spread into every corner of life. For more than a thousand years this mistaken path has found a place for itself among the people, spread into several other countries, formed into different denominations and become entangled in historical events. If we want to speak of its evils (since they should be discussed) and busy ourselves in historical episodes, we would be forced to write such a lengthy book. But we do not have the opportunity for that, and there is no need for such long compositions since our aim is merely to awaken people. Therefore we have summarised the discourses in the present work and will offer only several clear criticisms.

First, as we said, the basis of Sufism is 'the oneness of existence' (*vahdat-e vojud*). They say, 'God is that very simple existence' (absolute existence, *vojud-e motlaq*) that all things possess. As we said, the meaning of this is that there is no God, but we ourselves are God. Yet there are many sayings from [the Sufis] which do not accord with this. Many of their sayings confirm that God exists and we (or our spirits) are separate from Him. This in itself is a criticism that their views are contradictory.

Abu Bakr Razi,[35] who is considered one of the eminent Sufis, in *Mersad al-'ebad*[36] said on this topic that 'the human spirit has been brought down from the proximity of the Lord of the creatures to the world of bodies, the darkness of the physical elements, the desert of this world', and he says that occasionally people do not forget this fate, but remember their old state of proximity to God, and he composed a story about this (or should we say a fable) which is presented in the following. He said:

> In Nishapur Shaykh Muhammad Kufi (God have mercy on him) related that he had found Shaykh 'Ali Mo'ezzin who said, 'I'm reminded that I came from the realm of the Truth's proximity to this world, and they passed my spirit through to the heavens. The inhabitants in each heaven at which I arrived wept over me and said, "They sent this wretch from the station of proximity to the world, and they took him from the highest to the lowest, making him journey from the spaciousness of Paradise to the restrictions of the world." They sighed in regret at this and pitied me. Then an address from the Almighty reached them, "Do you imagine that taking him to that world was to abase him? By God's glory, it is better for him if, during his life in that world, on one occasion he pours a bucket of water from a well into an old woman's jar, than your being busy in worship in Paradise for a hundred thousand of your years. You buried your heads under the cloak of *"each person rejoicing in what they had"*. (30:31) Leave the divine affair to Us because *"We taught what they did not know*[2:30]."'[37]

But there have been many others who clearly took up the claim of divinity, indeed they praised everything as God:

> *We are the essence of the Master of Majesty, God, the Greatest,*
> > *We are the Holy essence, above all impurities.*
> *It is We, our essence is manifest in each particle,*
> > *Don't you know We are yet more than the trace of Our essence.*
> *I praise Myself to Myself in each attribute,*
> > *Sometimes We are the wine and the beautiful witness, and sometimes the cup.*
> *O heart, don't consider anything in existence without God's presence.*
> > *We are the essence of the Master of Majesty, God, the Greatest.*

Mehrbaba is one of the famous Sufis in India, and one of his followers wrote a book about him in which appeared many discourses on this topic. He wrote the following story using Mehrbaba's own words.

> One day someone asked Mehrbaba about the understanding of reality. 'O pivot of the universe, you have shaken and severely jolted the creatures because of your claim to divinity, prophecy, messengership, and truth. Everyone is scared after hearing these words and sentences. What should we do?'
>
> Mehrbaba said, 'Say to the pretenders and opponents of mine that I have not said that I am God. But I exclaim that I am God, you are God, he is God, we are God, all of you are God, they are God, my friends are God, my enemies are God, and my opponents are God. Indeed, I too am frightened by their words and I am shocked and surprised to hear that they see themselves as and call themselves servants and creatures, and regard themselves as this very trivial body. I don't merely call and see myself as God, but I regard all the others too, each one individually as God, and God is also them. There is no difference between me and them.'

If you read the *Masnavi* of Mawla-ye Rumi you will see that sometimes he suddenly becomes a Sufi and presents himself to that illusory world of the unity of existence:

> *Listen to the reed, as it tells its tale*
> *And complains of separation.*
> *'When they cut me from the reed-bed*
> *Men and women have cried out through my flute.*[38]

Sometimes too he forgets this and discusses and composes stories about God in such a way that is believable for Muslims. Not only him but others too have suffered this confusion.

Anyway, the criticisms of 'the unity of existence', according to whatever meaning they derive from it are:

(i) These discourses of the Sufis are illusory, and they do not have any proof for the unity of existence. This is an example of the philosophers' incoherence. One group's interpretation was that man reaches God, and another group tied Him to the animals and wild beasts, not recognising any separation between them.

(ii) This view is not compatible with the true recognition of God (which we have discussed before). Is it correct that human beings (who have come unwillingly to this world and leave unwillingly) should be called God?

(iii) People of God or people from God, say whatever you want, why are their eyes covered from pleasures? Why do they trouble themselves so much? Why do they regard this world as contemptible? What is the conclusion of all this? If it is true as you say that man is from God, then sooner or later he will return to Him, then what is the need of all this effort?

If their purpose is to purify man from the pollutants of the soul (such as desire, anger, hatred, and others), then this is not the path. The path is recognising the right meaning of humanity, and understanding the truths of life which we have made clear in other places.

Second, idleness and staying in the *khanaqah*, practices that the Sufis have chosen, are among their great sins. The result is sensual indulgence which has brought a curtain down upon the eyes of the wool-wearers, and they have not seen many obvious truths of life.

Everyone knows that in this life one must make an effort in order to obtain a satisfactory amount of food, drink, clothing, bedding and other necessities. Each person in his turn must make an effort and busy himself in work or a skill, and co-operate with other people. The person who does not make such an effort, but sponges, is dishonest with the people, and is a sinner. This situation occurs when someone does not make an effort but acquires food, clothing and other necessities from some other means. If someone does not have such a means he must resort to begging and vagrancy, just like the Sufis, and it is clear that his sin will double.

These are matters that everyone can comprehend, but the Sufis have not understood them, and they have adopted idleness and begging. Their boasting of God, their disgrace in begging, each one is worse than the other.

Perhaps people know as much that begging and vagrancy (which are well known because of the Sufis) have been the occupation of worthless, ignoble dervishes. But the truth is that their leaders and masters have also engaged in it. Shaykh Abu Sa'id Abi 'l-Khayr, who is accounted as one of their famous leaders, says himself that in the beginning [of his Sufi life] he spent a while too in begging, as these sentences of his show:

> For the sake of the dervishes, we started begging because we saw nothing more difficult for ourselves than this. At first, whoever saw us gave us a *dinar*, after a while the charity grew less until it was no more than one-sixth of a *dinar*. Then it decreased further until it was virtually nothing. And the people offered no more than this until finally they didn't give anything.

Abu Sa'id had a student called Bu Sa'd who wrote that he went to Baghdad and built a *khanaqah* and became famous.[39] This Abu Sa'id related that once in

Baghdad he entertained pilgrims travelling in a caravan from Khorasan to Mecca, and he set out a meal for them from [the fruits of his] begging. In his own words:

> A group of Sufis were in a caravan, and some of the merchants and people of this crowd consented and agreed [to set up their tents] . . . I rose and picked up a basket, and set out to beg. Every day, morning and evening, I provided meals, and at the five times I gave the call to prayer and acted as the prayer leader . . . in that way I begged and provided a meal.[40]

When Abu Sa'id became a shaykh and established a *khanaqah* in Nishapur, his task each day was merely sending . . . dervishes to this and that wealthy person to ask for money and other things. He made an enemy and spoke badly of the person who gave nothing, and he made such people fearful. A large book entitled *The Secrets of Unity in the Stations of Shaykh Abu Sa'id* has been published which is full of these kinds of stories. It is written in this book, 'The Shaykh asked a woman to invite the dervishes to dinner.' She said, 'I don't have anything.' He replied, 'Go and beg.'

While twenty or thirty fat, greedy, idle men spend their time in a *khanaqah*, this helpless [woman] was forced to go begging. This idleness had another harmful outcome. The Sufis sit [in the *khanaqah*] and weave useless thoughts and imaginings, they sit, sponge and talk rubbish.

> *We are the essence of the Master of Majesty, God, the Greatest.*
> *We are the Holy essence, above all impurities.*

They sit, sponge and give long sermons to the people.

> *May God curse the People of the World, the young and old, all of them.*

They sit, sponge, and spin shameful balderdash.

> How long should I be the taught about my Beloved in the seminary?
> *Send him to us to relax and play!*[41]

All of the verbal weavings of Mawla-ye Rumi in the *Masnavi* or his numerous *ghazals*, and all the spinning of Shaykh 'Attar in *The Conference of the Birds*,[42] or in his other books are all the result of sitting idle and sponging.

In order for it to be understood with what tasks these Sufis spent their days and in what way they occupied the faculties of their minds, we will present a story from *The Secrets of Unity*.

Our Shaykh said, 'When we were in Amol, one day I was sitting with Shaykh Abu 'l-'Abbas when two people came and sat in front of him and said, "O Shaykh, we have a difference of opinion. One of us says that an eternity of sorrow is more fitting, and the other says that eternal joy is better. Now Shaykh, what is your opinion?" Abu 'l-'Abbas drew his hand down over his own face[43] and said, "Praise belongs to God, for my station is neither sorrow nor joy," *There is neither morning or evening with your Lord.'*[44]

See with what futile and useless things they busied themselves. That question of the inquirer and the answer of Abu 'l-'Abbas (or in his own words the son of the butcher), each one is more futile than the other.

Third. The Sufis' not marrying is another of their great sins. God made men for women, and women for men, and He made their numbers equal. So the unmarried man is the source of misfortune for a woman. And having children and descendants is each person's duty. It is disobedience to God when a man does not marry.

Aside from the Sufis who did not marry, many of them engaged in obscenities. In other words, they engaged in paedophilia (or in their words, *shahed-bazi*)[45] which is among the ugliest of sins. It was widespread in the *khanaqah*, and this [was] more abominable since they [tried] to conceal such uncleanliness, and they connected it to 'love of God', to which they made a claim. They cited the following, '*allegory is a bridge to truth.*'

This was the method of the Sufis. They coined a good name for each evil act of theirs. For example, they called idleness 'not lowering the mind into the abject world'. They spoke of begging as 'asceticism' for crushing the 'ego' and selfishness. They called not marrying 'covering the eyes from pleasure', and they invented such terms too for paedophilia.

> *Those imaginings that are the trap of God's Friends*
> *Are the images of beautiful faces in God's garden.*

In *Nafahat al-Ons*, the name of one of the great Sufis, Shaykh Owhad al-Din Kermani (may God Most High bless him) is mentioned. It states, 'In witnessing the Truth he used to turn to manifestations of the upper body,[46] and he witnessed Absolute Beauty in fixed forms.'

The author wants to say Shaykh Kermani was a homosexual, but he clothes his ugly acts in other garments. He says, 'He contemplated the beauty of God in the faces of youths.' See the extent of their rudeness and shamelessness.

In the same book is the following story about Shaykh Hamed.

When he became excited during the *sama'*, he would tear open the shirts of the beardless youths, and dance with his breast upon theirs.

When he came to Baghdad, the Caliph who had a handsome son heard this and said, 'He is an innovator, and if the unbeliever performs this kind of action while associating with me, I will kill him once the *sama'* is in full swing.' The Shaykh understood [the Caliph's thoughts] through his charismatic power, and said:

It is easy for me to feel the point of a sword
    [It is easy] to lose one's head for the sake of the Friend.
You have come to kill the unbeliever,
    Since you are the lord I must be an unbeliever.

The Caliph and his son placed their heads at the Shaykh's feet, and became his followers.[47]

Fourth, rejection of the world and despising life (which has been a custom of the Sufis, indeed, has been the foundation of their life) is another of their sins.

Why have they poured scorn upon the world? Wasn't it God who created it? Isn't the world the place where we live? I admit that there is evil in the world but it is necessary to make an effort, and as far as possible eradicate that evil, not pour scorn and badmouth the world.

The result of the scorn for life that the Sufis (and for that matter, those who frequent the *kharabat*) have, is that the Iranian people and neighbouring countries are nonchalant about life, and spend their time in languor and laziness, and they just stare into the future. This nonchalance and weakness has resulted in their becoming captive and controlled by others.

It is surprising to me that from one perspective the Sufis regard existence as one, and the world, whatever is in it, has been separated from God (or rather, God Himself), and they have incessantly stated this in their writings:

The Friend discloses Himself, unveiled from behind gates and walls,
    Most worthy of being seen.
Was it not Moses who heard 'I am God!'[48]
    And if not, this murmuring under a tree[49] is nothing other than nothing.

And from another perspective they pour scorn and reproach on the world. Is it this or that? On the basis of Plotinus's statement that 'the human spirit descended from an exalted world, and was trapped in matter within this world', there is some justification in viewing this world with disgust. But with regard to the unity of existence (which is the foundation of eastern Sufism) where is the justification for disgust for this world? Without doubt, their reproaching of the world is the result of the Sufis' idleness and poverty. Since they had nothing, they busied themselves with reproaching and saying evil things. Another aim was to encourage the wealthy and rich to give charity and donations.

Fifth. The accounts of dancing, singing and love with God is another of the evil acts of the Sufis. In this regard, it is said that Plotinus – the founder of Sufism – explained in one of his discourses that 'when the human spirit separates from God, it must always desire and like good and beautiful things. It must desire God who is the source of all good and beauty, and it must have love for God in its heart.' His writings contained sayings like this.

This word love ('*eshq*) – it is not known whether or not it is correctly translated – became an excuse in the hands of the Sufis for their amorous talk with God. And in remembrance of Him during the *sama'*, they played the lute and flute, stamped their feet, clapped their hands, spun and jumped around in such a way that they foamed at the mouth, became dizzy and fell over. Everywhere, their writings are full of the word 'love':

> *Whatever you have, devote it all to love.*
>   *I would be an unbeliever if you are hurt in the slightest.*
> *From the dew of love, the earthly body of man became clay*
>   *And a hundred afflictions and troubles arose in the world.*
> *The tip of the lancet of love cut the vein of the spirit,*
>   *A drop fell, and its name was the heart.*[50]

It is clear that this section cited above was taken from the writings of Plotinus. Although he used the word 'love', his intention was 'thinking about God, revering and recalling His name, and performing works at His will'. It is not these kinds of futile, sensual practices. For what are these sorts of words of love with God worthy? In the words of Plotinus, first it is necessary that one wishes good things, and attempt to carry out good deeds, and then attain love. The thing that we hear less frequently from the Sufis concerns good deeds. The deeds of the Sufis were those that we have mentioned: idleness, sponging, paedophilia, begging, weaving illusions, and the like of these.

Anyway, this was an example of the Sufis' blindness to God. The behaviour of those who have called themselves 'gnostics' and 'friends of God' towards God has been this rudeness. The truth is that most of them witnessed either a beautiful youth or woman, and danced in memory of him or her.

Through ignorance some of them have called God '*shahed*',[51] indeed, they have added the ugly word '*harja'i*'[52] to that.

> *To whom can this thing be told?*
>   *My beloved is the beauty seen everywhere*[53] *and the one in seclusion.*[54]

This sin would be enough to blacken the Sufi's faces, even if they had committed no other sin.

In this regard there are disgraceful stories in the books of the Sufis themselves, and we shall present one of them. In *Nafahat al-Ons*, the name 'Shaykh Fakhr al-Din Ebrahim', famous as 'Eraqi, God bless his spirit' is mentioned, and it includes shameful stories about him. As an example, it states:

> At the age of seventeen, in some of the famous theological seminaries of Hamadan, teaching was in progress when one day a group of *Qalandar* arrived. Among them was a handsome boy and the wine of love overcame 'Eraqi and he was captivated by that boy. As long as the *Qalandar* were in Hamadan, 'Eraqi was with them. When they departed and several days passed, 'Eraqi could endure no more, and so he left in search of them. When he caught up with them, he adopted their manners, went with them to India, and enjoyed the association of Shaykh Baha' al-Din Zakariya. And they say that when the Shaykh prescribed isolation for 'Eraqi, he recited this *ghazal* after ten days of his *chelleh*, having experienced ecstasy (*wajdi*) and a [when a mystical] state had overcome him:

First wine that filled the cup
  they borrowed from the saqi's drunken eyes.

> He sang this loudly, and wept. When the People of the *Khanaqah* saw this and regarded it as contrary to the way of the Shaykh (because their method of isolation was nothing other than reciting the *zekr* or controlling the self), they objected about it to the Shaykh. He said, 'You are forbidden from this but he is not.' After several days, one of the deputies of the Shaykh passed the *kharabat* and heard the people singing that *ghazal*, accompanied with the lute and the clicking of fingers. He went back to the Shaykh and explained the circum-stances.[55] The Shaykh asked, 'What did you hear, tell me.' When he reached the part in his story when he heard the couplet '*They are so free with their secret – why then should they blame 'Eraqi?*' the Shaykh said, 'His task is finished!' He got up and went to the door of the cell where 'Eraqi was in isolation. 'Eraqi laid his head at the Shaykh's feet, and with his own hands the Shaykh raised 'Eraqi's head from the earth and no longer allowed him to practise isolation, but took off his own *kherqeh*, and put it on him.[56]

Meditate well on this story so that you can understand what meaning the 'love' of the Sufis has, and from what path it comes.

Sixth. Another sin of the Sufis is the hostility that they have shown to reason (*kherad*). Reason is the most precious thing given by God, and each person must recognise it, and it must be the guide in their activities. Those whose actions are irrational have shown their hostility to reason, and have busied themselves in voicing their scorn to it:

> *Love arrived and his intellect became a vagrant.*
> *Morning came and intellect's candle became useless.*[57]

> *The legs of the reasoners are wooden*
> *And wooden legs are too unstable.*[58]

> *Love arrived and plundered the intellect.*
> *O heart this is the good news.*[59]

'When a dervish once asked our Shaykh, "O Shaykh, what is intellect?" he said, "Intellect is the god of servitude. With intellect one cannot discover the secrets of lordship because [the intellect] is created, and there is no access for created things to the eternal."'

In Sufi books, there are many of these kinds of sentences: 'Since the intellect gets nowhere, commence the [Sufi] travelling and journeying (*sayr va soluk*) and seek [mystical] unveiling and witnessing,' and 'since the nail of reason does not untie the knot of the task, turn to love,' and 'as love settled in the heart, intelligence was busy with the house.'

With these sentences they wanted to make others understand that they existed in a world greater than reason and its dominion. They existed in a world where the basis of reason had no place. But the truth is that since their business was clearly irrational, inevitably they put reason to one side and made efforts to belittle it.

Sitting idle in the *khanaqah*, eating bread derived from the toil of others, begging in the bazaar, not taking a wife and having children, growing a beard, dancing, clapping hands and spinning themselves around have the least [degree of] compatibility with reason, let alone all the other irrational stories about them. Now I will relate one of them to serve as an example.

It was that very Mawlana who said, 'Love arrived and human intellect became a vagrant.' In *Nafahat al-Ons* there is the following story about him and his master, Shams-e Tabrizi.

> For a period of three months they were sitting for uninterrupted fasting, night and day, and they had not come out of isolation at all. No one had the gall to interrupt their isolation. One day Shams al-Din asked Mawlana for a *shahed*. Mawlana took his wife's hand, and led her to [Shams, Mawlana] said, 'She is the sister of my soul.' [Shams said], 'I want a beautiful boy.' In a second he brought his son, Sultan Valad.

He said, 'He is the son of my soul.' [Shams said] 'Now we shall enjoy ourselves if he will give a little wine.' Mawlana went out and filled up and brought back a jar from the Jewish quarter. Shams al-Din said, 'I have tested the strength of Mawlana's obedience. It is greater than whatever they say."[60]

Contemplate well on this story. Two people for three months in isolation, what did they do? The author says, 'uninterrupted fasting'. Can one spend three months in uninterrupted fasting? How can one reconcile uninterrupted fasting with desiring a woman or a boy and wishing for wine? On this point they say, 'the liar is forgetful'.

Is it not dishonourable to give one's own wife or son to another person? Is dishonour too appropriate in Sufism? What dishonour there is for Mawlana in this story, if it is the truth. If it is not the truth then what ignorance those people had who concocted these things in the name of their leaders and recorded them in books. This Mawlana is that very person whose *Masnavi* has been published time after time, and upon which much foolish praise has been lavished. He is that person whose book is considered equal in rank to the Qur'an.[61] The people who want to know about this type of Sufi disgrace read Jami's *Nafahat al-Ons* or 'Attar's *Remembrance of the Saints*.

The thing that I must state at the end of this chapter is that idleness and not taking a wife – which we regard as Sufi sins – have not existed among all [Sufi] orders. First, for a long time a Sufi was not able to engage in work or profession, but he could take a wife. Some of them took wives because it was clear [a Sufi] needs his food and household things, and his children too started begging. Then Shaykh Safi Ardabili and Shah Ne'matollah Kermani[62] recommended their disciples to get a job or profession. Shah Ne'matollah said, 'The friends of God can wear the clothes of workers and professionals too.'

Notes

[1.] *Payman* was a monthly journal begun by Kasravi in the 1930s.

[2.] *Parcham* was a daily newspaper, edited by Kasravi, the first issue of which was on 23 January 1942, and ceased publication on 8 December. Kasravi subsequently continued publishing his views through a variety of publications edited by himself. See Jazayery, 'Kasravi, Iconoclastic Thinker of Twentieth Century Iran', in *On Islam*, (Costa Mesa: Mazda, 1990) p. 6.

[3.] *Memoirs of the Saints* is a well-known Sufi text that has been rendered into English in an abridged form; see *Muslim Saints and Mystics: Episodes from the Tadhkirat al-Auliya'*, trans. A. J. Arberry (London/New York: Arkana, 1990).

[4.] The *Masnavi* of Mawlana is of course the famous six volumes of didactic Sufi Persian verse composed by Jalal al-Din Rumi. This has been translated into English by R. A. Nicholson, as *The Mathnawi of Jalalu'ddin Rumi* (London: Gibb Memorial Series, 1925–40).

5. The *chelleh* is a Sufi practice of remaining in isolation for a period of forty days for prayer and spiritual contemplation.

6. Kasravi's footnote. He does not state where he discusses this topic.

7. Kasravi does not state where he expresses these opinions.

8. The Persian reads: *nangeshan az nam va nameshan az nang*, which reflects Hafez's statement '*az nang cheh gu'i ke mara nam z-nang ast, vaz nam cheh porsi ke mara nang z-nam ast*' ('What do you say about ignominy, for me reputation comes from ignominy; and what do you say about reputation, because for me ignominy comes from reputation.') The Persian text is found in Arberry, *Fifty Poems of Hafiz* (Curzon: 1993), p. 45.

9. The Qalandar were a group of antinomian Sufis who had a reputation for shocking behaviour, including wearing green clothing (sometimes very little clothing at all), who shaved their heads and eyebrows, and wandered from place to place, having no fixed abode. For the Qalandar see A. Karamustafa, *God's Unruly Friends* (Salt Lake City, 1994).

10. Kasravi does not mention which book.

11. The *pir* is another name for the Sufi leader, guide or shaykh.

12. Kasravi states that these sentences have been taken from the book *The Course of Philosophy in Europe*. This is presumably the work of Muhammad Ali Forughi. Kasravi does not give the page number or the edition of the book.

13. The *kherqeh* is the Sufi cloak.

14. The *selseleh* is the chain of initiation, usually stretching back through a series of famous and celebrated Sufi masters to Muhammad.

15. A typical practice of the Qalandar Sufis.

16. This is the ecstatic expression commonly associated with Ma'ruf al-Karkhi (d. 815–16).

17. This is the ecstatic expression commonly associated with Bayazid Bastami (d. 874).

18. Reference to Hallaj, executed in 922, and famous for his exclamation 'I am the Truth.'

19. The *kharabat* (a Persian term) refers to places of ill-repute such as taverns, brothels, gaming houses. Kasravi associates the *kharabat* with the medieval Persian poets Khayyam and Hafez.

20 Mir Qavam al-Din Mar'ashi (or Mir Bozorg) was a member of the Shaykhiyyeh order of Shi'-ite Sufis, and established a Shi'-ite state – known as the Mar'ashi dynasty – in northern Iran in 1359. It was shortlived, and was conquered by Timur in 1391.

21 Shaykh Junayd Safavi emerged as leader of the Safavid Sufi order in the second half of the fifteenth century, and he died in 1460. For the Safavids, see R. Savory, *Iran Under the Safavids* (Cambridge University Press, 1980).

22 Shaykh Haydar was the son of Shaykh Junayd, who also inherited the leadership of the Safavid movement. He passed away in 1488.

²³ Shah Esma'il, one of Haydar's sons, established the Safavid state in Iran when he was crowned in 1501.

²⁴ Sana'i (d. 1131) is generally acknowledged as one of the founders of Persian Sufi poetry. For his work see De Bruijn, *Of Piety and Poetry* (Leiden: E. J. Brill, 1983).

²⁵ For the hagiography of Abu Sa'id see *The Secrets of God's Mystical Oneness*, trans. by J. O'Kane.

²⁶ 'Attar (d.c.1220) was the author of numerous mystical poetic works. The most famous in English is *Mantiq al-Tayr*, translated as *The Speech of the Birds*, by P. Avery (Cambridge: Islamic Texts Society, 1998). See also n. 3.

²⁷ Mawlavi, also known as Jalal al-Din Rumi. See n. 4.

²⁸ Owhadi (d. 1337); as far as I know, there have been no English translations of his mystical verse. He was initiated into the mystical tradition by Owhad al-Din Kirmani (criticised later in the text by Kasravi). Awhadi is famous in Iran for his *masnavi* entitled *Jam-e jam*, ed. S. Nafisi in *Kolliyat-e Owhadi-ye Esfahani ma'ruf ba-Maragheh'i* (Tehran: 1961).

²⁹ Jami (1414–92) was another great mystical poet who also composed works in prose, referred to and cited in Kasravi's text (e.g. *Nafahat al-Ons*).

³⁰ Shabestari (d.c. 1320) was the author of 'The Rose Garden of Mystery' (*Golshan-e Raz*) which portrayed the perfection of man through the path of gnosis. See L. Lewisohn, *Beyond Faith and Infidelity* (Richmond: Curzon, 1995).

³¹ Shebli (d. 945) is famous for his paradoxical statements, and also for the use of imagery that became commonplace in later Persian poetry. He is also associated with Hallaj. On his execution, the masses threw stones whereas Shebli cast a rose at him. See Schimmel, *Mystical Dimensions of Islam* (Chapel Hill: 1975).

³² Bayazid Bastami (d. 874) was probably the first Sufi to describe his mystical experience of the divine in a fashion that resembles Mohammad's own 'Night Ascent' through the heavens to God. He is also famous for his ecstatic statement 'Glory be to me, how great is my majesty.' For accounts of the Ascent of Bayazid Bastami, given in two Sufi medieval texts, see R. C. Zaehner, *Hindu and Muslim Mysticism* (London: Athlone Press, 1960, pp. 198–218).

³³ It is claimed that Sa'ri al-Saqati (d.c. 867) was the first to discuss the mystical states (*ahwal*), or mystical experiences of the Sufis, and he also spoke of the mutual love between God and man. He was the uncle of the great Sufi master Jonayd (d. 910).

³⁴· Ebrahim Adham (d. 776 or 790) is described as having a radical aversion to the world and its inhabitants. He is a model of Islamic ascetic practice and seems to have gathered a considerable following.

³⁵· [Najm al-Din] Abu Bakr Razi, also known as Najm al-Din Dayah (1177–1256) was a member of the Kobraviyyeh order and wrote several important mystical treatises including an esoteric commentary of the Qur'an, a work he took over from his master, Najm al-Din Kobra. He is most famous, however, for his book *The Path of God's Bondsmen from Origin to Return*, trans. Hamid Algar (Delmar, NY: Caravan Books, 1983).

³⁶· *Mersad al-'ebad*, i.e. *The Path of God's Bondsmen from Origin to Return*, ibid.

37. Ibid., pp. 130–1.

38. The famous opening to Rumi's *Masnavi*.

39. O'Kane, *The Secret of God's Mystical Oneness*, p. 544.

40. Ibid., p. 544.

41. This last line in Arabic is a quotation from the Qur'an (12:12).

42. See n. 26.

43. J. O'Kane has explained that this action is a customary gesture a person makes when he has recited a final prayer and brings an assembly to a close. *The Secrets of God's Mystical Oneness*, p. 606, n. 70.

44. Ibid., p. 123.

45. *Shahed-bazi*, as Jazayery states, is a Persian word for homosexuality, and refers to male homosexuality only, in particular, the role played by the male who penetrates his partner. In 'Ahmad Kasravi and the Controversy Over Persian Poetry', p. 198, n. 1.

46. Kasravi's text reads *Mazaher-e sadri*. Jami's text (ed. 'Abidi) reads 'he witnessed the absolute beauty of the Truth – may He be glorified – in created, sensual manifestations', p. 588.

47. This story with slight variations is found in Jami, ibid., p. 588.

48. A reference to the Qur'an 27:9.

49. The fire (of the burning bush) is referred to in 27:7.

50. 'Attar, *Divan*, ed. T. Tafazzoli (Tehran: Bungah-e tarjameh va nashr-e ketab, 1967), p. 493.

51. See n. 45. A *shahed* is a person who gives witness to the beauty of God.

52. *Harja'i*, literally means everywhere. From the perspective of *vahdat-e vojud*, it means that God can be witnessed in all existence.

53. Literally *shahed-e har-ja'i*.

54. *Gusheh-neshan*.

55. At this point Kasravi's text reads *baqi shaykh khak-and* – or 'the other shaykhs are earth [or worthless]'. 'Abidi's edition reads 'baqi shaykh-e hakem and'.

56. Jami, pp. 599–600.

57. Rumi, *Masnavi*, IV: 2109. Kasravi's text has the first line beginning with 'love' (*'eshq*), however, the standard texts begin with *'nuql'* (sweet). Nicholson translates the first line as: 'The Dessert came: his reason became distraught.'

58. Rumi, *Masnavi*, I: 2128.

59. Rumi, *Masnavi*, I: 2128.

60. Kasravi's text is again corrupt, as instead of wife (*haram*), the text reads *j.r.m*, which makes no sense at all. Again I have relied on 'Abidi's text, op. cit., p. 467.

61. A reference to Jami's famous words: 'Whoever recites the Mathnawi in the morning and evening, for him Hellfire be forbidden! The spiritual Mathnawi of Mawlana is the Qur'an in Persian tongue.' Cited in Schimmel, *The Triumphal Sun* (London and The Hague: East-West Publications, 1980), p. 367.

62. Shah Ne'matollah Kermani (1331–1431) founder of the Ne'matollahi order, which has been widespread in Iran at various times.

CHAPTER 8

Concerning the Wayfaring and Spiritual Journey of the People of Intellect[1]

'Allameh Sayyed Mohammed Tabataba'i

Kasravi's writings on Sufism are a good example of the opposition of some contemporary intellectuals towards Iran's mystical tradition, yet criticisms of this tradition have existed for centuries. Some Shi'-ite clerics have been so antagonistic to Sufism that they have used their influence and power to instigate what can only be called purges. Perhaps the most infamous of such clerics was Aqa Mohammed Baqer Behbehani (1731–1801), who earned the sobriquet 'Sufi-kosh' (Sufi-killer). The reasons for clerical distaste for Sufism hinges on a number of points, perhaps the most significant being the basis for the claim to knowledge and authority. For the Sufi, the pinnacle of knowledge comes through the ineffable mystical experience of the divine, which transcends any linguistic or rational explanation. The individual who enjoys such access to God surely does not need to have recourse to the advice and guidance of clerical authorities that base their authority on knowledge of the sacred texts, through which they claim to have the best possible under-standing of the probable will of the Hidden Imam. Knowledge, power and money are linked in a number of ways, and the antagonism between the clerical authorities and the Sufis may also be connected to the fact that both sides were laying claims to guidance, which also meant a battle for the donations that came through attracting followers, and which were used to pay the stipends given to the clerics' students. Another major contentious issue between the two concerned the understanding and interpretation of sacred texts. Many Sufis read Islamic texts in an allegorical fashion, witnessing 'secret' or esoteric meanings in the Qur'an and sayings of the Imams. In addition, there were some mystics who viewed a form of universalism in religion, and were quite favourable to utilising philosophical methods and discourse to reveal such a perspective. This was problematic for the clerical scholars because allegorical interpretation and philosophical enquiry belittle the 'literal' readings that contribute to the basis of Islamic law.

Of course there have been some clerics who believed in the compatibility of mystical speculation and philosophy with the juristic rulings of Shi'-ite law. Perhaps the most well-known exponent of both Sufism and Shi'-ite law in recent times was Ruhollah Khomeini, who composed a treatise on mysticism in 1930 entitled Mesbah al-Hedayat, *in which he explained the 'four journeys' (*al-Asfar al-Arba'eh*) described by Molla Sadra (1571– 1640) in a favourable and mystical fashion. Khomeini himself was a student of mysticism during his early years in Qom, but he mentions the difficulty of finding a teacher due to the suspicion and mistrust in which mysticism held there. Khomeini was to hold secret sessions in which he explained the 'four journeys' in which the mystic and the Perfect Man progressed on a journey away from humans to God and then returned to the human realm to instruct and advise Muslims. Similarly, and at about the same time, one of Iran's leading spiritual figures of the twentieth century, 'Allameh Seyyed Mohammed Tabataba'i (1901–81) was asked to teach Molla Sadra's 'four journeys'. His course became very popular, to the extent that over one hundred pupils attended, yet the stipends of all those who attended the lectures were curtailed by Grand Ayatollah Borujerdi, the leading clerical figure in Iran. Borujerdi's reason for this action is somewhat vague ('the open teaching of the Asfar in an official seminary setting, that is not appropriate'), but even more revealing is his admission that he had also studied the text as a student, but in secret.*[2] *'Allameh Tabataba'i's reason for teaching this text was because of his belief that it was Islamic philosophy and mysticism that had a better chance of challenging the secular ideologies that were becoming increasingly popular in Iran than the obscurantist literalism of some of the traditional Shi'-ite clergy.*

Tabataba'i's concern with mysticism and philosophy should not be regarded as merely intellectual, as it appears that he engaged in traditional Sufi ascetic practice (although not the antinomian variety), and certainly believed that he had received certain spiritual unveilings. The Kernel of the Kernel *includes Tabataba'i's account of a dream in which he was spoken to by the prophet Idris, and this dream 'was the first transformation that connected the material world of nature to the supernatural realm for me'.*[3] *Another indication of Tabataba'i's active engagement with the* 'erfani *tradition that went beyond mere speculation was his practice of bibliomancy (determining a course of action with reference to the message contained within a random* ghazal *from the* Divan-e Hafez*).*[4] *Moreover his description within the* Kernel of the Kernel *of what the wayfarer witnesses and experiences during the spiritual journey suggests that he may have believed that he had gone through something similar himself (although it may also be possible that he was drawing on the works of celebrated medieval Sufis such as Najm al-Din Kobra whose writings also describe such mystical, visionary journeys).*

In his 'erfani *perspective, Tabataba'i did not see any contradiction between mysticism and Shi'-ism, for he describes how the particular guide for the wayfarer is the Imam for*

> *the source of all that which finds concrete existence and manifestation in the world of creation is the Divine Names and Attributes, and the reality of the Imam is the same as the Names and Attributes of God . . . Accordingly, in the process of wayfaring, the traveller traverses within the planes of the Imam's luminosity. Any spiritual station he may ascend or status he may attain, the Imam already possesses and accompanies the wayfarer in that plane and station.*[5]

Moreover, Tabataba'i's portrayal of the spiritual journey is one that conforms to Shi'-ite piety and the observance of legal norms, and those who believe that they have reached such advanced spiritual stations that the shari'a *is no longer applicable to them merely make prevarications and false assertions.*[6]

The brevity of the Kernel of the Kernel *should not detract from its significance as an example of how a core of Sufi practice (such as the ritual of* zekr *and spiritual seclusion) and teachings (see Tabataba'i's description in Chapter 5 of the attributes that the wayfarer must possess in the path) is utilised and contained within a non-traditional Sufi order (*tariqeh*). Such a non-traditional order is outlined in the section from the* Kernel of the Kernel *that is presented below. Tabataba'i claims that his order is unlike the traditional chains of initiation, and only stretched back as far as the middle of the nineteenth century to Shaykh Sayyid 'Ali Shustari who was instructed by a mysterious weaver who is identified in a footnote as the 'hidden (twelfth) Imam [who] . . . appears from time to time to initiate certain individuals of exceptional spiritual realisation, without revealing his true identity'.*[7] *The* Kernel of the Kernel *also includes other intriguing points, such as the claim that non-Muslim spiritual wayfarers cannot enjoy the same extent of spiritual unveiling as Muslim travellers.*[8] *This belief is of interest given Tabataba'i's later engagement and interest in Western philosophy and other religious traditions, which was deepened with his association with the French scholar, Henri Corbin, that commenced in 1958.*

The text reproduced below is part of a work entitled Lobb al-Lobab dar sayr va soluk-i ulu 'l-albab *('Kernel of the Kernel Concerning the Wayfaring and Spiritual Journey of the People of Intellect'), which was a series of lectures delivered by Tabataba'i to his students between 1949-50. One of the students was Seyyid Muhammad Husayn Tehrani, who took extensive notes during the lectures, and a few years before his death in 1995 he compiled, edited and expanded his notes and published the work in Mashhad. The section reproduced below is interesting for its alternative route of spiritual enlightenment.*

This text should be considered significant if only because of the esteem in which Tabataba'i was (and is) held by many Iranians. He became an eminent and highly regarded spiritual leader within Iran and also the larger Islamic world, and his name is usually linked with his twenty volume Arabic commentary of the Qur'an, commonly known as al-Mizan *(the balance), which he wrote between 1954 and 1972. This exegesis was based on the principle that 'certain parts of the Qur'an are defined by certain other parts', in other words, the Qur'an was itself the scale or balance by which the meanings of the verses could be understood. This stood in contrast to the explanations of other clerics who were influenced by the prevailing scientific theories of the day.*

Notes

[1.] The main text in this chapter is taken from *Kernel of the Kernel: Concerning the Wayfaring and Spiritual Journey of the People of Intellect (Risala-yi Lubb al-Lubab dar Sayr wa Suluk-i Ulu'l Albab): A Shi'i Approach to Sufism*. From *The Teachings of Sayyid*

Muhammad Husayn Tabataba'i, compiled, edited and expanded by Sayyid Muhammad Husayn Husayni Tihrani (Albany: SUNY Press, 2003).

2. For the background to this event see Hamid Dabashi, *Theology of Discontent*, pp. 273–84.

3. *Kernel of the Kernel*, p. 72.

4. Hafez is the fourteenth century Persian poet, famous for his love poetry. Tabataba'i's practice of bibliomancy is mentioned by Dabashi, *Theology of Discontent*, pp. 282–7.

5. *Kernel of the Kernel*, p. 109.

6. Ibid., p. 37.

7. *Kernel of the Kernel*, p. 130, n.18.

8. Ibid., p. 60.

Further Reading

Hamid Dabashi, *Theology of Discontent* (Chapter 5: 'Allameh Sayyid Muhammad Hossein Tabataba'i: The Philosophical Dimension of Islamic Ideology') (New York University Press, 1993).

'Allamah Tabataba'i, *Shi'ite Islam* (translated Seyyed Hossein Nasr) (Albany: State University of New York Press, 1975).

——*The Quran in Islam: Its Impact and Influence on the Life of Muslims*, trans. Assadullah ad-Dhaakir Yate (London: Zahra Publications, 1987).

———•———

[The reality of gnosis (*'irfān*) originates from Amīr al-Mu'minīn 'Alī ibn Abī Ṭālib, may God's greetings be upon him. The number of orders that have accepted and spread this reality [his *wilāyah*] generation after generation and from masters to disciples exceeds more than one hundred. But the principal branches of *taṣawwuf* do not exceed twenty-five. All of these orders trace their origin to Ḥaḍrat 'Alī ibn Abī Ṭālib, may God's greetings be upon him. Among these twenty-five orders, two or three belong to the *khāṣṣah* (i.e., Shī'ites) and all the rest belong to *'Āmmah* (i.e., Sunnis). Some of these orders also trace their origin to Imām Riḍā, may God's greetings be upon him, through Ma'rūf al-Karkhī. However, our order, which is the same as that of the late Ākhūnd (Mullā Ḥusayn Qulī), does not originate from and is not related to any of these chains (*silsilahs*).

Let us now turn to a brief discussion of our order. Over a hundred years ago there was an eminent scholar in the city of Shūshtar [in southern Iran] named Āqā Sayyid 'Alī Shūshtarī who held the function of the judge and religious authority for the people of Shūshtar. Like other prominent religious scholars of the time, he performed ordinary functions like teaching, judging, and settling disputes between people, and acting as a source of emulation (*marja'īyat-i taqlīd*) in religious matters. It has been reported that one day someone knocked at his door. When asked who it was, the visitor told him to open the door as he had business to conduct with him. When the late Āqā Sayyid 'Alī opened the door, he saw a man whose appearance revealed that he was a weaver. When asked what he wanted, the weaver told him: 'Such and such judgment that you had issued in favour of a person concerning the ownership of such and such property on the basis of the testimony of witnesses was not correct; and that the said property – in fact – belonged to a minor, an orphan.' He then added that the deed of that property was buried in such and such location.

The weaver also told Sayyid 'Alī Āqā that: 'The path that you have adopted is not the right one; this path is not for you.' Āyatullūh Shūshtarī asked the man whether he had committed any wrongdoing or followed the wrong way. The weaver replied: 'I have already given my answer.' Having said this the weaver went away. The Āyatullūh was immersed in his thought and wondered who that man had been and what he had meant. After some investigation, it turned out that documents pertaining to the said property and proving the orphan's ownership of that were indeed buried in the same place as the weaver had indicated; and that the witnesses who had testified in favour of the other party had lied under duress and out of fear.

Sayyid Āqā 'Alī became dismayed and wondered whether many of the judgments he had issued had been of this sort. He was overwhelmed by fear and anguish. The following night the weaver again knocked at his door and told him: 'The true path is not the one on which you are travelling.' The third night the same episode was repeated in precisely the same manner. This time the weaver also told him to sell his house and all his belongings as soon as possible, and go to the city of Najaf in Iraq and carry on the tasks that he would assign to him. Then he added, 'After six months, wait for me in the Wādī al-Salām cemetery in Najaf Ashraf.'

Reportedly, the late Shūshtarī immediately began to carry out the weaver's instructions. He sold his house and gathered his belongings and made arrangements to depart for Najaf Ashraf. As soon as he arrived in Najaf, at sunrise he saw the weaver in Wādī al-Salām cemetery standing in front of him as though he had come out of the ground. The weaver gave him some more instructions and disappeared. The late Āyatullāh took residence in Najaf Ashraf and carried out the weaver's instructions until he reached a station that words cannot describe. May God be pleased with him and may His peace be upon him.

In Najaf Ashraf, out of reverence for Shaykh Murtaḍā Anṣārī,[1] Āyatullāh Shūshtarī attended the Shaykh's lectures on jurisprudence (*fiqh*) and Principles (*uṣūl*). In return, Shaykh Anṣārī also went to Shūshtarī's class on ethics. When Shaykh Anṣārī, may God have mercy on him, passed away, Shūshtarī, may God have mercy on him, took charge of the Shaykh's chair and continued the lectures where the Shaykh had left off. However, he did not live for very long and after six months departed towards God's eternal mercy. Once during that period, the late Shūshtarī sent a message to one of the most outstanding pupils of Shaykh Anṣārī, named Ākhūnd Mullā Ḥusayn-Qulī Dargazīnī Hamadānī. Hamadānī knew Shūshtarī while Shaykh Anṣārī was still alive and had benefited from his courses in ethics and gnosis. He planned to continue teaching the same subjects that Shaykh Anṣārī had taught, and had compiled the Shaykh's lectures and discourses. In that message Āyatullāh Shūshtarī reminded Hamadānī that that position (teaching) was not a perfect one for him, and that he should aim at attaining higher stations. This message transformed Hamadānī and guided him to the abode of the truth.

At any rate, the late Ākhūnd Hamadānī, who had studied sacred sciences under the late Āqā 'Alī Sayyid 'Alī several years before the death of the late Shaykh Anṣārī, became one of the wonders of his time and superior to his contemporaries in the fields of ethics, spiritual struggle, and sacred sciences. Moreover, he trained several outstanding disciples, each of whom was considered a citadel of gnosis and a manifestation of Divine Unity. Among his most eminent pupils one can mention the late Ḥājj Mīrzā Jawād Āqā Malikī Tabrīzī, the late Āqā Sayyid Aḥmad Karbalā'ī Tihrānī, the late Āqā Sayyid Muhammad Sa'īd Ḥubbūbī, and the late Ḥājj Shaykh Muhammad Bahārī.

Our revered teacher and master, the unrivalled gnostic, the late Ḥājj Mīrzā 'Alī Āqā Qāḍī Tabrīzī, may God be pleased with him, belonged to the circle of pupils of the late Āqā Sayyid Aḥmad Karbalā'ī. This is the chain (*silsilah*) of our masters and teachers that goes back to the late Āqā 'Alī Shūshtarī and ultimately to that weaver. As to the identity of the weaver and his connections or the source of his knowledge and instructions, nothing is known.[2]

Like our grand master and teacher Ākhūnd Mullā Ḥusayn-Qulī, the approach of our master and teacher the late Āqā Qāḍī Tabrīzī, was based on awareness and knowledge of the self (*ma'rifat al-nafs*). In the initial stages, he always prescribed concentration on one's soul in order to gain control over mind and thought. According to his instruction, every day a novice traveller must devote a certain amount of time, half an hour or more, just to concentrate on his soul and practise to control his mind and thought. As a result of this concentration, slowly he would gain [spiritual] strength and thoughts and other mental preoccupations will disappear. Gradually, he would attain knowledge of his soul, and God willing, would ultimately reach his desired spiritual destination.

Most aspirants who have succeeded in liberating their mind and cleaning and purifying it from memories and ordinary preoccupations to prepare it for the rise of the Kingdom of Gnosis (*sulṭān-i ma'rifat*), have done so in one of the two following states. The first is during recitation of the Glorious Qur'ān, contemplating and wondering who the actual reciter of the Qur'ān is, and ultimately feeling [being revealed to] that the reciter is none other than God Himself, Majestic is His Glory.

Second is by pleading to (*tawassul*) and seeking the intercession of Ḥaḍrat Abā

'Abd Allāh al-Ḥusayn, may God's blessing and peace be upon him, because he is graciously instrumental in lifting the veil and removing the obstacles on the path of God for the wayfarer.

As was mentioned in our discussion in previous pages, two factors play important parts in the theophany of the Kingdom of Gnosis. The first is constant attention (*murāqabah*) in its various forms and degrees of intensity; and second is concentration on the soul. When the traveller makes every effort to focus his attention on these two principles, gradually he will realise that the multiplicities of this world originate from and are nurtured by one wellspring, and anything that finds existence in the world derives its existence from one source. Any degree of light, beauty, glory, and perfection that may be present in any existing thing is derived from that single source that gives it the light of life, beauty, and majesty in accordance with its inherent capability (*qābilīyat-i māhuwī*). In other words, absolute and boundless grace emanates unconditionally from the Absolute Source and every existent receives its share in accordance with its qualifications and quiddity (*māhīyat*).

In any case, as a result of constant attention and persistent effort, gradually four [spiritual] realms will be revealed to the traveller.

The first realm is the world of Unity in deeds (*tawḥīd-i afʿāl*). That is, at first the traveller realises that whatever his eyes see, his tongue says, his ears hear, his feet, hands, and other bodily organs perform are all supported by his own soul, and the soul does what it wills. Then he realises that whatever actions that take place in the external world derive from and are supported by himself. In other words, his soul is the source of all his [external] acts. Soon, however, he realises that his soul subsists in the Divine Being and is only a gate for emanation of Divine Mercy and Grace; and therefore, all acts in the external world are supported by His Sacred Being.

The second realm is the world of Unity of Attributes (*Tawḥīd-i Ṣifāt*) and is revealed after the first realm. In this realm when the traveller hears, he does not regard the reality of hearing to belong to himself, but to God. Similarly, whatever he sees with his eyes, he perceives the reality of his sight as belonging to God. In short, he realises that every kind of knowledge, power, life, hearing, sight, and everything else that he notices in the existent things in the external world all emanate from and subsist in God, Exalted is He.

The third realm is the world of Unity of Names (*Tawḥīd-i Asmāʾ*) and it emerges after the second world. In this realm, the traveller understands that [Divine] Attributes subsist in His Essence. For example, he realises that only God, Exalted is He, is the [real] Knower (*ʿĀlim*), the Powerful (*Qādir*), and the Living (*Ḥayy*). In other words, he realises that his own knowledge is, in fact, God's knowledge; and believes that his power, hearing, and sight all belong to God and are in God. In general, he understands that in the entire universe there is only One who is Powerful, Knowing, Seeing, and Living and that is God, Glorious is He; and that every existent thing, in proportion to its own existential reality, alludes to and reflects a certain degree of the reality of the *All-Knowing*, the *All-Powerful*, the *All-Hearing*, the *All-Seeing*, and the *Living*.

The fourth realm is the world of Unity of Essence (*Tawḥīd dar Dhāt*), which is higher than the third realm and is revealed to the wayfarer through the theophany of the Divine Essence. That is to say, the traveller realises that the Essence by which all acts, attributes, and names are supported is One Essence and One Reality in which they all subsist. At this point, the wayfarer is no longer concerned about Attributes and Names but solely with the Essence. This is realised only when he bids farewell to and leaves behind his derivative existence (*wujūd-i 'āriyah wa majāzī*) and loses his identity and *selfhood* once and for all and annihilates them in the Sacred Essence of God, Exalted is He. This is the point of the theophany of the Essence. Of course, to name this station as the station of the Essence (*maqām-i dhāt*), the reality of the Essence (*ḥaqīqat-i dhāt*), or Unicity (*aḥadīyat*) or any other name is a waste of time and a meaningless and futile effort. For whatever can be expressed by the tongue or written by the pen is not beyond definition. Whereas the Sacred Divine Essence is above all definitions. One cannot find a proper name or description for It, nor can It be conceived in terms of states and stations. In fact, it is even beyond the boundaries of inability, for while inability implies negation, it still sets a limit for Him, and God the Almighty is above all limitations. When the traveller enters this realm, he loses his own identity and *selfhood*. He will not know himself, nor will he recognise any other person. In short, he will not know anyone except God, because ultimately only God can know Himself.

In the process of his journey in each of the fourfold realms, the traveller loses a part of his identity and selfhood – ultimately losing his total being and existence. In the first abode where he reaches the station of annihilation in the Act, he realises that it is not he, but God, who acts. He loses all signs of his effects pertaining to action. In the second realm, thanks to the theophany of Divine Attributes, the traveller understands that knowledge, power, and all other qualities are exclusive to the Divine Essence, Glorious and Exalted. At this point he loses his own attributes and no longer sees any trace of them in himself. In the third realm, as a result of the theophany of the Divine Names, the traveller understands that it is God, the Glorious, who is the Knower and the Powerful. Here he loses his names and no longer finds them in himself. Finally, in the fourth abode, which is the realm of the theophany of Essence, the wayfarer loses his own existence and dispossesses his essence. He no longer sees himself, for the only essence that he sees is the Sacred Essence of God.

This phase of witnessing, that is, the theophany of the Essence, is referred to by gnostics as the Griffin (*'Anqā*) or (*Sīmurgh*), a mythical bird that no hunter can trap. The *Sīmurgh* is that Pure Essence and Absolute Being, which is called variously the world of Non-Being (*'ālam-i 'amā*), the Hidden Treasure (*kanz-i makhfī*), the Invisible of all invisibles (*ghayb al-ghuyūb*), and the Essence that has no name and no identity (*dhāt mā lā isma lahū wa lā rasma lahū*).

> For another bird, go and set this snare,
> for the Griffin has a nest on inaccessible heights.

It is interesting to see how well Ḥāfiẓ, may God's mercy be upon him, described this profound [metaphysical] truth in his poetry and explained it in such a powerful metaphorical fashion in the following *mathnawi*:

> Lo! Wild gazelle, tell me where you are?
> I have had with you much intimacy.
> Two lonely and friendless wanderers in wilderness
> Wild beasts and snares lying in ambush up and down the way.
> Come, let us learn each other's plight,
> And if we can, fulfil each other's dreams and wishes
> So do I remember the old sage's words,
> Which I have never forgotten:
> That once a traveller in a certain land,
> Was told in a subtle way by a wandering beggar,
> 'O traveller what is it that thou carriest in thy bag,
> Come and set a snare if thou hast any grain.'
> He replied, 'Yes I do have a net,
> But I must the Griffin hunt.'
> He said, 'How shall you find its trace,
> For it is traceless and traceless is its nest.'
> He said, 'Though it should be an impossible task,
> But despair too is a calamity.'
> That old companion did not tolerate,
> For God's sake! O Muslims! O Muslims!
> Perhaps the Khiḍr, the blessed one will help,
> For he alone can guide this lonely one to the Lonely One.

Obviously, when the Griffin's nest is traceless one cannot hope to hunt the Griffin itself, unless when His Grace becomes the guide and leads the wanderers of the abode of love and the lovers of His eternal Beauty into the realm of Unity and annihilation (*wādī-yi tawḥīd wa fanā*). For the sake of the precursors of the abode of love, the standard bearers on the path of praise and Divine Knowledge (*ḥamd wa maʿrifah*), Muhammad al-Muṣṭafā and ʿAlī al-Murtaḍā and his eleven glorious sons in the descent of the Pure, Fāṭimah al-Zahrā' – may the peace of Allāh, the Exalted Sovereign, be upon them – O God, grant success to all your lovers and to us, to attain everything which pleases You and to join us with the Righteous Ones (*ṣāliḥīn*).

Praise be to God for his generosity, this noble treatise, which has been named *Kernel of the Kernel Concerning the Wayfaring and Spiritual Journey of the People of Intellects (Risāla-yi lubb al-lubāb dar sayr wa sulūk-i ulu'l-albāb)* and which was completed by the pen of this nondescript and poor being on the eighth night of the month of fasting in the year 1369 of Hijrah (24 June 1950).

> And to Him belongs all Praise, in the World and the Hereafter.
> May our last call be *alhamduli'llah rabb al-ʿālamīn* (All Praise
> belongs to God, the Lord of this world and the next).

This nondescript and poor being is Sayyid Muhammad Ḥusayn Ḥusaynī Tihrānī, at the holy city of Qum.

Notes

[1.] Shaykh Murtaḍā Anṣārī (d. 1281/1864) was the most prominent Shīʿite scholar and the *marjaʿi taqlīd* (Supreme Source of Emulation) in the nineteenth century (d. 1281 A.H./1864). Among his many works one can cite *Farāʾiḍ al-uṣūl* (Qum: 1987), *al-Makāsib* (Tabriz: 1955), and *Ṣirāṭ al-najāt* (Tehran: lithograph edition, 1290/1873).

[2.] This is an allusion to the initiatic authority of the Hidden (twelfth) Imām, Ḥaḍrat Ḥujjat ibn Ḥasan al-ʿAsgarī (May God's greetings be upon him). It is believed that He appears from time to time to initiate certain individuals of exceptional spiritual realization, without revealing his true identity.

CHAPTER 9

A New Perspective on Mysticism and Sufism: 'Abdollah Entezam

Introduced and Translated by Matthijs van den Bos

Seyyed 'Abdollah Entezam (1274/1895–1362/1983) was born from a family which produced illustrious men of state. His brother Nasrollah became a successful diplomat. His father, Entezam as-Saltaneh, had been a director-general of the Ministry of the Interior under Reza Shah. He had also been a Sufi authority[1] who held the dervish name Binesh 'Ali Shah.[2]

'Abdollah Entezam held a position in the Foreign Ministry after 1919, worked as a diplomat in various foreign stations and at various times between 1953 and 1956 served as Iran's foreign minister and vice-premier in the 'Ala' and Zahedi cabinets. He earned a reputation for firm integrity and had been one of the few in government who had dared to refuse the Shah's demand to kiss his hand at each audience.[3]

*Between 1957 and 1963, he was the director of the National Iranian Oil Company (NIOC). Moreover, he took part in an informal gathering (*dowreh*), the participants in which were ranked among the 307 most influential Iranians.[4] But Entezam was relieved of his NIOC directorship as he fell out of favour with the Shah, who had been infuriated by the unsolicited advice of several of his elite officials, among whom was Entezam. They had been worried about the state's harsh military reaction to the June 1963 uprising – which is now enshrined in Islamic Republican historiography.*

Fifteen years later, however, in the summer of 1978, with the revolution well under way, the Shah summoned Entezam to take part in a new government. This, he refused.[5] He did from then, however, present the Shah with advice[6] and was appointed a member of the Regency Council[7] that was to represent the Shah in his absence. Revolutionary turmoil easily sidetracked the Regency Council, but Entezam was spared persecution and would remain in Tehran.

*Like his father, Entezam had belonged to the Society of Brotherhood (*Anjoman-e Okhovvat*) within the Safi 'Ali Shahi (-Ne'matollahi) Sufi order. The society represented a mixture in organisation and symbolism of Sufism and Freemasonry. Entezam was a* *member since at least the 1960s and its leader from 1974.*[8] *Both Sufism and Freemasonry, then, had profoundly influenced his life as a mystic.*

Moreover, several Iranian Freemasonry lodges connected to the United Grand Lodges of Germany had operated from the premises of the Safi 'Ali Shahis' Brotherhood Society in Tehran. Entezam had been a founding member in 1960 of one of these, the Mehr lodge, and also guided another, the Safa lodge, which had been established in 1962. Finer details of his involvement in Iranian Freemasonry, however, remain unclear.

In 1977/8 Entezam wrote a series of articles entitled 'A New Perspective on Mysticism and Sufism' (Nazari tazeh be 'erfan va tasavvof). He used the pseudonym 'I do not know' (la adri), and the articles allegedly reported the question-and-answer sessions of a Sufi master. Thus he set out on a Socratic investigation of Iranian mysticism. The essays were gathered and republished after the revolution by Vahid Publishers, under the pseudonym of 'Abdollah Azadeh (1363/1984–85).

One will search in vain for spectacularly innovative aspects of Sufi doctrine in Entezam's texts, or even thorough renderings of Sufi tradition. Nevertheless, his prose is representative of a main development in post-war, late-Pahlavi-era Sufism in which elite notions of modernity provided a thematic grid for (Islamic) spirituality.

There were Sufis such as Mohammad 'Anqa and Mas'ud Homayuni who were well positioned within elite networks, held pro-regime views implicitly or explicitly, and syncretised mysticism via the natural sciences and theosophy respectively. The Society, many of whose leaders were part of the state elite, had subjugated the traditional master–disciple structure to a modern, non-shaykhal, collective board. In the 'New Perspective', one finds impatience with thoughtless old ways and pretentious Sufi masters:

> 'Can people not be educated with [. . .] Sufism? And be shown a new way? If
> you say no, then I say: but what have you accomplished? Is your conscience put
> at rest with the construction of a few lodges [. . .]? [. . .] Dear honourable
> Elders, I have spent more than fifty years of my time on these studies.
> Furthermore, I do not have any pretension. I am a lover of the School of Sufism,
> I have great expectations for this School [. . .] Do you *really* have faith in
> Gnosis and Sufism? [emphasis mine]'.[9]

In Entezam's essays, one also finds the stress on natural, hierarchical order – which by implication was that of late-Pahlavi Iran – in addition to several other themes of Iranian elite modernity. Islam is a noticeably weak presence in Entezam's rendering of Sufism, whereas the discourse on personal morality and development is central to it.

Anything which Entezam was going to say on mysticism through his shaykh was modest, and he stressed that complacency was to be avoided: 'Our understanding of the divine sphere (lahut) is limited to the perception of its traces, not its essence [. . .] No matter how much we ascend to high stations, we will not uncover this enigma".[10] Analogically, he pointed at the impotence of philosophy, which had from Plato to existentialism come up with illusory political solutions.[11]

But the importance of Sufism, he also held, could hardly be overestimated. Although lives in the service of others were incumbent on commoners and the elite alike, he especially recommended the participation of the high dignitaries of the country, who could be brilliant moral examples for the others: 'if a minister makes simplicity his adage in his own life [. . .] then all civil servants in [his] ministry will change [as well] and be turned into abstemious and dutiful people.'¹²

The selected texts consist of a practical description of Sufi exercises, built up classically as a progression of stages of self-reformation, and one rather more abstract reflection on the significance of Sufism in the transformation of individual and society (La Adri [= 'Abdollah Entezam] 1356/1977–78c, 'the fifteenth session'; 1356/1977–78a, 'the twentieth session'). The texts comprise unity, however, in the recurring humanistic themes of 'being a free man' (azadmardi) and 'human dignity' (sharafat-e ensani).

The footnotes in the translations include my explications of a limited number of points in Entezam's texts – which, generally, are fairly lucid and self-explanatory.

Notes

I would like to express my gratitude to Mr Mohamad Karim Eshragh for having scrutinised my translations and offered valuable recommendations as to their improvement

¹· Cf. Azimi, 'Entezam', in *Encyclopaedia Iranica*, 8 (1988), p. 461.

²· See M. van den Bos, *Mystic Regimes. Sufism and the State in Iran, from the Late Qajar Era to the Islamic Republic* (Leiden: Brill, 2002).

³· Milani, *The Persian Sphinx: Amir Abbas Hoveyda and the Riddle of the Iranian Revolution* (Washington, DC: Mage Publishers, 2000), p. 115.

⁴· Zonis, *The Political Elite of Iran* (Princeton, NJ: Princeton University Press, 1971), pp. 238–9.

⁵· Wright, 'Abdullah Entezam.' *The Times*, 23 April, 1983.

⁶· Milani, *The Persian Sphinx*, pp. 290–1.

⁷· Azimi, *Entezam*.

⁸· Homayuni, *Tarikh-e selseleh-ha-ye tariqeh-ye Ne'matollahiyeh dar Iran* (London: Bonyad-e 'Erfan-e Mowlana 1371/1992), p. 327.

⁹· Azadeh, Majles-e bistom. In *Nazari tazeh be 'erfan va tasavvof* (Tehran: Entesharat-e Vahid, 1363/1984–85), pp. 114–15.

¹⁰· La Adri (b), 'Nazari tazeh be 'erfan va tasavvof. So'al-javabi beyn-e yek juyandeh va yek mard-e 'aref. Majles-e hijdahom.' *Majalleh-ye Vahid* (209) (1356/ 1977–78), p. 36.

¹¹· La Adri (d), 'Nazari tazeh be 'erfan va tasavvof. So'al-javabi beyn-e yek juyandeh va yek mard-e 'aref. Majles-e shanzdahom.' *Majalleh-ye Vahid* (207) (1356/1977–78), p. 35.

¹²· La Adri (a), 'Nazari tazeh be 'erfan va tasavvof. So'al-javabi beyn-e yek juyandeh va yek mard-e 'aref. Majles-e bistom.' *Majalleh-ye Vahid* (211/212), (1356/ 1977–78), pp. 93–4.

References and Further Reading

'Abdollah Azadeh, Majles-e bistom. In *Nazari tazeh be 'erfan va tasavvof* (Tehran: Entesharat-e Vahid, 1363/1984–85), pp. 112–15.

Fakhreddin Azimi, 'Entezam', in *Encyclopaedia Iranica* 8 (1988), pp. 461–3.

Matthijs van den Bos, *Mystic Regimes. Sufism and the State in Iran, from the Late Qajar Era to the Islamic Republic* (Leiden: Brill, 2002).

Mas'ud Homayuni, *Tarikh-e selseleh-ha-ye tariqeh-ye Ne'matollahiyeh dar Iran* (London: Bonyad-e 'Erfan-e Mowlana, 1371/1992).

La Adri (a) 'Nazari tazeh be 'erfan va tasavvof. So'al-javabi beyn-e yek juyandeh va yek mard-e 'aref. Majles-e bistom' *Majalleh-ye Vahid* (211/212) (1356/1977–78), pp. 92–5.

——(b) 'Nazari taze be 'erfan va tasavvof. So'al-javabi beyn-e yek juyandeh va yek mard-e 'aref. Majles-e hijdahom,' *Majalleh-ye Vahid* (209) (1356/1977–7), pp. 36–8.

—— (c) 'Nazari tazeh be 'erfan va tasavvof. So'al-javabi beyn-e yek juyandeh va yek mard-e 'aref. Majles-e panzdahom', *Majalleh-ye Vahid* (206) (1356/1977–78), pp. 19–24.

——(d) 'Nazari tazeh be 'erfan va tasavvof. So'al-javabi beyn-e yek juyandeh va yek mard-e 'aref. Majles-e shanzdahom', *Majalleh-ye Vahid* (207) (1356/1977–78), pp. 32–7.

Abbas Milani, *The Persian Sphinx: Amir Abbas Hoveyda and the Riddle of the Iranian Revolution* (Washington, DC: Mage Publishers, 2000).

Denis Wright, 'Abdullah Entezam', *The Times*, 23 April 1983.

Marvin Zonis, *The Political Elite of Iran* (Princeton, NJ: Princeton University Press, 1971).

—•—

The Twentieth Session

[He stated: 'Today I wish to bring to an end the cycle of our discussions and I hope that the things that I have said until now have been useful to you.'

I said: 'I am extremely sad for the fact that this congregation is ending but I have to say, just like you encouraged me, that I feel myself to be a new person as the result of the instructions and the exercises. And I hope I will progress further than this.'

He stated: 'Even in a lifetime the relations between the two of us will not be severed. But given that a chain of interconnected topics was spoken about with respect to Sufism, sooner or later we would have to end it.

If you paid attention during this turbulent period, [then you know that] I have a major longing, which is the spread of Sufism. As I have pointed out several times, I am certain that if this doctrine spreads out, in such a way that from different classes of the people a number who are worthy of consideration will come to be its followers, that they will then change our ethical manner and social thought and that gradually, a humanity will be raised in the true meaning of the Free Man [*azadmard*], bound up with human dignity [*sharafat-e ensani*], endowed with laudable ethics, and innocent of the animal vices.

Such a humanity does not fail in the accomplishment of its social duties, it is compassionate with regard to the people, ready to grant every assistance to the helpless, and self-sacrificing and altruistic with respect to those who are in jeopardy.

Dervishhood and Sufism are not laziness. In all eras of Sufism, Sufis have been men of work and in the time of jihad they have not refrained from sacrificing their lives either. This erroneous reputation that has associated dervishes with laziness is the work of a number of beggars and parasites posing as dervishes, who in order to show themselves off come forward in dervish clothes and with hairs of the moustache growing beyond the upper lip [*shareb*] and the axe [*tabar*] and the cup suspended by a chain [*kashkul*] make claims to spiritual poverty and Sufism. What do these impostors have to do with the world of Sufism? It is true that the dervish is contented in his own personal life, does not amass goods immoderately and does not render himself miserable and wretched on the road of seeking ever more voluptuousness, and rivalry. He reckons repose and peace of mind higher than these things. The delights and tranquillity which the experienced dervish probes are higher than the pleasures which become available through intoxicants, or with sensual delights, or displaying gold and jewellery. If a dervish is employed, whether specialised or common, he has recourse to the upright members of staff and personnel for the progression of work in his institution, and he establishes a healthy environment in the surrounding of his own organisation, which constitutes an example for the others.

If in a people, God forbid, corruption should be established, the repelling thereof by means of force and severity is not very effectual. We should be aware that corruption is not limited to material issues. Corruption is not limited to theft, bribe taking, collusion, or fraud. It is perjury, breaking one's promises, being unchaste, maliciously deceiving, working little, impudence, selling one's honour, being authoritarian, shortcomings in the accomplishment of duties and hundreds of other disagreeable characteristics, which will cause corruption, and if we wish to prevent these vices by means of our bearers of authority, it is likely that these authorities themselves will not be without corruption!

But if a number of persons in various stages, ranks and professions incline towards Sufism, then after a relatively short period they will constitute a people with virtue. Not only will there not remain a sign of corruption among them but they themselves may also be mentors for the deviant and lead them the way towards the Straight Path [*serat-e mostaqim*]. In the same manner, these pure Sufis would educate their own families on the path of Sufism and from that very beginning inculcate ethical principles upon them. The result would not be available very swiftly, but like a tree rooted in soil, its produce will be lasting. Great, deep-rooted works will not emerge all of a sudden and if we are hasty in the accomplishment of the job, the result will be a construction which is outwardly alluring but whose foundation is built on sand.

I presume that the state authorities would well be able to assist in the labours on this road. On condition that they would not be despondent from that very beginning. My proposal is that they teach the bases of the prolegomena of Sufism as ethics in elementary and secondary schools, with a method simpler than that which I referred to in my previous sessions. This in itself would provide the foundation for the youngsters who incline towards Sufism.

In the same manner, the Ministry of Culture and Arts and the Ministry of Education (that only in its name, presently, stands for education) could arrange programmes with the co-operation of radio and television that encourage the thought of Sufism and Mysticism (not caricaturist imitation of Mowlavi's dances). If this is accomplished with sound programmes, it will be very influential. The high dignitaries of the country themselves may serve as high moral examples for the others. By nature we are imitators, so what better thing could we do than imitate good works? If a minister makes simplicity his adage in his own life, for instance: organises no reception that would produce a par-venu appearance, doesn't visit such parties, adorns his own work office with simplicity and hundreds of other things, then all employees in that ministry will change and turn into abstemious and dutiful people. They say that it is natural for some of the captains of industry who have attained to all things from nothing as a result of work and effort, that they should wish to arrange a life full of splendour for themselves, of which prodigality, extravagance, ostentation, squandering and other things are among the necessities. I am certain that if a Sufi man would talk to such people in a brotherly fashion and explain to them that these things are worthless, and make them understand the true value of ethics and the meaning of <u>human dignity and service [*khedmat*] to God and the people</u>, that it would not then take long before a particular change in their morality would occur and they would enter a path full of delight that initially they were unaware of.

Be not pessimistic. Do not say it will not be. The test is a simple matter. Ah, unknown addressee of mine, if you are a man, begin from yourself!

These are my words to the spiritual axes [*aqtab*], elders [*pirs*] and guides [*morsheds*] of the various spiritual lineages [*selselehs*]: Are my words baseless? Can people not be educated with the propagation of Sufism? And be shown a new way? If you say no, then I say: but what have you accomplished? Is your conscience put at rest with the construction of a few lodges [*khanaqahs*], congregating, communally and repetitively reciting a poem [*dam gereftan*], and eating *dig jush*?[1] Do you know your own disciples? Do you know that among them there are hundreds who not only are not Sufis but are even worse than Khuli?[2] Do not these elements put spiritual poverty [*faqr*] and Sufism to shame? Are you assiduous of their behaviour?

Do you intend to purify them or is this crowd of people, and these numerous disciples, sufficient? Dear honourable *pir*s. I have spent more than fifty years of my time on these studies. Furthermore, I do not have any pretension. I am a lover of the school of Sufism, I have great expectations for this school. I suffer from the fact that I see this pearl is hidden in a ruin and there is no one who is after its discovery. For this reason I humbly ask of you, great men, who all claim superiority: Is your conscience clear *vis-à-vis* 'Ali, the Commander of the Faithful (*Amir al-Mo'menin*) (on whom be peace), the great Imam of all, from whose Friendship [*vela*] you breathe. Is there nothing in the bottom of your heart that makes you ashamed? If you do not desire rank and position, and you have really reached the station of Subsistence in God [*baqa'*] after Passing Away [*fana*], then the world ought not to have any value to your eyes. It is only God's creatures [*khalq-e khoda*] who are needful of help. So why do you not unite and retire into assemblies together so that you may find a way to guide the people? I do not say: All come together under the banner of one person and elect him to the leadership. Because I know man and I know that you do not possess such moral heroism and altruism. Each person controls his own disciples. But in those associations of heads, which may possibly be secret, adopt overall ways for the education of the disciple in a way so that all share the same ideal. There may be slight variations in the secondary aspects, but the foundation is one. If such a thing takes shape, then the status of Sufism and Dervishhood will rise in the public opinion and the people will understand that the dervish is not that lazy or reckless man that they imagined. This approach will also add to your own fame (in case love of position would still remain in your hearts). The due respect you command in the eyes of the people will increase. As a result of the extension of service, spiritual retribution will reach higher levels. Are you ready? Do you have the courage? Do you really have faith in Gnosis ['*erfan*] and Sufism? If your answers are affirmative, then what are you waiting for?

I will speak to you in the clearest of terms
You may take them as either advice or offence

My dear, these are my words to you once more. You have listened to my words for a long time and jotted them down. Important matters which came to my mind I told you. I tried in particular to refrain from wordiness and idle specu-lation. The issues were told in a simple and practical way that everyone could put into practice. The exercises and assignments are not hard but they require eagerness and motivation. It is not by all means necessary for a person to reach the highest of the highest degrees. Those who have reached that station are few. To the extent that a person puts his preliminaries into practice and follows that value of human dignity, he develops into a different person who both discovers a different spiritual life for himself and becomes of particular value for the preliminary education of others.

I have tried in these conversations to raise you as a school teacher of Sufism so that you would be able to teach the introductory parts to a number of persons. In case you would come to thrive in this particular sphere, then be grateful to God, because not too much use has been made of the many claimants to the Pole-ship [*qotbiyat*].

Have faith in God. The merit of someone's service will not be lost. The more you are selfless, humble, and well-mannered, to that extent you will be rewarded and make progress in your work, which is the guidance of the people. Never be a preacher who does not practise what he preaches [*wa'ez-e qeyr motta'ez*]. If you have eaten dates yourself, then do not debar the eater of dates. I beseech God for your blessing and I entrust you to the master ['Ali].'

The Fifteenth Session

He stated: 'Some gatherings back I said that the preliminary stages of the Path [*soluk*] consist of Seeking and Spiritual Struggle [*Talab o mojahedeh*], Purification of the Soul [*tazkiye*], Self-examination [*mohasebeh*], Self-vigilance (while having God before one's eyes) [*moraqebeh*], and Self-abandoning [*taqeliya*]. Regarding Seeking and Spiritual Struggle I gave sufficient explication, and Purification of the Soul and Self-examination, which comprise practical exercises, we also discussed in detail. If we had put the exercises of Purification of the Soul into practice and the Book of Self-examination confirmed that we came out successfully from the exam, then we could say that we finished the elementary school and the high school of Sufism. Self-vigilance, which is our discussion topic of today, is an introduction to the university of Sufism. At the outset I have to say that many of the seekers have wished to enter into Self-vigilance without having passed through the stage of Purification of the Soul and have not reached their goal. The reason therefore also lies in the fact that in order for Purification of the Soul to render a result, as I explained in detail, first the mirror of the heart must be polished and cleaned so that it becomes possible for its images to be reflected clearly. If this mirror had not at all seen polish, then an image would not be reflected in it. And if it would be cleansed improperly, then the image which it reflects is dim or distorted, or in another simile, like photography equipment which has no sensitive film inside. Even though our camera would be perfect, it would then be incapable of making photographs, and if its film would be broken, then the photo which it takes would be dark and defective.

They have written a lot about the Self-vigilance of the Gnostics [*orafa'*] and the accounts of some are in conflict with the accounts of others. Sometimes they have even allocated Remembrance of God and Reflection [*zekr o fekr*] within [the stage of] Self-vigilance. As I promised at the outset, I refrain from phraseology, prolongations and detailed expositions and I try to explain the matter in as clear a way as possible, even where this procedure comes under criticism. One of the simplest narratives is where they say that <u>Self-vigilance is the guarding of the heart</u>. It is a very simple and appealing account, but which is its way of action? Then again they bring up the tale in which Junayd (God's mercy upon him)[3] states that he learned Self-vigilance from a cat who was lying in ambush for a mouse and was so absorbed in thinking about the mouse that not a hair fell from him. This is all very well, but since we are not mice, what are we to do? I say Self-vigilance is in the first degree concentration of the senses on a unique object, and in the second degree the complete eradication of the senses from the brain. In speaking, these two stages are very simple but in practice they are very difficult. The matter of Self-vigilance has been focused on in all mysticisms of the world, whether in Islam, or the Jewish, the Christian, the Buddhist, or Chinese and so forth varieties, and they have given it various names. In our days, new schools have also been founded in this field, and they have gathered followers as well. I want to make use of some of these methods in the exercise of Self-vigilance and to the extent possible render this Way easier.'

I said: 'Will turning to methods outside of our own Sufism not lead us astray?'

He said: 'We cook our own soup. Besides, they used to cook soup in a pot and on a hearth with firewood in the old days, whereas nowadays, we want to cook that soup on gas or electricity. The soup is that very same old soup of ours. But with the new means, it is possible to cook it faster and better.

The aim of Self-vigilance is concentration. The Sufi tries to concentrate his mind on one object. If we position a lens before the sun and place an inflammable substance in the focal point of the lens, then as a result of the concentration of rays of sunlight in the centre, heat is brought together in such a way that it inflames that inflammable substance. If, in the same way, we concentrate our thinking on one subject, then its power increases many times more.

As I said, Self-vigilance is a very difficult matter. It requires consistency, firmness of purpose, and persistency. These exercises are relatively easier for some and harder for others. In strengthening their disciples, sheikhs encourage them in the endurance of the *zekr* that they have taken. And if there would also be other ordinations, then these are verbal. No clear path has been indicated in the books of Sufism. Unfortunately, it is only a very small number of those who go on with the *zekr* these days, that have really attained to the station of Witnessing and Disclosure [*shohud va mokashefeh*]. One of the reasons for the inadequacy, to my mind, is that disciples have not done their utmost with respect to Purification of the soul and have not rendered themselves prepared for Self-vigilance. In addition, the instruction with respect to *zekr* has not been adequate. I believe that the method which I propose as a result of the experiences which I have obtained through long years, is both practical and in all probability will lead to result.

In order to commence Self-vigilance, both the body and the spirit must be prepared for the job. Because for Self-vigilance it is necessary that all limbs and organs and nerves and thinking and imagination be under control, and not a single distraction is to occur, or else this would cause the dissolution of the mind and the non-focus of the senses.

For this reason and in order for the terms of the exercise to be clear, we divide it into stages. We must become deft and ready during each stage and then involve ourselves in the next stage. Not following this way will cause the scattering of the work, the exercise to become difficult, and in the end, not reaching the goal. The first stage is the control of the limbs, the second stage is concentration of the mind and the third stage, which is the most difficult one, is emptying the brain of all kinds of reflection, which they call Self-abandoning [*takheliya*].

1. In the first place, one has to bring all one's muscles in a state of repose, in order for the body and the spirit of man to become ready for Self-vigilance, and in such a way that none of them is in a state of flexing and tension. Approximately like in the state in which man is asleep. (On condition that various dreams did not turn around the dormant person.) This is not a very difficult task; it only takes some practice. In the beginning we start out with the hand and the arm. We cause our fingers to be in a state of total relaxation, in such a way that when a person touches our fingers, the spot must have only lifeless fibres. In the same way we "loosen" the muscles of the wrist and the elbow and the forearm, so that when a person would raise and then drop our hand and arm, these would fall down besides us with their own natural weight, like a hand which had been fabricated out of cotton and in which there would be no sign of resistance. We carry on this exercise until we can bring our two hands and arms in a state of complete relaxation. Then we bring this about with the feet and the foreleg and thigh. That is, we sit on a chair and suspend our feet as if there were no life in them. Then we do the same thing to the muscles of the stomach and the chest. Naturally, we cannot completely bring our chest muscles to a rest and in a state without tension, because we breathe. But one has to try to breathe in a regular and tranquil way, and then to relax the muscles in the neck and the head. No sense of traction and tension must remain in the neck. The jaws must be in a state of complete relaxation, meaning: the teeth must on no account press upon one another. The eyelids, whether closed or open, must also be tranquil. After obtaining success in this stage, so that we could volitionally and instantaneously bring the muscles of the body in a state of relaxation, we engage in the next exercise.

2. We sit in a state of relaxation on a chair or in the tailor's seat on the floor. This task may possibly be accomplished by stretching out on a bed as well, but as we could enter into a state of sleep while relaxing the muscles, it is better to carry it out it while seated. This workout must be realised in a surrounding of seclusion, without noise, and in solitude.

3. After we sit down on a chair or on the floor, we render all muscles in a state of relaxation in the way that we have previously exercised. That is, we start from the feet until it reaches the muscles of the head and the neck.

4. In this state we close our eyes and take a deep regular breath from our nose. Not to such an extent that this leads to the distraction of the senses.

5. In this state we try, to the extent possible, to prevent the distraction of the senses.

6. We keep up this state for about ten minutes. If we would get weary in the beginning, it would be better to breach the work, because continuing it in a state of being tired prevents the concentration of the senses.

7. After we advance in this part, we start with the second stage, which has the nature of Meditation/Remembrance of God [*zekr*]. Again we sit on a chair or on the floor in a secluded surrounding, we bring our muscles in a state of relaxation, we close our eyes and we co-ordinate our breathing with the invocation of <u>*Ya Hu!*</u>. This is to say, when we inhale our breath we say <u>*Ya!*</u>; when we exhale our breath we say <u>*Hu!*</u>. This "rhythm" of the breath causes our thinking to be aware of the <u>*Ya Hu!*</u> meditation and prevents the distraction of the senses.

8. We maintain this exercise for ten to twenty minutes. Thereafter we open our eyes and relax for some minutes.

This state of relaxation and concentration is not yielded quickly, but one should not become disappointed. One needs to pursue the exercise and if the spirits get dissipated, one should not assign importance to it. With persistence we are going to progress and gradually we will accomplish the concentration of the senses.

These days, the bases of this method of the relaxation of the muscles and the nerves are pursued from a scientific point of view in the world, and we also make use of it, because it is completely compatible with Sufism's introductory method of Self-vigilance.

In some medical centres they have experimented with this method and reached conclusions which concern only the viewpoint of bodily health. It has been useful for persons with high blood pressure and those who suffer from muscle tensions or mental anxiety. The soothing of the nerves and getting rest are very useful for people who are distressed in this world. But from a spiritual point of view, the results obtained have been diverse. In some states ecstasy [*khalsa*] occurred, in some others rejoicing [*neshat*] and mirth [*farah*], and generally speaking, people have enjoyed a special relaxation. But for us who look at that from the point of view of Sufism, like I said, this Self-vigilance would bring about the desired result some time after we traverse the state of <u>Purification</u>. Obviously, a person who has not been liberated of the vices of the lower soul [*raza'el-e nafsani*] and has not gone through the stages of ethical virtues [*marateb-e faza'el-e akhlaqi*] cannot attain to that relaxation and repose which are essential to Self-vigilance. The superiority of our method lies in the combination of the foundations and introductions of Sufism on the one hand and this state of relaxation of the muscles on the other, which causes success in the exercise of Self-vigilance.

But when these exercises should be accomplished is dependent on the situation of the persons in question. In my opinion, the best time is early in the morning. But after this exercise becomes second nature to us and we are able to relax the muscles any time we wish, we could do the exercise each time of the day when we have the opportunity for some minutes. Some imagine that the results will increase if they elongate the exercise. This is a mistake, because if we tire ourselves as a result of over-indulgence and become susceptible as a natural result, then in short it may be possible for that state to get transformed into a delirium and some state of melancholia. This is very detrimental and leads us astray from the desired path. Here also, one must not let go of <u>Temperance</u> [*e'tedal*].

But the third stage is the last stage. After advancing ourselves on this path, we get to a place where, with the continuation of the *Ya Hu!* invocation, our senses become perfectly aware of this meditation, and the distraction of the senses becomes less. That is the time when little by little we may get expectations of this vigilance. In the beginning, we express this *Ya Hu!* invocation, and it is even useful to render present the word *Ya Hu!* before our eyes in the imaginal world and to unify it with the uttering of the Remembrance of God, so that it contributes further to the advancement of our goal. But gradually we get to a place where we speak the Remembrance of God in our heart and it doesn't require to be spoken in language any more. If we would progress from even here, we would get to a place where we would submerge into ourselves in such a way that there is no further necessity for Remembrance of God. This is the beginning of <u>Self-abandoning</u>, and Self-abandoning is one of the most difficult exercises for the Sufi. Self-abandoning is removing all thoughts from our brain in the moment of Self-vigilance and opening the door for entrances. If we would, in the way that I described earlier, have reached a stage in prayer [*namaz*] where we voice each word with the presence of the heart, then we make use of that in our exercise of today.

For Self-abandoning after Self-vigilance and the utterance of the Remembrance of God, we attempt, slowly, to remove all thought from the head, even the thought of Remembrance of God, and to think of nothing. If we would succeed, in the beginning, to do this for half a minute, then this would inspire hope. Gradually, we must try to elongate this duration. If one day we would be able to perform Self-abandoning for five minutes, then we may claim to have reached some place. One of the ways that aids Self-abandoning is realising before us, when we have closed our eyes, a dark crater which has no close, and directing our thought to that darkness. For the Sufi, Self-vigilance and Self-abandoning have material results which may be his incentive for further progress. For instance, if there is a difficulty in your life, lying ahead of you, which you find hard to resolve, then resort to God and enter into the state of Self-vigilance. Mostly, it happens that a solution becomes manifest to you in the shape of spiritual insight. Needless to remind, this aspiration and wish must not in the least be contrary to the Shari'a and the Spiritual Way [*tariqeh*]. It is possible for those who advance in Self-vigilance and Self-abandoning after attaining quietude of the heart [*sakineh-ye qalbi*], which is the wish of every Sufi, that divine love contracts friendship with them and divine contingencies [*varedat*] happen to them which are beyond words. This is the gate of Disclosure [*mokashefeh*] and Epiphany [*tajalli*].

Like I said from the beginning, I was thinking of teaching preliminaries and elementary and secondary school courses of Sufism. I believe that I have fulfilled this commitment so far, and that we are now on the threshold of the university of Sufism. Further progress requires a *pir* who, from this point onward and step by step, guides the disciple forwards and watches over his manners and demeanour. The *pir* shows him a way out of the well and guides the disciple to the extent that he himself is gifted. God passes on the hand of the seekers to such an authority.

Now let us imagine that you have not yet been able, presently, to acquire such ways. Come and take account of yourself and pass judgement impartially. Have you not become a different human being while going through the preliminaries? Are you not a human being who, through tranquillity of the spirit and the acquisition of moral virtues and quietude of the heart, has probed the meaning of human dignity [*sharafat-e ensani*] and of being a Free Man [*azadmardi*]? Do you believe that you could guide a number of others along this road? Have these blessings been worth their trouble? The judgement lies with yourself.

In this session, I bring the teachings to a close. During future discourses, I will address the work of Gnostics on the Spiritual Journey [*seyr o soluk*] and what they generally have said, and occasionally, I will also criticise their method.

My discussions in the future will have more of the character of a condensed programme in the university of Sufism, not the teaching of its lessons.'

Notes

[1.] *Dig jush* is a ritually prepared Sufi meal that usually involves lamb and often accompanies the admission of new dervishes (cf. Richard Gramlich, *Die schiitischen Derwischorden Persiens. 3: Brauchtum und Riten.* Marburg, Wiesbaden: Deutsche Morgenländische Gesellschaft, 1981; Kommissionsverlag Franz Steiner, *Abhandlungen für die Kunde des Morgenlandes*, 45 (2), pp. 49–51).

[2.] Khuli b. Yazid Asbahi took part in the battle against Imam Hosayn at Karbala in 680 and took his severed head to Kufa's governor Ibn Ziyad. Shi'-ite historiography represents him as a throughly abject person.

3. Abu 'l-Qasim al-Junayd of Baghdad (d. 910) was one of Islam's most famous and 'respectable' Sufis, best known for his doctrine of the ultimate stage of 'survival' as equivalent to 'sobriety' (see Julian Baldick, *Mystical Islam. An Introduction to Sufism.* (New York: New York University Press, 1989, pp. 44–6).

CHAPTER 10

The Outline of a Disease[1]

Jalal Al-e Ahmad

In 1941 British and Soviet troops entered Iran, fearing that the Nazis might gain a stronghold in the region. Reza Shah was forced to abdicate, and his young son, Mohammad Reza, became the new monarch. For a period, the Iranian political atmosphere was cleansed and political parties could draw fresh breath, and so towards the end of 1941 the socialist Tudeh Party (1941) was created, and it grew quickly and was popular especially in the north and among trade unions. However, the appeal of the Tudeh Party suffered because of the movement for autonomy in Azarbayjan in 1945 which was led by socialists, some of whom had spent time in the Soviet Union. Moreover, its fortunes were also detrimentally affected by the Soviet demand for a concession for oil in the north of the country.

Another major political movement during this post-war period was the nationalist group led by Mohammad Mosaddeq (an elderly politician who had been elected to the Parliament prior to the establishment of the Pahlavi dynasty). In 1951 he became the Iranian premier, leading a nationalist coalition named the National Front. Mosaddeq had gained in popularity because of his opposition to the Anglo-Iranian Oil Company (which enjoyed the rights to exploit Iranian oil); in particular, he voiced the common resentment that the AIOC's profits far exceeded the royalties that it paid to Iran. He was committed to the nationalisation of Iranian oil, a policy which was ratified by the Parliament in April 1951. The British were reluctant to lose Iranian oil without a fight, and the Americans feared that the Tudeh Party would usurp Mosaddeq and lead Iran into the Soviet camp. In 1953 Mosaddeq fell from power in a coup that was engineered by the USA, Britain, and which also enjoyed the support of the Shah, the clerics and merchants. Following the fall of Mosaddeq, the Shah began to assert himself within the political domain, acting increasingly like his dictatorial father, banning all forms of genuine political opposition (notably the Tudeh Party), developing close links with the United States, belittling Islam and promoting an Iranian identity which leaned heavily on its pre-Islamic heritage.

Jalal Al-e Ahmad was born in 1923 into a religious family. As a teenager, he was attracted to the ideas of Ahmad Kasravi[2] but in 1943 was sent to Najaf by his father to *become a cleric. However, he decided not to follow this path, and after a few months he returned to Tehran and pursued a more secular education, and was soon to join the Tudeh Party. However, he withdrew from the party, perhaps as a result of the policies of the Soviet Union regarding its attempts to secure an oil concession in the north of Iran, and also Soviet support for the independence movement in Azarbayjan. In any case, Al-e Ahmad returned to the political scene in co-forming the Iran Toiler's Party, and later the Third Force. However, the 1953 coup in which Mosaddeq was removed from power disillusioned Al-e Ahmad who thenceforth concentrated more on literary activities, although his writings were deeply political.*

His most famous work is entitled Gharbzadegi *(a term which is difficult to render into English, and has been translated as Weststruckness, Westoxication, Plagued by the West, Westamination and others). It was a report that he had prepared for the Ministry of Education which decided that it could not be published because of its strongly critical appraisal of the Pahlavi regime. Nevertheless, Al-e Ahmad published the work privately, and soon it achieved widespread appeal among students and Iranian intellectuals. As Dabashi observed, 'Westoxication was read and discussed in high schools and universities as the first bibliographical item on a hidden syllabus with which the Iranian youth of the 1960s came to political consciousness. You were accepted into cliques of political activists by virtue of your ability to quote passages from the text verbatim.'*[3]

This work of some 180 pages in English translation identifies the political and socio-economic ills of Iran as originating in the dominance of machines that were produced in the West which subsequently resulted in the West's hegemonic political and cultural power over Iran, and the internal confusion that this new technology produced (including urbanisation, conflicts between old ways and new, consumption patterns, lifestyles and values, etc). Al-e Ahmad was severely critical of several elites in Iranian society. One such group was made up of the clerics who remained quiescent despite the onslaught of the West, and preferred to concentrate on matters of ritual purity and piety, or else on superstitious matters.[4] *One particular exception was Shaykh Fazl Allah Nuri, who Al-e Ahmad describes as a champion who tried to resist* Gharbzadegi: *'To me, the corpse of that great man hanging on the gallows is like a flag they raised over this country after two hundred years to symbolise the ascendency of* Gharbzadegi.'[5] *He was also critical of Sufism, in particular the Sufism that emerged from the Safavid period onwards ('. . . we descended into the cocoon of Safavid Sufism . . .')*[6] *and tended towards isolation rather than engaging in promoting the interests of Iran.*[7]

The intellectuals who had internalised Gharbzadegi *were also criticised heavily because such individuals contributed the spine of Iran's schools and universities. They were subservient to the West's own intellectual legacy and were keen to show such knowledge by citing the works of Western scholars rather than those of Iranians.*

The government is also criticised for promoting the interests of the Western governments and its capitalists. He despaired of any remedy for Gharbzadegi: *'[The government is] . . . self-interested because there's no refuge from it, no hope, no freedom, and no rights.'*[8] *Interestingly he applauds the government's attempt at 'granting freedom to women' (which is one of the requirements of* Gharbzadegi – *to encourage women to become workers outside of the home and generate income in order to take up the surplus production). However, Al-e Ahmad chastises the government for 'feigning liberation of women' by merely removing veils and not permitting them real social and economic rights.*[9]

Al-e Ahmad's Gharbzadegi *is perhaps the best text from an Iranian that manifests the evils of dependency of a Third Country on the West. It also serves as a fine example of nativism, which has been defined as 'the doctrine that calls for the resurgence, reinstatement or continuance of native or indigenous cultural customs, beliefs and values'.*[10] *Yet Al-e Ahmad's* Gharbzadegi *falls into the trap so often found in nativist works, namely, in responding to an essentialised version of their own culture and religion (usually posited by colonial or post-colonial powers), nativists re-act by producing a chariacature of the civilisation, culture and world view of their opponents. For example, Al-e Ahmad says little positive about the West,*[11] *and castigates it for its promotion of the machine, despite the hardships that technology causes. This is despite the fact that technology and machines most probably provided some workers a great deal of relief in their working lives. Moreover, Al-e Ahmad offered little that was positive in terms of a vision of a future Iran that had somehow loosened the noose of* Gharbzadegi. *In essence, the text focused upon the evils of the West and a description of those who supported its policies. Of major significance, however, were his references to an 'authentic' Iran, which was based upon Islam and Shi'-ism, and his remarks about the potential power of this Islam during the Constitutional Revolution are worth citing here because they were applicable also to his own era during the 1960s (for as he comments,'ninety per cent of the people in this country live by religious values and criteria'):*[12] *'If the clerical establishment had realised – with the belief that it isn't necessary to obey leaders – what a precious jewel lay hidden in the hearts of our people, like a seed for any uprising against a government of oppressors and the corrupt.'*[13]

Notes

[1] From *Gharbzadegi* [Weststruckness]. Translated from the Persian by John Green and Ahmad Alizadeh (Costa Mesa: Mazda Publishers, 1997), pp. 11–23.

[2] Dabashi (see below), pp. 45–6.

[3] Ibid., 76.

[4] Ibid., p. 84.

[5] *Weststruckness*, p. 59.

[6] Ibid., p. 44.

[7] Ibid., p. 57.

[8] Ibid., p. 134.

[9] Ibid., p. 80.

[10] Boroujerdi (see below), p. 14.

[11] Al-e Ahmad does indeed note that some in the West perceive that their civilisation is in a crisis (typified by Camus and Ingmar Bergman) (p. 185), and some Western intellectuals are turning to the East's criteria in culture, art and

literature, and gradually to the East's criteria in politics. He comments that such attention to Eastern politics is a requirement for an escape from machinestruckness (p. 185).

12. *Gharbzadegi*, p. 81.

13. Ibid., p. 61.

Further Reading

Jalal Ale-Ahmad, *Gharbzadegi*, translated from the Persian by John Green and Ahmad Alizadeh (Costa Mesa: Mazda Publishers, 1997).

Hamid Dabashi, *Theology of Discontent* (New York: New York University Press, 1993), Chapter 1 (pp. 39–191), 'Jalal Al-e Ahmad: The Dawn of Islamic Ideology'.

Mehrzad Boroujerdi, *Iranian Intellectuals and the West* (Utica, NY: Syracuse University Press, 1996), Chapter 3 (pp. 52–76), 'The Other-ing of the West'.

꘎

[I say that *Gharbzadegi* [Weststruckness][1] is like cholera. If this seems distasteful, I could say it's like heatstroke or frostbite. But no. It's at least as bad as sawflies in the wheat fields. Have you ever seen how they infest wheat? From within. There's a healthy skin in place, but it's only a skin, just like the shell of a cicada on a tree. In any case, we're talking about a disease. A disease that comes from without, fostered in an environment made for breeding diseases. Let's look for the characteristics of this disease, its cause or causes, and if possible, a cure.

This *Gharbzadegi* has two heads. One is the West, the other is ourselves who are Weststruck. By ourselves, I mean a part of the East. Rather than two heads, let's say two poles, or two extremities, because we're talking about two ends of a single continuum, at least, if not two sides, of the world. Instead of the west, let's say to a certain extent all of Europe and Soviet Russia and all of North America, or let's say the advanced countries, or the developed countries, or the industrialised nations, or any country able to bring raw materials to a state of refinement with the aid of machines and put them on the market as merchandise. These raw materials are not only iron ore, petroleum, gut, cotton, or gum tragacanth. There's also mythology. There are also belief systems. There's also music. There are also celestial worlds. Instead of ourselves, who are part of the other pole, we can say Asia, Africa, or the underdeveloped countries, or developing countries, or non-industrialised nations, or that group of countries who are consumers of products manufactured in the West, products whose raw materials – the very ones I listed – come from that same part of the world, meaning from countries in the process of growing. Petroleum from the shores of the

Persian Gulf, jute and spices from India, African jazz, silk and opium from China, anthropology from the South Sea Islands, and sociology from Africa. These last two come from South America too, from the Aztec and Inca tribes, who were totally victimised by the advent of Christianity. Yes, everything comes from somewhere, and we're in the middle. With these latter groups our points of commonality are more numerous than our differences.

It's not within the scope of the present work to define these two poles or extremities from the point of view of economics, politics, sociology, psychology, or civilisation. Those are exacting tasks for specialists. You will see, however, that I will be compelled from time to time to make use of all of these disciplines. The only thing left to say here is that in my view, East and West are no longer two geographical concepts as such. To a European or an American, the West means Europe and America and the East means Soviet Russia, China, and the Eastern European countries. To me, however, West and East have neither a political nor a geographical meaning. Instead, these are two economic concepts. The West means the countries with full stomachs, and the East means the ones that are hungry. To me the Union of South Africa is a little piece of the West too, even though it's at the southernmost extreme of Africa, and most of the Latin American nations are part of the East, although they're on the other side of the globe.

In any case it's true that to measure an earthquake one must consult the university's seismograph, but before the seismograph records anything the villager's horse, even though he's balky and stupid, has fled and taken refuge in the desert. Yes, this writer would like to sense, with a sharper nose than a sheepdog, and with sharper eyes than a crow, those things that others have passed over deliberately, or the presentation of which has appeared to offer no advantage to livelihood or welfare in the next world.

Let me list, therefore, the collective general characteristics of the countries in the first group: high wages, low mortality rates, low birth rates, well-organised social services, adequate nutrition (at least 3,000 calories a day), annual per capita income of more than 3,000 tumans [$430] per year, and a democratic façade inherited from the French Revolution.

The corresponding characteristics of the second group are these: low wages, high mortality rates, higher birth rates, no social services, or merely the pretence of social services, poor nutrition (1,000 calories a day at most), annual per capita income of less than 500 tumans [$75] per year, no concept of democracy, and a legacy of colonisation since its earliest days. We're obviously in the second group, the group of hungry nations, the first group being all the nations with full stomachs, as Josue de Castro[2] puts it in his The Geography of Hunger. You see that not only is the gap between the two extremities very wide, but, as Tibor Mende said, 'It is a bottomless pit that gets deeper and deeper every day.' Thus wealth and poverty, power and impotence, knowledge and ignorance, prosperity and desolation, and civilisation and savagery have become polarised in the world.

One pole is controlled by the satiated, the rich and powerful and the makers and exporters of manufactured goods, the other by the hungry, the poor and the weak, the consumers and importers. The heartbeat of evolution on that side of the world is progressive, while the stagnant pulse on this side is on the verge of stopping. This disparity does not simply arise because of the separation in space and time, nor is it quantifiable. It's a qualitative disparity between two widely separated and mutually repellent poles. On the other side is a world that has become frightened of its own dynamism, and on our side is a world that has not yet found a channel of leadership for its scattered movements, which dissipate instead into nothing. Each of these two worlds is looking for something in its own way.[3]

So the time is now past when we divided the world into two 'blocs', the two blocs of East and West, or communist and non-communist. Although the first articles of most of the constitutions of the governments of the world still contain that huge twentieth-century sham, the flirtation between the United States and Soviet Russia (the two supposedly unrivalled leaders of those blocs) over the Suez Canal and Cuba showed how the owners of two neighbouring villages can sit down together comfortably at the same table, and following that the nuclear test ban treaty and other instances. Therefore our time, besides no longer being a time of confrontation between the rich and poor classes inside borders, or a time of nationalist revolutions, is also not a time of confrontation between 'isms' and ideologies. Behind the scenes at every riot, *coup d'état*, or uprising in Zanzibar, Syria, or Uruguay, one must look to see what plot by what colonialist company or government backing it, lies hidden. Furthermore, regional wars of our time can no longer be called wars between differing ideas – even superficially. These days any schoolchild not only sees the expansionist aims of mechanised industry on both sides of the dispute at work behind the scenes in the Second World War, but also sees that the things that were happening in Cuba, the Congo, the Suez Canal, and Algeria were disputes over sugar, diamonds, and oil. The bloodshed in Cyprus, Zanzibar, Aden, and Vietnam was for achieving a bridgehead to protect trade routes, which are the first determinant of the policy of governments.

Our time is no longer a time when they scare the people with 'communism' in the 'West' and with the bourgeoisie and liberalism in the 'East'. Now even the kings of nations can be superficial revolutionaries and speak charismatically, and Khruschev can buy wheat from America. Now all these 'isms' and ideologies have become pathways to the exalted throne of 'machinism' and machines. The most interesting development in this regard is the deviation taken by the political compasses of leftists and leftist pretenders throughout the world in their turn towards the East. They have made a ninety-degree turn from Moscow to Peking, because Russia is no longer 'the leader of the world revolution'. Rather it is a top contender in the circle of those who possess atomic missiles. A direct telegraph line operates between the Kremlin in Moscow and the White House in Washington, showing that there is no longer even the need for British mediation in these dealings. Even those who hold the reins of power in our country have realised that the danger of Soviet Russia has diminished. The pasture Soviet Russia was grazing in was the abominable spoils of the First World War. The time has come to phase out Stalin, and Radio Moscow has come out backing the referendum of the sixth of Bahman![4] In any case Communist China has taken Soviet Russia's place. Why? Because it is calling all the world's underfed people to unite in the hope of reaching paradise tomorrow, just as Russia did in 1930. If Russia had a population of some 100 million then, China now has a population of 750 million.

It's true, as Marx said, that we now have two worlds in dispute, but these two worlds have become somewhat more extensive since his time, and that dispute has much more complicated characteristics than a dispute between workers and management. Our world is a world of confrontation between the poor and the rich in a worldwide arena. Our time is a time of two worlds. One is on the side of manufacturing, distributing, and exporting machines; the other is on the side of using, wearing out, and dismantling them. One is a producer, the other a consumer. And where is the arena of this conflict? The world market. And its weapons? Besides tanks, artillery, bombers, and missile-launchers, themselves the manufactures of that Western world, there is UNESCO [United Nations Educational, Scientific and Cultural Organisation], FAO [United Nations Food and Agriculture Organisation], the United Nations, ECAFE [United Nations Economic Commission for Asia and the Far East], and other so-called international institutions that seem to be international and universal, but the truth of the matter is that they're Western tricksters who bring colonialism to that second world in a new suit, to South America, to Asia, to Africa. And this is where the basis of the *Gharbzadegi* of all non-Western nations lies. This is not a discussion about rejecting or refusing machines, as the utopians[5] imagined in the early nineteenth century. Not at all. The inundation of the world by machines is a historical inevitability. It's a discussion about the nature of our encounter with machines – as a growing nation, and we already saw the people of the nations in the second group – and about the fact that we don't make machines, but because of economic and political necessity – and that international confrontation between rich and poor – we must be docile and humble consumers of Western products, or at best must be poorly paid, contented, and submissive repairmen for whatever comes from the West.

These things, of themselves, make it necessary for us to adapt ourselves, our government, our culture, and our daily lives to the pattern of machines. Everything must conform to the specifications of machines. If those who manufacture machines, in the wake of the gradual changes of two to three hundred years, have gradually become accustomed to this new God and its heaven and hell, what does the Kuwaiti say, who just got his machine yesterday, or the Congolese, or what about me, the Iranian? How are we going to jump out of this three-hundred-year historical pit? Forget about other people. Let me deal with directly with us. The basic thesis of this short essay is that we've not been able to retain our own cultural/historical personality during our encounter with machines and in the face of their inevitable assault. In fact, we've been destroyed.[6] The point is that we've been unable to take a calculated and well-assessed position in the face of this monster of the new century, not even to the extent that Japan has done. The point is that as long as we don't perceive the nature and philosophical basis of Western culture, and continue to behave as Westerners superficially, we'll be like the donkey who posed as a lion and ended up being eaten by one. If the one who builds machines is now screaming and suffocating, we don't even complain about having become slaves to machines. We even brag about it. For two hundred years we've been like a crow who tries to be a partridge (if we can be sure which is the crow and which is the partridge).

An obvious principle emerges from all this. It's obvious that as long as we only use machines and don't make them, we're Weststruck. Ironically, as soon as we start building machines we'll be afflicted by them, like the West, which is now suffering from the effects of runaway technology.[7]

Never mind that we didn't even have the capability Japan has, which undertook to understand machines one hundred years ago, made itself a competitor with the West in its affliction with machines, defeated the Tsars (1905) and America (1941), and took their markets away from them before that. The West ended up smashing them with the atomic bomb to teach them the consequences of playing with fire, and now too that the western 'free world' has opened the world's vast markets to Japanese goods, it's because they have invested in all the Japanese industries. They also intend to recover the military costs of protecting those islands, whose leaders, having come to their senses since the Second World War, are now totally inept where weaponry, armies, and militarism are concerned. And perhaps it's also because the simple American wants to ease the burden of conscience that made a madman of that abominable bomber[8] pilot who repeated the story of Ad and Thamud[9], at Hiroshima and Nagasaki.

Something else is obvious to us as well, and that is that since the time the 'West' called us – from the Eastern shores of the Mediterranean to India – the 'East' as it arose from its hibernation of the Dark Ages seeking the sunlight, and spices, silk, and other goods, they've been coming to the East, first as pilgrims to the holy shrines (to Bethlehem, Nazareth, and so on), then in the armour of the Crusades, then in the guise of tradesmen, then under the protection of their treasure-laden warships, then as Christian missionaries, and finally in the name of promoting civilisation. This last one was a veritable celestial mission. After all, 'colonisation' draws its roots from 'development', and whoever engages in 'development' inevitably takes part in civilisation.

It's interesting that among those countries who were beneath the heel of the colonialist vanguard, Africa was the most receptive and promising, and do you know why it was more promising? Because besides the raw materials it had (and abundant they were: gold, diamonds, copper, ivory, and many other raw materials), its natives walked in no urban tradition or widespread religion. Every tribe had its own god, chief, customs, and language. And so scattered! And inevitably, so receptive to authority! Most important of all, all its natives went around naked. It was too hot to wear clothes. They celebrated and prayed in Manchester when Stanley, a world traveller in the tradition of the English humanitarian, brought this good news back to his country from the Congo. After all, a metre of cloth every year for every man and woman of the Congo to put on, become 'civilised', and wear to Sunday services would equal 320 million yards of Manchester cloth every year.[10] We know that the colonialist vanguard included Christian missionaries, and that they built churches in the vicinity of every merchant throughout the world and, by means of subtle trickery, persuaded the native people to attend them. And now, with the removal of the feast of colonialism from those areas, for every commercial outlet that closes, a church door closes too.

Africa was also more promising and receptive for those gentlemen because the African natives were raw material themselves for the use of all kinds of Western laboratories in the development of the fields of anthropology, sociology, ethnology, linguistics, and a thousand other kinds of 'ologies' based on the background of African and Australian experience, enabling the professors of Cambridge, the Sorbonne, and Leiden to become established in their chairs using these same 'ologies', and to see the other side of their own urban civilisation in African primitivity.

We Middle Easterners were neither so receptive nor so promising. Why? Because if we want to speak more personally, that is, to speak of ourselves, we must ask why weren't we Muslim Easterners more receptive? You can see that the answer is embedded in the very question, for within our Islamic totality we apparently weren't worth studying.

It was for this reason that the West, in its encounter with us, not only came into conflict with our Islamic totality (in the instances of the bloody encouragement of Shi'ism at the beginning of the Safavid dynasty, the sowing of conflict between us and the Ottomans, the encouragement of the Baha'i movement in the middle of the Qajar dynasty, the parcelling of the Ottoman Empire after the First World War, and finally in confrontation with the Shi'i clergy in the disturbances of the Constitutional Revolution and afterwards), but it also tried to disrupt that fragmented totality, which was only a totality in appearance, from within as quickly as possible. They also tried to make us into raw material like the African natives, and then to take us to their laboratories. This is why the *Encyclopaedia of Islam* is at the top of the list of Western encyclopaedias. We ourselves are still asleep, but the Westerner has taken us to his laboratory in this encyclopaedia.

India, after all, was a place something like Africa, with that 'Babel' of tongues and the dispersion of races and sects. And South America had instantly turned Christian at the points of the Spaniards' swords. And the Pacific was itself an archipelago of islands, which is to say the ideal setting for sowing discord. Thus, in appearance and in the reality of the Islamic totality, we were the only barrier to the spread (colonialism = Christianity) of European civilisation, meaning to Western industry's search for markets.

The Ottoman artillery that stopped at the gates of Vienna was the end of a process that had begun in 732 A.D. in Andalusia.[11] What do we call this twelve-century period of conflict and rivalry between East and West if we don't call it a conflict between Islam and Christianity? In any case, now – in this age we're living in – I as an Asian descendant of that Islamic totality, and that African or Australian descendant of savagery and primitivity – both equally and to the same extent – are perfectly welcome from the standpoint of the civilised nations(!) of the West and the machine builders to content ourselves with being museum exhibits, to remain simply something worth studying in a museum or a laboratory and nothing more. Don't you dare tamper with this raw material!

Now it's no longer a matter of their wanting the petroleum from Khuzestan or Qatar in unrefined form, the diamonds from Katanga in the rough, or the chromite from Kerman unsmelted. What matters now is that I, as an Asian or an African, must even preserve my literature, my culture, my music, my religion, and everything else I have in perfect condition just like an artifact right out of the ground, so that these gentlemen can come and gawk, and take it to their museums and say, 'Oh yes, here's another form of primitivity!'[12]

Now, after this introduction, allow me, an Easterner with his feet planted firmly in tradition, eager to make a two- or three-hundred-year leap and obliged to make up for so much anxiety and straggling, and sitting in the middle of that fragmented Islamic totality, to offer the following definition of *Gharbzadegi*.

[It is] all the symptoms that have been created in the life, culture, civilisation, and manner of thinking of the peoples on this side of the world without any historical background or support from tradition, and with no thread of continuity through the changes. They are merely the by-products of machines, or, better yet, they are their preliminary substitutes. Having said this, it is clear that if it be said that we are one of those peoples, since the discussion in this booklet in a primary way pertains to the regional environment, language, tradition, and religion of its author, it is also even clearer that if we have machines, that is to say if we build machines, there is no further need for their by-products to serve as preliminaries and substitutes.

Gharbzadegi is therefore a characteristic of an era in which we haven't yet obtained machines and don't understand the mysteries of their structure and construction.

Gharbzadegi is a characteristic of a period of time when we have not become familiar with the prerequisites for machines – meaning the new sciences and technology.

Gharbzadegi is a characteristic of a time in our history when we're compelled to use machines because of the market and economic constraints on us to use machines and because of the incoming and outgoing petroleum.

What brought on this era? What happened that other people, ignoring us completely while they changed and developed their machines, built, carried out plans, and moved in and out of our midst and we awoke to find every oil derrick a spike impaling the land? Why did we end up Weststruck?

Let's go back to history.

Notes

[1.] I borrowed this term from Mr Ahmad Fardid. He's written several other things and given some talks under the same title which are most readable. It is the hope of this writer that he will be encouraged to continue discussing this matter[A].

[2.] *Josue de Castro*. The Geography of Hunger *(Boston: 1952)[Tr.]*.

[3.] *Freely translated from* Jahani Miyan-e Tars va Omid *[A world in the midst of fear and hope], by Tibor Mende, translated by Khalil Maleki, Tehran 1339 [21 March 1960–20 March 1961] [A]. Tibor Mende,* Reflexions sur l'histoire d' aujourd' hui, entre la peur et l'espoir *(Paris: 1967)[Tr.]*.

[4.] The referendum took place on 26 January 1963. Its purpose was to produce a show of popular support for the Shah's land reform bill, which was designed to break up big estates and distribute land to peasants, and also for a law giving Iranian workers a 20 per cent share of the net profits of their factories. The election, called by the Shah to bypass the National Assembly, which normally approved his decrees, marked the first time women were permitted to vote in Iranian history. It was vigorously opposed by the Muslim clergy, the National Front, the communists, and the major landowners, all of whom boycotted the polls[Tr.].

[5.] Referring to the spate of utopian movements that flourished in the United States in the early nineteenth century – the Rappites, the Oneida Community, the Shakers, New Harmony Indiana, and Brook Farm – to name some of the most prominent, all of whom were threatened by the disruptions of industrialisation and hoped to form ideal, self-contained communities[Tr.].

[6.] I gave a perfect example of this in *Jazireh-ye Khark, Dor-e Yatim-e Khalij* [Khark Island, orphan pearl of the Persian Gulf] (Tehran: Entesharat-e Danesh)[A].

[7.] See *La France contre les robots* (Paris: 1955), by Georges Bernanos, a contemporary French writer[A].

[8.] This pilot's name was Claude Eatherly. See the book below, which is his correspondence with an Austrian writer with an introduction by Bertrand Russell.

This book was translated in *Ferdawsi* magazine in a series of issues in 1342 [21 March 1963–20 March 1964] by Iraj Qarib under the title 'The Demolition of Hiroshima'. *Avoir detruit Hiroshima*, ed. Robert Laffont, Paris[A]. As a point of fact, Claude Eatherly was not the pilot of the aircraft that was used to drop an atomic bomb on Hiroshima. Major Eatherly piloted a plane called the *Straight Flush*, which overflew Hiroshima prior to the actual bombing on the same day. The *Enola Gay*, which actually was used to bomb the city, was piloted by Colonel Paul Tibbets. See Claude Eatherly, *Burning Conscience: the Case of the Hiroshima Pilot, Claude Eatherly, Told in His Letters to Gunther Anders* (New York: 1962)[Tr.].

9. Ad and Thamud were two ancient tribes said to have been among the first peoples to inhabit the Arabian peninsula. They were destroyed en masse by God (according to accounts given in the Qur'an) for disobeying their prophets. See R. A. Nicholson, *A Literary History of the Arabs* (Cambridge: 1956), pp. 1–3[Tr.].

10. *Du Zambese au Tanganika, 1858–1972, by Livingston and Stanley (Paris: 1958)[A].*

11. I'm referring to the defeat of 'Abdol Rahman Amavi (one of the Andalusian Islamic caliphs) by the French General Charles Martel at Poitiers and the stopping of the expansion of the Western Islamic caliphate in the beginning of the eighth century A.D. And you'll remember that this 'Martel' is today the name of a famous cognac![A]. This Andalusian caliph is known in Western literature as 'Abd al-Rahman B. 'Abd Allah al-Ghafiki, governor of Spain, who was killed along with most of his army by Charles Martel between the cities of Tours and Poitiers at a battleground known to Arabs as Balat al-Shuhada' (Pavement of the Martyrs)[Tr.].

12. Mr Semin Baghchenban, a musician friend of mine, has some notes (unpublished) concerning the Music Congress of Farvardin of 1340 [21 March–20 April 1961] in Tehran. There he writes: 'For [Alain] Danielou (the French representative) nothing is more interesting than the fact that we lived during the age of the Sassanian kings and are available for him, who arrived in the heart of the twentieth century, to study, so that he, with his precise instruments and the latest tape-recording systems, can find his way to the Sassanian court, record a concert by Barbad and Nakisa, and then return to Paris on an Air France jet from an airstrip near the Sassanian capital built especially for orientalists and experts on poetry, painting, and music'[A]. Barbad was a famous vocalist and lutist, Nakisa a harp player. Both were prominent entertainers in the Sassanian court of Khosraw II at the turn of the sixth century A.D.[Tr.].

CHAPTER 11

Civilisation and Modernisation[1]

'Ali Shari'ati

Although the Islamic Revolution is associated by most in the West with Ayatollah Khomeini, it is unlikely that the revolution would have unfolded as it did without the contribution made by 'Ali Shari'ati, who died a year before the events that led to the departure of the Mohammad Reza Pahlavi. Indeed, it has been speculated that Shari'ati's death in London in 1977 (held by some to have been instigated by the Shah's secret police) resulted in a series of memorials and demonstrations that eventually escalated beyond the control of the Pahlavi dynasty.[2] These demonstrations were supported by Iran's leading modern intellectuals, and most importantly, the newly educated Iranians who found the clerics too obscurantist and the Marxists too removed from Iran's Islamic heritage. Shari'ati's significance in formulating an alternative world view from those of the secularists, clerics and the monarchy is illustrated in descriptions of him by leading scholars: 'If the Iranian intellectual panorama of the 1960s was dominated by Jalal Al-e Ahmad, that of the 1970s undoubtedly belonged to Ali Shari'ati';[3] he was 'the outstanding intellectual of the . . . whole of contemporary Iran,'[4] 'the ideologist of the revolution',[5] and 'the most furious revolutionary among the ideologues of the Islamic Revolution'.[6]

Part of Shari'ati's appeal for the newly educated class of young Iranians was his firm faith in the compatibility of Islam with the requirements of the modern age in providing a just and egalitarian society. By his own admission, 'Ali Shari'ati was greatly influenced in his youth by his father's Islamic leaning. Mohammad Taqi Shari'ati had trained to be a cleric, but he was more inclined to teach the new generations of Iranians about the dangers of Kasravi's Deism and the Tudeh Party's secularism, and established the Centre for the Propagation of Islamic Truths in Mashhad in 1944. Moreover, Mohammad Taqi's views on Islam must also have contributed to its appeal among the reform-minded, even if he was criticised by the more conservative clerics of the time.[7] The Centre for the Propagation of Islamic Truths attracted university students and some clerics (including Seyyed 'Ali Khamene'i, the present leader – Rahbar – of the Islamic Republic). The society was 'propelled . . . into the forefront of Iranian intellectual life, making its presence known well beyond the city limits of Mashhad'.[8]

'Ali Shari'ati's understanding and presentation of Islam developed as it was filtered through the prisms of Western social sciences. Between 1959 and 1964 Shari'ati studied for a PhD in Paris, and he became familiar with existentialism, liberation theology, German philosophy (Hegel, Marx and Husserl), and the anti-colonialism of George Gurvitch and Frantz Fanon. While in Paris Shari'ati was politicialy active, as he contributed articles that were critical of the Pahlavi regime to a number of journals, and he was also sympathetic to the National Liberation Front which was seeking to establish independence in Afgeria from French rule. On his return to Iran in 1964 Shari'ati was arrested, and he was a frequent guest in Iran's jails before he left Iran for good in 1977.

Between 1967 and 1971 Shari'ati was employed to teach the history of Islam at Mashhad University, and this offered him the opportunity to formulate his ideas on Islam and Western social sciences into a 'coherent' whole, and also to present these ideas to a captive and receptive audience. He was able to establish a devoted following among the students who were attracted, perhaps, by both the modern message and the passionate style of Shari'ati's presentation. (The passionate and poetic style of Shari'ati's lectures can still be felt in some of his writings, and a notable example of this is his work on Hajj. Such writings stand in contrast to the scholastic essays of some of the clerics who accused Shari'ati of historical and theological inaccuracies.) His major writing from this period was Islam-shenasi *(Recognising Islam) in which he viewed Islam as compatible with reason, democracy and social and economic equality. Moreover, this work also attacked the clergy and the monarchy for promoting polytheism, as they had both substituted themselves for God because they encouraged blind imitation to themselves, rather than leading the people towards God by nurturing human reason. Shari'ati's religious idealism led him to believe that people themselves could initiate a change in unjust social situations once they had removed the veils of ignorance, fear and acquisitiveness. This adherence to human agency did not, in Shari'ati's opinion, contradict his advocacy of ideas that were derived from Marxist ideology, such as his hatred of capitalism and the petit-bourgeoisie, and class struggle (which was expressed in history through the conflict between monotheism and polytheism).[9] Shari'ati explained that his world view was different from that of Marxists by claiming, 'Marx makes economics the infrastructure of man, but we [hold] precisely the opposite view.'[10] Yet the call for socialism, justice for all, and the use of modern terminology made Shari'ati's discourses very appealing to the newly educated generation of Iranians.*

Despite his anti-Marxist claims, Shari'ati's thought betrays deep Marxist leanings, and this is evident in his opinion of the clergy, as he considered that Islam had been corrupted by the close links between the seminaries and the bazaar. The jurists had produced laws that were designed to promote the interests of the bourgeoisie (the bazaar) because they were dependent on the religious taxes and charity of the property-owning classes. Unsurprisingly, Shari'ati had little time for the obscurantist clerics, and believed that instead of the clerics leading the revolt against the corruption of the Pahlavi monarchy and the capitalist states that supported the regime, it would be the intellectuals to guide the masses.

Shari'ati's opportunity to increase his audience came in 1971 when he could no longer lecture in Mashhad, and so having been sent to Tehran, he commenced lecturing in the Hosayniyeh Ershad, *a religious institution where clerics such as Morteza Motahhari propagated a different form of Islam. In fact, Motahhari resigned from the managing board of the institution because he believed Shari'ati was promoting a sociological understanding of Islam rather than one that was grounded in its intellectual dimension.*[11] *Shari'ati became more radical during this period, perhaps in response to the pomposity and arrogance of the Shah's celebration of 2,500 years of monarchy in Iran, and the increasing insurrectionary activity of a Marxist-Leninist organisation, the Feda'iyan of Iran. In the winter of 1972, Shari'ati started to declare in public that armed struggle was permissible as an appropriate strategy for Shi'-ite Islam. Consequently the Hosayniyeh Ershad was closed down by the state in November 1972, and subsequently Shari'ati spent periods under surveillance and in prison until he left Iran in 1977. He died in England in the same year of a heart attack (although some Iranians expressed their suspicions that the Shah's notorious secret police, SAVAK, were in some way involved in his death).*

Within the text of this chapter, 'Civilisation and Modernisation' (dated to 1969), the influences upon Shari'ati's thought are easily discernible: Jean-Paul Sartre, Western sociology, and anti-imperialist discourses of Fanon, Marxist critiques of capitalism, and Gharbzadegi. *There is little in the text that is specific to Iran or Islam, as its message is primarily censure of the capitalist and bourgeois societies of the West. The message is simple and its general appeal to Iranians is strengthened by referring to images that have a universal appeal, such as Charlie Chaplin's* Modern Times. *(Interestingly, Chaplin's films were also mentioned in Jalal Al-e Ahmad's* Gharbzadegi*).*[12] *By utilising such images, Shari'ati distanced himself from the discourses of clerics (some of whom had probably never seen a film in their lives before, indeed, the fatwa of Shaykh Fazl Allah Nuri denouncing the cinema is well known in this regard).*[13] *The 'modernity' of the text is ironically revealed in citations from and references to European intellectuals. However, what is significant for the Iranian reader of this text in the 1970s was its 'scientific' nature − evidenced by its familiarity with Western scholarly thought. Here there is a great difference between Shari'ati and Jalal Al-e Ahmad who condemned scholars who tended to cite the works of Westerners as if they held ultimate truths at the expense of Iranian and Islamic intellectuals. However, the perceived scientific and universal message of the text was significant because it suggested to its readers that the backwardness and alienation that Iranians felt were not unique to Iran. This alienation and backwardness are themes that have occurred in the writings of previous intellectuals, and some have witnessed the cause in Sufism, others in Islam and the clergy, and still others in Western capitalism. This text suggests that Shari'ati saw the problem primarily as one that has been caused by Western capitalism, but in his other publications, Shari'ati was critical of Sufism (though not to the same extent as Kasravi) and also the clergy–bazaar alliance. Yet Shari'ati held that a purified version of Islam could help to resolve the problems that beset Iranian society. His ultimate recourse to religion and human agency recalls the Qur'anic verse, so fondly repeated by Afghani, that 'God changes not what is in a people, until they change what is in themselves.'*[14]

Notes

1. 'Ali Shari'ati, *Tamaddon va Tajaddod* (Civilisation and Modernisation) (Ettehadiyeh-e Anjomanha-ye Islami-ye Daneshjuyan dar Urupa va Anjomanha-ye Islami-ye Daneshjuyan dar Amrika va Canada) (no date or place of publication).

2. A. Rahnema, 'Ali Shari'ati: Teacher, Preacher, Rebel', in A. Rahnema (ed.), *Pioneers of Islamic Revival* (London: Zed Press, 1994), p. 245.

3. M. Boroujerdi, *Iranian Intellectuals and the West* (Utica, NY: Syracuse University Press, 1996), p. 106.

4. Abrahamian, *Iran Between Two Revolutions*, (Princeton, NJ: Princeton University Press, 1982), p. 464.

5. Y. Richard, 'Contemporary Shi'i Thought', in N. Keddie, *Roots of Revolution*, p. 215.

6. H. Dabashi, *Theology of Discontent* (New York University Press, 1993), p. 106.

7. Such a reformed version of Islam advocated 'the necessity of women's literacy . . . the possibility of interpreting the Qur'an differently, seeking non-theological reasons for natural disasters as earthquakes and tornadoes, and not believing in polygamy' (M. Boroujerdi, *Iranian Intellectuals and the West*, p. 103).

8. Ibid., p. 102.

9. Some scholars have noted inconsistencies in Shari'ati's thought, such as S. Akhavi, who questions how free human agents can know 'reality' when Shari'ati the phenomenologist admits, individuals can only comprehend material objects and signs as indications to the truth, see A. Akhavi, 'Shari'ati's Social Thought', in N. Keddie (ed.), *Religion and Politics in Iran* (New Haven, ER: Yale, 1985), p. 131.

10. Cited in Dabashi, *Theology of Discontent*, p. 143.

11. A. Sachedina, 'Ali Shari'ati: Ideologue of the Iranian Revolution', in J. Esposito (ed.), *Voices of Resurgent Islam* (Oxford University Press, 1983), p. 206.

12. Jalal Al-e Ahmad, *Gharbzadegi* (translated by John Green and Ahmad Alizadeh), p. 164. In the same chapter, on page 170, Al-e Ahmad discusses service to machines and the necessity to turn their wrenches so many times.

13. The famous Iranian film director Mohsen Makhmalbaf has mentioned that as a child his grandmother believed that watching films was a sin. (See L. Ridgeon, 'Makhmalbaf's Broken Mirror: The Socio-Political Significance of Modern Iranian Cinema', *Durham Middle East Papers,* 2000). It is of interest too that Makhmalbaf became one of Shari'ati's supporters having listened to him speak at the Hosaynieh Ershad. See H. Dabashi, *Close Up: Iranian Cinema, Past, Present and Future* (London: Verso, 2001), p. 167.

14. Qur'an, 13:10 (cited in A. Hourani, *Arabic Thought in the Liberal Age*, p. 128).

Further Reading

A. Akhavi, 'Shari'ati's Social Thought', in N. Keddie (ed.), *Religion and Politics in Iran* (New Haven, ER: Yale, 1983).

M. Boroujerdi, *Iranian Intellectuals and the West* (Utica, NY: Syracuse University Press, 1996), pp. 105–15.

H. Dabashi, *Theology of Discontent* (New York University Press, 1993), pp. 102–46.

A. Rahnema, 'Ali Shari'ati: Teacher, Preacher, Rebel', in A. Rahnema (ed.), *Pioneers of Islamic Revival* (London: Zed Press, 1994), pp. 208–50.

—— *An Islamic Utopian* (London: I.B. Tauris, 1998).

Y. Richard, 'Contemporary Shi'i Thought' in N. Keddie (ed.), *Roots of Revolution* (New Haven, ER: Yale University Press, 1981), pp. 203–30.

A. Sachedina, 'Ali Shari'ati: Ideologue of the Iranian Revolution', in J. Esposito (ed.), *Voices of Resurgent Islam* (Oxford University Press, 1983), pp. 191–214.

A. Shari'ati, *Hajj* (Bedford: Free Islamic Literatures, 1978).

——•——

In the name of God.

Dear readers! The treatise in your hands is the text of a speech given by Doctor 'Ali Shari'ati at the Society of Sociology Teachers of Khorasan. Those addressed in this speech are the intellectuals and the educated who seek a remedy and a cure to liberate them from the pain and sickness of West-toxification and modernisation. Considering the importance of the subject, the sociological analysis, the speaker's accuracy in presenting the problems related to modernisation – and the comparison with civilisation – the speech has been prepared in the form of this pamphlet that you have before you today, the original speech having been recorded on a tape. It is hoped that the importance and significance of the text has not been diminished in this preparation.

In the name of God, the Merciful and Compassionate.

Debate concerning what is culture and what is barbarism, and who is the civilised person and who is the modern person are hidden in the message of Islam. And this is one of the main problems that must be considered, not only by each Muslim in the name of Islam but (also by) the intellectuals and educated in particular, who are attached to Islamic society. They are responsible for the direct message of modernisation or for their civilisation and society, and for coming face to face with it.

This is one of the most critical problems (perhaps the most critical and sensitive problem) that must be set out for us today, but unfortunately until now it has not been mooted. It is the problem of modernisation that we face today in all non-European and also Islamic societies. What is the relation between modernisation and civilisation? Is it the case that what we have been made to understand – that modernisation is a synonym for civilisation – or is it otherwise, that modernisation is the cause of something else, another social phenomenon that is unrelated to civilisation? Unfortunately, in the name of civilisation, modernisation is considered appropriate for non-European societies.

In these 100–150 years in which all non-European societies including Islamic societies were put in touch with the West and Western civilisation, and had to become modernised, the West undertook the responsibility of modernising these societies. But they modernised us in the name of becoming civilised and acquainting these societies with civilisation. This 'us' to which I refer includes all non-European societies, and they defined (modernisation) in such a way that (they said) 'this is civilisation.' For many years our intellectuals should have paid attention, made the people understand and made it clear for us that modernisation is one thing and civilisation is something else. They should have made us understand that it is not possible to attain civilisation through modernisation. But they did not do so!! In these 100–150 years in which Europe undertook the responsibility of modernising these societies and whose aim was modernising all non-Europeans, weren't the educated and the intellectuals of the non-European societies aware of this problem? I will explain the reason for their (lack of awareness) in the course of this discussion.

In my discussion there are several terms and if their meaning is unclear, then the whole of my discussion will be unclear. Therefore I will define the terms which are the essential key to understanding my discussion so that I can then proceed into the main discourse.

Firstly: Intellectual.

This is an everyday, common term that is widespread in our society and all societies of the world – European and non-European. What does it mean? What person do we call an intellectual? Who are the intellectuals? What message and plan are they responsible for in their societies?

In a word, an intellectual is a person who is aware of his own 'human condition' in an historical time and place, and in the society in which he lives. This 'self-awareness' gives him a sense of responsibility. 'It is the self-aware, responsible person that has the responsibility for the plan for the scientific, social and revolutionary leadership of the society.'[1]

Secondly: Assimilation.

This word is the foundation of all the disputes and troubles that we non-Europeans and Muslims face. Assimilation, in other words, is when a person intentionally or not makes himself resemble someone else. When someone has this disease he is unaware of his personality, origin and qualities, If he is aware of his personality, origin and qualities then he detests them. In order to remove all personal and societal qualities, and even his own national qualities, he makes himself resemble someone else with a limitless and unconditional intensity and obsession until the shame that he feels within himself and that he feels has been attributed to him is remote and he enjoys all the glory and virtues that he feels in another person.

Thirdly: Alienation.

Alienation, in other words, is becoming a stranger to oneself. That is to say, alienation is when a person becomes unfamiliar with himself and he feels something and someone else in his place. This is a serious social and spiritual disease. Alienation exists in several shapes and forms and it depends on several factors. One of these is the tools of work. In sociology and psychology it is recognised that whoever has more contact in the course of his life with a single tool or one kind of work gradually forgets his own independent and real personality, and he feels that the tool substitutes his identity. For example, the feelings, thoughts, emotions and all the human qualities will all be inactive and suspended in the person who always works from eight until twelve in the morning, and from two or three in the afternoon until six or seven in the evening at a single machine or turning screws. His only duty is to pick up a tool and complete a single, special, mechanical task. For example, a conveyor belt passes in front of him and he must tighten every third screw that passes.

This person who has various emotions, abilities, thoughts, tastes, tensions, hates, feelings, and aptitudes becomes a creature that turns screws in the daytime, his time of work when he is at his most active. He is merely an instrument. For ten, eleven or twelve hours his task is a single, boring act which he has to carry out. All his human qualities are inactivated. There are many examples to illustrate this problem, but the clearest example of all is provided by Charlie Chaplin. In *Modern Times* Chaplin acts the role of a man who at first is a free man, having different feelings. He is besotted with his girlfriend, respects his father, and he is excited when he meets his old friends. He also has needs, becomes sad on occasions and likes to sit down and discuss problems with others. In respect of the different aspects of life he has various needs and reacts in a variety of ways, and he has diverse talents. When this man sees his mother in the street he feels like a son who has not seen his mother for a long time. And when he sees the friend that he has not met for ages he wants to sit in a corner with him and chat and talk about life and old times. When he sees his girlfriend he feels love and affection, and he wants to sit with her so that they can whisper secrets and desires. When he sees his enemy, he feels hatred and enmity in his heart, and wants to fight, insult and take revenge on him. In short he is a human being with diverse needs. When he sees something beautiful he feels an aesthetic delight, and when he witnesses something unpleasant he feels aversion and regret. This is the natural state of a free human being.

Then he goes to work in a factory which is so huge and complicated that he could never have imagined its size. He doesn't know what all the vast technical installations produce and how they are co-ordinated. He only goes to an office, and fills in some identity forms, and then he is told to go to room number so and so. Off he goes to room number so and so and sits down. He is to work for ten hours each day. He is led to his workplace and is told, 'This is your job.' 'What is my job?' he asks. Nothing. There is a huge hall which is the workplace, and here there is an assembly line where there is a conveyor belt moving. The conveyor belt enters the hall from one side and exits at the other side, into other rooms and other machines. He does not know where this conveyor belt comes from or where it goes and what it is doing. Seven or eight people are standing here side by side. His task consists of letting two nuts on a machine placed on the conveyor belt pass by, but he must tighten the third that reaches him with one turn, and then two more nuts pass him by and he tightens the third with two turns, and then two more nuts pass by and he tightens the third with half a turn. Then the same process is repeated: one turn, two turns, half a turn, one turn, two turns, half a turn. He continues with this routine from eight or nine in the morning until a bell rings and then he can go home. He has no other job. He does not know what the nuts were for, why he did what he was told, where the conveyor belt came from or to where it went. Beside him were seven or eight people who were unable to talk to one another because the conveyor belt moved with such speed that if one of the workers glanced at the person next to him to see who it was, then the nut would pass and the whole of the factory would have to grind to a stop. Then the managers would come and fine him and fire him.

This man has two eyes only for the nuts. The human tasks that he performs, this human being, consist of one turn, two turns, and half a turn, and that is all.

But among the qualities of the human being is that firstly he considers a task, and secondly there is a purpose in mind for the task selected to which he is inclined. Once the purpose has been established he begins the first stages of his task and then in due course he feels aware of the task (and says to himself): 'I have undertaken this job because it will help me reach my goal.' Aside from feeling this during the work itself, that is to say, being aware of his work, he is a human being who possesses various feelings and different needs.

But this worker, Charlie Chaplin, sees his mother, fiancée and friend who have come to see him at the factory. This individual has not yet become accustomed to this tough order and this boring, repetitive aspect of machinery. While working he sees his beloved, or mother, or son or friend and he lets the nut pass him by. He goes and greets his beloved and starts to chat.

Suddenly he sees the policemen rushing in and the red lights are flashing, and the sirens are ringing and the inspectors come. What has happened? The control system of the whole of the factory has realised that a single nut has not been turned and everything grinds to a halt. They come and grab him by the collar and shout, 'What have you done? Why didn't you tighten the nut?'

A single, simple and very natural human feeling in this individual has been the reason for the breakdown in the whole system. In other words, in the present order of things it is impermissible for a person to have the slightest human feeling. But gradually they train this individual who has had these sentiments, and little by little they turn him into a machine, until after twenty years of work the following descriptions that 'the human is a rational animal' or 'the human is a worshipping animal' or 'the human is a self-conscious and creative animal' and others like these are no longer valid.

So what is this human being? 'An animal that tightens nuts.' This human being passes down the street and sees a policeman coming towards him. He sees that the policeman's buttons on his uniform are like nuts, and so he immediately takes out his spanner to tighten them!! He sees a woman with a design on her hat or coat and all at once he feels that he must go and twist it once or twice or give it half a turn.

The whole world for him is 'skip two and tighten the third'. This is the philosophy of his life. This is his meaning, his essence and his human reality. Why does he tighten the nuts? To eat. Why does he eat? To tighten the nuts. A circular man.

This is a man does not feel that he possessed within himself those feelings, desires, needs, weaknesses, sensibilities, memories, and virtues. They have all vanished, in the words of Marcuse[2] he is a 'one-dimensional man', or to use the phrase of Rene Guenon[3] he has become a 'man lessened, diminished'. In the words of Chandel[4] he has become a 'circular man'. Production for the sake of consumption, consumption for the sake of production.

This man who was a microcosm, a mini-world, was like God and had the attributes of God, but has been transformed into an extension of a spanner. In other words, the attributes of machines, nuts, and mechanical movement have permeated his being. He does not recognise himself as such and such a person, the son of so and so, of a certain house of a certain family, of this race with these characteristics. Indeed he feels that he is, in truth, only a tool for a machine.

Sometimes this alienation comes in the form of a severe sickness which a doctor must cure. Sometimes when it becomes so severe it manifests itself as an illness that requires a psychoanalyst to take him to an asylum. This alienation has penetrated into humans through machines and inhumane discipline. Humans have become trapped in it. Alienation may be caused by technology and sometimes it appears because of bureaucracy. In the words of a sociologist, I don't remember if it was Marx, Weber or Marcel Mauss,[5] in a great big bureaucratic institution which has a thousand numbered counters, the man who sits at number 345 and who has worked there for twenty or thirty years and continually performed the same task for the whole of his life, considers himself as 'counter 345'. It is generally construed that he has no attachment in the world except to 'counter 345'. The feeling appears in even 'Mr Counter 345' himself that he is Mr Counter 345 and not so and so, son of so and so, with his own characteristics.

This is the alienation caused by bureaucracy.

Alienation as a word means 'a *jinn* takes possession of a person'.[6] In times past people believed in *jinn*, and when someone became insane they said that a *jinn* had possessed him and displaced his reason which subsequently no longer functioned, and he no longer sensed himself, but rather he felt the *jinn* in himself.

It is this word 'alienation' that today sociologists and psychologists use for this sickness.

Just as in the past people were possessed by the *jinn*, today too people are moulded by a certain tool for a machine or by a single cog in the vast network of a merciless bureaucracy into one of the tools of that very machine or bureaucracy. Moreover, he no longer recognises his particular qualities. He is 'lost'. Just as they used to say, a *jinn* or a demon has possessed the mind of a person who became mad or insane, now the tools of a person's job or the type of job possess his mind. Gradually he loses his authentic, sound human personality and the qualities of the machine, the tool of the job, the type of job, the chain of the bureaucratic order possess his mind. He feels them within him, replacing his self.

Another kind of '*jinn* control' or possession that alienates a person from himself or a class from itself is an alienation more frightening and real in which we Eastern people, Iranians, Indians, Africans and Muslims have become trapped.

This is not the alienation caused by technology, and neither have we become alienated by machines. No machine or bureaucracy is involved. A few departments of bureaucracy and some officials will not bureaucratise someone, and the bourgeoisie has not yet matured that it can alienate us. But what he has been trapped in and is more frightening and dangerous is 'cultural alienation'.

What is cultural alienation? Didn't we say that alienation, in whatever shape or form it appears, is when a person does not recognise himself as he is, but feels that something has taken his name or his place. This is the alienated person. Now, it does not matter whether this thing that he feels in his place (and which is not his self) is money, a machine, counter 345, ascetic practice or his beloved. What it is depends only on chance and taste.

What is culture? I do not want to list the different interpretations of culture here. However culture is defined, it is an expression for all artistic, historical, religious and abstract manifestations (the latter being in the form of symbols, signs, customs, habits, traditions, effects and acts of the group) and all the feelings of a people which in the course of history have produced those very people and given them a special form.

These manifestations explain the people's pains, desires, qualities of spirit and nature, social characteristics, material life and finally social relations and economic structures.

When I feel my own religion, literature, emotions, sufferings, pains, and needs through my culture then in truth I feel my self: the social and historical 'self' not the individual me. In other words, it is the spring from whence this culture gushes and has its origin. Therefore culture is the expression of the basis of my society, its real existence and history. But artificial factors, most often of a suspicious nature, appear in a society which displays particular social conditions or social relations in a certain historical period. These factors acquaint it with the particular pains, sufferings, emotions and sensitivities that have been caused by a different spirit, a different past, a different background and a different material and economic society. They eliminate my culture from my mind and then replace it with another culture that is suited to another time and stage of development, another history, another economic level and structure, and another system of social and political relations. And then when I want to recognise my self, I feel another culture's culture in place of my own. I complain of sufferings which are not even my own, and lament the pessimism that is not suited for my cultural, philosophical, and societal realities, and I discover aims, ideals and sufferings which are natural for that other society and belong to that society and its social, economic, political and historical conditions, but which do not pertain to my society. Yet I find those pains, sufferings, and aims are my own!

In this way I have become alienated by another culture. The black people in Africa, the Berbers of North Africa, and the Iranians and Indians in Asia, each possesses a particular history and unique present condition, but they discover that the sufferings which are called 'their own sufferings' are derived from the period of the Middle Ages, the Renaissance of the sixteenth century, the Enlightenment of the seventeenth century, Scientism of the eighteenth century, the age of the Ideologies of the nineteenth century and capitalism after the two world wars.

So how does it concern you? Which one of these pertains to you so that now its sufferings, ideas or cures, or the feeling of it, its reactions or effects pertain to you?

It is as if I had a pain in the foot but complained of my nerves. Why? Because I was in contact with someone that I thought was more clever, wealthier and respect-worthy who had 'nervous problems'. Even though I have a pain in the foot I seek a cure for my nerves, whatever the nervous disorder I feel another psychological disorder within myself rather than the pain in my foot.

So I do not feel 'me' or 'myself' as I really am, rather I feel someone else in the way that he or she exists. In other words, I am alienated. Don't you see that in a society where hunger and illiteracy are common its intellectuals think, feel, and have pains and desires like the new generation of Americans or British or French? The suffering of this intellectual is the abundance of blessings and prosperity and his deficiency is spiritual weakness. He pursues comfort and an easy life, and he becomes sick through the strict discipline that technology has imposed upon him. He complains of the pains that this discipline has caused. But as for me, I have the pain of having no technology yet complain of the pains of technology!

It is so absurd! It is as if we had been crushed by a machine and emerged with bones broken, teeth shattered and bloody faces and heads. Yet we empathise with the person who was in control of the machine that had crushed us, who was fed up of and depressed by sitting at the machine and crushing people.

So in this way non-European societies become alienated by European societies. They become foreign to themselves; in other words, the educated or the intellectual of Eastern society does not feel or complain or hope like an Eastern person, and he does not strive in a way commensurate with the pains of his own society; rather, he feels the sufferings, pains, sensitivities and pains of a European in the final stage of capitalism and mature, material prosperity.

This is the greatest suffering and perversion that exists in human society today. It is the psychological perversion of non-European personality types, the realities of which are different from the European kind. But non-European people feel something alien within them; they feel another person there. In times past the non-European countries existed as authentic selves, and if we visited these countries two hundred years ago it is probable that today's European civilisation did not exist; rather, each non-European country possessed its own civilisation, sensitivities, hopes, ways of doing things, its own forms of spirituality, amusement, style, sensuality, worship, its own good and bad acts, its own art and aesthetics, its own way of philosophical thinking, and its own way of religious thinking. Everything in the non-European country was authentic.

If I had visited a country like India, for example, or an African country, I would have known this was an African country, or this was India. Their tastes and buildings would have been unique to themselves. They composed their own unique poetry and painted in a style unique to themselves. Their poets felt the pains of India, thought in the way that the rest of Indian society thought. The people had their own colours, sicknesses, hopes and religions. Everything belonged to the people themselves. With regard to the level of civilisation, everything that they possessed was theirs, but material prosperity was low. Although they were not sick, they were poor. But today, European society has been able to export the trappings of its civilisation to non-European societies, and it has made these societies use its tools and its modern, new manufactured products to the same extent that it has been able to export its unique philosophy, beliefs, tastes, manners to these countries, these societies that were never compatible with European manners, its despair, its way of thinking, and its tastes. In the words of Alined Yope, one of the greatest black intellectuals, a number of societies have been produced out of European civilisation – including our society – mosaic societies. But what is the meaning of a mosaic society? A mosaic is composed of hundreds of tiny, coloured tiles in different colours and shapes that have been pressed within a mould. But what shape have they yielded? No shape!

This single mosaic has various colours and is composed of stones with different shapes, but no final shape has been produced. Why? These civilisations are mosaic civilisations. That is to say they are civilisations composed of some elements left over from the past and from some formless and rootless elements from Europe that produce a mosaic called 'a half civilised and half modernised society'. It is a mosaic because in the creation of our own civilisation we did not even choose the elements that were utilised for European civilisation. We did not know what civilisation was or what shape it had. They gave the shape of civilisation to us!

Therefore without knowing what we should construct in this society and without deciding how we should shape our own society in our own way, we took some elements from our own society and some from others and without a plan commenced this construction. We added different elements from all directions, one on top of the other; some from Europe and others indigenous to our own society; some from the past and others from the present. But this method of adding ingredients on top of each other was formless and ill planned and created a new shapeless and aimless society. These societies are non-European societies that in a century or a century and a half have been able to acquire material from Europe in the name of civilisation. What is the root of the mosaic civilisation in non-European countries, or to use my expression 'camel–cow–leopard' societies which have no special form or goal? What is the root of a society about which it is not known what kind it is, where its people and intellectuals cannot understand why they are alive, nor do they know what their aims and futures are, nor do they know what their belief is? Mechanical technology advanced in Europe during the seventeenth, eighteenth and nineteenth centuries, and machines were owned by capitalists and the rich. One of the characteristics of a machine is that its balance of production must continually increase. This is the requirement of a machine. If a machine does not increase its production in the course of ten or eleven years it will cease to be of use, and it will not be able to continue its function or compete with other machines. Why? Because if the balance of its production does not increase, then other machines that produce the same product will make it available for the people more cheaply. Therefore the product of the machine that does not increase will be left on the shelf. The machine must be able to increase its production more each day so that it can pay its worker's wages that grow larger on a daily basis and so that it can sell its produce on the market at a price lower than its rivals. Science and technology have improved the machine and caused the face of contemporary humans to change. We don't think that this is one of the problems that is discussed in the world today; rather, no problem other than this has caused these two centuries of suffering. All the problems that Europe has caused in the world today are because of this.

Each year a machine must increase its production, and to avoid stockpiling it must create a demand for consumption that matches the increase in production. But people's consumption does not increase in proportion to that of the machine's production. It is possible that a society increases its consumption of paper by 30 per cent during ten years, but in the same period the paper-producing machine increases its production by 300 per cent. Ten years ago a machine produced five kilometres of paper every hour, but now it produces fifty kilometres of paper per hour even though the consumption of paper has not risen and cannot increase accordingly. So what should be done with this excess production? What should be done with all this excess paper? A new market for consumption must be created. Each European society has a particular level of consumption; their populations do not exceed 40 million, 50 or 60 million. Although production increases at a delirious rate, the people cannot be forced to increase their consumption. It would be impossible! Therefore just as the machine must increase its production it must cross its national boundaries and find a foreign market. Human fate became determined in the eighteenth century when machines and the new technology and science fell into the hands of the capitalists. Each person on earth was compelled to become a consumer of the produced merchandise. European markets were saturated very quickly, and there was no alternative but to export the excess production to Africa and Asia, and the inhabitants of these areas had to consume all the European goods. This is what the machine necessitated.

Is it possible to carry these goods so easily to the East where the way of life does not necessitate the consumption of such products, and is it possible to impose the consumption of these goods on the East? It is impossible! When we visit Asian societies we see Asian clothes which have been made by Asian women or indigenous Asian workers. They have local clothes and they wear their own clothing. Factories that make machines, clothes and fabrics which produce modern, European fabrics are not in demand here. When we visit Africa we see that all the hopes, tastes and amusement of the people are confined to horse riding, and their pleasure lies in the appreciation of the horse. They have no highways or chauffeurs, and the conception of a car doesn't even exist in their minds. In fact they have no need of a car. Production and consumption accord with their life, customs, tastes, needs, and styles. Therefore they do not need European cars. In Europe a factory produces modern, fancy goods very quickly in great variety and numbers, and it is necessary to export these goods to African and Asian countries – in the eighteenth and even nineteenth century it would have been impossible for Asian and African men and women to use these goods, even if they were placed at their disposal free of charge because they had their own specific designs and their own unique and authentic sense of aesthetics. An African or Asian woman had no need for these goods or this rubbish to make herself beautiful, or wear attractive clothes, or put on her make-up. She had her own special, fancy things, her own unique make-up and cosmetics, and she both used and liked these things. She didn't even feel the desire to change them in any way.

Therefore the goods of the European capitalists remained unsold because these people lived with their own way of thinking, with their own needs and with their own tastes, and moreover, they themselves produced in their own society whatever they needed. There was no way that they could become consumers of the products of the capitalists and industry of eighteenth-century Europe. So what could the capitalists do? It was necessary to make these people in Asia or Africa consumers of European goods, to reorganise their society in such a way that they would purchase these goods: 'change the nation'. They must transform a nation, transform the individual so that he would be able to change his clothing, his consumption, his adornment, the furniture in his house and the shape of his city. What part of him must they change? His spirit! Who could change the spirit of a nation, or the way a society thinks? Neither the European capitalist or engineer, nor those who produced the goods could have done this. Here the European intellectual had to sit down and devise a particular plan that would change the tastes, thoughts and lives of non-European people. This change would not conform to the desires of the non-European because it would have been possible that the changes would result in his not consuming European products. Rather, the changes would be in such a way that his tastes, pleasures, sufferings, sorrows, aims, ideals, aesthetics, customs, social relations and amusements would compel him to become a consumer of European industrial goods. So the great producers and capitalists of nineteenth- and twentieth-century Europe let the intellectuals devise the programme for change.

The programme was that all people on the face of the earth would conform to a single pattern; they would live in the same way and have the same way of thinking. But it is impossible for all nations to think alike. What things make the personality, spiritually and mentality of one person or a nation? Its religion, history, culture, past civilisation, education and customs are all the collection of elements that make up the personality, spirituality and mentality of one person and a nation. These elements differ from society to society; they take one form in Europe and another shape in each corner of Asia and Africa. They all have to conform to a single pattern! In order to conform to a single pattern all the different mentalities that we see in each nation, region and society must be destroyed and they would all follow the same pattern. What is a pattern? The pattern is prepared by Europe and it is shown to all of the East, Asia and Africa just how they should be, how they should wear clothes, how to be sorrowful, how to build a house, how to conduct their social relations, how to hope, how to consume, how to believe and how to worship. After a while we would see that once more a new culture appears in the name of modernisation across the whole world.

Modernisation was the best blow that could empty the way of thinking and personality from any form, mould or mentality of the non-European person in all non-European societies. The only thing that Europe had to do was to create the temptation for 'modernisation' in all societies, whatever form they may have had. They knew that if they created the temptation for modernisation in some way or another, then the Eastern people would co-operate with them to negate everything from their past and deny each element that made up their non-European personality. And with the assistance of the Europeans the Eastern people would destroy and drag through the mud all the aspects that composed their unique culture, religion, and personality.

Therefore, the common duty of all the countries of the Far East, Middle East, Near East, Islamic countries and the countries of black people was to create the temptation and longing for modernisation. 'Modernisation' was an expression for becoming 'European-like'. Modernisation, in other words, modernisation in consumption. He who becomes modernised becomes modern through consumption. The consumption of modern goods means that a person consumes modern ways of life. These new ways of life, these goods that the Eastern person consumes are not compatible with the kinds of products and the kind of lifestyle and customs of his past, and they are not compatible with his origin, society or nation. Rather, they are the kinds that are imported from Europe. Therefore the non-Europeans must become modernised for the sake of consumption. But the Europeans could not say to the non-Europeans, 'We want to insert the desire for the new inventions and creations in your intellects, minds and personalities,' for fear of creating opposition.

So the Europeans wanted to modernise non-European societies (in other words, to avail themselves of new consumers for their goods). They had to make the non-European think that 'modernisation' meant 'civilisation' so that everyone desired civilisation. The Europeans defined modernisation for the non-Europeans as civilisation to the extent that the non-Europeans persuaded themselves to co-operate in modernisation. It was the non-European intellectual (even more than the agents of the bourgeoisie and capitalists, and the agents of European industry) that tried to change the consumption of goods and the way of life in non-European societies. But non-European societies could not produce these new products by themselves, and therefore they became dependent on those machines that were made for them and which expect these societies to purchase.

When I was studying in Europe I heard about the owner of car company who was offering a well-paid job for a student of sociology and psychology.

I went after the job. I was intrigued to know what need a factory that produced cars had of a sociologist or psychologist. So I went there to find out. In the interview which I had with the public relations officer, he said, 'You must be wondering why we invited you for this interview when you have studied sociology, for usually we employ students who have studied sciences!' 'Yes,' I replied. He continued, 'I want to explain this to you,' and he brought out a map of the whole of Asia and Africa and said, 'The factory's cars sell well in cities X, Y and Z where there are many consumers, but in societies A, B, and C the cars do not sell well. Engineers cannot solve this problem, but a sociologist should be able to discover what tastes the people in these societies have and why they don't buy cars, so that we can either change the colour or the design of the car, or else change their tastes.' He then told me about how some European sociologists had been successful in modernising a tribe in Africa.

He pointed out a land of jungle and mountains on the banks of the River Chad in Africa, where many ancient tribal peoples lived. They did not wear clothing and they kept cattle. He pointed out several places where groups of people lived around the chief's fortress, and he pointed out that this tribe still had no school or roads, and that the ordinary people had no proper clothes, and they had no houses for they usually lived in tents. Then he said that the chief of this semi-wild tribe parked two new Renaults with gold stripes along their sides in front of the fortress.

He wanted to say that the interests of the people of this land were in horses. The person who had the best horse was the most famous and the people envied him. Everyone was thinking of rearing a horse better than his. A horse was the means to self-glorification and dominance.

[He said] 'As long as this mentality ruled over the minds of these tribespeople, no one would buy a car. Everyone bought horses, yet we do not produce horses. So we had to think of a way to make the tribes people buy a car that had been made in Europe. The women of this tribe put on the best kind of make-up which is made from gum and sap of the trees of the jungle, and everyone likes it. They dress in the local costume, dance in the local manner, and eat the local food. It is obvious that in these circumstances no woman would buy the cosmetics of Christian Dior, and the men would not buy a Renault car. Europe would never be able to bring its merchandise to such a tribe. Anyway, much preparation was necessary so that the European sociologists in this location, before anything else, could change the tastes of the indigenous peoples. The chief of the tribe used to tie two beautiful horses in front of his fortress with his best hunting dogs. Now he has changed in a way that conforms to his taste, in other words, we have modernised him, for whereas he used to be proud of tying two beautiful, pedigree horses in front of his fortress, now he is proud to park two Renaults with gold trimming there.'

I asked, 'Where are the roads?' He replied, 'Temporarily, they have built seven to eight kilometres of roads around the fortress. When the chief of the tribe first bought the cars he would drive it a little way each morning, and the people would gather and look at the car. The chief didn't have a driver, and so they brought over one from here, and he spent seven or eight months driving there, and they gave him a monthly salary. There were no petrol stations, and so they had to bring petrol from afar by boat.'

So in this way we see that the aim of the capitalist was not to civilise the tribe, but in fact it was to modernise it. The person who used to take pride in horses and ride them now takes pride in his cars and drives them. The chief of the tribe or an Asian or non-European in truth has become modernised. But we must be really simple or judge superficially if we say that they have become civilised too.

Modernisation means changing customs and various consumption patterns of a material nature from old to new because the people themselves made the old goods, and those machines of the nineteenth and twentieth centuries make the new.

Therefore it was necessary for all non-European people to be modernised, and in order to make them modernised they had first to wage war with their religion because religion is the reason that each society perceives its identity. In other words, religion is a meaning, and each person attaches himself to that exalted meaning. If that meaning is crushed, shattered and humiliated, then the person who has accepted that meaning will also be humiliated and shattered. Suddenly, therefore, in the East, in Asia and Africa, resistance movements against prejudice appeared among the indigenous intellectuals.

Fanon[7] said, 'Europe wants all non-Europeans to be slaves to machines. Is it possible for a human being or a society to be a slave to a machine or to a particular European producer before stealing away his personality? Therefore the personality must be destroyed.'

Religion, history, culture, under the rubric of all meaning, thought, the accumulated treasure of art and literature give society its personality, and therefore they must all be destroyed.

In the nineteenth century I would have felt as an Iranian that I was attached to the great civilisation of the fourth, fifth, sixth, seventh and eighth Islamic centuries, which was without equal in the world and, moreover, the whole world came under its influence. I would have felt attached to a culture that was more than two thousand years old, which has created in various ways new intellectuality, literature and art in the world of humanity. I would have felt attached to an Islam which was the greatest, newest and most universal religion, and which created all that intellectuality, and which dissolved all of those other civilisations into itself, thereby creating a great civilisation. I would have felt attached to an Islam that created the most beautiful spirits and the most sublime faces of humanity. And I would have been able to feel, as a human, a human personality in relation to the world and all the people. So how could they change such an 'I' into a tool whose only worth is to consume new merchandise?

They must empty him of his personality. They negate the 'I' that he feels within himself. And they compel him to believe that he is attached to a weaker civilisation, culture and way of life. He must believe that European civilisation, Western civilisation and race are superior. An African must believe that he has been wild in order to create the temptation in him to become civilised. He places his fate in the hands of the Europeans in order to become civilised. But he does not understand that they are modernising him rather than civilising him. For this reason, we see that suddenly Africans of the eighteenth and nineteenth century were described as cannibals and savage. But the African who had dealings with Islamic civilisation was never known as a cannibal. Suddenly, a black African becomes a cannibal, and he has a particular smell and has a special race. The grey cells of his brain do not work, and the forepart of the Easterner's brain is shorter than the European's.

Even their medical doctors and biologists have proved (!!) that the Westerner's brain has an additional grey layer which is not found in Eastern man or negroes, and which assists in the intelligence and the sensitivity of Western man. They have also proved that the Western man's brain has an additional part (which the Easterner lacks) that is the reason for his greater talent and intelligence.

So we see that a new culture is created on the basis on the 'superiority of the West' and the 'superiority of its civilisation and its people', and they have made us and the world believe that the Westerner has a strong intellectual and technical ability, the Easterner has a stronger emotional and gnostic ability, and the negro is good in dancing, playing, music, painting and sculpture.

Therefore, the world has been divided into a race that can think – only Europeans, from ancient Greece to the present day – and a race that can only feel or compose poetry well – the East – that is, a race that only has Sufi and mystical feelings, and negroes who can only sing, dance and play jazz well.

So this way of thinking which has been presented to the world as a foundation in the belief for modernising non-European societies, determines the basic thought of the educated non-Europeans. As we see they caused a hundred years' war between the 'modernised' and 'old-fashioned' in non-European societies, which was, and is, the most futile of wars that humanity has started.

'Modernism' in what? In consumption not in thought.

'Old-fashioned' in what? In the form of consumption.

It was natural that the war ended in favour of modernisation, and if the war had ended in favour of the old-fashioned it would not have been to the benefit of the people. In this war between modernisation and civilisation, the standard-bearer was Europe and it was victorious in the name of modernisation. Then for a hundred years and more, non-European societies progressed by means of their own educated individuals.

How did they make these educated individuals? In the introduction to the book '*The Wretched of the Earth*', Jean-Paul Sartre says:

> We would bring a number of young people from Africa and Asia to Paris and London . . . for a few months, and we would show them around, change their clothes, their make up, and teach them customs, manners, social etiquette and some fragments of language. In short, we emptied them of the contents of their own culture and then sent them back to their own countries. These were people who no longer would speak (for themselves), for they were now our loud-speakers. We would cry out the slogans of humanity and equality, and then the mouths of Africa and Asia opened and they fortified the last part of our words . . . 'ity' . . . 'ity'.

These were persons who could make the people understand that they must put aside prejudice, forget religion and cut off from themselves their indigenous culture which had made them fall behind European societies, and they must become Westernised from head to toe.[8]

How is it possible to become Westernised through exportation or transfer? Is civilisation a piece of merchandise that can be exported from one place and imported into another location? No, but modernisation is an expression for the totality of all new products that can be imported into a society in the course of a year, two years or five years. A society can be completely modernised in the course of several years.

Likewise, an individual can become completely modernised overnight, even more so than a European. You can change his consumption and he becomes modernised. The Europeans did not aim for anything more than this.

But it is not possible to change a society so easily. Civilisation and culture are expressions for goods and merchandise not made in Europe, and their possession [the European products?] does not make one civilised. But they have made us believe that they all result in civilisation!

With enthusiasm we have cast aside everything that we had – even the personality of our society, our morals and our intellect. And we have become an existent that is thirsty to drink whatever a European drops into its mouth, namely, modernisation.

Then a human appeared who was empty of any kind of past. He was alienated from his history and religion, alienated from whatever his race, history and forefathers had built. He was alienated from his own human characteristics. He was a second-hand human being. He was a human being who had changed his pattern of consumption, and his thinking had not just been changed, but he had not even guarded his old thoughts, or past glories or intellectuality, and so he has been emptied.

In the words of Jean-Paul Sartre, in these societies an 'assimilae', in other words, a pseudo–intellectual or educated person, has been created, not real intellectuals or enlightened individuals.

An enlightened person is one that recognises his society and its pains, and can determine its fate, knows what its past is and its meaning, and can choose for himself.

The people too were glued to what these pseudo-enlightened thinkers said. Who were these pseudo-intellectuals in non-European societies? They were the intermediaries between the person who had merchandise and the people who had to change and be the consumers of this merchandise. They were intermediaries who knew European languages and the indigenous language. They facilitated the path for the Europeans, of colonisation and exploitation.

For this reason they created the native enlightened thinkers, but they do not have the courage to choose, discern or decide for themselves, and they do not understand at all their own reality.

Then, in such societies they created people that when asked, did not have the courage to say whether the juice that they drank tasted good or not, or whether they thought that the music to which they listened sounded good or not, or whether they liked the clothes that they wore. This was because it was no longer this person who made this decision.

He must be told that the Europeans like these clothes in order for him to like them. They tell him that today Europeans eat this food (which for him tastes like snake poison), which he does not like, and so we see that he too eats it, and does not have the courage to say, 'I don't like it.'

Therefore, we see there are people in America and Europe who do not like jazz music, who in fact detest it; they complain loudly when they are somewhere where jazz is being played. But in Eastern countries no one has the courage to say, 'Jazz is rubbish, I don't like it.' Why?

Because they have not left him the smallest amount of humanity to have the courage to choose the colour of his own clothes and the flavour of his drink. As Fanon said, in order for non-European societies to become imitators of Europe and to imitate her like a monkey, they had to show to the non-Europeans that they did not have the same qualities as Western humans, and they had to belittle their history, literature, religion and art, and as a result they were made strangers. We see that they have done just that. They created humans who do not recognise their own culture; rather, they hold it in contempt. They do not understand Islam, in fact they say bad things about it. They cannot recite a single, simple poem; instead they curse it. They do not understand their history; rather, they criticise it. Yet they enthuse about everything from Europe without a single reservation or condition.

In conclusion, a human has been made, first, a stranger to his religion, culture, history and his past, and second, hating all of these. He believed that he was inferior to Europeans. When such a belief appeared in him all of his effort and his hopes were spent in denying himself, and severing all of his connections which had been attached to him. He wanted to make himself resemble a human who did not possess such inferiority, in other words, into a European. He wanted to say, 'Thank God that I'm not Eastern. I have been able to modernise myself to the European level.'

Whereas the non-European is happy that he has been modernised, the European capitalists and bourgeoisie laugh to the depths of their hearts that he has become a consumer of theirs.

Notes

1. On the topic of the intellectual refer to 'Where Shall We Begin' and 'The Intellectual and His Responsibility in Society', by Doctor Shari'ati.

2. Herbert Marcuse (1898–1978) was a famous philosopher of the Frankfurt

School. His most famous books include *One Dimensional Man* and *Eros and Civilisation* [Ed.].

3. Rene Guenon (1886–1951) was a Frenchman interested in comparative philosophy and spirituality, reflected in his book *Orient and Occident*. Another well-known book of his is *The Crisis of the Modern World*. He is considered to be the founder of the so-called Traditionalist School, which was interested in Sufism and esoteric traditions. He spent much time in Egypt and became a Muslim, calling himself Abd al-Wahid Yahya. He died in 1951 [Ed.].

4. Professor Chandel had a degree in *ejtehad* from the centres of learning in North Africa and was a friend of the leading existentialists. He was not a real character but one that Shari'ati invented who could 'say what he could not say, give further authority to his views and help him out when he needed the intellectual support of one who would say exactly what Shari'ati wanted him to say.' See A. Rahnema, *An Islamic Utopian* (London: I.B. Tauris, 1998), p. 162 [Ed.].

5. Marcel Mauss (1872–1950) was a student of Durkheim who wrote on gift-exchange and the concept of *habitus* [Ed.].

6. A *jinn* is a creature described in the Qur'an as made of fire, and tradition holds that they can 'possess' humans [Ed.].

7. Frantz Fanon was born in 1925 and was to become a great champion of anti-colonialism. He supported the Algerian independence movement against the French, and wrote major anti-colonialist works, such as *The Wretched of the Earth*. He died in 1961 [Ed.].

8. Shari'ati adds in a footnote that this kind of thinking was advocated by Seyyed Hasan Taqizadeh.

CHAPTER 12

The Necessity for Islamic Government[1]

Ayatollah Khomeini

In chapter eight reference was made to Khomeini's mystical inclinations, and his discussion of the four journeys in which the mystic travels from the world of creation to God, and returns back to mankind to engage in perfecting humans. The identity of the individual who completes these four journeys is left somewhat ambiguous in Khomeini's writings, but an acceptable view would be that he is a prophet or a Shi'-ite Imam. Some scholars, however, have claimed that Khomeini himself believed that he had completed the four journeys.[2] This belief has important consequences, as it ultimately denies political legitimacy to rulers such as the Pahlavi monarchs whose autocratic rule saw little room for Islamic sentiments and democracy. Indeed, Khomeini's Islamic government viewed the clerical authorities as having the responsibility of forming a government, even though the traditional Shi'-ite view is that Islamic government was the prerogative of the Imams. However, once the Twelfth Imam went into occultation he could no longer provide the function of government, although in theory he retains political legitimacy. This has been the source of potential conflict between clerical authorities and the various dynasties in Iran since the emergence of the Safavid dynasty. Yet, Khomeini argued that Islamic government was necessary: 'When we say that after the Occultation, the just faqih *[jurisprudent] has the same authority that the Most Noble Messenger and the Imams had, do not imagine that the status of the* faqih *is identical to that of the Imams and the Prophet.'[3] The necessity for the clerical authorities to engage in government is therefore paramount in Khomeini's world view and is not necessarily tied to the 'four journeys' (and some scholars are more hesitant than Moin and Ha'iri Yazdi in claiming that Khomeini believed he had undergone the four journeys). Yet the following remarks by Hamid Algar seem fair: 'For . . . Khomeini, however, spirituality and mysticism have never implied social withdrawal or political quietism, but rather the building up of a fund of energy that finds its natural expression on the socio-political plane.'[4]*

Khomeini's mystical writings were produced when he was in his twenties and thirties, but his works became more explicitly political with the overthrow of Reza Shah. However, he was not able to criticise the policies of the new Shah because he was obliged to pay due respect to the most senior cleric, the marja' taqlid, *Ayatollah Borujerdi, who according to most accounts was politically quiescent and co-operated with the monarchy to preserve law and order.*[5] *However, on Borujerdi's death Khomeini, perhaps, no longer felt restrained, as he was recognised by some as a legitimate* marja' taqlid *in his own right. In 1962 Mohammad Reza Shah launched a series of reforms known as the White Revolution, which Khomeini opposed due to the perceived threat to traditional Islamic interests. A showdown ensued between Khomeini and the Shah, and the conflict became serious in 1963 when the Shah's paratroopers attacked the Fayziyeh seminary in Qom and Khomeini was subsequently arrested and then exiled to Turkey, from where he then was able to go to Najaf in Iraq and continue his opposition to the Shah's regime.*

It was in Najaf that Khomeini gave a series of lectures on Islamic government, which emerged because of a dispute with Ayatollah Khoi, who had argued that there was no obligation for clerics to participate directly in politics.[6] *'Islamic government' was in fact a series of lectures that Khomeini had given in early 1970 in Najaf, and which had been recorded, transcribed and published in book form by one of his students. In its English translation, the work is 122 pages long and is divided into four sections: an introduction, the necessity for Islamic government, the form of Islamic government, and the programme for the establishment of an Islamic government.*

Khomeini's theory of Islamic government is significant because it provided an alternative in the 1970s to the non-clerical works of intellectuals such as Jalal Al-e Ahmad and 'Ali Shari'ati. Moreover, it continued the trend of clerical figures responding to the changing circumstances under which they were forced to operate, including the new secular ideologies and the changing nature of a modernising, centralising and increasingly complex society. For example, Ayatollah Taleqani had played a major role in discussions with clerical and lay figures in the early 1960s concerning the reform of the clergy. Their conclusions included suggestions that collegial decisions should be made and that leading clerics should specialise in specific areas.

Islamic government is built upon the claim that there is no distinction between religion and politics in Islam, and Khomeini offers the example of Islamic taxes and the shari'a *as indications of the all-encompassing nature of a complete social system. With the occultation of the Twelfth Imam, the legitimacy of rule falls upon the shoulders of the* faqihs, *or the clerics. The governance of the* faqih (velayat-e faqih) *is the ideal form of government, and the appropriate* faqihs *to rule are those who are 'learned in matters pertaining to the function of judge . . . [are] just . . . [and] the third qualification is that he should be an imam, in the sense of a leader'.*[7] *Khomeini is frustratingly brief about the* faqihs *and the form of government, although the following is worthy of consideration:*

> *The authority that the Prophet and the Imam had in establishing a government executing laws, and administering affairs, exists also for the* faqih. *But the* fuqaha [pl. of faqih] *do not have absolute authority in the sense of having authority over all other* fuqaha *of their own time, being able to appoint or*

dismiss them. There is no hierarchy ranking one faqih *higher than another or endowing one with more authority than another.*[8]

This point becomes significant in the light of the treatment meted out to clerics who opposed Khomeini's understanding of velayat-e faqih (such as Ayatollah Shari'atmadari) who envisaged a much less political role of supervision for the clergy in its relations with political leaders. Moreover, the absence of hierarchy seems all the more difficult to substantiate with the removal of Ayatollah Montazeri, who was 'forced' to resign as Khomeini's successor.[9] Khomeini does states that the fuqaha can establish a government collectively (perhaps he had in mind the group of mojtaheds mentioned in the Supplementary Fundamental Laws that emerged in the wake of the Constitutional Revolution, and which had been promoted by Shaykh Fazl Allah Nuri),[10] or individually.

Khomeini must have been conscious that his understanding of velayat-e faqih (by which the clergy became the supreme political rulers) was controversial, if not an innovation. And to counter criticisms he gave examples of leading clerics who had issued fatwas that amounted to governmental rulings. He cited Mirza Hasan Shirazi's famous fatwa against the use of tobacco, Mirza Mohammed Taqi Shirazi's fatwa for jihad against the British in Iraq at the end of the First World War, and he also claimed that Kashef al-Ghita (a leading Shi'-ite scholar based in Iraq who died in 1954) expressed the same opinion about velayat-e faqih.[11]

It is beyond the scope of this introduction to describe the events leading to Khomeini's return to Iran, the fall of the Pahlavi dynasty, and the implementation of velayat-e faqih. This doctrine has never been wholeheartedly embraced by all Iranians, even all clerics, as the cases of Ayatollahs Khoi and Shari 'atmadari have shown. Moreover, with the election of Mohammad Khatami in 1997 to the position of President there has been increasing criticism directed at the doctrine from both clerics and lay individuals. Given the 'routinisation of charisma' and the death of Khomeini this perhaps was inevitable, but the appointment of 'Ali Khamene'i, who at the time was a relatively junior clerical figure, to the leadership of the Islamic Republic revealed that the leadership of the velayat-e faqih was different from marja' iyyat (or the role of being a marja' taqlid). Indeed, 'Ali Akbar Rafsanjani (one of Khomeini's early disciples and former President of the Islamic Republic) claimed that Khomeini had said that marja'iyyat was not a condition for the leadership and that any faqih (even if he was not a mojtahed) could be the vali.[12] In effect, such an argument leads to the conclusion that the religious and political spheres are separate. The qualities that the jurist should possess according to Khomeini's idealised view (delivered in an address in 1989) suggest the difficulties facing the leader of the Islamic Republic:

A mojtahed should be fully aware of his time. It is not acceptable that he should say that he will not express an opinion regarding political issues. Familiarity with the methods of dealing with the tricks and deceits of the culture governing the world, the possession of an economic understanding and knowledge . . . familiarity with policies and even politicians . . . An authoritative interpreter *should possess the intelligence and shrewdness necessary for managing and safeguarding a great Islamic or even a non-Islamic society. He should in addition to possessing piety and sincerity, and asceticism befitting a mojtahed, be a skilful manager.*[13]

Although this ideal mojtahed *remains an ideal, it is also a reflection of extreme pragmatism. The* mojtahed *must now get involved in worldly affairs and dirty his hands in political intrigues, not just simply engage in discussions of ritual purity and asceticism. Khomeini's political pragmatism is not a recent development, necessitated by circumstances, as in his lectures on Islamic government in the 1970s he remarked: 'Anyone who rules over the Muslims, or even human society in general, must always take into consideration the public welfare and interest, and ignore personal feelings and interests. For this reason, Islam is prepared to subordinate individuals to the collective interest of society and has rooted out numerous groups that were a source of corruption and harm to human society.'*[14] *If one leaves aside the ominous reference to the subordination of individuals and focuses on the collective interest of society, it is possible to see a consistency in Khomeini's doctrine that Islamic government is the priority. This message resurfaced nearly thirty years later when he remarked that:*

> *Government is a branch of Mohammad's absolute vice-regency, and is one of the first precepts of Islam. It takes precedence over all religious practices such as prayer, fasting or the Hajj pilgrimage . . . I openly say that the government can stop any religious law if it feels that it is correct to do so . . . the ruler can close or destroy the mosques whenever he sees fit.'*[15]

Velayat-e faqih is a doctrine that for Khomeini amalgamated various strands of Islamic thought, including the mystical and the legal. Not without its opponents, Khomeini's interpretation and that offered by those who endorse the current spiritual leader, 'Ali Khamene'i, has resulted in some confusion between the role of the leader of the Islamic Republic and that of the individual marja' taqlids. *The ideal* mojtahed *that Khomeini described cannot possibly exist given the complexities of modern society, and such specialised knowledge can exist only among several individuals, as was recognised in the discussions initiated by Ayatollah Taleqani in the 1960s and prior to that in the Constitutional period when Supplementary Fundamental Laws envisaged a body of no fewer than five* mojtaheds. *It is ironic indeed that the institution by which Khomeini attempted to weld politics and religion together now reflects the difficulty and perhaps the failure of the Islamic Republic to unite these two spheres.*

Notes

[1.] 'The Necessity for Islamic Government' is the second chapter in Khomeini's work *Islamic Government*, translated by Hamid Algar, and contained in *Islam and*

Revolution: Writings and Declarations (London: KPI, 1985), pp. 40–54. Reproduced with permission.

[2.] See B. Moin, 'Khomeini's Search for Perfection', in A. Rahnema (ed.), *Pioneers of Islamic Revival* (London: Zed Books, 1994), p. 74. Moin's claim is based upon a discussion with Professor Mehdi Ha'iri Yazdi, the son of Ayatollah Ha'iri who was a former student of Khomeini's.

[3.] *Islam and Revolution,* p. 62.

[4.] "Introduction", *Islam and Revolution,* p.14.

[5.] M. M. J. Fischer, 'Imam Khomeini' in J. Esposito (ed.), *Voices of Resurgent Islam* (Oxford University Press, 1983), p. 152.

[6.] Ibid., p. 157.

[7.] Khomeini, *Islam and Revolution,* trans. Hamid Algar, p. 84.

[8.] Ibid., p. 64.

[9.] On the disputes surrounding the *velayat-e faqih* in post-revolutionary Iran see D. Menashri, *Post-Revolutionary Politics in Iran,* pp. 13–46.

[10.] 'There shall be at all times a council of not less than five persons who are mojtaheds or jurists, well versed in the religious law, and aware of the exigencies of the age.' See Vanessa Martin, *Islam and Modernism: The Iranian Revolution of 1906* (Syracuse University Press, 1989), p. 120.

[11.] Imam Khomeini, *Islam and Revolution,* p. 124.

[12.] D. Menashri, *Post-Revolutionary Politics in Iran,* p. 18.

[13.] From a message addressed by Khomeini to the instructors and students of religious seminaries, February 22, 1989. Printed in the *Guardian* (6 March 1989).

[14.] Imam Khomeini, *Islam and Revolution,* p. 89.

[15.] *Middle East International,* 317, 23 January 1988, p. 18.

Further Reading

M. Boroujerdi, *Iranian Intellectuals and the West* (Utica, NY: Syracuse University Press, 1996) (Chapter 4, 'The Clerical Substructure', pp. 77–98).

M. Fischer, 'Imam Khomeini: Four Levels of Understanding', in J. Esposito (ed.), *Voices of Resurgent Islam* (Oxford University Press, 1983), pp. 150–74.

V. Martin, *Creating an Islamic State: Khomeini and the Making of a New Iran* (London: I.B. Tauris, 2000).

D. Menashri, *Post-Revolutionary Politics in Iran* (London: Frank Cass, 2001) (Chapter 1, 'The Guardianship of the Jurisconsult: The Ideological Dilemma', pp. 13–46).

B. Moin, *Khomeini: Life of the Ayatollah* (London: I.B. Tauris, 1999).

—•—

[A body of laws alone is not sufficient for a society to be reformed. In order for law to ensure the reform and happiness of man, there must be an executive power and an executor. For this reason, God Almighty, in addition to revealing a body of law (i.e., the ordinances of the *Shari'a*), has laid down a particular form of government together with executive and administrative institutions.

The Most Noble Messenger (peace and blessings be upon him) headed the executive and administrative institutions of Muslim society. In addition to conveying the revelation and expounding and interpreting the articles of faith and the ordinances and institutions of Islam, he undertook the implementation of law and the establishment of the ordinances of Islam, thereby bringing into being the Islamic state. He did not content himself with the promulgation of law; rather, he implemented it at the same time, cutting off hands and administering lashings and stonings. After the Most Noble Messenger, his successor had the same duty and function. When the Prophet appointed a successor, it was not for the purpose of expounding articles of faith and law; it was for the implementation of law and the execution of God's ordinances. It was this function – the execution of law and the establishment of Islamic institutions – that made the appointment of a successor such an important matter that the Prophet would have failed to fulfil his mission if he had neglected it. For after the Prophet, the Muslims still needed someone to execute laws and establish the institutions of Islam in society, so that they might attain happiness in this world and the hereafter.

By their very nature, in fact, law and social institutions require the existence of an executor. It has always and everywhere been the case that legislation alone has little benefit: legislation by itself cannot assure the well-being of man. After the establishment of legislation, an executive power must come into being, a power that implements the laws and the verdicts given by the courts, thus allowing people to benefit from the laws and the just sentences the courts deliver. Islam has therefore established an executive power in the same way that it has brought laws into being. The person who holds this executive power is known as the *vali amr*.[1]

The Sunna[2] and path of the Prophet constitute a proof of the necessity for establishing government. First, he himself established a government, as history testifies. He engaged in the implementation of laws, the establishment of the ordinances of Islam, and the administration of society. He sent out governors to different regions; both sat in judgment himself and appointed judges; dispatched emissaries to foreign states, tribal chieftains, and kings; concluded treaties and pacts; and took command in battle. In short, he fulfilled all the functions of government. Second, he designated a ruler to succeed him, in accordance with divine command. If God Almighty, through the Prophet, designated a man who was to rule over Muslim society after him, this is in itself an indication that government remains a necessity after the departure of the Prophet from this world. Again, since the Most Noble Messenger promulgated the divine command through his act of appointing a successor, he also implicitly stated the necessity for establishing a government.

It is self-evident that the necessity for enactment of the law, which necessitated the formation of a government by the Prophet (upon whom be peace), was not confined or restricted to his time, but continues after his departure from this world. According to one of the noble verses of the Qur'an, the ordinances of Islam are not limited with respect to time or place; they are permanent and must be enacted until the end of time. They were not revealed merely for the time of the Prophet, only to be abandoned thereafter, with retribution and the penal code of Islam no longer to be enacted, or the taxes prescribed by Islam no longer collected, and the defence of the lands and people of Islam suspended. The claim that the laws of Islam may remain in abeyance or are restricted to a particular time or place is contrary to the essential credal bases of Islam. Since the enactment of laws, then, is necessary after the departure of the Prophet from this world, and indeed, will remain so until the end of time, the formation of a government and the establishment of executive and administrative organs are also necessary. Without the formation of a government and the establishment of such organs to ensure that through enactment of the law, all activities of the individual take place in the framework of a just system, chaos and anarchy will prevail and social, intellectual, and moral corruption will arise. The only way to prevent the emergence of anarchy and disorder and to protect society from corruption is to form a government and thus impart order to all the affairs of the country.

Both reason and divine law, then, demonstrate the necessity in our time for what was necessary during the lifetime of the Prophet and the age of the Commander of the Faithful, 'Ali ibn Abi Talib (peace be upon them) – namely the formation of a government and the establishment of executive and administrative organs.

In order to clarify the matter further, let us pose the following questions: from the time of the Lesser Occultation[3] down to the present (a period of more than twelve centuries that may continue for hundreds of millennia if it is not appropriate for the Occulted Imam to manifest himself), is it proper that the laws of Islam be cast aside and remain unexecuted, so that everyone acts as he pleases and anarchy prevails? Were the laws that the Prophet of Islam laboured so hard for twenty-three years to set forth, promulgate, and execute valid only for a limited period of time? Did God limit the validity of His laws to two hundred years? Was everything pertaining to Islam meant to be abandoned after the Lesser Occultation? Anyone who believes so, or voices such a belief, is worse situated than the person who believes and proclaims that Islam has been superseded or abrogated by another supposed revelation.[4]

No one can say it is no longer necessary to defend the frontiers and the territorial integrity of the Islamic homeland; that taxes such as the *jizya, kharaj, khums* and *zakat* [5] should no longer be collected; that the penal code of Islam, with its provisions for the payment of blood money and the exacting of requital, should be suspended. Any person who claims that the formation of an Islamic government is not necessary implicitly denies the necessity for the implementation of Islamic law, the universality and comprehensiveness of that law, and the eternal validity of the faith itself.

After the death of the Most Noble Messenger (peace and blessings be upon him), none of the Muslims doubted the necessity for government. No one said: 'We no longer need a government.' No one was heard to say anything of the kind. There was unanimous agreement concerning the necessity for government. There was disagreement only as to which person should assume responsibility for government and head the state. Government, therefore, was established after the Prophet (upon whom be peace and blessings), both in the time of the caliphs and in that of the Commander of the Faithful (peace be upon him); an apparatus of government came into existence with administrative and executive organs.

The nature and character of Islamic law and the divine ordinances of the *shari'a* furnish additional proof of the necessity for establishing government, for they indicate that the laws were laid down for the purpose of creating a state and administering the political, economic, and cultural affairs of society.

First, the laws of the *shari'a* embrace a diverse body of laws and regulations, which amounts to a complete social system. In this system of laws, all the needs of man have been met: his dealings with his neighbours, fellow citizens, and clan, as well as children and relatives; the concerns of private and marital life; regulations concerning war and peace and intercourse with other nations; penal and commercial law; and regulations pertaining to trade and agriculture. Islamic law contains provisions relating to the preliminaries of marriage and the form in which it should be contracted, and others relating to the development of the embryo in the womb and what food the parents should eat at the time of conception. It further stipulates the duties that are incumbent upon them while the infant is being suckled, and specifies how the child should be reared, and how the husband and the wife should relate to each other and to their children. Islam provides laws and instructions for all of these matters, aiming, as it does, to produce integrated and virtuous human beings who are walking embodiments of the law, or to put it differently, the law's voluntary and instinctive executors. It is obvious, then, how much care Islam devotes to government and the political and economic relations of society, with the goal of creating conditions conducive to the production of morally upright and virtuous human beings.

The Glorious Qur'an and the Sunna contain all the laws and ordinances man needs in order to attain happiness and the perfection of his state. The book *al-Kafi*[6] has a chapter entitled, 'All the Needs of Men are Set Out in the Book and the Sunna', the 'Book' meaning the Qur'an, which is, in its own words, 'an exposition of all things'.[7] According to certain traditions, the Imam[8] also swears that the Book and the Sunna contain without a doubt all that men need.

Second, if we examine closely the nature and character of the provisions of the law, we realise that their execution and implementation depend upon the formation of a government, and that it is impossible to fulfil the duty of executing God's commands without there being established properly comprehensive administrative and executive organs. Let us now mention certain types of provision in order to illustrate this point; the others you can examine yourselves.

The taxes Islam levies and the form of budget it has established are not merely for the sake of providing subsistence to the poor or feeding the indigent among the descendants of the Prophet (peace and blessings be upon him); they are also intended to make possible the establishment of a great government and to assure its essential expenditures.

For example, *khums* is a huge source of income that accrues to the treasury and represents one item in the budget. According to our Shi'i school of thought, *khums* is to be levied in an equitable manner on all agricultural and commercial profits and all natural resources whether above or below the ground – in short, on all forms of wealth and income. It applies equally to the greengrocer with his stall outside this mosque and to the shipping or mining magnate. They must all pay one fifth of their surplus income, after customary expenses are deducted, to the Islamic ruler so that it enters the treasury. It is obvious that such a huge income serves the purpose of administering the Islamic state and meeting all its financial needs. If we were to calculate one fifth of the surplus income of all the Muslim countries (or of the whole world, should it enter the fold of Islam), it would become fully apparent that the purpose for the imposition of such a tax is not merely the upkeep of the *sayyids*[9] or the religious scholars, but on the contrary, something far more significant – namely, meeting the financial needs of the great organs and institutions of government. If an Islamic government is achieved, it will have to be administered on the basis of the taxes that Islam has established – *khums, zakat* (this of course, would not represent an appreciable sum),[10] *jizya,* and *kharaj.*

How could the *sayyids* ever need so vast a budget? The *khums* of the bazaar of Baghdad would be enough for the needs of the *sayyids* and the upkeep of the religious teaching institution, as well as all the poor of the Islamic world, quite apart from the *khums* of the bazaars of Tehran, Istanbul, Cairo, and other cities. The provision of such a huge budget must obviously be for the purpose of forming a government and administering the Islamic lands. It was established with the aim of providing for the needs of the people, for public services relating to health, education, defence, and economic development. Further, in accordance with the procedures laid down by Islam for the collection, preservation, and expenditure of this income, all forms of usurpation and embezzlement of public wealth have been forbidden, so that the head of state and all those entrusted with responsibility for conducting public affairs (i.e., members of the government) have no privileges over the ordinary citizen in benefiting from the public income and wealth; all have an equal share.

Now, should we cast this huge treasury into the ocean, or bury it until the Imam returns, or just spend it on fifty *sayyids* a day until they have all eaten their fill? Let us suppose we give all this money to 500,000 *sayyids*, they would not know what to do with it. We all know that the *sayyids* and the poor have a claim on the public treasury only to the extent required for subsistence. The budget of the Islamic state is constructed in such a way that every source of income is allocated to specific types of expenditures. *Zakat*, voluntary contributions and charitable donations, and *khums* are all levied and spent separately. There is a *hadith* to the effect that at the end of the year, *sayyids* must return any surplus from what they have received to the Islamic ruler, just as the ruler must aid them if they are in need.

The *jizya*, which is imposed on the *ahl adh-dhimma*,[11] and the *kharaj*, which is levied on agricultural land, represent two additional sources of considerable income. The establishment of these taxes also proves that the existence of a ruler and a government is necessary. It is the duty of a ruler or governor to assess the poll-tax to be levied on the *ahl adh-dhimma* in accordance with their income and financial capacity, and to fix appropriate taxes on their arable lands and livestock. He must also collect the *kharaj* on those broad lands that are the 'property of God' and in the possession of the Islamic state. This task requires the existence of orderly institutions, rules and regulations, and administrative processes and policies; it cannot be fulfilled in the absence of order. It is the responsibility of those in charge of the Islamic state, first, to assess the taxes in due and appropriate measure and in accordance with the public good; then, to collect them; and finally, to spend them in a manner conducive to the welfare of the Muslims.

Thus, you see that the fiscal provisions of Islam also point to the necessity for establishing a government, for they cannot be fulfilled without the establishment of the appropriate Islamic institutions.

The ordinances pertaining to preservation of the Islamic order and defence of the territorial integrity and the independence of the Islamic *umma*[12] also demanded the formation of a government. An example is the command: 'Prepare against them whatever force you can muster and horses tethered' (Qur'an, 8:60), which enjoins the preparation of as much armed defensive force as possible and orders the Muslims to be always on the alert and at the ready, even in time of peace.

If the Muslims had acted in accordance with this command and, after forming a government, made the necessary extensive preparations to be in a state of full readiness for war, a handful of Jews would never have dared to occupy our lands, and to burn and destroy the Masjid al-Aqsa[13] without the people's being capable of making an immediate response. All this has resulted from the failure of the Muslims to fulfil their duty of executing God's law and setting up a righteous and respectable government. If the rulers of the Muslim countries truly represented the believers and enacted God's ordinances, they would set aside their petty differences, abandon their subversive and divisive activities, and join together like the fingers of one hand. Then a handful of wretched Jews (the agents of America, Britain, and other foreign powers) would never have been able to accomplish what they have, no matter how much support they enjoyed from America and Britain. All this has happened because of the incompetence of those who rule over the Muslims.

The verse: 'Prepare against them whatever force you can muster' commands you to be as strong and well-prepared as possible, so that your enemies will be unable to oppress you and transgress against you. It is because we have been lacking in unity, strength, and preparedness that we suffer oppression and are at the mercy of foreign aggressors.

There are numerous provisions of the law that cannot be implemented without the establishment of a governmental apparatus: for example, blood money, which must be exacted and delivered to those deserving it, or the corporeal penalties imposed by the law, which must be carried out under the supervision of the Islamic ruler. All of these laws refer back to the institutions of government, for it is governmental power alone that is capable of fulfilling this function.

After the death of the Most Noble Messenger (peace and blessings be upon him), the obstinate enemies of the faith, the Umayyads[14] (God's curses be upon them) did not permit the Islamic state to attain stability with the rule of 'Ali ibn Abi Talib (upon whom be peace). They did not allow a form of government to exist that was pleasing to God, Exalted and Almighty, and to his Most Noble Messenger. They transformed the entire basis of government, and their policies were, for the most part, contradictory to Islam. The form of government of the Umayyads and the Abbasids,[15] and the political and administrative policies they pursued, were anti-Islamic. The form of government was thoroughly perverted by being transformed into a monarchy, like those of the kings of Iran, the emperors of Rome, and the pharaohs of Egypt. For the most part, this non-Islamic form of government has persisted to the present day, as we can see.

Both law and reason require that we not permit governments to retain this non-Islamic or anti-Islamic character. The proofs are clear. First, the existence of a non-Islamic political order necessarily results in the non-implementation of the Islamic political order. Then all non-Islamic systems of government are the systems of *kufr*,[16] since the ruler in each case is an instance of *taghut*,[17] and it is our duty to remove from the life of Muslim society all traces of *kufr* and destroy them. It is also our duty to create a favourable social environment for the education of believing and virtuous individuals, an environment that is in total contradiction to that produced by the rule of *taghut* and illegitimate power. The social environment created by *taghut* and *shirk*[18] invariably brings about corruption such as you can now observe in Iran, the corruption termed 'corruption on earth'.[19] This corruption must be swept away, and its instigators punished for their deeds. It is the same corruption that the Pharaoh generated in Egypt with his policies, so that the Qur'an says of him, 'Truly he was among the corruptors' (28:4). A believing, pious, just individual cannot possibly exist in a socio-political environment of this nature and still maintain his faith and righteous conduct. He is faced with two choices: either he commits acts that amount to *kufr* and contradict righteousness, or in order not to commit such acts and not to submit to the orders and commands of the *taghut*, the just individual opposes him and struggles against him in order to destroy the environment of corruption. We have in reality, then, no choice but to destroy those systems of government that are corrupt in themselves and also entail the corruption of others, and to overthrow all treacherous, corrupt, oppressive, and criminal regimes.

This is a duty that all Muslims must fulfil, in every one of the Muslim countries, in order to achieve the triumphant political revolution of Islam.

We see, too, that together, the imperialists and the tyrannical self-seeking rulers have divided the Islamic homeland. They have separated the various segments of the Islamic *umma* from each other and artificially created separate nations. There once existed the great Ottoman State, and that, too, the imperialists divided. Russia, Britain, Austria, and other imperialist powers united, and through wars against the Ottomans, each came to occupy or absorb into its sphere of influence part of the Ottoman realm. It is true that most of the Ottoman rulers were incompetent, that some of them were corrupt, and that they followed a monarchical system. Nevertheless, the existence of the Ottoman State represented a threat to the imperialists. It was always possible that righteous individuals might rise up among the people and, with their assistance, seize control of the state, thus putting an end to imperialism by mobilising the unified resources of the nation. Therefore, after numerous prior wars, the imperialists at the end of the First World War divided the Ottoman State, creating in its territories about ten or fifteen petty states.[20] Then each of these was entrusted to one of their servants or a group of their servants, although certain countries were later able to escape the grasp of the agents of imperialism.

In order to assure the unity of the Islamic *umma*, in order to liberate the Islamic homeland from occupation and penetration by the imperialists and their puppet governments, it is imperative that we establish a government. In order to attain the unity and freedom of the Muslim peoples, we must overthrow the oppressive governments installed by the imperialists and bring into existence an Islamic government of justice that will be in the service of the people. The formation of such a government will serve to preserve the disciplined unity of the Muslims; just as Fatima az-Zahra[21] (upon whom be peace) said in her address: 'The Imamate exists for the sake of preserving order among the Muslims and replacing their disunity with unity.'

Through the political agents they have placed in power over the people, the imperialists have also imposed on us an unjust economic order, and thereby divided our people into two groups: oppressors and oppressed. Hundreds of millions of Muslims are hungry and deprived of all form of health care and education, while minorities comprised of the wealthy and powerful live a life of indulgence, licentiousness, and corruption. The hungry and deprived have constantly struggled to free themselves from the oppression of their plundering overlords, and their struggle continues to this day. But their way is blocked by the ruling minorities and the oppressive governmental structures they head. It is our duty to save the oppressed and deprived. It is our duty to be a helper to the oppressed and an enemy to the oppressor. This is nothing other than the duty that the Commander of the Faithful (upon whom be peace) entrusted to his two great offspring[22] in his celebrated testament: 'Be an enemy to the oppressor and a helper to the oppressed.'

The scholars of Islam have a duty to struggle against all attempts by the oppressors to establish a monopoly over the sources of wealth or to make illicit use of them. They must not allow the masses to remain hungry and deprived while plundering oppressors usurp the sources of wealth and live in opulence. The Commander of the Faithful (upon whom be peace) says: 'I have accepted the task of government because God, Exalted and Almighty, has exacted from the scholars of Islam a pledge not to sit silent and idle in the face of the gluttony and plundering of the oppressors, on the one hand, and the hunger and deprivation of the oppressed, on the other.' Here is the full text of the passage we refer to:

> 'I swear by Him Who causes the seed to open and creates the souls of all living things that were it not for the presence of those who have come to swear allegiance to me, were it not for the obligation of rulership now imposed upon me by the availability of aid and support, and were it not for the pledge that God has taken from the scholars of Islam not to remain silent in the face of the gluttony and plundering of the oppressors, on the one hand, and the harrowing hunger and deprivation of the oppressed, on the other hand – were it not for all of this, then I would abandon the reins of government and in no way seek it. You would see that this world of yours, with all of its position and rank, is less in my eyes than the moisture that comes from the sneeze of a goat.'[23]

How can we stay silent and idle today when we see that a band of traitors and usurpers, the agents of foreign powers, have appropriated the wealth and the fruits of labour of hundreds of millions of Muslims – thanks to the support of their masters and through the power of the bayonet – granting the Muslims not the least right to prosperity? It is the duty of Islamic scholars and all Muslims to put an end to this system of oppression and, for the sake of the well-being of hundreds of millions of human beings, to overthrow these oppressive governments and form an Islamic government.

Reason, the law of Islam, the practice of the Prophet (upon whom be peace and blessings) and that of the Commander of the Faithful (upon whom be peace), the purport of various Qur'anic verses and Prophetic traditions – all indicate the necessity of forming a government. As an example of the traditions of the Imams, I now quote the following tradition of Imam Riza[24] (upon whom be peace):

> 'Abd al-Wahid ibn Muhammad ibn' Abdus an-Nisaburi al-'Attar said, 'I was told by Abu'l-Hasan 'Ali ibn Muhammad ibn Qutayba al-Naysaburi that he was told by Abu Muhammad al-Fadl ibn Shadhan al-Naysaburi this tradition. If someone asks, 'Why has God, the All-Wise, appointed the holders of authority and commanded us to obey them?' then we answer, 'For numerous reasons. One reason is this: Men are commanded to observe certain limits and not to transgress them in order to avoid the corruption that would result. This cannot be attained or established without there being appointed over them a trustee who will ensure that they remain within the limits of the licit and prevent them from casting themselves into the danger transgression. Were it not for such a trustee, no one would abandon his own pleasure and benefit because of the corruption it might entail for another. Another reason is that we find no group or nation of men that ever existed without a ruler and leader, since it is required by both religion and worldly interest. It would not be compatible with divine wisdom to leave mankind to its own devices, for He, the All-Wise, knows that men need a ruler for their survival, it is through the leadership he provides that men make war against their enemies, divide among themselves the spoils of war and preserve their communal solidarity, preventing the oppression of the oppressed by the oppressor.
>
> 'A further reason is this: were God not to appoint over men a solicitous, trustworthy, protecting, reliable leader, the community would decline, religion would depart, and the norms and ordinances that have been revealed would undergo change. Innovators would increase and deniers would erode religion, inducing doubt in the Muslims. For we see that men are needy and defective, judging by their differences of opinion and inclination and their diversity of state. Were a trustee, then, not appointed to preserve what has been revealed through the Prophet, corruption would ensue in the manner we have described. Revealed laws, norms, ordinances, and faith would be

altogether changed, and therein would lie the corruption of all mankind.'[25]

We have omitted the first part of the *hadith*, which pertains to prophethood, a topic not germane to our present discussion. What interest us at present is the second half, which I will now paraphrase for you.

If someone should ask you, 'Why has God, the All-Wise, appointed holders of authority and commanded you to obey them?' you should answer him as follows: 'He has done so for various causes and reasons. One is that men have been set upon a certain well-defined path and commanded not to stray from it, nor to transgress against the established limits and norms, for if they were to stray, they would fall prey to corruption. Now men would not be able to keep to their ordained path and to enact God's laws unless a trustworthy and protective individual (or power) were appointed over them with responsibility for this matter, to prevent them from stepping outside the sphere of the licit and transgressing against the rights of others. If no such restraining individual or power were appointed, nobody would voluntarily abandon any pleasure or interest of his own that might result in harm or corruption to others; everybody would engage in oppressing and harming others for the sake of their own pleasures and interests.

'Another reason and cause is this: we do not see a single group, nation, or religious community that has ever been able to exist without an individual entrusted with the maintenance of its laws and institutions – in short, a head or a leader; for such a person is essential for fulfilling the affairs of religion and the world. It is not permissible, therefore, according to divine wisdom, that God should leave men, His creatures, without a leader and guide, for He knows well that they depend on the existence of such a person for their own survival and perpetuation. It is under his leadership that they fight against their enemies, divide the public income among themselves, perform Friday and congregational prayer, and foreshorten the arms of the transgressors who would encroach on the rights of the oppressed.

'Another proof and cause is this: were God not to appoint an Imam over men to maintain law and order, to serve the people faithfully as a vigilant trustee, religion would fall victim to obsolescence and decay. Its rites and institutions would vanish; the customs and ordinances of Islam would be transformed or even deformed. Heretical innovators would add things to religion and atheists and unbelievers would subtract things from it, presenting it to the Muslims in an inaccurate manner. For we see that men are prey to defects; they are not perfect and must needs strive after perfection. Moreover, they disagree with each other, having varying inclinations and discordant states. If God, therefore, had not appointed over men one who would maintain order and law and protect the revelation brought by the Prophet, in the manner we have described, men would fall prey to corruption; the institutions, laws, customs, and ordinances of Islam would be transformed; and faith and its content would be completely changed, resúlting in the corruption of all humanity.'

As you can deduce from the words of the Imam (upon whom be peace), there are numerous proofs and causes that necessitate formation of a government, and establishment of an authority. These proofs, causes, and arguments are not temporary in their validity or limited to a particular time, and the necessity for the formation of a government, therefore, is perpetual. For example, it will always happen that men overstep the limits laid down by Islam and transgress against the rights of others for the sake of their personal pleasure and benefit. It cannot be asserted that such was the case only in the time of the Commander of the Faithful (upon whom be peace) and that afterwards, men became angels. The wisdom of the Creator has decreed that men should live in accordance with justice and act within the limits set by divine law. This wisdom is eternal and immutable, and constitutes one of the norms of God Almighty. Today and always, therefore, the existence of a holder of authority, a ruler who acts as trustee and maintains the institution and laws of Islam, is a necessity – a ruler who prevents cruelty, oppression, and violation of the rights of others; who is a trustworthy and vigilant guardian of God's creatures; who guides men to the teachings, doctrines, laws, and institutions of Islam; and who prevents the undesirable changes that atheists and the enemies of religion wish to introduce in the laws and institutions of Islam. Did not the caliphate of the Commander of the Faithful serve this purpose? The same factors of necessity that led him to become the Imam still exist; the only difference is that no single individual has been designated for the task.[26] The principle of the necessity of government has been made a general one, so that it will always remain in effect.

If the ordinances of Islam are to remain in effect, then, if encroachment by oppressive ruling classes on the rights of the weak is to be prevented, if ruling minorities are not to be permitted to plunder and corrupt the people for the sake of pleasure and material interest, if the Islamic order is to be preserved and all individuals are to pursue the just path of Islam without any deviation, if innovation and the approval of anti-Islamic laws by sham parliaments[27] are to be prevented, if the influence of foreign powers in the Islamic lands is to be destroyed – government is necessary. None of these aims can be achieved without government and the organs of the state. It is a righteous government, of course, that is needed, one presided over by a ruler who will be a trustworthy and righteous trustee. Those who presently govern us are of no use at all for they are tyrannical, corrupt, and highly incompetent.

In the past we did not act in concert and unanimity in order to establish proper government and overthrow treacherous and corrupt rulers. Some people were apathetic and reluctant even to discuss the theory of Islamic government, and some went so far as to praise oppressive rulers. It is for this reason that we find ourselves in the present state. The influence and sovereignty of Islam in society have declined; the nation of Islam has fallen victim to division and weakness; the laws of Islam have remained in abeyance and been subjected to change and modification; and the imperialists have propagated foreign laws and alien culture among the Muslims through their agents for the sake of their evil purposes, causing people to be infatuated with the West. It was our lack of a leader, a guardian, and our lack of institutions of leadership that made all this possible. We need righteous and proper organs of government; that much is self-evident.

Notes

1. *Vali amr*: 'the one who holds authority', a term derived from Qur'an, 4:59: 'O you who believe! Obey God, and obey the Messenger and the holders of authority (*uli 'l-amr*) from among you.'

2. Sunna: the practice of the Prophet, accepted by Muslims as the norm and ideal for all human behaviour.

3. Lesser Occultation: *ghaybat-i sughra*, the period of about seventy years (260/872–329/939) when, according to Shi'i belief, Muhammad al-Mahdi, the Twelfth Imam, absented himself from the physical plane but remained in communication with his followers through a succession of four appointed deputies. At the death of the fourth deputy no successor was named, and the Greater Occultation (*ghaybat-i kubra*) began, and continues to this day.

4. The allusion is probably to the Baha'is, who claim to have received a succession of post-Qur'anic revelations.

5. *jizya*: a tax levied on non-Muslim citizen of the Muslim state in exchange for the protection they receive and in lieu of the taxes, such as *zakat*, that only Muslims pay. *Kharaj*: a tax levied on certain categories of land. *Khums*: a tax consisting of one fifth of agricultural and commercial profits. *Zakat*: the tax levied on various categories of wealth and spent on the purpose specified in Qur'an, 9:60.

6. *al-Kafi*: one of the most important collection of Shi'i *hadith*, compiled by shaykh Abu Ja'far al-Kulayni (d. 329/941). Two fascicules of this work have recently been translated into English by sayyid Muhammad Hasan Rizvi and published in Tehran.

7. Qur'an, 16:89.

8. The reference is probably to Imam Ja'far as-Sadiq, whose sayings on this subject are quoted by 'Allama Tabataba'i in *al-Mizan fi Tafsir al'-Qur'an* (Beirut, 1390/1979), XII, 327–8.

9. *Sayyids*: the descendants of the Prophet through his daughter Fatima and son-in-law 'Ali, the first of the Twelve Imams.

10. *Zakat* would not represent an appreciable sum presumably because it is levied on surplus wealth, the accumulation of which is inhibited by the economic system of Islam.

11. *Ahl adh-dhimma*: non-Muslim citizens of the Muslim state, whose rights and obligations are contractually determined.

12. *Umma*: the entire Islamic community, without territorial or ethnic distinction.

13. Masjid al-Aqsa: the site in Jerusalem where the Prophet ascended to heaven in the eleventh year of his mission (Qur'an, 17:1); also the complex of mosques and buildings erected on the site. The chief of these was extensively damaged by arson in 1969, two years after the Zionist usurpation of Jerusalem.

14. Umayyads: members of the dynasty that ruled at Damascus from 41/632 until 132/750 and transformed the caliphate into a hereditary institution. Mu'awiya was the first of the Umayyad line.

15. Abbasids: the dynasty that replaced the Umayyads and established a new caliphal capital in Baghdad. With the rise of various local rulers, generally of military origin, the power of the Abbasids began to decline from the fourth/tenth century and it was brought to an end by the Mongol conquest in 656/1258.

16. *Kufr*: the rejection of divine guidance; the antithesis of Islam.

17. *Taghut*: one who surpasses all bounds in his despotism and tyranny and claims the prerogatives of divinity for himself, whether explicitly or implicitly.

18. *Shirk*: the assignment of partners to God, either by believing in a multiplicity of gods, or by assigning divine attributes and prerogatives to other-than-God.

19. 'Corruption on earth': a broad term including not only moral corruption, but also subversion of the public good, embezzlement and usurpation of public wealth, conspiring with the enemies of the community against its security, and working in general for the overthrow of the Islamic order. See the commentary on Qur'an, 5:33 in Tabataba'i, *al-Mizan*, V, 330–2.

20. It may be apposite to quote here the following passage from a secret report drawn up in January 1916 by T. E. Lawrence, the British organiser of the so-called Arab revolt led by Sharif Husayn of Mecca: 'Husayn's activity seems beneficial to us, because it marches with our immediate aims, the breakup of the Islamic bloc and the defeat and disruption of the Ottoman Empire . . . The Arabs are even less stable than the Turks. If properly handled they would remain in a state of political mosaic, a tissue of small jealous principalities incapable of political cohesion.' See Phillép Knightley and Colin Simpson, *The Secret Lives of Lawrence of Arabia* (New York, 1971), p. 55.

21. Fatima az-Zahra: Fatima, the daughter of the Prophet and wife of Imam 'Ali.

22. I.e., Hasan and Husayn.

23. See *Nahj al-Balagha*, ed. Subhi as-Salih (Beirut, 1397/1967).

24. Imam Riza: eighth of the Twelve Imams, born in 148/765 and died in 203/817 in Tus (Mashhad). According to Shi'i belief, he was poisoned by the Abbasid caliph Ma'mun, who had appointed him as his successor at first, but then grew fearful of the wide following he commanded. His shrine in Mashhad is one of the principal centres of pilgrimage and religious learning in Iran.

25. The text of this tradition is to be found in Shaykh Sadduq, *'Ilal ash-shara'i'* (Qom, 1378/1958), I,183.

26. That is, in the absence of the Imam or an individual deputy named by him (as was the case during the Lesser Occultation), the task devolves upon the *fuqaha* as a class.

27. Here the allusion may be in particular to the so-called Family Protection Law of 1967, which Imam Khomeini denounced as contrary to Islam in an important ruling. See Imam Khomeini, *Tauzih al-Masa'il*, n.p., n.d., pp. 462–3, par. 2,836, and p. 441.

CHAPTER 13

Challenges and Complicities: Abdolkarim Sorush and Gender

Ziba Mir-Hosseini

The text in this chapter is taken from a book entitled Islam and Gender: The Religious Debate in Contemporary Iran, *written by Ziba Mir-Hosseini, and first published in 1999. The reason for including this chapter in this reader is because it highlights two major issues in Iran post-Khomeini, namely, the issue of gender and the methodology that some intellectuals are employing in the reinterpretation of Islam. This chapter differs from preceding chapters because it consists of an introduction in which the life of one of Iran's leading intellectuals and 'dissidents' is presented, and this is then followed by conversations between the two.*

Ziba Mir-Hosseini is a social anthropologist whose primary academic interest lies in the field of gender, which is reflected in her publication about family law in Islam[1] and more recently in her collaboration with Kim Longinotto in the making of two award-winning documentary films, Divorce Iranian Style *and* Runaway. *Her 1999 publication,* Islam and Gender, *continues and expands on the themes addressed in her previous works. Interestingly, in the introduction to the book Mir-Hosseini describes herself as an Iranian and Muslim who understands and relates to issues as an Iranian Muslim woman, and who values and respects her religious and cultural heritage.[2] The self-reflexive section in the introduction is frustratingly brief; however, Mir-Hosseini's 'Islamicity' becomes clearer as the book traces her threefold classification of contemporary perspectives of gender in modern Iran (1995–98). Her sympathies lie with the group described in the final chapters of the book, which she calls 'modernists', and representatives of this group are Abdolkarim Sorush and Hojjat al-Islam Sa'idzadeh. They offer a vision of Islam which is based upon a radical reinterpretation of Islam which holds that its ethical teachings are neutral in terms of gender, and the discrimination and lack of equality between the sexes exists because of wrong interpretations that reflect the successful attempts by some males to gain powerful positions in society. The difference that Mir-Hosseini sees in the views of Sorush and Sa'idzadeh, however, lies in their position towards* feqh. *The latter believes that* feqh *cannot be discarded, indeed, his reinterpretation of Islam and specific gender issues is rooted in the particular methodology of* feqh. *'First he introduces the issue – for instance, women's right to serve as judges, both Shi'i and Sunni, he then scrutinises these opinions in the light of the Koran, Hadith, Consensus, Reason, and the practice and custom of the time, finally he refutes those that are contrary to the principle of equality and elaborates on those that accord with it.'[3] On the other hand, Sorush is much more critical of the* feqh *tradition, and sees the legal debates as secondary, preferring to use theoretical and philosophical debates (including the perspectives of mystics such as Rumi and Ebn 'Arabi)[4] as his point of departure. Sorush admits that we are all trapped in the hermeneutic circle and therefore the old* feqh *rulings cannot guarantee adequate guidance for the contemporary age. It is for this reason that he claims it is necessary to rely on divine revelation,[5] and this point seems somewhat at variance with his statement that the starting point for a reformulation of gender issues should be the guidance offered by the mystics. Sorush is criticised by Mir-Hosseini for being too abstract, whereas Sa'idzadeh receives approval because his grounding, which is in* feqh, *results in more specific treatment of contemporary issues in Iran.*

Yet it must be said that ultimately the views of both Sorush and Sa'idzadeh concerning the ethical imperative are not startlingly new, as similar ideas have been expressed by scholars such as Fazlur Rahman (which Sorush himself points to).[6] Moreover, if the views of these two scholars are taken to their logical conclusion, one has to question what would be left of traditional Shi'-ite Islam, and this perhaps is exactly why Sorush's thought has become so problematic for many conservative religious groups in Iran (which Mir-Hosseini mentions in the introduction to the chapter in this text). If much of the Shi'-ite tradition (the hadith, histories and other sacred texts such as the Nahj al-Balagheh *(a book composed of the sayings of Imam 'Ali) – in the words of Sa'idzadeh 'The 'Ali of* Nahj al-Balagheh *is a brutal man'[7] – are unreliable then the basis for understanding the Qur'an itself is severely shaken and makes reinterpretation extremely difficult (a point acknowledged by both men).*

Another point of interest is the context in which these ideas concerning gender are discussed. The difficulty and fear experienced by Sorush as an academic and by Sa'idzadeh as a cleric in Qom in expounding their views reflects the power of both 'traditionalist' clerics and of the patriarchal world view of Iranian society. Yet, the apparent growing number of clerics in Qom who are receptive to these ideas, or at least, those of the 'neo-traditionalists' (Mir-Hosseini's second group) suggests that reformist ideas within the seminaries in Qom mirror the 'realities' of family life (in which both partners work outside the home) which question the tradition of the male duty to support his wife. One wonders about the validity of the claim made by the 'neo-traditionalists' that the promotion of women's equality was advanced by Khomeini, who they claim endorsed the right of women (via judges) to divorce their husbands. Khomeini declared, 'Caution demands that first, the husband be persuaded, or even compelled, to divorce, if he does not (then) with the permission of the judge, divorce is effected, but there is a simpler way, (and) if I had the courage (I would have said it).'[8]

The second group Mir-Hosseini discusses is the 'neo-traditionalists', the views of whom are represented in discussions with Seyyed Zia Mortazavi (the editor of Payam-e Zan [Woman's Message] which is a monthly journal that focuses on gender issues) and Mohammad Hasan Sa'idi of the propagation office of the journal. The views on gender of these neo-traditionalistsas represented by Mir-Hosseini are a mix of the 'traditional' world view that Islamic regulations respond to the differences in nature between the sexes,[9] and the more progressive opinions that women should have an active role in society. This is exemplified by the view that wearing the hejab has permitted women to participate in society rather than remaining unseen in the home. Yet the journalists of Payam-e Zan guard a rather conservative view of Islam that endorses the male right of polygamy, the 'unequal' worth between the sexes in payment of blood money and the duty of maintaining his wife (even if she works and earns more than her husband). This is justified by adhering to the principle of balance (rather than equality), for Islamic laws are based on justice, and so the individual who has the most onerous burdens or duties should also receive greater rights and privileges. Mir-Hosseini criticises this perspective because of its failure to respond to modern circumstances in Iran where in practice the burdens are more equally shared between the sexes than the presumptions upon which the feqh rulings are based. However, the neo-traditionalists appeal to the feqh principle of 'denial of harm' by which a woman is sometimes able to attain a greater degree of freedom (divorce from her husband) and acheive a better level of parity of rights with her husband.

The 'Traditonalists' represent a group that believes that differences between the sexes are based on nature but they differ from the neo-traditionalists in that the former seek a far greater restriction on women's particpation in society, despite the permission granted to women by the Islamic Republic of Iran to engage in the political process and in society. A typical traditionalist argument is that there are 'two defects in women, one of which is their love of luxury and display, and the other is lack of knowledge and strong reasoning'.[10]

This introduction has not provided any detailed background to Abdolkarim Sorush because this is given in Mir-Hosseini's text. The significance of this text is not just related to Sorush's opinions on gender, but rather the broader issue of Islamic hermeneutics. His call for a more democratic and open discussion about religion is refreshing, but it is easy to understand why his critics dislike his world view, which could be construed as relativist. The following quote in which he discusses the ambiguous (mutashabihat) and clear verses (muhkamat) of the Qur'an demonstrates the radical threat he has presented to entrenched and conservative Islamic thinking:

> Interestingly enough, the Qur'an itself does not give any clue as to how the mutashabihat can be determined and distinguished from other verses, and the whole history of Islam clearly shows that virtually every verse of the Qur'an has been suspected at one time or another of being mutashabih, which is clear evidence in favour of the suggestion that all this stems from the nature of interpretation and interpreters' presuppositions.[11]

Notes

[1.] *Marriage on Trial: A Study of Islamic Family Law: Iran and Morocco Compared* (London: I.B. Tauris, 1983).

[2.] *Islam and Gender* (London: I.B. Tauris), p. 19.

[3.] Ibid., p. 250.

[4.] Ibid., p. 245.

[5.] Ibid., p. 231.

[6.] Sorush, 'Contraction and Expansion of Women's Rights' found on www.seraj.org/zanan.htm.

[7.] *Islam and Gender*, p. 264.

[8.] Ibid., p. 165.

[9.] Ibid., p. 94.

[10.] Ibid., p. 57.

[11.] Abdul-Karim Soroush, 'The Evolution and Devolution of Religious Knowledge', in C. Kurzman (ed.), *Liberal Islam* (Oxford University Press, 1998).

Further Reading

J. Cooper, 'The Limits of the Sacred: The Epistemology of 'Abd al-Karim Soroush', in J. Cooper, R. Nettler and M. Mahmoud (eds), *Islam and Modernity: Muslim Intellectuals Respond* (London: I.B. Tauris, 1998), pp. 38–56.

Z. Mir-Hosseini, 'Women's Rights and Clerical Discourses: The Legacy of 'Allameh Tabataba'i' in N. Nabavi (ed.), *Intellectual Trends in Twentieth-Century Iran* (Gainesville: University of Florida Press: 2003), pp. 193–217.

A. Soroush, 'The Evolution and Devolution of Religious Knowledge', in C. Kurzman (ed.), *Liberal Islam* (Oxford University Press, 1998).

—— *Reason, Freedom, and Democracy in Islam*, trans. and ed. M. Sadri and A. Sadri (Oxford University Press, 2000).

———•———

[I began studying the works of Abdolkarim Sorush in autumn 1995, after the second of my debates with *Payam-e Zan*, and following the disruption of his lectures by the Ansar-e Hezbollah, 'helpers of Hezbollah'.[1] On 11 October, Sorush was invited by the Islamic Students Society to address a meeting in Tehran University; as he began his lecture, he was attacked and injured by about a hundred youths from off campus, members of Ansar. Their leader, in a debut public speech, claimed that Sorush's ideas were subversive to Islam and undermined the *velayat-e faqih*, vowed that he would no longer be allowed to disseminate them, and demanded a public debate with him. Another meeting at which Sorush was to speak had been disrupted in a similar manner in Isfahan University in June. On both occasions, the authorities had ignored student warnings. Press coverage was polarised: some papers condemned the attacks as blatant violations of constitutional rights to freedom of thought and speech; others applauded the legitimate right of Hezbollah to intervene if necessary.

Abdolkarim Sorush is perhaps the most influential and controversial thinker the Islamic Republic has so far produced. In the early years, his lectures were broadcast regularly on national radio and television; I remember watching him in television debates with secular and leftist intellectuals, using Islamic mystical and philosophical arguments to demolish Marxist dogmas. I was curious to find out for myself what it was in Sorush's ideas that now, sixteen years into the Islamic Republic, put him on the other side of the fence and enabled women like those in *Zanan* to reconcile their faith with their feminism.

As I made my way through Sorush's vast corpus of publications – over twenty books – I could see why and how his ideas created such varied passions and reactions. He is a subtle and original thinker, who has found a new language and frame of analysis to re-examine hallowed concepts. He approaches sacred texts by reintroducing the element of rationality that has been part of Shi'i thought, and enabling his audience to be critical without compromising their faith. He is making it legitimate to pose questions that previously only the ulema could ask.

I could see some interesting parallels and differences between Sorush and Shari'ati. Both have been immensely popular with the youth, distrusted and opposed by the clerical establishment, and dismissed by secular intellectuals as lightweights. But their visions and conceptions of Islam are fundamentally different. For Shari'ati, the most important dimension in Islam was political; he sought to turn Islam into an ideology, to galvanise revolutionaries, and to change society. For Sorush, on the other hand, Islam is, as he puts it, 'sturdier than ideology'; all his thinking and writing are aimed at separating the two.

Abdolkarim Sorush is the pen name of Hosein Dabbagh, born in 1945 in a pious but non-clerical family in southern Tehran.[2] Sorush was among the first graduates of Alavi High School, established by a group of pious bazaaris in the late 1950s with a curriculum integrating modern sciences with traditional religious studies. He then studied pharmacology at Tehran University and, after completing his military service in 1972, he went to England to continue his studies. Obtaining a Master's degree in analytical chemistry from London University, he went on to study history and philosophy of science at Chelsea College. While in London, he joined a group of Iranian Muslim students who held meetings in a building in west London,[3] where Shari'ati's funeral service was held and where Ayatollah Motahhari spoke when he came to London. Sorush was close to both men, and was a regular speaker there. He returned to Iran just as the Pahlavi regime was about to collapse.

In 1981 Sorush became one of seven members of the Council for Cultural Revolution, appointed by Ayatollah Khomeini when the universities were closed in order to contain the students and to eliminate leftist groups from the campuses. The council's task was to oversee the Islamisation of higher education and to prepare the ground for the reopening of the universities. This occurred in 1983, after a massive ideological purge of students and teachers; and Sorush started teaching philosophy of science in Tehran University. Not longer after, he resigned from the council, disagreeing with the direction it was going.[4] Since then he has held no official position within the ruling system of the Islamic Republic, although his lectures continued to be broadcast until the late 1980s and he remained close to centres of power, acting as adviser to several government bodies until the early 1990s.

In 1984 Sorush began teaching courses in philosophy of religion (known as modern theology), comparative philosophy, and mysticism to both university students in Tehran and Houzeh students in Qom. In 1988, he started a series of weekly lectures in Imam Sadeq Mosque in north Tehran, on *Nahj ol-Balagheh*, the collection of Imam Ali's sermons and hadith. In the early audiences were members of the political and religious elite, including some government ministers. By autumn 1994, when the lectures were suspended, the audience was different: younger, and largely students. Not only had Sorush acquired a following among students who found his ideas and approach intrinsically appealing but he was beginning to set the tone for more public debates.

Disruption of his lectures began in April 1995, after the publication in *Kiyan* of his lecture 'Liberty and the Clergy'. He argues there that the clergy as a group functions as a guild, with religion as their source of livelihood, which limits both their own freedom in interpretation and that of others.[5] This article was denounced as 'subversive to Islam', and brought the Hezbollah back to campus.[6] After the attack in Isfahan in June, a letter of protest signed by 104 writers and university teachers was sent to the president of the Islamic Republic.[7] With the emergence of the Ansar following the October incident in Tehran University, Sorush was no longer able even to give his regular university lectures. The showdown came in the spring of 1996. He wrote an open letter to the president, calling on him to 'remove this rot' and to ensure freedom of speech and thought.[8] But to no avail. In mid-May, Ansar members surrounded Amir Kabir University in Tehran, where Sorush was due to talk in a meeting to mark the anniversary of Ayatollah Motahhari's death. Clashes ensued between the students and Ansar, arrests were made on both sides, and Sorush sent a message announcing his withdrawal. Soon after, unable to teach and fearing for his life, he went abroad on a lecture tour, not returning until April 1997.

As with Shari'ati, most of Sorush's writings are edited texts of public lectures, delivered in a variety of forums. If read chronologically, these volumes reveal the development of not only his ideas but his relationship with the Islamic Republic. Up to 1983 they mostly constitute a critique of the leftist ideologies espoused by Iranian intellectuals and groups then politically active.[9] After 1983, Sorush's writings show his concern with themes in philosophy and epistemology. They include translations of English books on philosophy,[10] a volume of collected essays and lectures on ethics and human sciences,[11] as well as several articles in cultural periodicals.

The breakthrough in his work came with his seminal articles on the historicity and relativity of religious knowledge: 'The Theoretical Expansion and Contraction of the Shari'a'.[12] These articles – in which Sorush distinguished religion from religious knowledge, arguing that whereas the first was sacred and immutable, the latter was human and evolved in time as a result of forces external to religion itself – appeared intermittently between 1988 and 1990 in the quarterly *Kayhan-e Farhangi*, published by the Kayhan Publishing Institute, which had come under the control of the Islamic faction shortly after the revolution. The heated debate that followed the publication of these articles led to a kind of intellectual coup and the birth of an independent journal, *Kiyan* (Foundation) in October 1991.[13] Sorush's writings form the centrepiece in each issue of *Kiyan*; they reveal the concerns and thinking of a deeply religious man who is becoming increasingly disillusioned by the domination in the Islamic Republic of what he calls '*feqh*-based Islam'.[14]

This began a new phase in Sorush's writings, comprising volumes of collected essays, largely published originally in *Kiyan*; most are edited texts of lectures and talks delivered in universities and mosques in which he expands his epistemological arguments to develop a critique of government ideology and policies of the Islamic Republic and to argue for democracy and pluralism on religious grounds. Each volume bears the title of one of the essays, and has gone through several editions and impressions.

In the vast amount of his published work I could find nothing on women, apart from two paragraphs, both merely asides commenting on the incongruity between texts taught in the seminaries and the current state of knowledge and world views.[15] So I looked for his unpublished work, and acquired recordings of two lectures in which he had addressed the issue of women, both of them in the series on *Nahj ol-Balagheh*. The first was delivered in Imam Sadeq Mosque in January 1989; Sorush used the occasion of Women's Day to comment on Imam Ali's harsh views on women, contained in a sermon delivered after the Battle of the Camel, led by Ayesha, the Prophet's widow; it reads:

> O people! Women are deficient in Faith, deficient in shares and deficient in intelligence. As regards the deficiency in their Faith, it is their abstention from prayers and fasting during their menstrual periods. As regards deficiency in their intelligence it is because the evidence of two women is equal to that of a man. As for the deficiency in their shares that is because of their share in inheritance being half of men. So beware of the evils of women. Be on your guard even from those of them who are (reportedly) good. Do not obey them even in good things so that they may not attract you to evils.[16]

As Sorush recited and translated the sermon, some women in the audience – as in all mosques, the women's section was curtained off from the men's, where Sorush was speaking – cried out in protest, to be promptly silenced by a man shouting: 'It's the Imam's words the Doctor is quoting: do you object even to them?'[17] But the protests continued and stopped only when Sorush asked to be allowed to finish his commentary and explain. His commentary, however, betrayed his ambivalence on the issue of women in Islam, and also suggested that he was not prepared for such a reaction, nor for a man to shout the women down. He had intended to confine his discussion of women to one session, but the reaction persuaded him to continue the following week. He repeated and elaborated the content of the discussion in his second lecture, and I shall discuss his views in that context.

The second lecture was delivered in Isa Vazir Mosque in central Tehran in 1992, as part of an extended commentary on Imam Ali's letter to his son, known as the Will, the closing sentences of which contain the Imam's advice to his son about women. Again Sorush had intended to devote only one session to the theme of women and gender relations, but at his audience's request he continued for four more sessions. Although he was more explicit in his views, and expanded on what he had said in 1989, his position on gender, and the thrust of his arguments, remained the same. In 1995, *Zanan* gave me an abridged transcript of the 1992 sessions, prepared earlier for publication as 'The Perspective of the Past on Women'; but they never carried the article and, so far, neither lecture has appeared in print.[18]

The main part of this chapter consists of selected passages from the 1992 sessions, which touch directly on gender and reveal Sorush's perspective. I conclude with extracts from an interview with him in London in October 1996 when I was able to discuss the 1992 sessions with him, to ask about the audience, and raise my objections to his gender perspective.

The 1992 lecture was spread over five weekly sessions from 8 October to 5 November, each lasting nearly two hours. The audience of about one thousand, including many university students, was both more numerous and younger than that which attended his 1989 lecture. The sessions have an informal but uniform structure. On the tapes, as Sorush is speaking, one can hear children's voices, greetings by new arrivals, and so on. He begins each session with a short Arabic prayer, the same as in 1989 before his commentary on the *Nahj ol-Balagheh*, then summarises the main points covered in the previous session, before reviewing and developing them further. When he has finished, there is a break, during which those who have questions submit them anonymously and in writing; the session ends with Sorush reading out and answering a selection of these questions.

Sorush is a gifted orator; his voice is calm and mesmerising. He talks without a script, and often without notes. I present a summary of each session, retaining the order in which he introduces his points and using his words as much as possible. There is a clear structure and purpose to each lecture, during which he takes his audience through layers of religious concepts and philosophical arguments, interjecting Qur'anic verses, hadith, and mystical poems. He does this knowledgeably, clearly, and honestly. His style and language are as important as what he has to say. His command of literature and his memory are formidable; he appears to know by heart the Qur'an, the *Nahj ol-Balagheh*, Rumi's *Mathnavi*, and Hafez's *Divan*.[19]

Sorush's Lectures on Women

From the opening summary, we gather that the previous session's theme was ethics and religion. Sorush repeats two points: that political ethics are separate from religious ethics, and that although religious ethics are primarily personal in nature, they can be a source for a sound political ethics. Imam Ali's letter to his son is one such source. Addressed to a future leader, it contains the Imam's advice on several political and social matters. Sorush recites and translates the closing sentences:

> Do not consult women because their view is weak and their determination is unstable. Cover their eyes by keeping them under veil because strictness of veiling keeps them [good]. Their coming out is not worse than your allowing an unreliable man to visit them. If you can manage that they should not know anyone other than [you,] do so. Do not allow a woman matters other than those about herself because a woman is a flower, not an administrator. Do not pay her regard beyond herself. Do not encourage her to intercede for others. Do not show suspicion out of place because this leads a correct woman to evil and a chaste woman to deflection.[20]

He continues:

> In an earlier discussion on *Nahj ol-Balagheh*, we said it contains words that are uncongenial to women, and infringe cultural notions and democratic values that have come to fill human societies in the past two centuries. For this reason, words that were once acceptable – that no commentator found forbidding to interpret or to justify – are now problematic. They demand a new interpretation or a new defence. Our forebears had no qualms in either interpreting or defending such words . . . As such a position for women wasn't contested, no one doubted these words . . . But today women – even men – don't accept or believe in such a position.

Nahj ol-Balagheh contains two kinds of statements on women: those based on reasoning and those not. Taken at face value, both are offensive to women. Among the latter, for instance, is the Imam's address to the people of Basra after the Battle of the Camel. He says; 'You were the army of a woman and in the command of a quadruped. When it grumbled you responded and when it was wounded you fled away.'[21] Or: 'As regards such and such woman, she is in the grip of womanly views while malice is boiling in her bosom like the furnace of the blacksmith.'[22] Or: 'Woman is evil, all in all; and the worst of it is that one cannot do without her.'[23] These statements contain no reasoning. But in other statements the Imam has reasoned; they include those famous ones: that women are deficient in belief, in reason, and in worldly gain, because they do not pray or fast during menses; the testimony of two women equals that of one man; and their share of inheritance is half a man's. In this part of the letter that we have recited, the Imam also advises his son not to consult women because their views are weak.

Put together, these statements suggest that seeking women's advice and involving them in affairs of society should be avoided; that is, it's Muslim men's duty to keep their women secluded, to control them, and not to allow them a say. If we add *feqh* rulings, the picture that emerges is even more devastating for women. There's no denying that in an Islamic society women are granted fewer rights and fewer opportunities than men.

If one of the *ulema* of a century ago could be reborn and see the conditions of our society and the women, undoubtedly he'd have a fright. Such a level of women's [public] presence – which isn't by any means ideal – would be unthinkable for him. The very fact that it's now accepted that a woman's presence in society doesn't violate her womanhood and Muslimhood is due to the immense changes that have occurred in the realms of thought and practice; these have also found their way into our religious consciousness and our society. Women's presence in society is now as natural and logical as their absence once was. This tells us the extent to which, in our understanding and practice of religion, we act unconsciously and involuntarily; this isn't to be taken negatively but in the sense that we're guided by elements that aren't in our control. They do their work, shape our lives, our minds, our language . . .

You know, and I have already said, that there have been several reactions to these hadith of the Imam and similar ones. These reactions are instructive, too. Specific justifications have been made; for instance, some of our clerics say that the Imam's comment on women's deficiencies was made after the Battle of the Camel, and was due to the insidious role that Ayesha played in it. Such hadith, they argue, refer only to Ayesha or women like her. Some say the Imam uttered such words about women because he was upset and angry. Neither argument works. We must remember that reason derives its validity and universality from its own logic, not from what its user wishes to impose on it. That is, once we contend that a certain hadith of the Imam was influenced by anger or an event, then we have to admit the probability that other emotions and events influenced other hadith. In that case, no hadith can ever again be used in the sense that they have been so far. Likewise, we can't say this hadith referred only to Ayesha. Its logic and content convey universality: it's not only Ayesha but all Muslim women who inherit half a man's share, and so on . . .

But the explanation we gave [in 1989] about those hadith of the Imam that are based on reasoning was that once a hadith is based on reasoning then it must be approached through its own reasoning. In fact, the credibility of such a hadith is contingent on the force and validity of its reasoning, not on the authority of its utterer. This has been our method in dealing with all sacred texts. For instance, we read in the Qur'an: 'If there had been in them any gods but Allah, they would both have certainly been in a state of disorder' [Sura Anbia, 22]. This is a reasoning whose acceptance doesn't rest on its being the word of God but on its force and soundness, so that it can become a backbone for our thinking . . .

One can take issue with the Imam's reasoning and say that if women don't pray or don't fast at certain times [during menses], this isn't a token of deficiency in their faith. It's in fact the very proof of their faith, as His prophet tells them not to pray at such times. Obeying His prohibitions is like obeying His commands. In God's eyes what matters is the spirit of an act, not its form . . . As to women's deficiency in material gain, it's true that their share in inheritance is less, but this isn't proof that they're less than men and we can't conclude from it that women shouldn't be consulted, or assigned certain social and political status. No logical connection can be made here. If they inherit less, it's because they are told so.

Such an approach might work, of course, with ahadith based on reasoning. But what about the others that aren't? Our solution here is to say that these hadith are 'pseudo-universal propositions' (as logicians have it); that is, they reveal the conditions of women of their time. In addition, since what an Imam or a sage says is in line with the society in which he lives, we need a reason to extend it to other epochs . . . Here we're faced with two jurisprudential principles and positions: one holds that *shari'a* idioms – whether legal or ethical in nature – speak of societies of their time and thus we need a reason for extending them to other societies or times: and the other argues the opposite, that we need a reason *not* to apply such ahadith and Rulings to all other societies and times. These two positions can't be reached from the words [of sacred texts] but only when we examine them from outside and apply our own reasoning to them.

Contrary to the Imam's advice, today in the Islamic Republic women are consulted. As for women's entry into Parliament, the problem is theoretically resolved: women don't directly decide for Islamic society. Although it seems to me the *ulema*'s thinking on the issue hasn't changed, since the argument put forward then against women's entry into Parliament was that the Prophet said that a society ruled by a woman is doomed.[24] Both Shi'i and Sunni *ulema* have argued that if women are in Parliament, their votes will be counted among the rest and thus they can influence the passing of a bill, which is a kind of *velayat* for women, although it isn't personal. At present, as you know, in our country the Majles is [only] the adviser of the *vali-ye faqih*. The notion of legislation as understood in other parts of the world doesn't exist in our country; that is, the Majles doesn't have an independent view, and the *vali-ye faqih* can alter its decisions or act counter to them. So you could argue that women's presence in Parliament doesn't contradict the Prophet's hadith. It bans women from *velayat*, which at present only the *vali-ye faqih* exercises. But what about the ban on consulting women? As far as I remember, before the revolution when the Houzeh opposed women's entry to the Parliament, they made no reference to such arguments or ahadith, either because they didn't find them acceptable or [they didn't think it] suitable to invoke them.

Anyway, these words exist in *Nahj ol-Balagheh*, and solutions must be sought for them, and the search for solutions, as I said already, is decisive and can't be confined to words. If we challenge their authenticity, then our entire [corpus of] sacred sources will come into question. If we say they're pseudo-universal propositions, then not only women but men and many other rulings based on them will be affected. If we accept them as they are, then we must resolve the consequences of their incongruity with our present society. What we can say is that there's a kind of absolute neglect regarding such ahadith. They aren't addressed seriously, so no serious solutions are found for them. This is because the hold of democratic values and notions of human rights is so strong that men and women don't allow themselves to think of contradicting them and prefer to keep silent in the face of

incongruities. This isn't limited to our time, nor to religious knowledge, but [it's true of] all times and all branches of knowledge. It's also
the case in science. A cultural view, a theory, sometimes takes such
hold and captures minds and imaginations to such an extent that no
one dares think otherwise. So, in every era, part of religious thought,
views, or ahadith is overshadowed and ignored, and another part is
highlighted and welcomed.

All we can say is that such issues must be left for history to resolve,
in time. When our minds tell us not to think about this issue [women
in sacred texts], then we can't hope to find a suitable solution. In the
past, this and many other issues were so much in line with popular
culture that there was no need for thinking. In our time such ahadith
have been dealt such devastating blows that no one finds it expedient
to tackle them or to confront such a formidable torrent. The most we
can do is to become familiar with the problem and its cause and leave
the solution to time and later thinkers.

On this note, Sorush brings the session to an end. He has repeated essentially
what he said in 1989 about the Imam's famous words on women's deficiencies,
applying his theory of 'Expansion and Contraction of the Shari'a' descriptive,
explanatory, and normative, all at once. He argues both that understanding of
sacred texts is time-bound and that the *ulema*'s opinions are influenced by what
he calls 'extra-religious knowledge'. Changes in knowledge render natural and
Islamic some matters that were once considered 'unthinkable' and 'non-Islamic'.
He despairs at the *ulema*'s unwillingness to admit this at a theoretical level and
to take consciously planned steps to revise their understanding in the light of
current realities. He also implicitly criticises the institution of *velayat-e faqih* by
pointing to the contradiction in having a parliament yet subordinating it to the
rule of *vali-ye faqih*.

Despite this heady stuff, and Sorush's fresh approach, listening to him I could
not help thinking that he too, as a religious intellectual, was avoiding the issue
by skirting around any discussion of women's legal rights in Islam – the domain
of *feqh*. This may have been a concern voiced by his audience,[25] since, even
though he had declared the theme of women closed, he returned to it at the next
session, a week later (15 October), because 'some friends, especially sisters, asked
for more'. But once again he skirted around *feqh* and moved instead into religious
literature to shed light on the sources from which jurists derive their conceptions
of women's rights. This time he framed his discussion in the context of changing
conceptions of the human role and place in the universe, and asked why there is
such a focus on women's rights in Muslim societies. He demonstrated that there
is nothing sacred in our understanding of the *shari'a*, which is human and evolves
in time and is filtered through our own cognitive universe.

The recording begins with the usual prayer and summary of key points from the previous discussion, before Sorush continues:

> Friends know that in our time certain views have emerged about mankind, women included. In our society in recent decades these views have centred on women's legal rights. The problem facing our thinkers has been to explain to believing Muslim women why certain differences in rights between women and men exist in Islamic thought. Confronted with the notion of gender equality, they try either to explain these differences away or to argue that Islam upholds sexual equality but rejects similarity in rights. Some have argued for differences not in rights but in the duties of each sex, stemming from the differing abilities of each sex and the natural division of labour. Others have tried to explain by connecting differences in rights to physical, psychological, and spiritual differences between the sexes . . .
>
> The nub of the matter is that it's assumed that equality between men and women – which women demand in our time in various parts of the world – means equality in legal rights. Here I want to explain the exact meaning of this [notion of] equality between men and women – in the sense that some are now seeking – and then see whether the common understanding of women's rights and duties in Islam admits such a notion of equality; and how most of our *ulema*, thinkers, and jurists have conceptualised women and their status and the basis for their views. I stress, it's not for me to judge but only to offer a historical report of understandings that have so far existed. Nor do I claim that the door of understanding is closed, that no other understanding will emerge on this issue. Nevertheless, what has existed so far must be recognised and known.
>
> We can have two views, both of which are rooted in our conception of women's purpose in creation . . . In a nutshell, one holds that woman is created for man: her whole being, disposition, personality, and perfection depend on union with man. The other view denies such a relationship and holds that a woman has her own purpose in creation, her own route to perfection . . . The first view – that woman is created *of* and *for* – sums up past perspectives, including those of Muslims. Both qualifiers [of and for] are important.

In poetic and mystical language, Sorush discusses at some length what these qualifiers entail, how they create asymmetry in rights and shape relations between the sexes. A woman is created to mediate man's perfection, to prepare him to fulfil his duty, to enable him to manifest his manhood, to make him worthy of God's call. This is the essence of womanhood, and that is why she attains perfection through union with a man. But for a man, union with a woman is not the end but only the beginning of his path to perfection. Sorush opens two caveats: to say that woman is created of and for man does not mean she is created for, or to be at the mercy of, man's whim; and to say that woman's perfection rests on union with man does not necessarily imply marriage, although formation of a family is one manifestation of such connection and an arena for complementarity and mutual perfection.

On the second view, which he says has captured the hearts and minds of Muslim women of our time, Sorush is less eloquent or forthcoming:

> [The] second view, demanding equality between the sexes, says nothing more than that woman is not created *of* and *for* man. This philosophical and existentialist conception, of course, defines the scope of women's legal rights, shapes their status and relations between the sexes, and so on. Here I don't want to discuss the implications of such a conception for women in the sphere of gender relations, nor shall I enter philosophical and legal discussions. These are to be found in the works of the late Motahhari and other thinkers such as Allameh Tabataba'i. Perhaps what can be said in defence of difference and non-similarity [of gender rights] has been said in these works, and I don't intend to add anything here. Nevertheless, I will make one point. One of those who judiciously understood yet denied [the implications of the two views] was Ayatollah Motahhari: in his book *Women's Rights in Islam* he clearly states that in the Islamic view woman isn't created for man. But I should say that this is not the general presumption of our *ulema*. An understanding of equality between man and woman won't be possible unless we understand the basis correctly and know contemporary men's and women's understanding of it. This is the formulation of the problem, the two claims that confront each other . . .

Having identified the core contradiction in the gender discourses of contemporary Muslim thinkers, such as Motahhari, Sorush delves into religious literature to show the kinds of theories and master narratives on which they are based. He observes that although no Muslim thinker has said in so many words, 'woman is of and for man', they all subscribe to the thesis; he offers three kinds of evidence for this: first, that religious sources are male-oriented: whatever their genre, they solely or primarily address men, even when they deal with apparently genderless themes, such as rules for praying or ethical issues such as lying or cheating. In this, Sorush says, scholars have followed the example of the Qur'an, which most often addresses men. For instance, many of the blessings promised in paradise – such as black-eyed perpetual virgins – appeal only to men.

The second kind of evidence is the way religious literature describes marriage. Here again, men are treated as the main beneficiaries, even though marriage is by definition a joint affair. He examines legal and ethical sources to list the kinds of benefit Muslim scholars identify in marriage, ranging from immunity from Satan's temptations to achieving the peace of mind that enables men to prepare for greater duties in life, such as gaining knowledge and serving God. He also relates ahadith of the Prophet, that 'women are among Satan's army and one of its greatest aids'; and a story from Rumi's *Mathnavi* that when God created woman, Satan rejoiced, saying 'now I have the ultimate weapon for tempting mankind' – meaning, of course, men.

Similar is the sort of advice given to men on how to respect women's rights and pay them their dues. Sorush reads a passage from Feiz Kashani's *al-Mohajjat ol-Beiza* (The Bright Way), a book on ethics and morals. Feiz, a sixteenth-century Shi'i scholar, defines marriage as a kind of enslavement, and a wife as a kind of slave, advising men: 'now you have captured this being, you must have mercy on her, cherish and respect her, etc.' Sorush points out that it was in the light of such a conception of marriage and women's status that scholars read and understood the hadith, and shows the internal flaw in such understandings. He recites ahadith attributed to Shi'i Imams, telling men not to teach women Sura Yusef from the Qur'an, but Sura Nur instead, and to forbid women to go to upper floors of the house in case they are tempted to look down at unrelated men passing in the street.

> The point is not what the real meaning of these ahadith is, nor whether or not they are authentic. The point is, what meanings have been attributed to them [by] our religious scholars [who] have taken them seriously. My point is phenomenological, not theological. I don't judge, I simply say that in Islamic culture and history they've been taken seriously, and religious scholars have based their views on them.

Sorush's final argument to show the absolute hold of the 'woman is for man' thesis is from mystical and philosophical literature. He cites two contrasting passages, one from the celebrated Sufi Ibn Arabi (d. 1240), the other from the philosopher Molla Hadi 'Hakim' Sabzevari (d. 1878), and argues that they reveal the same conception of women, although expressed in two different idioms. Inspired by a hadith about the creation of Eve from Adam's rib, Ibn Arabi says that, like a rib, woman has the inborn ability to bend in her love without breaking: she is the symbol of divine love and mercy, created from 'affection', and love toward man is implanted in her essence. Thus woman's role and destiny is to bend in love; in so doing she joins man and makes him whole again. Man's love for woman, on the other hand, is like the love of the whole for a part; looked at this way, man's love for woman does not infringe his love for God. Compare this, Sorush tells his audience, with Hakim Sabzevari's view that women are in essence animals; God gave them human faces so that men will be inclined to marry.

> I apologise to the sisters present here for the insult implied in these words, but it's important to know them. Today in our society there's an unacceptable cover-up, even by our Muslim thinkers, who hide what's been said . . . There's no reason, no point in hiding it, it'll be clear to those who care to think and search. It's important to face it with an open mind, to know better the dark tunnel we've come through, and how to contemplate our future.

His excursion into religious literature ended, Sorush concludes his talk with three further points.

> First, in the sphere of women's rights we cannot think and talk only in *feqh* categories, of forbidden and permitted acts; we must also think in terms of interpreting religious texts, of man's and woman's purposes in creation, of traditions and social customs. Second, if Muslim scholars defined women's status in a way we find unacceptable today, it is not because they wanted to humiliate women or undermine their status, but because that is how they understood and interpreted the religious texts. Women in the past accepted their status not because they were stupid or oppressed but because they had no problems with such understanding and interpretation. In the past two centuries, however, the myths and theories that made such understandings acceptable to men and women have been challenged by scientific theories, including evolution. Changes in our world view have also made women's legal rights an issue in Islam. Finally, the problem cannot be resolved by providing new justifications to defend an outmoded world view, hoping women will be lured back into accepting them; after all, acceptance is a matter of belief rather than reasoning. What we can do is try to understand the basis for, and implications of, old and new views on women. Only then can women clarify for themselves where they stand in relation to each view, and where they want to be.

Sorush invites his audience, in particular the women, to do this. The session continues with Sorush answering four questions. Two invoke a Qur'anic verse and a hadith to negate the 'woman is for man' thesis, to which Sorush replies: 'True, there are also many others, but so far the other side is stronger, in the sense that their reasonings and evidences dominate.' A third question asks for comment on women's status in present society; he answers that this can best be dealt with by a sociologist. After a lengthy pause, Sorush reads out what must be part of the final question: 'In our history, women have said nothing about themselves.' He responds with a critique of feminism:

> Yes, it has been the case, and even if [women] said [something] their voices haven't reached us. There are several theories here. The argument of feminist movements – that now exist in the world as so-called supporters of women, demanding equal rights between men and women on all fronts – is that differences between men and women, which their rights are based on, result from socialisation. That is, boys and girls are socialised differently: boys are taught they are superior to girls, sexes are assigned different roles, they are valued differently, this sets a pattern and men and women have come to accept their roles; this has been the case in most societies from the start, and so on. I once witnessed a debate abroad between one of these feminists and an opponent, who argued that you must explain why this pattern was set in the first place, why men and women accepted it, and why it continues today; perhaps there's a reason for it, perhaps there [really] is a difference between the sexes – not [necessarily] that one is better than the other – but why do you want to deny difference?

This leads into a digression on the philosophy of history; Sorush affirms his own view that 'the history of mankind has been natural', and asks whether the fact of women's oppression at certain periods can be taken as contrary evidence. Although he admits that his theory cannot be falsified, he seems to imply that history will show men's domination to be natural, too.

That last question seems to me to haunt the three sessions on gender relations that follow. They are more discursive in style and full of incomplete statements and arguments. Unlike in the first two sessions, Sorush pursues neither a central argument nor a sustained critique of old readings of the sacred texts, but tries instead to make sense of the Imam's words, to provide the basis for debate and a new positioning. This he makes clear at the outset. In his summary of the previous discussion, he repeats his criticism of current understandings of the sacred texts, voices his scepticism of the new view, which he sees as seeking to 'put women in men's place', then continues:

> The old view has passed its test, and religious societies that lived by its rules have revealed what they entail for men, women, and the family. On the other hand, societies that have opted for the new view, putting women in men's place, have also shown their hand. In both camps, many now feel the need for revision. But since these views aren't

philosophically neutral, revision is always slow and painful. They're tied up with a mass of baggage, and it's impossible to remain impartial when dealing with them . . . Until very recently – in the West, too – men have been the main theorists on women's nature and role in creation and society. This must make us cautious. When women replace them, they too are tied to their own baggage, however different. This is one of those rare cases where the door of judgement is closed to us, as both science and reason can be influenced by our emotions. You can't apply cold reason to an issue in which your entire being is immersed. There can be no guarantee that mistakes made in previous centuries won't be repeated . . .

I say all this to affirm that we must rely here on Revelation and seek guidance in the words of religious leaders and those pious ones who are free of such baggage; the path of human reason here passes through the path of divine Revelation; if we explore and invest in this path, perhaps we'll obtain worthwhile results.

Having set the tone and the theme, Sorush returns to the closing sentences of Imam Ali's letter to his son, quoted earlier. He relates them to the concepts of *hejab*, sexual honour and jealousy (*gheirat*), and worth (*keramat*). On *hejab* he is brief, confining himself to two points: that its form and limits have always been bound up with culture and politics; and that what God permits, man should not forbid. To drive both home, he relates what Ayatollah Motahhari told him about how he began research for his book on *hejab*. Motahhari said he was afraid to enter a minefield of divergent opinions, but as his research progressed he found an astonishing degree of consensus among Shi'i and Sunni jurists: all – bar one Sunni – held that women's hands and faces need not be covered. He also found that all *fatwas* recommending stricter covering were issued after Reza Shah's unveiling campaign. Sorush leaves his audience to draw the moral from the anecdote: that advocating *chador* as the 'superior form of *hejab*' has more to do with culture and politics than sacred texts. 'We all know that *chador* is not "Islamic *hejab*", but it's rare to find a cleric who allows his womenfolk to venture out without wearing one. What Motahhari said on *hejab* – which was what he found in *feqh* texts – shocked the *ulema* of his time, who interpreted it as a licence for promiscuity.'

On the second concept, jealousy (*gheirat*), Sorush is more explicit. He first defines jealousy as 'preventing another sharing what one has', and distinguishes it from envy (*hesadat*), which he defines as 'wanting what belongs to another'. The first is a positive ethical value that is extra-religious and should be encouraged, he argues, but the second is negative and should be controlled. He refers to another hadith of Imam Ali: 'the jealousy of a woman is heresy (*kofr*), while the jealousy of a man is part of belief ',[26] and tries to shed light on what heresy can mean in this context. It has an ethical rather than a religious connotation, arising from the asymmetry inherent in the way the sexes relate to each other. Women are entrusted to men, they become not only part of men but part of their honour. Men can take more than one woman as spouse at the same time, while the opposite cannot happen. Without asking whether such asymmetry is defined by laws of nature or culture, Sorush ends the session by saying there is another jealousy, manifested in creation, but he will leave it for next week.

In the next session (28 October), Sorush continues with the theme of jealousy, but on a mystical level. He starts with Rumi's interpretation of a hadith about divine jealousy and relates it to love (*'eshq*), devoting the entire session to this. Here he is in his element, weaving his own narrative into a rich body of mystical concepts and poems to make a case for love, which he argues must be treated with jealousy, that is, protected from those who do not have it.

I find this session the most engaging and important, and yet the most difficult to assess. I am taken by Sorush's eloquence, his perception, and his courage in tackling such a delicate issue in a mosque. He makes a strong case for love, keeping it out of the *feqh* domain – yet I am puzzled by the clear male bias in his narrative. I can't decide whether he is telling his audience the whole story or is talking in innuendo. He begins by pointing to a duality, a paradox, in Persian literature, which reflects a cultural ambivalence towards the subject of love and women. Love is the main theme in Persian literature, yet one is never sure whether the writer is talking about divine or earthly love.

> Our poets have perfected the art of ambiguity. In our culture, the same ambivalence can be seen when women are concerned . . . It's enough to look at our own current society. I suppose there are few societies in the modern era for which sex and women are such a problem, yet we pretend the issue is resolved, that no problem exists. It's enough just to see the places that come under certain people's control; the kinds of separation and segregation [imposed] speak of the obsession, of the state of minds, and show the size of the problem and the distance that must be crossed for it to be resolved naturally.

He talks about the role of earthly love in the lives of those such as Ibn Arabi and Hafez, and recites poems in which they talk of their love. He relates the story of Ibn Arabi's falling in love with a learned and beautiful Isfahani woman in Mecca, and her influence on his mystical development.[27] He also tells two stories from the Qur'an that speak of women's love for men: those of Zoleikha for Yusef (Sura 12) and the daughter of Sho'eib for Musa (Sura 28). He relates both stories in detail, seeing their message as endorsing the naturalness of attraction and love between men and women.[28] Unlike others, he emphasises not Zoleikha's cunning and her attempts to seduce Yusef but his beauty and ability to resist temptations. God put love for him in her heart; he is so beautiful and desirable that other women, having at first blamed Zoleikha, sympathise with her when they see him, and plead with him to respond to her love. The two stories, he says, must be taken in conjuction with Sura Nur; he recites verse 31, which deals with women's covering and chastity. He asks, can love between men and women be recommended on ethical and religious grounds, or must it be condemned? In either case, what are the consequences, and how should a religious society deal with it?

In the rest of the session, Sorush presents a broad review of love in the history of Islamic thought. On the one hand are the moralists, who denounce love and tolerate no mention of it; on the other are those who recognise its blessing and power and resist denouncing it in the name of religion. Mystics argue that earthly love is a passage to divine love, a metaphor leading us to the Truth; but this is also an attempt to theorise a successful experience. The force of their argument is such that even philosophers have to contemplate love, although some reduce it to sex drive.[29] Those who readily issue *fatwas* dividing love into *halal* and *haram*, not only mistake lust for love but also forget that love, as Sufis argue, is involuntary; it is in its nature to undermine the will, thus it is not a matter on which there can be a *feqh* ruling. Instead of condemning it, our thinkers should contemplate love – whether earthly or divine – and propagate it. We must not let love be treated as a disease, something that defiles. It is healing and purifying, and can cure both individuals and societies of many afflictions and excesses. *Feqh*, more oriented to piety than love, must approach mysticism, which is more inclined to love than piety. Then they can overcome the duality, the rupture, in our cultural history and moderate the excesses of both.

Concluding his review, Sorush returns to jealousy. What he says here, it seems to me, not only reveals his male bias but undermines the case he has made for love.

> Thus man's jealousy towards women isn't only about honour but also about love. It's said that women are the repository for love and men the repository for wisdom; we can put this better, and say that women are objects of love, and men are not. If we accept that great loves have led to great acts in history, then we must admit that women have played a great role, and it's unwise for women to try to be men; they can't, they can only forfeit their womanhood. This is to negate one's blessing. It does [neither sex] any good, if someone, or a group, doesn't appreciate their worth and their place and also if others try to dislodge them from their place.

Sorush seems to have forgotten that only a moment earlier he told his audience two Qur'anic love stories in which, as he himself pointed out, men

(Joseph and Moses) not women were the objects of love. Or does the lapse betray his own ambivalence?

Also puzzling, I find, is Sorush's final observation on love in contemporary Iranian poetry. He says he will touch on it only briefly, inviting his audience to do their own research and draw their own conclusions. Love still dominates our poetry and occupies our poets' minds, he says, but its manifestations are no longer pure and spiritual. In the past the poet was part of a closed world defined by religious values: 'even if the poet chose to fix his gaze on the earth, the sky above him cast its shadow on his world.' This is no longer the case; he makes the point by reciting a poem by Forugh Farrokhzad, where she says she never wanted to be a star in the sky or to be the companion of angels, she never separated herself from the earth.[30] This identity – never wanting to be part of a celestial world – Sorush argues, is evident in her approach to love and some how degrades it. Adding 'some of her poems, if you don't know they're hers, you'd think they're by a mystic', he recites one of her love poems, but stops as he reaches lines in which she expresses yearning for her lover, saying that a mosque is not the place for it.[31] He ends his defence of love by returning to the mystical realm, where earthly love is a metaphor for, and a means of experiencing, a greater truth.[32]

In the final session, Sorush concludes his commentary on Imam Ali's words on women with a discussion of *keramat*, which he glosses as 'the limit, the purpose, the proper place of each being'. He approaches the concept from a philosophical angle, placing it in the context of the two competing world views discussed earlier. The first, to which the Imam's words belong, accepts the world and its order as designed by the Creator, and has no dispute with the place assigned to His creation. The second, which makes the Imam's words difficult to digest, sees the world and its order as accidental, and wants to define the role of creation. The first view (that of Islamic thinkers) sees women as created for men and the roles of the sexes as non-interchangeable. In the second (that of modern times) women aspire to men's place in the order of things. Sorush embarks on a long discussion, examining the pros and cons of each of these world views. Critical of both but not totally rejecting either, he resorts to the Qur'an to shed light on women's place in the divine order of life. As he continues, it becomes clear that his own understanding of the Qur'anic position is in line with that of Islamic thinkers whose texts he earlier analysed critically. He recites and elaborates on a Qur'anic verse: 'And one of His signs is that He created mates for you from yourselves that you may find rest in them, and He put between you love and compassion; most surely there are signs in this for a people who reflect' (al-Rum, 21). Earlier, when speaking of love, he found a kind of symmetry in the ways men and women relate to each other; now he finds asymmetry and complementarity:

The most important role for women, as understood from this verse, and as recognised by most of our *ulema*, is to restore to man the peace he has lost, to correct the imbalance that prevents him from fulfilling his role. This is the role assigned to woman; this is the status bestowed on her by creation. You can, of course, disagree and believe that woman is malleable and can assume whatever role she is given, and man likewise; who says woman should be confined to this role – she can have better roles in society . . . Fine, this is a theory that some maintain today. But as I said, what we find at the root of Islamic thought is that men's and women's roles are assigned, defined, and not interchangeable; in this view, woman fulfils her role in society through man, that is, she restores to men, the main actors in society, their lost balance and peace.

If we accept this as a proper understanding of religious texts, then, when the Imam says: 'don't allow a woman matters other than those about herself, because a woman is a flower, not an administrator', he means that [gender] roles in society are not changeable. Those who say otherwise are those who say we [are the ones who] define roles, that people can be prepared for roles through socialisation, education, etc.

Typical to his style, Sorush now poses a question and a counter-argument that subvert the claims of conventional understandings.

But if we accept the view that [gender] roles are defined and their limits set, we face the question: what are these limits? Who says these limits have been correctly defined? How do we know the roles men and women have played so far are the male and female roles they should have played? This is an important question. In theory, we might accept that man should remain man, and woman should remain woman, but who has defined what men should do, and what women should do? We have three sources to consult: religion, science, and history.

To find the answer, Sorush invites his audience to consult each of these sources, telling them to focus on history, which he sees as natural, as reflecting the human nature in which men and women have shown their characteristics. He expands his response to a question a few weeks earlier about the philosophy of history.

I know you'll object that women weren't allowed to find their own status. But this objection isn't valid, whether in this case or in others. We must ask why and how men succeeded . . . We can look at history from an ethical angle and reach certain conclusions; but if we suspend ethical judgement and look at history in terms of possibilities, we'll reach different ones. I suggest that if women occupied a position we now see as oppressed, then they saw this as their proper place in life; they didn't see themselves as oppressed and didn't ask for more, as they saw their *keramat*, their worth, as being women, not as being like men. We can't impose our own values on the past, and assume that what we now consider to be injustice, or essential rights, were valid then – that's the worst kind of historiography. I suppose we're at the start of a new epoch; in fact it began almost two centuries ago, with the rise of protesters, who see themselves as making and designing their own world. It remains to be seen how.

Although science, the second source, Sorush argues, can tell us more about the characteristics of each sex, it cannot give us the final answer. Religion, whose answer he has been exploring in these lectures, is no longer consulted, since:

> Men and women of this age – whether religious or not – now inhabit a world where they give an absolute value to expressing dissatisfaction and protesting at their lot. They're not prepared to hear the clear answer of religion, nor does anyone tell them. So we must only wait for the third source – history – to make our places clear to us. It's only then that humans can hear and understand the delight of surrender to God's will.

So Sorush concludes his discussion of women and gender roles. He talks for another half an hour, dealing with questions, but makes no further points.

Sorush in London

In October 1995, when I first listened to recordings of these lectures in Tehran, I did not know what to make of them. I was taken by Sorush's rational approach to sacred texts, by his eloquence, by his willingess to see different sides to an argument, by his courage in opening up and speaking of taboo subjects (such as Farrokhzad's love poetry) in a mosque, to an audience for whom women like her had been demonised in the past seventeen years. On the other hand, I found his own position on gender problematic, and was frustrated and annoyed by what I saw as skilled evasion of any kind of serious debate over women's legal rights. I could also see that his position, and to an extent his approach to women's issues, was very close to that of Shari'ati. They both criticise not just old understandings of women's status in Islam but also the advocates of equal rights; both refuse to enter the realm of *feqh*.

I decided there was no way I could include Sorush among the supporters of gender equality in Islam. Clearly he subscribed to the view that in the divine order of things women are for men, as they are men's 'calm', their anchor. I shared my misgivings about Sorush's gender position with Shahla Sherkat, editor of *Zanan*. She conceded that she had pressed him to let her publish a transcript of his lectures, but when the text was prepared Sorush delayed approving it for publication. Finally, she herself abandoned the project. She gave me a copy of the transcripts.

I could not understand how and why Sorush's ideas had inspired women in *Zanan*, who like me objected to his gender position.[33] Only later, when I was well into writing this book, did I understand that I must shift my focus. It was not his position on gender but his conception of Islam and his approach to sacred texts that empowered women in *Zanan* to argue for gender equality, just as they also, I realised, made possible my debate with the *Payam-e Zan* clerics, even though they did not agree with his approach to the texts any more than I agreed with his gender position. The tension in the last session of our debate – I now realised – had partly to do with my increasing self-confidence in locating my objections within an Islamic framework, which I had internalised by listening to Sorush's tapes and reading his work in the intervening months.

Between May and December 1996 Sorush gave a number of talks in London, mostly in Persian and to audiences largely of Iranian students, including a series of eleven lectures on Rumi and mysticism. I attended most of these talks, and whenever I had a chance I asked questions and tried to draw attention to gender issues. The opportunity to hear Sorush in person helped me place his 1992 talks on women in the context of his wider analytical method and his later thinking. By now I could see how his approach to Islam could open up space for a radical rethinking of gender relations, among other issues. Yet whenever I or other women in the audience asked him pertinent questions, he was evasive. For example, at a Middle East Forum meeting at the School of Oriental and African Studies, London, in June, I asked him why he had not addressed women's questions in print. He replied that it was not easy, they cannot be addressed without discussing human rights, and anyway women do it themselves. In September, at a seminar in London, 'Obstacles to Development in Iran', organised by the Islamic Society of Iranian Students, where Sorush was one of four panellists – all male – I asked why none of the speakers had said a single word about women's rights or gender issues. Again Sorush's answer was vague, in line with his 1992 talks.

After listening to the 1992 tapes again, I still could not decide what he was actually saying. There were different layers. Although I agreed with some points, I could not accept others. Sometimes he seemed to be arguing in line with the traditionalists. I agreed with his identification of the main contradiction in the

Islamic Republic's discourse on women, but his own arguments seemed to me just as problematic. What Sorush was arguing, and urging on Muslim women, was to resolve the contradiction by accepting the role they were given in creation, their 'position'. He called this 'the step that must be taken'. To me, this was the voice of a conservative philosopher, not a reformer and thinker trying to reconcile democracy and Islam. Didn't he consider gender equality, too, to be part of democratic and human rights?

Then in October I had a private meeting with him, in which I raised my objections to the gender position he took on the tapes, and tried to draw him into a more specific discussion. I started by summarising his arguments and the issues he raised in the 1992 talks, interjecting comments of my own. Dealing with Imam Ali's views on women, he says we find them difficult to accept because they reflect an old world view. He criticises the two ways they are now dealt with (casting doubt on their authenticity; interpreting them as only concerning Ayesha), saying that neither will solve the problem. He suggests dealing with them by reasoning; but this, I said, is not enough.

AKS: Enough for what? That depends what conclusions you want to draw. In that talk I laid an important foundation whose implications for religious literature, in my view, can't be appreciated now. I said that unquestioning obedience to the words of a religious leader when he reasons isn't obligatory. In certain situations we follow and submit unconditionally: we're Muslims and pray as the Prophet says; here there's no room for questioning. But this isn't the case when there's reasoning in the words of a religious leader.

ZMH: That is, we can refute it?

AKS: Of course we can. If not, what is reasoning for in the first place? not just to persuade but also to evaluate. If Imam Ali reasons with us, he invites us to reason back, to use our critical faculties. There I tried to present a counter-argument, and pointed out that we can't deduce from the Imam's words that women are defective in faith [because they don't pray or fast at certain times]. If we say that, then we must also say that those who can't afford to go on Hajj pilgrimage are also defective in faith; but we say that it's not obligatory for them.

Such a foundation can be a torch for you when entering the religious literature, to put aside fear and clarify matters for yourself. You can say that such reasonings satisfied the logic of people of that age, or that since the reasoning is false it's impossible that the Imam would deduce such a Ruling from it. What conclusion you draw from these arguments depends on your own perspective and intentions. That's the essence of what I said there; it can have many applications if we use it consistently and methodically.

I continued with my summary, and pointed out that, despite the many insights he provides into the old view, there is a kind of fallacy in his arguments, particularly as regards what he calls 'the new view'.

> ZMH: When it comes to discussing the new view that 'woman is not for man', you oversimplify a complex debate and reduce women's demands for equal rights to 'wanting to take man's place', which in your discourse becomes not valuing God's design for humanity. It's in this context that you introduce the concept of *keramat* to define the true place and boundaries of created beings, and you examine it in the context of two competing world views: the old and the new. You criticise the *ulema*'s understanding of women's role, but as you go on, it becomes evident that yours isn't very different. You too hold that in the divine order of things women are for men, as they are men's 'calm', their anchor. What do you mean by this?

At this point, I quoted a passage from Ayatollah Javadi-Amoli's book, where he, like Sorush, bypasses *feqh* Rulings and tries to place the whole gender debate on a spiritual plane – even invoking the same Qur'anic verse.[34] Unaware that Javadi-Amoli was Sorush's most articulate and powerful clerical adversary, I pointed out how Sorush's position and understanding of gender in sacred texts, even some of his arguments, resemble those of Javadi, whose approach is theological. As I blundered on, Sorush kept repeating (probably in disbelief): '*'Ajab! 'ajab!*' (how odd!). I went on:

> You close your discussion of women and gender roles by inviting your audience to look for the answer in history. That is, you tell them implicitly that women's roles in society will be the same as before, since there is a reason why they have played such roles so far. There are several problems with this argument. History has many narratives: the one you are talking of is written by men; the history of mankind might be natural, as you say, but that doesn't mean it's just; there's no reason to say that the Lawgiver wanted it to be this way, or that it will always remain such; slavery was with us for much of our history, and other examples abound. Gender equality is a Principle, a prevailing value of our age; whether it's here to stay, or a passing fashion, is another matter. The question then is why you, a religious intellectual, also choose to ignore it. What does Revelation have to say on this? What is your own understanding?
>
> Incidentally, you employ a rhetorical device – like the *ulema* when they talk of pre-Islamic views and practices. You criticise past thinkers' outlandish views on women, which somehow diverts attention from a

discussion of current views. For instance, you quote views such as those of Feiz Kashani [woman is an animal created so that man will be inclined to mate] . . .

AKS: He takes it from Ghazzali.

ZMH: And Feiz develops it. That is, you give the men in your audience a false sense of generosity and pride that they don't think like that, and women a sense of gratitude that they aren't thought of that way. I don't know whether or not you do this deliberately, but it sets the tone and the course of the debate. You also do the same when dealing with feminism: focusing on excesses and pre-empting a debate.

AKS: [laughing] You're rather angry!

ZMH: I do find what you say infuriating! I can't accept the basis of what you say there.

AKS: And what is that basis?

ZMH: Perhaps if there's an anger, it's because of the ambivalence in what you say. You say there's a status for women, there's a purpose, but you never say clearly what they are. You reduce this purpose for woman to being man's calm, his anchor in life. But the same could be said of men. And there's more to feminism, to women's demand for equality, than what you told your audience; there are many debates and positions within feminism; no one says that women are identical to men, difference is now brought into the picture, some even argue that apart from their bodies women differ from men in psychology and the way they relate to the world.

AKS: Look, there's a need for these debates, they've mellowed feminists, earlier they went too far and these [religious] counter-arguments gradually made them aware that woman should demand status by keeping her womanhood. I'll give some general explanations and hope they address your questions.

First, we must make a distinction. The majority of our *ulema* – even men of politics – when talking about women, their guide is *feqh*, that is, their ideas, their images come from a set of Rulings they have in mind, then they create an image of women to reflect it.

ZMH: But behind these Rulings lie world views, value systems . . .

AKS: Exactly. I mean, we have two points of departure: if your guide is *feqh* then you define women as such to conform with its Rulings. I claim to be the greatest critic of such thinking. Among the objections I have raised is that *feqh*, as the lowest-ranking religious science, shouldn't become the centre of religious thought. I took the basis of this argument from Ghazzali, and expanded it in a lecture I gave at Harvard last year, entitled 'The Place of Feqh in Islamic Teachings' . . . One of the main differences I see between pre- and post-revolutionary Islam is that our present Islam is *feqh*-based, whereas before it was spiritual. That Islam was appealing; Islam since the revolution no longer appeals, it displays a stern legalism. In my last article in *Kiyan*, based on a talk I gave at UNESCO, when I reach *feqh* I say it's a kind of stern legalism that brings alienation.[35] . . . Of course, it isn't easy to talk of *feqh* in these terms . . . [but I continue to do so] since I see it as one of the ills of current religious thinking, precisely because of what you mentioned: *feqh* holds within itself a world view, but some ignore this, take its Rulings as immutable, then go on to define women accordingly. In a recent article, I argue that a religious Ruling is not the same as a *feqh* Ruling; I discuss [the *ulema*'s] understanding of religious Rulings as like *feqh* Rulings.[36] This fallacy must be eradicated.

I want you to know how I think on such issues. *Feqh* is not my point of departure, and the question of women . . .

ZMH: But you can't totally ignore or bypass *feqh*.

AKS: No, I'll get there in the end. The question is where *feqh* should be placed, at our point of departure or at our destination. To enter a debate on the women's question via the path of women's rights is incorrect, and I consciously don't pursue it. Not because I don't believe in them or want to ignore them, but because I believe that this isn't a starting point and will lead us astray. I start from your question: what's the status of women? Women's status mustn't be reduced to law; it's much broader. In the past, women's status wasn't what we say. Look at the religious literature. When I first quoted what Hakim Sabzevari said on women, some [*ulema*] got angry, and denied the authenticity of my quotation. In the text Molla Sadra wrote that several types of animals are created, one of which, woman, is created for men to mate with. Then Hakim Sabzevari comments on the text, saying the great man made a just point; he relies on it too in his interpretations of the religious texts: men are guardians of women because women are animals whom God gave human faces . . . Someone even wrote that I made this up. I had quoted it from memory, but when I checked, it was correct; I have given the reference in an article which came out in *Sturdier than Ideology*.[37] It's important that someone like Molla Sadra had such views, I tell you our jurists thought the same.

ZMH: Some still do.

AKS: I'd be surprised if it were otherwise. What school teaches them otherwise? These texts are still taught in the Houzeh, there isn't one on human rights. They base their logic, the Principles of Jurisprudence, on these philosophers' views. Unless a people's understanding of the women's question is changed, there'll be no basic change; women will remain less than second-class citizens; if they're given rights, it's from charity or necessity. Look, this is the milieu in which I'm talking, as a person; this is where the status of women must be corrected; in my opinion, we'll get nowhere by haggling about women's legal rights.

ZMH: Mr Motahhari, and today others, didn't think like this.

AKS: I accept that. I'm talking about the dominant rule; they're exceptions, all influenced by outside [the Houzeh]. I don't believe one can enter a legal debate with these gentlemen [*ulema*]; they can produce a hadith to silence you, but not if we start with broader concepts. We must first establish whether woman is human or, as Hakim Sabzevari says, animal; how God conceives of them, regardless of their place in relation to men. Is association with women defiling or enhancing to men? We must say that men can attain spiritual growth through love and friendship with women. This is a path I've been following in recent years in my teachings on Hafez. Hafez believes that humans aren't brought into the world to be ashamed; they've a right to exist and must honour this right. Someone like Rumi or Ghazzali didn't think this way. If we can correct such ideas then we can easily take the next step. That's why I see legal debates as secondary, and favour theoretical and philosophical debates. At present in our society, among our students, we have a problem: how to look at women with religious eyes. Once ideas and views change, laws will change . . . In the West too, ideas on these matters changed first, then women's place in life, in work, and family changed accordingly. *Zanan*, or anyone who works on women, should devote 70 per cent to these broader debates and 30 per cent to legal ones.

ZMH: Do you know that so far *Zanan* has had no article on [philosophical rather than legal views on women]?

AKS: Yes, that's a failing. Not many dare to write on this. It's also a difficult matter.

ZMH: It's a problem. There aren't many women competent to deal with theoretical debates on Islamic grounds. Women in the Houzeh seem to have no qualms about its views on women; some are even worse than men. To some degree this is to be expected: women who enter a patriarchal institution must accept its values in the first place, otherwise there's no place for them. Perhaps this is a stage; women in the Houzeh can't enter such debates at present. Some [religious] women, such as those in *Zanan*, haven't the expertise and others [non-religious] refuse to frame their discussions in Islamic terms. Male religious intellectuals, such as yourself, won't enter gender debates at all; for instance, there isn't a single reference to women's questions in

Kiyan, which considers them outside the realm of concern for religious intellectuals.

AKS: No . . . but they're involved in other debates; perhaps one day they will; perhaps they think there's no need, since there's *Zanan*. But I accept that in the realm of religious intellectuals, the women's question is neglected.

ZMH: Why do you think it's neglected?

AKS: Women are always seen through the eyes of *feqh* . . . Women themselves – including socially active intellectuals – tend to define themselves through a series of *feqh* duties. This is an important point.

ZMH: Of course, only some – that is, they've accepted . . .

AKS: I don't mean they shouldn't accept *feqh*; after all, a Muslim man or woman has a set of duties they must fulfil. What I mean is that they don't know their own 'existence', as existentialists would say. I see the difference between old and new men, old and new women, as lying in self-knowledge. That is, in recognising what it is to love as a woman, to be anxious as a woman, to demand rights as a woman. These they [old women?] lack; they think it's a sin to think about men, and don't see themselves as having the right to know. This is the problem: we must first make women aware of themselves. It's extremely difficult. It's like swimming in acid, which is heavy and burns your limbs. It takes a long time to explain to these women that there are some issues that have nothing to do with religion; these are meaningless taboos which are not imposed by God and His Messenger, you have imposed them on yourself and have distorted human relations. What is a woman with this image of herself to do with equal rights? That's why I say: debates on rights should come later. In our society, delicate theoretical work is needed, and when women know themselves, then you can say: now define your relationship with men, define your status, and yet remain Muslim and live according to the *shari‘a*. These relations [defined in *feqh*] aren't sacrosanct, they come from minds with distorted world views; many arose in situations when women didn't undertake social responsibilities. In our society, women work and are present, but some still want to enforce outmoded ethics. No one says where they came from, what era they belong to. The only thing that's done is to tell girls not to wear this or that.

ZMH: It's after all a transitional stage . . .

AKS: Of course, but this transitional stage must be paved with awareness, for us to reach more fundamental issues . . . We must change the image humans have of themselves . . . In my talk on Houzeh and university,[38] I said [to the *ulema*]: if you have a Women's Day in this country, then you must also declare that you reject what

Hakim Sabzevari says: you publish it in your books, yet without criticising it, and if you don't, someone like me will – and then you'll protest . . .

If you ask the same question about men—what's the purpose in their creation? – I would say, I don't know; certainly there's a purpose, but we don't know.

ZMH: Then why do you raise it [when it comes to women]?

AKS: Permit me. I mean that one level of the story goes to God, but at the other level, if you ask the question in broader terms – that is, what's the purpose in creation of mankind, which is divided into two sexes? – my answer is: what men, what women are we talking about? Men or women of yesterday or today? The answers differ. In my opinion, men and women should know each other and define their relationships. The only thing I can say is that we think women can be this or that and assume this or that role. Now whether [what we think] really is their purpose, I don't know. One thing is that in religious thought the greatest status a creature can be accorded is to be on the road to his or her spiritual perfection, not to be a director or a prime minister. In my talks I made it clear that, contrary to Ghazzali's view – that women are among Satan's army and their very essence is to prevent men from reaching God – I say that it's to help men. It's important for women for such a status to be recognised; on that basis their rights will be regulated. Looked at from a religious viewpoint, I think this is the story, and it's worth saying it, since when it's accepted that women bring men closer to God, then we must ask, what women? A woman who doesn't know herself and has no place in society? Or a woman who's found herself and has social rights?

ZMH: These things must be debated; they haven't yet been. When our religious intellectuals don't bring them up, then the field is left to the *ulema* and those who address them outside the realm of religion.

AKS: If there's moderate thinking in the realm of religion, then I think women have a very good position. I know some women who have good places and use them properly, depending on their tact and knowledge.

ZMH: Look, what you say implies inequality; the very fact that you think women must have a place . . .

AKS: No; why inequality? Obviously, if it isn't there you must talk about it for a long time in order to establish it. Don't you accept this? Second, women *are* different from men, this difference is undeniable, so their roles are different.

ZMH: Certainly. But when we say that women's purpose in creation is to restore peace to men and enable them to get closer to God, then it follows that they should stay at home to care for the children, to cater for his needs, enable him to fulfil his role and duties, and so on.

AKS: This is one job woman can have, and it's an important one. If a woman can only do this, she shouldn't feel ashamed; it's a valuable job and men should be grateful. But it's not right to make it an imperative [woman should only do this, or never do it]. These days it's thought that a woman should feel ashamed to be a housewife, when her husband is doing well in society. In my view, it's no less important than any other [role]. Many of our mothers lived like this, burned like a candle and gave light to others. One characteristic of our society is that it doesn't allow exclusive roles for women; they can work and perform roles, which bring changes in defining their rights in relations with men, etc. We see that these things have happened, and changes are coming about naturally. But a proper basis for them must be established, it mustn't be allowed to take a pragmatic and unconscious course. We must start from a basis that's acceptable to people themselves, that is, from what Rumi and Ibn Arabi said. True, they were people of their time, but their insights can come to our aid. Rumi says: 'Love belongs to the world of humans and doesn't define relations between males and females of other species.' We must start from here, or what Ibn Arabi says, or some of the ahadith of the Prophet; then you can open the way and proceed step by step. But I admit that the issue hasn't been tackled from this angle; or if it has, little work has been done; or it took a legal turn, or certain considerations intervened, or they wanted to introduce something in line with *feqh* Rulings, which to me is a misguided approach. I accept what you say, that the debate is in the hands of those who didn't know how to approach [the *ulema*] or the non-religious ones.

Now let's see what secularists have done in recent years. What they did at the time of the Constitutional Revolution [1906–09] was very positive and achieved things without which women would have little place in our society . . . They yielded their fruit at the time of the Islamic Revolution; nobody then imagined women demonstrating in the streets. But now the secularist slogan is faded; they've nothing new to say. Unless we go to the roots, nothing will change . . . What we want from secularist thinkers is to contribute to debates at root level, for instance what elements of feminism they accept.

We talked for a while about the recent work and ideas of those dealing with women's issues in Iran and outside, and about gender developments since the revolution. I said that, judging from my own work in Qom and following the debates there, I felt that we were on the threshold of a major shift in discourses and perspectives on women. Sorush reiterated the necessity to go to roots and fundamentals, and develop theoretical grounds, but saw little prospect of this: 'Our society – both men and women – is now too ideological . . . even intellectuals still take their models from *feqh*, they haven't severed that umbilical cord.' He admitted that some important changes have taken place in large towns, but was not optimistic that they would lead to a fundamental shift in perspective, since 'they need theoretical backing', and this was missing.

To me, Sorush's ambivalence on gender comes from the very framework and agenda he set himself. Like Shari'ati, his refusal to address the issue of women through *feqh* leaves him little choice but to talk in abstractions. This brings his views and position on gender close to those of Javadi-Amoli, despite vast differences in their visions and approaches to Islam. Both men bypass *feqh* – Javadi-Amoli taking a theological turn and Sorush, as he puts it, a 'phenomenological' one – and they end up with similar readings and understandings of sacred texts when it comes to gender.

Notes

1. A group of religious and political zealots who emerged in the spring of 1995, becoming prominent through their violent disruptions of Sorush's lectures. The group is small in numbers but reportedly enjoys the support of Ayatollah Ahmad Jannati (a member of the Council of Guardians) and has links with the Revolutionary Guards and the Ministry of Information (Intelligence).

2. For details and dates, I have relied on 'A Biography of Dr. Abdol Karim Soroush' dated July 1996, available at 'Seraj Homepage', a website 'dedicated to coverage and analysis of his ideas': www.seraj.org.

3. After the revolution the Iranian government bought the building (*imam-bareh*); it is now called Kanun-e Touhid (Centre of Unity) and is run by students closely linked to the Iranian ruling establishment.

4. In an April 1997 interview with the Seraj website, Sorush responds to criticism about his role in the cultural revolution, which is a sore point and a major reason why he is rejected by secular intellectuals.

5. 'Abdol Karim Sorush, 'Horriyat va Rouhaniyat' (Liberty and the Clergy), *Kiyan*, 24 (1995/1374), pp. 2–11.

6. Another spur to the disruption was probably Robin Wright's article calling Sorush the 'Luther of Islam'; 'An Iranian Luther Shakes the Foundations of Islam', *Guardian*, 1 February 1995 (reproduced from the *Los Angeles Times*).

7. *Kiyan*, 25 (1995); 61.

8. For the English text see 'Seraj Homepage'.

9. See 'Abdol Karim Sorush, *Qesseh-ye Arbab-e Ma'refat* (The Tale of the Masters of Knowledge) (Tehran: Sarat Cultural Institute, 1994/1373), Preface, p. 29.

10. Such as Alan Ryan's *The Philosophy of the Social Sciences*; E. A. Burt's *Metaphysical*

Foundations of Modern Physical Sciences, D. Little's *Varieties of Explanation in Social Sciences.*

[11.] 'Abdol Karim Sorush, *Tafarroj-e Son': Goftar-ha'i dar Ma'qulat-e Akhlaq va San'at va 'Elm-e Ensani* (Essays on Ethics, Arts and Human Sciences) (Tehran: Sarat Cultural Institute, 1994/1373)[the volume].

[12.] 'Abdol Karim Sorush, *Qabz va Bast-e Te'urik-e Shari'at* (Theoretical Contraction and Expansion of the Shari'a) (Tehran: Sarat Cultural Institute, 1994/1373).

[13.] Nouchine Yavari-d'Hellencourt, 'La difficile réémergence d'une presse indépendante en Iran: *Kiyan,* une revue en quête de modernité islamique', *Cahiers d'Etudes sur la Méditerranée Orientale et le Monde Turco-Iranien,* 20 (July–December 1995), pp. 91–114. [In 1995 . . . Kiyan. See] Ziba Mir-Hosseini, 'Women and the Shari'a in the Islamic Republic of Iran: A Changing Relationship'. Paper presented at the Carsten Niebuhr Institute of Near Eastern Studies Conference, 'Women, Culture and Modernity', Copenhagen, 18–21 February 1996.

[14.] Valla Vakili, *Debating Religion and Politics in Iran: The Political Thought of Abdol karim Soroush* (Studies Department Occasional Paper Series, no. 2) (Washington, DC: Council on Foreign Relations, 1996) and Robin Wright, 'Islam and Liberal Democracy: Two Visions of Reformation', *Journal of Democracy,* 7(2), pp. 64–75; for his contribution to modern Islamic discourse, see Mehrzad Boroujerdi, 'The Encounter of Post-Revolutionary Thought in Iran with Hegel, Heidegger, and Popper', in Serif Mardin (ed.), *Cultural Transformations in the Middle East* (Leiden: E. J. Brill, 1994), pp. 236–59; Mehrzad Boroujerdi, *Iranian Intellectuals and the West: The Tormented Triumph of Nativism* (Syracuse, NY: Syracuse University Press); John Cooper, 'The Limits of the Sacred: The Epistemology of 'Abd al-Karim Soroush', in John Cooper et al. (eds), *Islam and Modernity: Muslim Intellectuals Respond* (London and New York: I.B. Tauris, 1998); Afshin Matin-asgari, 'Abdolkarim Sorush and the Secularization of Islamic Thought in Iran', *Iranian Studies,* 30(1–2), pp. 95–115.

[15.] 'Abdol Karim Sorush, *Qabz va Bast-e Te'urik-e Shari'at* (Theoretical Contraction and Expansion of the Shari'a) (Tehran: Sarat Cultural Institute, 1994/1373), pp. 81–3; 'Abdol Karim Sorush, *Farbehtar az Ide'uluzhi* (Sturdier than Ideology) (Tehran: Sarat Cultural Institute, 1994/1373), p. 39.

[16.] Nabia Abbott, 'Women and the State in Early Islam', *Journal of Near Eastern Studies,* 1, pp. 106–26; Denise A. Spellberg, 'Political Action and Public Example: 'A'isha and the Battle of the Camel', in Beth Baron and Nikki Keddie (eds), *Women in the Middle Eastern History: Shifting Boundaries in Sex and Gender* (New Haven, CT: Yale University Press, 1991).

[17.] I later asked Sorush who the man had been. He said he was sitting close by but he thought it was the first time he had come to the mosque. He had asked Sorush to talk to his son, who had a number of questions to ask, but he never came again.

[18.] 'Abdol Karim Sorush, *Hekmat va Ma'ishat* (Wisdom and Life), vols 1 and 2 (Tehran: Sarat Cultural Institute, 1995/1373; 1997/1376).

[19.] The first time I heard Sorush in person, in Imperial College, London, in May 1996, the large Iranian audience was electrified; later I attended his lectures on Rumi's *Mathnavi*, which he clearly knew by heart, talking without notes.

[20.] *Nahj ol-Balagheh*, pp. 434–5, Letter 31 (Will).

[21.] Ibid., p. 81, Sermon 13.

[22.] Ibid., p. 257, Sermon 154.

[23.] Ibid., p. 539, Saying 235.

[24.] Fatima Mernissi, *Women and Islam: An Historical and Theological Enquiry*, trans. Mary Jo Lakeland (Oxford: Blackwell, 1991), Ziba Mir-Hosseini, 'Stretching the Limits: A Feminist Reading of the Shari'a in Iran Today', in Mai Yamani (ed.), *Feminism and Islam: Legal and Literary Perspectives* (London: Ithaca, 1996), pp. 284–320.

[25.] The recording of the first session ends with Sorush's talk, a reading and recitation of a mystical story from the *Mathnavi*. If there was a question/answer follow-up, as in other sessions, it was not recorded.

[26.] *Nahj ol-Balagheh*, p. 515, Saying 123.

[27.] Reynold A. Nicholson, *The Tarjuman al-Ashwag (Interpreter of Desires): A Collection of Mystical Odes by Muhyi'ddin Ibn al-Arabi* (London: Theosophical Publication House), p. 8.

[28.] Barbara Stowasser, *Women in the Qur'an: Traditions and Interpretations* (New York: Oxford University Press), pp. 50–61.

[29.] He refers to Molla Sadra's *Asfar*, which has a chapter on love, and Molla Hadi Sabzevari, who defines love as sexual gratification.

[30.] Forugh Farrokhzad, *Tavallod-e Digar* (Another Birth) (Tehran: Morvarid , 1991/1370), p. 24. For her life and poetry, see Farzaneh Milani, *Veils and Words: The Emerging Voices of Iranian Women Writers* (Syracuse, NY: Syracuse University Press), pp. 127–52.

[31.] Forugh Farrokhzad, *Tavallod-e Digar* (Another Birth) (Tehran: Morvarid, 1991/1370), p. 55.

[32.] The audience's questions ask for clarifications, and elicit no new points. For instance, one asks why the Prophet and Imams were polygamous, and why Ghazzali reached such high status without love.

[33.] I found it liberating and promising that, despite its devotion to Sorush's ideas, *Zanan* validated Forugh Farrokhzad, whose poetry Sorush had described as 'too worldly'; see *Zanan*, 16 (Winter 1993), 20 (Autumn 1994), and 25 (Summer 1995). It is interesting that in early 1998 Sorush gave a series of thirty-five talks on Hafez and his philosophy, in which one of the main themes was the importance of earthly love.

[34.] 'Abdollah Javadi-Amoli, *Zan dar A'ineh-ye Jalal va Jamal* (Women in the Mirror of Glory and Beauty) (Tehran: Reja' Cultural Press, 1993/1372), pp. 38–9.

35. 'Abdol Karim Sorush, 'Zehniyat-e Moshavvash, Hovviyat-e Moshavvash' (Confused Mentality, Confused Identity), *Kiyan*, 30 (1996/1375), pp. 4–9.

36. 'Abdol Karim Sorush, 'Tahlil-e Mafhum-e Hokumat-e Dini' (Analysis of the Concept of Religious Rule), *Kiyan*, 32 (1996/1375), pp. 2–13.

37. 'Abdol Karim Sorush, *Farbehtar az Ide'uluzhi* (Sturdier than Ideology) (Tehran: Sarat Cultural Institute, 1994/1373), pp. 39–40.

38. 'Abdol Karim Sorush, *Farbehtar az Ide'uluzhi* (Sturdier than Ideology) (Tehran: Sarat Cultural institute, 1994/1373), pp. 21–43.

CHAPTER 14

Women's Political Rights After the Islamic Revolution[1]

Mehrangiz Kar

Translated by Haleh Anvari

Mehrangiz Kar was born in 1944 and educated at the College of Law and Political Science at the University of Tehran. After graduating she worked for the Institute of Social Security and began to publish on social and political issues in respected journals and magazines. By her own admission, Kar has been politically active since the age of twenty-four, and her writings reflected her disagreement with the politics of the Pahlavi regime. On the other hand, she was recognised for being non-religious, which became a problem with the establishment of the Islamic Republic in 1978. Nevertheless, Kar continued her politico-academic works and published a number of books including two volumes of The Quest for Identity: The Image of Iranian Women in Pre-History and History *(co-edited with Shahla Lahiji),* Women and the Iranian Labour Market *(1974),* The Legal Structure of the Family System in Iran *(1999), and* Violence Against Women in Iran *(2000). The conflict between Kar and elements within the Islamic Republic came to a head following her participation in a conference in Berlin (in April 2000 entitled 'Iran After the Elections') and she was subsequently charged on a variety of counts, including 'spreading propaganda against the regime of the Islamic Republic' and 'violating the dress code at the Berlin conference'. Kar was held in Evin prison but released on bail, and subsequently was permitted to leave Iran to receive medical treatment. (Her jail sentence was initially for a period of four years, but was later reduced to six months.) Having been released on bail, Kar was able to leave Iran to receive medical treatment, and she is currently in the USA. Her troubles have not yet ceased, as her husband, the journalist Siamak Pourzand, disappeared in Tehran, and it became clear that this was an attempt by the anti-Kar factions within the Islamic establishment to silence her and her daughters while abroad, but their policy failed, as she has spoken out about her husband's circumstances. In May 2002 the seventy-three-year-old Pourzand was sentenced to eight years' imprisonment.*

Kar's unflinching determination to raise the issue of inequality within Iranian society and her continuing efforts to voice her opinions have resulted in international recognition. She was confirmed as International Woman of the Year in 2000 by Italy and Canada, was awarded the prestigious 'Ludovic Trarieux International Human Rights Prize' in 2002, and some Iranians have expressed their opinion that the Nobel Peace Prize of 2003 which was given to the Iranian lawyer, Shirin Ebadi, should have been presented to Kar herself.[2] In her own opinion, Kar has remarked, 'While I think Shirin is very deserving of this award, I think this was a political statement by the Nobel Committee, with a message to the Iranian people that the international community is aware of their struggle and their ability to address political change.'[3]

The challenge that Kar presents to the established Islamic order in Iran has been made explicitly clear since her departure from Iran. She has mentioned one school of thought in Iran that argues that 'we need a total separation of religion and state. This last group would not even enter the debate on the compatibility of Islam, human rights and women's rights. I follow the latter; I believe that it is not possible to combine these two together.'[4] The following text, however, is more cautious, perhaps reflecting its publication in book form in Iran. Indeed, the text works from within the Islamic tradition in an attempt to undermine the arguments that are designed to prevent women's political participation from an 'Islamic' perspective. Kar provides lengthy quotes from leading religious figures who argue that not only can a woman become a marja' *(a source of emulation – a senior clerical figure) and issue* fatwas *that can be followed by men, but it is also possible for a woman to be the* vali-ye faqih, *the supreme leader of the Iranian political system. The present political system and culture prevent women from enjoying full political rights and equality, however, and Kar gives the examples of gender inequality in testimony before courts of law, the prohibition against women becoming judges, and the law of* qesas, *in which if a woman is murdered, her family have to pay half of the blood money, whereas this is not the case for the relatives of a male who has been murdered. Kar believes that Iranian society cannot remain static, as information technology and education increase daily, and under such circumstances it is impossible to tell women to 'go back to your homes'. Yet she argues that women must be more vocal and establish links with leading clerics in order for women's rights to advance.*

Kar's chapter works within the Islamic tradition (despite her own comments – cited above – that are at pains to distance herself from Islam). It would be very difficult to question the 'Islamic commitment' of this chapter, especially as Kar cites Ayatollah Khomeini and other high ranking ayatollahs and clerics to support her perspective. Moreover, her criticisms of the Constitution of the Islamic Republic are carried out in an academic fashion, recognising that there is a distinction between equality of human beings on the one hand and those which are then conditioned by Islamic standards, and it is such standards that need to be revised by the mojtaheds. This chapter from Women's Political Participation in Iran *was published well after Mohammad Khatami's victory in the 1997 presidential elections which heralded a period of social reform in Iran.*

It is appropriate to end this reader with such a chapter because it functions not just as an excellent example of the ongoing arguments about women's rights, but also as an example of the struggle that Iran faces in its quest for identity. The attraction of the West and its claim to respect universal human rights remains a goal for many Iranians, while this has been something that some factions within the Islamic Republic have rejected because of its perceived threat to Islamic tradition and Iranian culture. This quest for an authentic Iranian culture and the relation to it of both Islam and the West has been the underlying theme in the writings and speeches in this reader, and no doubt, as new perceptions of what 'authentic' Iranian and Islamic culture really are, these debates will continue for another hundred years and more.

Notes

[1.] From *Women's Political Participation* (Tehran: Rawshangaran va Mutala'at-i Zanan, 2001).

[2.] Private correspondence with Haleh Anvari. For Kar's comments about Shireen Ebadi see 'Mehrangiz Kar Speaks on Nobel Laureate Shirin Ebadi' <www.isop.ucla.edu/article.asp?parentid=5537>, posted 12/11/2003.

[3.] Ibid.

[4.] 'Interviewing Mehrangiz Kar' (28 May 2004) <www.irandokht.com/TV/Tvmore.php?PID=22>.

Further Reading

M. Kar, 'Second Class: The Legal Status of Iranian Women', <www.iranian.com/Opinion/2000/April/Women> (18 April 2000).

——'Mehrangiz Kar Speaks on Nobel Laureate Shirin Ebadi', <www.isop.ucla.edu/article.asp?parentid=5537> (12 November 2003).

(no reference given) 'Interviewing Mehrangiz Kar' (28 May 2004) <www.irandokht.com/TV/Tvmore.php?PID=22>.

—•—

Introduction

In the Islamic Republic too, there have been men and women who have been present in the election arena of the Parliament (*Majles*) during legislative terms. In general, those women who believed in the principles of the regime and were at one with and homogenous with official values, were declared (as candidates) and those who held other political views and belonged to other parties and opposing organisations did not find their way in.

Because of this, only the dominant pattern of participation by women has been registered in the Iranian women's political dossier in the periods 1962–79 and 1979 onwards. And there are no signs of the presence of the various classes and the differing trends among women's votes in the Iranian legislative institution.

But during the revolution, because of its religious characteristics, religious women of extreme traditional background who were imprisoned in their homes and had grown resentful of the Pahlavi era, left their houses to join the revolutionary demonstrations. They also had great impact at times of war and political crises on the consolidation of the Islamic Republic, which helped them form a political image, albeit clichéd and of the grassroots level.

This positive incident in itself, however, should not stop us from critiquing the one-dimensional blueprint for political participation in Iran by women. The presence of women in the legislative process alone is not a solution for gender inequality. The cultural structure of the government must be able to attract women from all social, political and ideological backgrounds and classes, to the political arena, with the help of parties, societies and independent organisations. It must create the possibility of participation for all the people in the law-making process without an inclination to monopoly.

The present paradox (which on the one hand emphasises the empowerment of women because of the eradication of *Shari'a* obstacles for women's presence in the political arena, while on the other hand amplifying their house-bound role) can be solved thus. While necessary facilities are created for independent women's organisations, the Islamic Republic's government should concurrently perform its role according to the constitution, and implement numerous cultural and social plans with the aim to improve and increase the scientific and personal abilities of women to learn skills and specialisations in a suitable environment in order to access new jobs. Should this happen, a large group of those women who have entered the centre stage from the margins and who have been familiarised with the alphabet of politics due to the influence of the revolution and war, will be transformed into a constructive, specialist and deserving force, and in time will learn to choose the logical routes in the battle to demand their rights. On the other hand, should the fluid force of these women (who have flown from their nests in order faithfully to reshape their homeland) be left unattended with the government feeling no sense of duty towards them, these women will be destroyed without leaving a lasting mark and assume a destructive and harmful role in the area of politics and morality. For this reason it is essential that Iranian women (should) communicate their legal demands with reference to certain points of the constitution, especially the second and third articles.

Article 2

The Islamic Republic is a system based on belief in:

1. The One God (as stated in the phrase 'There is no god except Allah'), His exclusive sovereignty and the right to legislate, and the necessity of submission to His commands;
2. Divine revelation and its fundamental role in setting forth the laws;
3. The return to God in the Hereafter, and the constructive role of this belief in the course of man's ascent towards God;
4. The justice of God in creation and legislation;
5. Continuous leadership (*imamah*) and perpetual guidance, and its fundamental role in ensuring the uninterrupted process of the revolution of Islam;
6. The exalted dignity and value of man, and his freedom coupled with responsibility before God in which equity, justice, political, economic, social, cultural independence and national solidarity are secured by recourse to:
    1. continuous *ejtehad* of the fuqaha possessing necessary qualifications, exercised on the basis of the Qur'an and the Sunnah of the immaculate ones (*ma'sumun*), upon all of whom be peace;
    2. sciences and arts and the most advanced results of human experience, together with the effort to advance them further;
    3. negation of all forms of oppression, both the infliction of and the submission to, and of dominance, both its imposition and its acceptance.

Article 3

In order to attain the objectives specified in Article 2, the government of the Islamic Republic of Iran has the duty of directing all its resources to the following goals:

1. The creation of a favourable environment for the growth of moral virtues based on faith and piety and the struggle against all forms of vice and corruption;
2. Raising the level of public awareness in all areas, through the proper use of the press, mass media, and other means;
3. Free education and physical training for everyone at all levels, and the facilitation and expansion of higher education;
4. Strengthening the spirit of inquiry, investigation and innovation in all areas of science, technology and culture as well as Islamic studies by establishing research centres and encouraging researchers;
5. The complete elimination of imperialism and the prevention of foreign influence;
6. The elimination of all forms of despotism and autocracy and all attempts to monopolise power;
7. Ensuring political and social freedoms within the framework of the law;

8. The participation of the entire people in determining their political, economic, social, and cultural destiny;
9. The abolition of all forms of undesirable discrimination and the provision of equitable opportunities for all, in both the material and intellectual spheres;
10. The creation of a correct administrative system and elimination of superfluous government organisations;
11. All-round strengthening of the foundations of national defence to the utmost degree by means of universal military training for the sake of safeguarding the independence, territorial integrity, and the Islamic order of the country;
12. The planning of a correct and just economic system, in accordance with Islamic criteria in order to create welfare, eliminate poverty, and abolish all forms of deprivation with respect to food, housing, work, health care, and the provision of social insurance for all;
13. The attainment of self-sufficiency in scientific, technological, industrial, agricultural, and military domains, and other similar spheres;
14. Securing the multifarious rights of all citizens, both women and men, and providing legal protection for all, as well as the equality of all before the law;
15. The expansion and strengthening of Islamic brotherhood and public co-operation among all the people;
16. Framing the foreign policy of the country on the basis of Islamic criteria, fraternal commitment to all Muslims, and unsparing support to the oppressed of the world.

What is evident is that the religious sources who led the Iranian Revolution have solved the difficult problem of women's presence in its general format. In the present circumstances it is the government's duty to encourage the many women who are enthusiastic towards growth, elevation and specialisation. The fourteenth section of the third principle of the constitution has paid adequate attention to the provision of all-round rights for women.

As a result, less than twenty years after the bloody events of 5 June 1963, during the first public elections after the revolution in 1979, the right of women to vote has been recognised officially as a definite right and far from un-Islamic. Religious sources even declared women's participation in the referendum of 31 March 1979 as necessary and promised them that their rights would be heeded after the referendum.

Ayatollah Khomeini in a meeting that took place on 28 March 1979 – i.e. three days before the referendum – with his women supporters, took this position:

> One way or another you are free to say yes or no or whatever you wish to write on the ballot, no one will stop you. But if they spread this among the people that Islam does not give women their rights

and what will happen after the referendum, this is one of those topics that agents of foreigners are bringing to the fore and it is agents of foreigners who are creating divisions between our people in various ways and do not wish this referendum to be concluded, and maybe they have a hope that the monarchy should be preserved or to bring about another regime. One way or another, the rights of women are set forth as are the rights of men, Islam has favoured women more than men, Islam has considered the rights of women more than men. This is the meaning of what will happen next: women have the right to vote. This provision that we are allowing for women is higher than the West. They [women] have the right to vote, the right to choose and the right to be elected. All this exists; they have control over their business deals and are free, free in choosing jobs. Naturally, there are limitations on men and those limitations are for the good of the men. And those limitations, in other words where there is evil for men, Islam prohibits gambling, Islam prohibits wine drinking, Islam prohibits heroin, because these are corruptors. There are limitations for everyone, divine and *Shari'a* limitations, limitations that are for the good of the society, it's not that something is beneficial for society and limitations are set on them. We promise you that in an Islamic government all and everyone is free, all and everyone will achieve their rights and all these debates that are brought forth before the referendum and they are working on, these are to the benefit of outsiders, come and rescue your own country. Tomorrow we all go to the ballot boxes and I will go to the ballot box myself and cast my own vote. All of you together go forth, God willing, for the creation of a free country, an independent country, a country that will be for ourselves and where we will toil in it and use it ourselves.

Visions in Opposition

Since the Constitutional Revolution, there has been a constant conflict between the religious and political viewpoints regarding the effective presence of Muslim women in social activities and political decision-making. Finally, almost one century after the justice-seeking Constitutional Revolution and twenty-one years after the Islamic Revolution, the crisis arising from this conflict became more serious, and forced the different levels of the country's policy-making body into action. The latest news indicates that the religious viewpoint towards women's rights expressed by some *ulema*, and *mojtaheds* (theologians) has been affected by social developments and that they have chosen to lean towards flexibility and an attunement with global and geographical conditions based on reason.

A group of deputies of the Majles discussed some of the problems facing women in a meeting with Grand Ayatollahs Sane'i and Jannati. Shahrbanu Amani, the representative for the people of Orumieh, said, 'Islam and Shi'-ism are dynamic religions. So to resolve the obstacles that exist in the path of women, we called on the *marja'* (source of imitation) and asked their opinion.' She added, 'The gentlemen's opinions were progressive and completely derived from the core of religion.' She also added, 'The religious academic community (hawzeh) must be ready to answer new questions that are raised in society at all times and to try to establish blueprints that are acceptable by the majority of society who will set these as their models; it is not enough to simply write books and disregard the acceptance of the people.'

The member of the sixth Majles representing the people of Orumieh continued, 'This discussion must be initiated by the Grand Ayatollahs, in other words they should debate with their colleagues in order to demonstrate the evolutionary side of religion in society."[1]

At the same time however, another newspaper wrote:

The debate about a woman's rights and her judgement as a court judge is one of the most important and controversial of Islamic debates. Some religious authorities have expressed their particular vision on this subject. Hojjat al-Islam Mehrizi in a conversation with Iranian Students' News Agency (ISNA) said, 'Some senior clerics in Shi'-ism who do not believe in women's right to judge, cite certain parables as their point of reference. For example they say that in such and such a verse from the Qur'an or parable the word "man" has been used and they set this as the principle and conclude that the verses and parables have addressed men only and not women. In answer to these clerics one can say that the word "*rajol*" does not mean man as opposed to woman. Whenever this word is used in the Arabic language in relation to general issues in such a way that there is no symmetrical opposite, it refers to all people. And as can be seen, there are many such interpretations in the Qur'an which makes the reasoning of this group of clerics problematic.'

Ayatollah Musavi Tabrizi, referring to this topic, said, 'Some clerics who oppose the role of women as judges quote Imam Sadeq (peace be upon him) in a hadith from Ebn Khadija, where he has said, "Be careful not to go to an unjust ruler and look to a Shi'-ite man who understands some of the rules and make him a judge for yourself." Some believe that the interpretation of this hadith leaves the right to judge to men only, because the Imam has said, "Look to a Shi'-ite man," whereas the word *rajol* is all-encompassing in language and one cannot say that the use of the word *rajol* per se excludes women from this law. And moreover there is no existing consensus against the right of women to judge.'

Ayatollah Sane'i, while emphasising the point that Islam has granted an equal status for men and women in tens of instances, reiterated, 'In my opinion the confession of woman, her judgement, her role as a *marja'* and her right to leadership have all been accepted and these are definite.' He added, 'As for the credibility of testimony, one must say that firstly, testimony of a witness is not an advantage; it is a headache. Secondly these days testimony is not the main point, what is important is evidence. In reality today, testimony is not credible because it is testimony per se, but testimony is credible as a sign or a pointer.'[2]

The objection of some religious sources in the matter of judgement and testimony by women is important because it gives the political system of the country, *Shari'a* licence to keep half the population away from those areas where final decisions are made in political, social, judicial and economic matters and to forbid them from being involved in such matters.

As we saw in our quick survey of the political developments from the Constitutional Revolution onwards, it has been the religious-political outlook that has dominated the affairs which denied the right of judgement and testimony to women. So it is only right that we should look at the opposing discussions that are taking place about the judgement and testimony of women in order to assess the situation in which we now find ourselves on the threshold of the third millennium, and which is reason for much astonishment.

In this 100-year period of development in Iran's political history, plenty of positive and negative opinions from an Islamic viewpoint have been published about the position of women in political and social activity. But in some instances, not only do we find conflicting and contradictory statements, but the opponents' views themselves are also expressed with contradictory content. The view that expresses itself in a positive and agreeable mould, despite its lack of immunity from contradictions, sets out the subject matter thus:

In Islam women, like men, have a suitable position and station and are not banned from social movements and group activity. In fact according to indisputable instructions in the Qur'an and the hadith, there are many social responsibilities that are the same for men as they are for women. Of course women have been relieved of the duty of primary 'Jihad' and offensive war.[3] But only Jihad and not other aspects of war such as preparation or accompaniment or following the war. And even then, women being excused from such duties is only to serve women and their dignity.[4]

Scholars have sometimes pointed to real examples of the active presence of women in various political and social spheres in order to challenge those views, which are absolutely negative on this topic or which try to hide their negative position under the guise of morality. They have chosen distinct examples from the lives of female personalities and have used as reference the circumstances in which these personalities have been politically active in their own time as proof of participation:

1. The life of Mother of the Faithful, Lady Khadija Kobra (God's heaven be hers).
2. The life of Mother of the Faithful, Uma Salma (God's heaven be hers).
3. The life of Mother of the Faithful, Hafsat (God's paradise be hers).
4. The lives of many women of Mecca during the difficult circumstances of the harsh rule of the Quraysh which led to the order of the Prophet (blessings and peace of God be with him and his household) to migrate to Abyssinia and the life of Muslim women in Medina after the *Hejira* (migration from Mecca to Medina).
5. The life of lady Zahra (peace be upon her) after the passing of the prophet (peace be upon him); her excellency was involved in leading political activity with regard to the rule of Islamic society after the Prophet through her contacts with prominent members of the migrants' and Ansar communities.
6. The life of Mother of the Faithful, 'A'isha, after the passing of the Prophet. She organised an extensive political campaign against the policies of the Caliph Othman bin Afan and provoked the people against his rule, uniting both the rulers and the commoners against him. This political campaign was one of the biggest and strongest elements that expedited the revolution against Othman and granted the revolutionaries legitimacy and political authority. Neither the grandees of followers (*Sahabeh*) nor the average people of society judged her interference at the highest levels of political rule to be incorrect or unbecoming.

   During the rule of the Commander of the Faithful, 'Ali (peace be upon him) too, 'A'isha promoted political intrigue against the Caliph and went so far as to turn political action into an extensive military campaign against Imam 'Ali (peace be upon him) and his rule; an incident which became one of the biggest tragedies in the fate and history of Islam [and was] an act in which 'A'isha made an error and for which she was criticised by Muslims. She even confessed to her error and expressed remorse. 'A'isha continued her political activity and intervention even during the Ommayad dynasty.
7. Biographies and history books from Imam 'Ali's time and after mention

women who strongly and effectively participated in political activities; some of them according to reports by hadith tellers and historians, were Shi'-ites who played an important role in the political confrontation during his exellency's time, such as Sawdeh,[5] and Zargha,[6] etc.[7]

This search therefore shows that the relation of Muslim women with political activity at the beginning of Islam is an image that conforms to the realities of history. But the same researcher, despite references in historical realities of the early years of Islam, cannot deny that the fields of political activity are multifarious and varied and that women's rights for entry into all these fields are controversial. Among *faqihs* (religious jurists), some negate the advisability in the *Shari'a* of women's involvement in any activity in society except family relations and matters pertaining to children and family. Some reject the competence of women according to the *Shari'a* in choosing candidates and members for municipal councils, let alone allowing women to become deputies and ministers themselves.

Another group believes that women are competent enough to elect deputies but not competent enough to be elected themselves. One group accepts the competency of women to become Majles deputies but regards them as lacking the competence for managerial or ministerial posts. And other *faqihs* believe that women can assume all these posts according to the *Shari'a*. But what is common belief among jurists of yesteryear and the present day – with the exception of a few rare people – is that women according to the *Shari'a* cannot be the head of government.[8]

Rule by Women

There are many differing opinions on the subject of women's rule and still the dominant opinion is that the rule of women is not acceptable. Some justify this from a *Shari'a* viewpoint and some do not tolerate the rule of women based on local custom and habit or by emphasising women's biological characteristics and their domestic role. One way or another, the problem is a serious one, especially as women's *Shari'a* rights are still defined according to the mind-set of the rulers of the day in Islamic societies, making the topic highly political. In certain circumstances, such as the case of Iran, this appears to have potential for a crisis.

The recognition of the importance of women's rights has led some reputable *marja'* bravely to attend to this topic. For example, Ayatollah Yusef Sane'i, in September of 1999, in an interview with a lawyer specialising in *Shari'a* matters, declared certain viewpoints which will have future repercussions and consequences. In his view:

> Moqadas Ardebili's opinion is that a woman can become a judge. We also hold this opinion. Others have also declared the same. In our

opinion a woman can be *vali-ye faqih* (supreme jurist). Personally I do not see being a man as a prerequisite in *fegh* (jurisprudence), *marja'iyat*, or *ejtehad*. Being a man is not a condition in theology or being a source of imitation. Therefore a woman can become a *faqih* and can become a *marja'*.

'*Faqihs* must be trustees of prophets.'[9] Gender is not the issue here. 'The *ulema* must be the inheritors of prophets.'[10] This hadith is not just about male *ulema* and gender has not been considered in it. So we see that Islam has allowed equal stature for men and women not once not twice but in tens of cases . . . in my opinion the confession of woman, her judgement, her *marja'iyat*, her leadership, her Presidency have all been accepted and proven. It is even mentioned in the Constitution about the President being a 'religious individual' (*rejal*) so women can become presidents too. There are no problems about *velayat* either. If you accept the possibility of judgement by women about which I and Moqadas Ardebili have spoken, then there is no obstacle in accepting *velayat*. When you say, '*Faqihs* are the guardians of Islam'[11] then in reality you have accepted *velayat* (for women) too, because *ulema* does not have a gender. His excellency Imam (Khomeini) has quoted this hadith in the book of *Velayat-e Faqih* and there has been no mention there either that by theologian we mean male theologians. '*Faqihs* are the guardians of Islam' has no gender.[12]

In response to this comment that some hadiths indicate the opposite, Ayatollah Yusef Sane'i said: 'All those hadiths suffer from a weakness of documentation.'[13]

In spite of these types of views that fit the needs of society, in women's entry into areas of political rule, Iran still faces obstacles of opinion. Although the slogan of meritocracy has become popular in various stages of government, the majority of intellectual and expert women have been left with no access to the structure of governance. Even despite many religious schools for women, which have created suitable opportunities for reaching religious posts, they rarely volunteer to enter decision-making arenas at top levels of political management.

Social Transformations and Its Effect on Religious Viewpoints

Based on the ever increasing social needs which manifest themselves in all cultural and political aspects, one can cite examples in the *fatwas* of six of the religious sources.

Women can be Prayer Leaders of Women in Prayer: in a report by the head office of the ministry of education in the province of Tehran, Mr

'Ali Asghar Nuri, in charge of the prayer HQ in the third district of Karaj, said that a woman can be Imam for *Jama'at* prayers for women. He also said that he felt using women to act as prayer leaders for other women would solve the problem of group prayers in girls' schools and said, 'In order to encourage female students to group prayers in schools we asked religious sources for solutions and subsequently this *fatwa* was issued in order to encourage female students to pray and attract them to group prayer'.[14]

The serious social needs which lead to such *fatwas* in a country where religion and politics are intertwined holds this warning: in a society that is moving towards modernisation and where the number of students and the educated is on the increase, one can no longer insist on old interpretations. As a result some religious experts are trying to adapt themselves to the times. For example, in answer to the question, 'To what extent can there be a ruling for the *ejtehad* of women based on verses of Qur'an and parables?' they answer:

'Theologians and *mojtaheds* have not accepted the expertise of women in religion absolutely (meaning that a woman issues a *fatwa*, and men and women follow her *fatwa* in the same way as they would the *fatwa* of a man). In the history of Islam we have had women *mojtaheds* who have reached the level of issuing *fatwas*. Two such examples are Ameneh Beygom, the daughter of the first 'Allameh Majlesi[15] and in our own time Mrs Amin Isfahani.[16] But their *fatwas* were not for instruction of the public, like male *mojtaheds*. Of course if they were asked questions about women's issues and in their own opinion they issued a *fatwa*, there was no problem, and perhaps to some extent this is the way it was. For example the mother of Seyyed Morteza[17] and Seyyed Razi,[18] by the name of Fatemeh and daughter of Taher Zu al-Monaqeb, is an argument for women. Sheikh Mofid (d. 1022) wrote the book 'Rules for Women' (*Ahkam al-nesa*) because of her request and for her. Or Sheikh Baha'i's wife, the learned daughter of Shaykh Ali Mansha-Ameli, who was a lady to whom Sheikh Baha'i (1546–1622) referred other women in order to get the answers to their questions; perhaps they gave their theological verdict as a *fatwa* in matters specially pertaining to women. The wife and daughter of Shahid-e Avval[19] were like this too. In my opinion, lady theologians who have the knowledge of other theologians' opinions and *fatwas* can issue *fatwas* in matters relating to ladies, and there is nothing wrong in their *fatwas* being put into practice and maybe their religious expertise and *fatwas* are better and stronger than *fatwas* and expertise by men!'[20]

In answer to this question, 'Do we have a woman in the history of Islam from whom a *fatwa* is quoted?' it is said:

At the time of the Prophet (peace be upon him) and the saintly Imams (peace be upon them), we have had women who were narrators of those saintly beings. Even the Prophet and the innocent Imams would refer other women to these ladies for religious problems. In the book of *Rejal* too they would dedicate a chapter to them and would talk about them. It needs someone who knows the scientists of the time to extract this from the pages of the book of *Rejal* and from the pages of history and hadith. It will be interesting. We have had knowledgeable women other than the wives of the prophets and Imams in the following centuries who have permitted men and many men have asked their permits in theology and hadith and science because they were experts in these fields.' In the interpretation of the *ulema*, women have always been home-makers; in theory it has been said that they should have a social role but in practice it has not been so.

At the time of the Prophet and the innocent Imams (peace be upon them) and according to their biographies and history women were not merely home-makers. The Prophet in most of his trips whether for war or Jihad took one of his wives with him. He called his wives clearly by name and even his followers would converse with them. The Prophet himself would say my wife Khadijeh and my daughter Fatemeh and everyone knew what the names of the Prophet's wives and daughter were. A practice that was later abandoned.

There were women who participated in wars and would nurse the wounded or bring water to the men. In the Ohod war her excellency Zahra (peace be upon her), the Prophet's aunt Safieh and other women from Medina came to the front and were witnesses to the war first hand. The warriors too would see them and were able to see their behaviour and the way they talked first hand. Some of the followers of Imams also would meet with their mothers or their wives and would show their respect and would hear them speak, and this has been described in books. So women's place in the home and their absolute isolation has come about in the following centuries and was not the Prophet's or the Imams' way. The late 'Allameh Tabataba'i would say: 'I don't know when it became the custom for us to be cautious about mentioning the names of our wives and daughters, and to try and avoid it! The Prophet and the Imams would call their wives and daughters by name and this was also common practice amongst their followers. Everybody knew that Zaynab and Omm Kolthum were the daughters of Imam 'Ali (peace be upon him) and what the names of the prophet's four daughters and his wives were, but this changed later. Of course all this would take place under complete Islamic instructions; women's *hejab* and the extent of their social role was such that there was no contention. If a man spoke with Muslim women it would be to a suitable extent and as far as it was needed, not without limit or when necessary. Men and women must have interaction. In our time too, women's interaction and social role must be to the necessary and required level.'[21]

Ayatollah Musavi Bojnurdi, who is a member of the Islamic Human Rights Commission, recently stated in an interview with ISNA:

'*Shari'a* rule is subject to evolution and the Islamic legislator; edicts are established as obligatory or prohibited according to his judgment of good and evil which is in his jurisdiction.' He added, 'The truth and humanity of men is not assessed by their body. But humanity is based on cognition which transcends gender. Men and women are equal in their rights and there is no difference between them in this matter except in circumstances where some rights specifically belong to men or women which create different responsibilities. Basically the nature of legislation in law is common and the first principle of law is the commonality of law.'

Ayatollah Musavi Bojnurdi said, 'The majority of *faqihs* see maleness as a condition of judgement and claim that it is consensus (*ejma'*) and in the same way they cite some parables as the reason for their stand, and of course one can say that this condition of maleness is itself subject to exception to the rule (*lays be shart*) and a person whether man or woman can become a judge if he or she has the common requirements for judgement.'

He added, 'What has been related in parables and hadith is a matter of example, not that the subject was only men, and when they say a judge should be a *mojtahed*, a *mojtahed* can be man or woman and the consensus of *faqihs* on this matter is of no value.' This member of the Islamic Human Rights Committee added, 'Each person's understanding is a reason (*hojjat*) for himself and this cannot be forced on others. Otherwise it will be against the principle of freedom and each *mojtahed* can think freely within his own vision. Naturally *ejtehad* must be dynamic and a *mojtahed* must consider the time and place of every edict and not separate himself from them.' In conclusion he said, 'Islam is a universal religion and cannot be confined to a particular time or place. A religion such as this cannot separate its edicts from time and place and must be able to accommodate the progress and the developments which are taking place in the world; if religion fails to provide appropriate answers, this is against the goals of Islam.'[22]

Ayatollah Amini, in answer to the question, 'Does your excellency consider women competent in accepting responsibility as *Marja' Taqlid* (source of imitation)?' answered:

'*Marja'iyat* has different questions and special circumstances and the measure is that there should be a *faqih* who has virtue (*taqva*) is a just man and has the traits which allow him to grasp questions well. Now if a woman has reached the level of understanding and can grasp the questions, like a woman who can be a source of cure in the field of medicine, she can be the same in the field of *marja'iyat* of religion. This of course is for when they reach that level, if they haven't reached that level, naturally a man should be approached as a *marja'* if he is a greater *faqih*. Anyway, what I was referring to in that last meeting when I said that women must follow their own path and get their rights was exactly this. Why should we not have enough educated ladies and have to resort to men to teach in our girls' high schools?! Why should a woman be a receptionist and a man be a doctor?! Women should be specialist physicians and their receptionists should be women too and they should provide the injections and other services themselves. It is not a status for a woman to be the receptionist for a male doctor, or perhaps be his assistant in surgery. A woman's status is such that she must move in higher spheres and not just be content to be a nurse in some hospital. It is true that nursing is a noble profession and women can perform it better, but does this mean that being a specialist is not within her abilities?! We have many talented women. They must pursue these jobs; this is what will afford them dignity. Women should do something to show their status to men. If they want to they can. I have seen some women who are excellent in science and other fields, even better than some men. Sadly men's self-centredness sometimes means that they will not allow women to reach higher levels. For example I have heard that typically male physicians don't allow a lady to come and learn a specialisation under their tutelage because they fear that soon she will push them aside! In my opinion we must reduce the number of male students in medicine according to statistics and instead accept more female students for these subjects so that their numbers can be balanced at all the levels of general practice, specialisation and above. That is when women can say we pursued our own independence and we are now truly independent. Growth and independence isn't about, say, doing sports. Sport is a good thing, but it's tricking women when we come and excessively encourage them to do sports. Because women are like men when it comes to sports, they can do it themselves. It's no big deal if you allow women to play sports and make them feel indebted for it. Let them go and become specialists. Encourage them to that end. Encourage them to go and get what is their right. I am surprised by the women too. They honestly sometimes overlook their own value and rights and go after such things; let us have jobs, but jobs at what? Only in lower jobs like being the receptionist to a male doctor? This is not the only value of women. In the area of theology and *hawzeh* (seminary) it is also the same. What I honestly say is that if we do this job properly and plan properly, half the *talabeh* (seminarians) should be women. Naturally it is obvious that they should study specific lessons that are suitable for them and they should be independent in doing so and have their own specialties. Of course this question is open to debate that although women have the right to study all the sciences, is it prudent for them and society as a whole to be involved in all the sciences and whether some subjects have a special suitability or priority. Anyway, we must not ignore women's issues and their special circumstances, the family and even society.'[23]

The Challenges are Serious

Iranian society is moving in a direction that makes its modern aspects dominant over its traditional aspects. Sociologists constantly point to the fact that this move towards modernity is inevitable and insist that we have had an imbalanced society since the Qajar era. An imbalanced society oscillates between tradition and modernity and there is a serious challenge going on, with the traditional aspect having a dominant role. At the time of the Constitutional Revolution the country's population was 90 per cent rural and 10 per cent urban. In 1978 the population became 55 per cent rural and 45 per cent urban. In other words, on the threshold of the Islamic Revolution's victory, Iran was still a semi-traditional society. In the last statistics taken in 1996 these figures have been reversed, i.e. 55 per cent are now urban and 45 per cent are from rural areas. Perhaps this figure has reached 60 per cent or more by now. And maybe as far as women's participation and formation of trade unions are concerned, we are now moving towards a society that is finding some order and management despite its imbalanced nature. Perhaps this lack of balance will remain for many years in our country, but eventually the modern aspect will overpower the traditional one. Maybe this change in the real structures of society will lead to our having civic institutions, or institutions that support democracy and parliament in a more genuine way. But it will be impossible for these institutions to disappear in challenging each other; I do not hold such pessimistic views.

In the light of this structural change, the population of cities is growing fast; we have 21 million students at schools and universities. The active presence of women on the social stage is another encouraging sign. In the past year 52 per cent of our university students were women; in other words for the first time in Iran's history women entrants were in greater numbers than men. This will have its own special consequences. Women will inevitably enter the job market and the socio-political arena, although there will be obstacles in their way of occupying the senior management levels of the country. That is why women's position in management has not changed in the past thirty years. But women's rate of literacy has been higher than the growth in population; our population has doubled while the number of more educated women appears to have increased by four- to six-fold.

We are facing the growth of mass media and the flow of information in our society that cannot remain entirely under the control of government and the groups that hold the power. Telephone, fax, computer, internet and foreign and domestic television networks are in operation. The collection of these elements is real and irreversible. It is no longer possible to tell the majority of literate and educated women, 'go back to your homes, be illiterate'. This is irreversible. You cannot switch off the televisions. Our projection of the future is that eventually we will establish those special institutions that will order and manage these changes and we will reach a stage where the imbalanced society with the traditional aspect being dominant will be replaced by an imbalanced society with the modernist aspect being dominant. The special institutions also will take us further towards a more desirable parliament, where we no longer just set our hopes on the minority faction, where the representatives actually have people they represent. Is it possible to reach these ideals by eradicating women from areas of government and ignore the challenges?

Taboos are in the Process of Being Broken

Women's rights, especially in the area of government, are entwined with the crisis in demands for freedom and reforms in today's Iran. As taboos are in the process of being broken, the taboo of women's entry into the arena of government is now a topic for discussion. But only if the majority of literate women become convinced about the necessity of this discussion and extensively participate in it.

The history of the development of women's position in Iran requires that women should demand their rights separately while keeping their association to the general political trends, and become involved in creating organisations, and producing cultural goods in connection with their full human potential.

For various reasons, women have not shown themselves as active and enthusiastic enquirers and have failed to establish a relationship with religious schools, credited *marja'* and organisations that are influential in overall decision-making in order to demand answers to their everyday problems. The fact that anyone who critiques the laws governing the rights of women may become prone to the charge of insulting the sanctities and foundation of Islam, is first due to there being no single and cohesive definition of *Shari'a* rules in the topical laws of the country, and second because women rarely take part in the discussions in connection to their rights.

So, the unfortunate situation that exists today cannot be remedied by the governing body alone. The role of women in the field of religious or non-religious criticism has hardly been stellar, and while this pattern remains, the position of women, especially in the higher echelons of political management of the country and important areas of government, will not change dramatically. A religious government requires that women should become active in order to receive the *Shari'a* permits for their own effective presence in the arena of government and stop waiting for favours from the gentlemen. They should lift themselves to the status of an informed enquirer and demand answers from accredited *marja'* and subject their opposing answers to a debate.

Equality in Law, Discrimination in Practice

Although the right to vote is one of the first basic human rights, in most countries women were denied this right until the end of the Second World War. At the advent of Islam a form of voting system (*bay'at*) existed between women and the prophet and the Caliphs. Women, in order to indicate their acceptance of the ruler, would submerge their hand in a bowl of water in which the ruler's hand was already placed. But in the majority of Islamic countries the granting of the right to vote has become law later than in industrialised countries.

In Iran in 1963 women were given the right to vote and to be elected to the parliament, an event that had political consequences verging on a crisis. Even now, after the establishment of the Islamic Republic of Iran, the right of women to vote and to be elected to parliament has never been taken away from them. The cultural, educational and political situation would not allow the opponents to take this right away from women. So this right to vote is still in place, but cultural problems and differing viewpoints create their own obstacles.

The present situation indicates that it is possible that equality in law may not necessarily lead to the eradication of discrimination because of the cultural fibre of societies. Some women's rights experts believe that the mere expression of the concepts of equality between men and women and the eradication of discrimination within the internal laws of a country is not enough. In other words *de jure*[24] equality can contain *de facto*[25] discriminations. As is the case in the constitutions of many countries, there are no prohibitions or limitations on women in occupying high political posts, but we seldom see a woman in such posts. In reality, the obstacle of *de facto* shows resistance to the licence which is granted by the *de jure* laws and in effect prevents the improvement in the legal position of women. But if societies were able to create basic changes in their social and cultural structures, *de facto* equality would become effective.

These experts point out that the subject of eradication of discrimination has been set forth in a general way in most human rights documents, but in these documents no attention is paid to the differing situations of women as far as education, upbringing, social and cultural factors are concerned. Consequently, women's total presence and participation in (their country's) affairs is impossible in practice; for example, if employment regulations are set in such a way that there is no special attention paid to gender and simply set according to equal treatment of men and women, in practice, because of the difference in women's situation from that of men, only rare opportunities are created for employment of women. This will effectively lead to a systematic deprivation of the women; *de facto* prejudice becomes effective which is harmful, even if prejudice in the form of *de jure* has been destroyed.

The Constitution of the Islamic Republic of Iran gives women a high status in its preface and promises: 'Because women have suffered a greater oppression under the regime of *Taghut*[26] vindication of their rights will be greater.' And in another place, women as the main member of the family will leave their position as objects and tools in the service of propagating consumerism and exploitation. Women will be fellow soldiers in the active fields of life alongside men, having rediscovered their crucial and honourable role of motherhood in training educated pioneers. They therefore have a more important responsibility, and in the eyes of Islam are deserving of a higher value and special attention. To this end, 'The government must ensure the rights of women in all respects, in conformity with Islamic criteria' and create policies that 'create a favourable environment for the growth of woman's personality and the restoration of her rights, both the material and intellectual'.[27] Also women's equal status to men has been considered and the government is duty bound 'to safeguard their full rights whether male or female and . . . to observe . . . equality of all in law'.[28]

In spite of all the emphases (on the dignity of women), the challenge of law and custom that in a religious government can also be interpreted as a challenge between law and current and traditional interpretations of religion, manifests itself to the detriment of women's presence in executive affairs. This is how.

The equality of human beings that has been confirmed many times by the Constitution has been delineated within the framework of Islamic standards and as such is provisional and conditional. In this way, 'All citizens of the country, both men and women, equally enjoy the protection of the law and enjoy all human, political, economic, social, and cultural rights, in conformity with Islamic criteria.'[29] As a result, wherever Islamic law sets specific legal differences between men and women, the Islamic Republic's rulership will believe in and be loyal to that principle and internal laws cannot be proposed, passed or carried out without being deferential to them.

For example, when all the current interpretations of religion are such that maleness is declared as a prerequisite for sitting as a judge, how can the judiciary eradicate this principle from internal laws despite the repeated emphases of the Constitution that women should benefit from all human, political and social rights? In order for development in the position of women's rights in Iran, therefore, it is necessary that a group of experts in religious affairs, *faqihs*, sociologists and generally people who recognise the needs of the time co-operate and debate the Islamic standards in accordance with the socio-political developments and customs. This is the only way that the Constitution will be able to implement change in the position of women. If not, the limitations that have been mentioned will be an obstacle (to change).

A judicial structure that is more in line with the ancient customs can, at times, create a serious obstacle and be a preventative force in the path of equality seeking tendencies within the Constitution. For example, the fourteenth section of the third principle of the Constitution, as has been mentioned, is a powerful law and a beacon of hope for equality of all in law in the matter of advancement of women's rights. But this same law, if it is subjected to study in the judicial structure of Iran, will be identified as one of the obstacles in the growth of women's rights.

Equality of all in the eyes of the law alludes to this, meaning that men and women enjoy equal rights in the present laws of Iran. But in the present situation the law focuses on inequality and as a result equality cannot be provided. Because when the law does not contain equality for people of two genders, equality in law cannot aid the eradication of discrimination against women and the words 'equality in the eyes of the law' will not contradict discrimination by itself. This section from the third principle of the Constitution is one of the obvious signs of the existence of ambiguity in the proclamation of women's rights.

For example, when a woman is murdered, it is true that based on the afore-mentioned section, the relatives of the victim, whether male or female, have the right to claim against the murderer, but *qesas* (retaliation of an eye for an eye) of the murderer can be carried out only after the family of the victim pay half the price of the murderer's blood money. So, men and women both have the right to claim and can initiate litigation against the murderer, but the judge is forced into a prejudicial judgment because of laws that must be adhered to. As a result, observing equality of men and women in important and fundamental rights such as the right to life is an impossible task.

The term 'Islamic standards' which is mentioned in most of the principles of the Constitution on the topic of women's rights constantly adds to the ambiguity. But according to experts in religious matters, this ambiguity can be remedied with the efforts of *faqihs*, accredited *mojtaheds* and independent religious *hawzeh*. Because if they consider the requirements of the time as their basis for revision within the framework of Shi'-ite *feqh*, many discriminatory instances in internal law can be alleviated. On this topic, some *ulema* make some points that can be useful. They maintain that Shi'-ism is capable of adapting to the conditions of time and place:

> It is not the case that whatever is said in *feqh* constitutes Islam, *feqh* is based on the deduction of *faqihs*, on jurisprudence which *faqihs* make. This is *feqh*, and it is possible to change this. It is not the case that it is variable, anyway we see that the deduction of *faqihs* is different throughout time. One *faqih* declares something forbidden (*haram*) whilst another identifies it as permitted (*halal*). Why? Because of the deductions which they take from the four proofs.[30] Now if *feqh* and the community of *faqhis* say that a woman cannot inherit land from her deceased husband, this is not the definite opinion of religion and can be changed, because it is possible for us to deduce from the four proofs that it is otherwise, the Qur'anic verses do not differentiate between the method of inheritance of man from woman or woman from man, and men and women inherit from their deceased partner's legacy. We always see these ebbs and flows in the history of Shi'-ite *feqh* until recently, when the late Imam (Khomeini) opened this topic that time and place have an effect on the edicts. Not that he changed the law of God, for the law of God cannot be changed, God's edict, if it is a genuine edict and preserved in tabula cannot be changed. But as I told you, whatever is in *feqh* is not necessarily in religion. We see the question of women's testimony, the problem of women's inheritance from a deceased husband, the problem of the method of retaliation (*qesas*), the problem of blood money, the problem of women's judgement and other problems that pertain to women's rights in our civic and criminal *feqh* which is regarded as discriminatory by the world and others. In my opinion if the *faqihs* and lawyers revise these instances and take a new look at the problems, many of these edicts will change because many of these have come about because of consensus (*ejma'*)[31] and not based on *Nass-e sarih* (explicit wording of a text).[32] I believe that it is possible to make some theological changes in those edicts that are in use today and where there is discrimination between men and women. My opinion is that the rights that exist for women in Shi'-ite *feqh* now, are not absolute and can be changed.'[33]

Based on what has been said, it is possible to understand that although differentiation between man and woman exists in Islam, it is not the case that equality of rights will be made impossible. Therefore critique of religious tradition and directing it towards the ultimate goal of eradicating legal discrimination against women is the best solution which can create the requisite opportunities for the law-making institutions of the country to review the laws to the benefit of women. Despite enlightened opinions expressed by some sources (*marja'*) and religious experts, the prevalent *Shari'a* opinion is that women cannot become active in areas of government. For example Ebn Qodamah Hanbali is quoted as saying: 'Women do not have the competence for Imamat (religious leadership) or the running of the country. According to what has been handed down to us, neither the Prophet nor any of his successors and nobody else after them has chosen a woman to run a city or to judge. If it was advisable (for women to occupy these positions) history would not be empty of examples of it.'[34]

Despite the differences in opinion, some which we have mentioned here, and the debates that exist on this topic within the religious schools (*hawzeh*), Islamic societies cannot easily accept women in important and sensitive areas of government. Perhaps it is based on this reality that in the Islamic Republic of Iran, from the beginning of its establishment to this day, an effort has been made to emphasise the participation of women in the course of law-making, planning and in the general policy-making. We seldom come across words such as equality or egality in political expressions or legal ratifications. In those cases where the political managers of the country have targeted and justified the participation of women in political, social, economic and cultural areas, they have immediately added the proviso 'conditional to the preservation of the status of the family and values and standards of Islam'. No unified definition which is compatible to the eclectic society of Iran has been presented to its people for the term 'preservation of family status and Islamic values and standards'. As a result, all managers and others in positions of responsibility permit themselves to impose their own personal definition within the boundaries of their power. The present situation appears suitable for the limited participation of women. But it will prevent and inhibit their effective and widespread participation. The elucidation of the outlook of Islam on this topic, therefore, is the crux of the problem in explaining, preparing and reforming and changing of laws and regulations that pertain to women and their socio-political situation in today's Iran.

Stipulating the observance of Islamic standards has in most cases become an obstacle that prohibits the growth and elevation of women, because there is a difference of opinion between *ulema* and the *faqihs* on the definition of Islamic standards. As a result participation of women is expressed by some in a very limited and miserly fashion, and by others who are not effectual in high decision-making levels as devoid of gender considerations.

The Constitution of the Islamic Republic of Iran has managed to open the way for deserving women through the use of legal terms despite the differences of opinion and the dominant *Shari'a* outlook that does not tolerate the entry of women into government. But to what extent can legal terms establish the political participation of women in a country that, first has a religious rulership and, second, insists on its dominant *Shari'a* outlook against the presence of women in government? The dominant outlook is expressed in a clear and forthright manner and urges the women it addresses to beware of equality-seeking:

> Today some malicious or ignorant people use the slogan of equality of men and women and pursue a goal which will not just give no value to women but endanger all her values. Honourable sisters! For a woman being appointed as a judge or not has no effect on her achieving higher human accomplishments, equality in inheritance or lack of it or the amount of blood money or the difference or lack of difference in testimony, and it has no effect on the spiritual or celestial aspects of her soul. Seek yourself and your own truth and do not heed the false problems that are set forth by some ignorant and malicious people.
>
> Know that some theological edicts on women (which on the surface give the impression of limitation or imperfection for them) are regarded by people of knowledge and perception as protection and reverence for bigger and more important duties which many men cannot perform. Ask yourself is being a woman an obstacle in reaching a life of purity which is the definite promise of god? You know the Qur'an has insisted, *'Are those who are knowledgeable equal to those who are ignorant?'* (39:9) but it has never said, 'Are men and women equal.'[35]

The Islamic Revolution and Changes in Viewpoint

Faqihs, interpreters and preachers prevented the social presence of women up until the revolution of 1979 and issued a *fatwa* for the veneration of women's presence in society. These *fatwas*, interpretations and sermons, with titles such as 'necessities of women staying at home', 'veneration of singing and songs of women', 'the veneration of looking at women', 'the veneration or lack of necessity of training women', 'the veneration of women horse-riding', 'the veneration of describing women', 'the veneration of displaying jewellery', 'prevention of women in mass prayer, the death prayer, the prayers for 'Ayd and Friday prayers', 'the prohibition of consulting women' and so on, would reach the populace and the public opinion would be primed in preventing the presence of women in society.

In very rare and exceptional instances when a *fatwa* was issued for women to leave the four walls of their homes, or when they received permission to speak, they were required to follow an unwritten book of regulations. Some of the points of these regulations included the following: they must not speak more than five words, they must walk close to a wall, they should not walk so that their feet make a noise . . . and these viewpoints, which still have some followers, were abandoned in the heat of the revolution without being subjected to debate and criticism.[36] Women were present in demonstrations. The *faqihs* and the politico-religious leaders not only did not challenge their presence but insisted on the necessity of their being there.

In the past twenty-one years in which the followers of the *Shari'a* have acknowledged the presence of women as a correct practice and have accepted that women should leave their homes and provide their energy for aiding the revolution and the Islamic government, this question constantly arises: why should they be imprisoned in the limited roles of civil servants and middle managers and not be allowed to take the seat at high political posts such as president, higher levels of management, ministerial or judicial posts? What is certain is that women caused the abandonment of *Shari'a* obstacles for their presence (in society) by their extensive presence during the revolution. And the religio-political leaders of the revolution, too, endorsed the legitimacy of this presence by the orders and commands that they issued. So the cultural background for their continuing presence and empowerment was provided. But the abandoned viewpoint remained active in religious circles and was able to block women from entry into higher levels of management by relying on the force of supporters who have the tools of decision-making at all levels, whether official or non-official, and can exert pressure. This viewpoint acted even during the course of law-making and implementation of laws against women's entry into arenas of decision-making and government. Despite the fact that the abandoned viewpoint is active within the rulership, it does not appear possible after twenty-one years of legitimacy[37] of women's presence on the scene, that reference to those same *fatwas* will be able to force women to marginality and mere observers of policy-making.

The important event in the social existence of women in Iran which is closely bound to the revolution of Iran is that the presence of women in society has been recognised as legitimate and as a result their demands for the symbols of their presence such as political rights cannot be prohibited by religion.

Notes

[1.] *Hamshahri*, 2195 (14 August 2000), p. 14.

[2.] *Aftab-e Yazd*, 181 (11 September 2000), p. 9.

[3.] Primary jihad is the one led by the Prophet or by an innocent Imam, the purpose of which is to invite people to join Islam.

[4.] *Ketab-e Naqd*, special edition on women's rights, 12 (Autumn 1999), 'The Social and Political Station of Women', Dr Fatemeh Fakuri, p. 30.

5. Sawdeh, daughter of Ashtar Hamedani, is reported to have had her properties plundered by Mu'awiya, and so she went to his court seeking justice. She remained defiant at his court and declared her loyalty to 'Ali [Ed.].

6. Zargha, daughter of Ebn Ghays Hamedani (d. 680), was present in the Battle of Siffin between 'Ali and Mu'awiya, and composed poems calling people to support the cause. After the battle she spoke with Mu'awiya who was amazed at her eloquence [Ed.].

7. *The Limits of Women's Political Participation in Islam*, Ayatollah Mohammed Mehdi Shams al-Din, trans. Mohsen Abedi (Be'sat Publications, 1997), pp. 39–40.

8. Ibid.

9. *Osul-e Kafi*, Book 1, hadith. 5, p. 46.

10. *Ibid.*, 'Sefat al-'elm va fazl al-'olama', hadith 2, p. 32.

11. *Ibid.*, Book 1, 'Feqh al-'olama', hadith 3, p. 38.

12. *Ettela'at*, 21731 (24 September 1999), p. 11, 'Gender and the Edicts of Punishment in Islam'. Interview with Ayatollah Yusef Sane'i by Dr Hosyan Mehrpur.

13. Ibid.

14. *Iran*, 1584 (2 August 2000), p. 16.

15. 'Allameh Majlesi (1628–99) was the greatest Shi'-ite scholar of his era, writing over sixty books, and urging believers to reject the beliefs of Sunnis, Sufis and mystical philosophers [Ed.].

16. Mrs Amin Isfahani, also known as 'Lady Amin', was born in 1866, the daughter of a famous merchant. She was educated by the leading jurists of the day, and subsequently became an important *mojtahed* in her own right, composing works related to women's issues. She died in 1983 [Ed.].

17. Seyyed Morteza (967–1044) was a great theologian, grammarian and poet who lived in Baghdad. He was one of the most influential Shi'-ites of the time, and his most famous works include *Kitab al-shafi fi 'l-imama* and *al-Ghurar wa 'l-durar* [Ed.].

18. Seyyed Razi (970–1016) is regarded by many as the compiler of *Nahj al-Balagheh*, one of the most important texts in the Shi'-ite canon, as it is a compendium of the sayings of Imam 'Ali. Razi was also a celebrated poet in his own time [Ed.].

19. Mohammad ibn Makki al-Amili al-Jizzini (1333–84) [Ed.].

20. The text does not reveal the identity of the person who gave this long answer, [Ed.].

21. *Zan* newspaper first year, 39, (20 September 1998), p. 8. A conversation with Hojjat al-Islam 'Ali Davani.

22. *Hamshahri*, eighth year, 2178 (July/August 2000).

23. *Payam-e Zan Monthly*, 9, December 1996, conversation with Ayatollah Amini.

24. Equality based on law.

25. Discrimination based on custom.

26. The name of an ancient pre-Islamic idol used as an alias for the Shah's rule [Tr.].

27. The twenty-first principle of the Constitution.

28. Section fourteen of the third principle of the Constitution.

29. The twentieth section of the Constitution.

30. The four proofs are the Qur'an, hadith, consensus and comparison.

31. *Ejma'* is the third source of law-making in Islam and it refers to the unity of opinion and consensus of all Islamic scientists on a *Shari'a* edict in one particular era. The first source of law-making is the book and the second is tradition.

32. *Nass-e sarih* is the first source of law-making in Islam. *Nass*, whether of the book or tradition, supersedes other sources and all branches of Islams are agreed on this. In cases where the book or tradition orders an edict clearly, to the extent that there is no possibility of doubt in one's mind, there is no necessity for *ejtehad*, i.e. on God's commandments, the promotion or prohibition must be accepted without exception.

33. Interview with Ayatollah Bojnurdi, *Farzaneh* quarterly, third year, 8 (Winter 1996), p. 15.

34. *Al-Mughni*, book 11, p. 380, quoted from *The Limits of Women's Political Participation in Islam* by Ayatollah Mohammad Mehdi Shams, trans. by Mohsen Ebadi, Be'sat Publications, p. 47 (Ebn Qodamah was a famous Sunni theologian from the thirteenth century – Ed.).

35. Extract from a speech by Grand Ayatollah Fazel Lankarani to the Scientific Conference of Chastity in Jame'eh Al-Zahra Seminary, Qom, quoted from the *Yalesarat al-Husayn* weekly, year 7, 96 (20 November 2000), p. 2.

36. Abandoning some parables in Shi'-ite theology has some precedent, the main reason for which is political goals and incentives. In this case because the political factor has a prominent role, now words are spoken about the correctness or incorrectness of the parables and they are abandoned even if they are correct without being researched or critiqued.

37. Despite views that women's presence in social and political scenes are against the *Shari'a*, the policy of making women active was implemented before the revolution. Women had become active in ministerial posts, as representatives of Majles and the senate and heads of courts. This presence was not approved by the *faqihs*.